Lecture Notes in Artificial Intelligence   12641

Subseries of Lecture Notes in Computer Science

More information about this subseries at http://www.springer.com/series/1244

Fredrik Heintz · Michela Milano ·
Barry O'Sullivan (Eds.)

Trustworthy AI –
Integrating Learning, Optimization and Reasoning

First International Workshop, TAILOR 2020
Virtual Event, September 4–5, 2020
Revised Selected Papers

 Springer

Editors
Fredrik Heintz (iD)
Department of Computer
and Information Science
Linköping University
Linköping, Sweden

Michela Milano (iD)
ALMA-AI Research Institute
on Human-Centered AI
University of Bologna
Bologna, Italy

Barry O'Sullivan (iD)
Department of Computer Science
University College Cork
Cork, Ireland

ISSN 0302-9743   ISSN 1611-3349   (electronic)
Lecture Notes in Artificial Intelligence
ISBN 978-3-030-73958-4   ISBN 978-3-030-73959-1   (eBook)
https://doi.org/10.1007/978-3-030-73959-1

LNCS Sublibrary: SL7 – Artificial Intelligence

This Springer imprint is published by the registered company Springer Nature Switzerland AG
The registered company address is: Gewerbestrasse 11, 6330 Cham, Switzerland

Preface

The current European scientific artificial intelligence (AI) landscape is fragmented with many research groups working individually or in smaller constellations, often in disjoint scientific communities. Machine reasoning, machine learning, and optimization are examples of such communities. The 1st TAILOR Workshop, held online as part of the European Conference on Artificial Intelligence (ECAI) 2020, brought together many of these researchers and groups to discuss scientific advances in the integration of learning, optimization, and reasoning, to provide the scientific foundations for Trustworthy AI.

TAILOR is an ICT-48 Network of AI Research Excellence Centers funded by EU Horizon 2020 research and innovation programme Grant Agreement 952215. The TAILOR community includes more than 100 research labs and companies in Europe and around the world. The purpose of the TAILOR project is to build the capacity of providing the scientific foundations for Trustworthy AI in Europe by developing a network of research excellence centres leveraging and combining learning, optimization, and reasoning. TAILOR will do this based on four powerful instruments: a strategic research roadmap; a basic research program to address grand challenges; a connectivity fund for active dissemination to the larger AI community; and network collaboration activities promoting research exchanges, training materials and events, and joint PhD supervision.

The workshop, which was held during 4–5 September, 2020, addressed the following main scientific topics:

- *Trustworthiness.* How to learn fair AI models, even in the presence of biased data? How to develop explainable and interpretable AI decision processes? How to develop transparent AI systems and integrate them into the decision process for increasing user trust?
- *Learning, reasoning, and optimization.* How to integrate AI paradigms and representations for reasoning, learning, and optimization in order to support trustworthy AI? Integrated approaches to learning, reasoning, and optimization should allow AI systems to bridge the gap between low-level perception and high-level reasoning, to combine knowledge-based and data-driven methods, to explain their behaviour and allow for introspection of the resulting models.
- *Deciding and Learning How to Act.* How to empower an AI system with the ability of deliberating how to act in the world, reasoning on the effects of its actions, and learning from past experiences, as well as monitoring the actual or simulated outcome of its actions, learning from possibly unexpected outcomes, and again reasoning and learning how to deal with such new outcomes?
- *Reasoning and Learning in Social Contexts.* Agents should not reason, learn, and act in isolation. They will need to do it with others and among others. So, this topic is concerned with how AI systems should communicate, collaborate, negotiate and

reach agreements with other AI and (eventually) human agents within a multi-agent system (MAS).

- *AutoAI.* How to build AI tools, systems, and infrastructure that are performant, robust, and trustworthy and have the ability to configure and tune themselves for optimal performance? How can we support people with limited AI expertise and highly-skilled experts in building such AI systems?

We received 49 submissions to the workshop. Each submission was reviewed single-blind by at least two reviewers and at most by three. In total, 36 papers were accepted to the workshop: 25 long papers, 6 extended abstracts, and 5 position papers. For this post-proceedings three new papers were submitted and all the papers were reviewed again by at least one reviewer, and in most cases at least two, and often three, reviewers. In total, 23 papers were accepted to the post-proceedings: 11 long papers, 6 extended abstracts, and 6 position papers. The final papers were reviewed by at least three, and in most cases four or more, reviewers.

We are very grateful to all those who made the workshop such a huge success: the organizing committee members, the programme committee members, and of course, the authors for contributing their research work. We are also grateful to the more than 100 workshop attendees who participated in the workshop, which was held online due to the COVID-19 pandemic.

March 2021

Fredrik Heintz
Michela Milano
Barry O'Sullivan

Organization

Organization Committee

The workshop was organized by the TAILOR H2020-ICT-48 project by the following people:

Fredrik Heintz (Chair)	Linköping University, Sweden
Luc De Raedt	KU Leuven, Belgium
Peter Flach	University of Bristol, UK
Hector Geffner	ICREA and Universitat Pompeu Fabra, Spain
Fosca Giannotti	National Research Council, Pisa, Italy
Holger Hoos	Leiden University, Netherlands
Michela Milano	University of Bologna, Italy
Barry O'Sullivan	University College Cork, Ireland
Ana Paiva	University of Lisbon, Portugal
Marc Schoenauer	Inria, France
Philipp Slusallek	DFKI, Germany
Joaquin Vanschoren	Eindhoven University of Technology, Netherlands

Program Committee

Giuseppe Attardi	Università di Pisa, Italy
Roman Barták	Charles University, Czech Republic
Maria Bielikova	Slovak University of Technology, Slovakia
Vicent Botti	Universitat Politècnica de València, Spain
Miguel Couceiro	Inria, France
Saso Dzeroski	Jozef Stefan Institute, Slovenia
Huascar Espinoza	CEA LIST, France
Elisa Fromont	Université de Rennes 1, France
Luis Galárraga	Inria, France
Maria Garcia De La Banda	Monash University, Australia
Randy Goebel	University of Alberta, Canada
Marco Gori	University of Siena, Italy
Dimitrios Gunopulos	University of Athens, Greece
Jose Hernandez-Orallo	Universitat Politècnica de València, Spain
Andreas Herzig	CNRS, IRIT, and University of Toulouse, France
Lars Kotthoff	University of Wyoming, USA
Sarit Kraus	Bar Ilan University, Israel
Krzysztof Krawiec	Poznan University of Technology, Poland
Gerhard Lakemeyer	RWTH Aachen University, Germany
Andrea Lodi	École Polytechnique de Montréal, Canada
Pierre Marquis	CRIL, CNRS, and Artois University, France

Contents

AutoAI

Trustworthy AI

Towards Automated GDPR Compliance Checking

Tomer Libal[(✉)] [iD]

Luxembourg University, Esch-sur-Alzette, Luxembourg
`tomer.libal@uni.lu`

Abstract. The GDPR is one of many legal texts which can greatly benefit from the support of automated reasoning. Since its introduction, efforts were made to formalize it in order to support various automated operations. Nevertheless, widespread and efficient automated reasoning over the GDPR has not yet been achieved. In this paper, a tool called the NAI suite is being used in order to annotate article 13 of the GDPR. The annotation results in a fully formalized version of the article, which deals with the transparency requirements of data collection and processing. Automated compliance checking is then being demonstrated via several simple queries. By using the public API of the NAI suite, arbitrary tools can use this procedure to support trust management and GDPR compliance functions.

Keywords: Automated reasoning · Compliance checking · Data protection

1 Introduction

Computer systems are playing a substantial role in assisting people in a wide range of tasks, including search in large data and decision-making; and their employment is progressively becoming vital in an increasing number of fields. One of these fields is legal reasoning: New court cases and legislations are accumulated every day and navigating through the vast amount of complex information is far from trivial. In addition, the understanding of those texts is reserved only for experts in the legal domain despite the fact that they are usually of interest to the general public.

This characteristic of the law goes beyond simply keeping the public well informed. In some domains, such as privacy and ethics of AI, there is a strong need to regulate and govern over a vast amount of applications and possible infringements. On the 8th of April this year (2019), an independent expert group on AI, set up by the European Commission (EC), has published ethical guidelines for trustworthy AI[1]. These guidelines, which respond to an earlier publication

---

[1] European Commission, Independent High-Level Expert Group on Artificial Intelligence. Ethics Guidelines for Thrustworthy AI. https://ec.europa.eu/futurium/en/ai-alliance-consultation, April 2019.

© Springer Nature Switzerland AG 2021
F. Heintz et al. (Eds.): TAILOR 2020, LNAI 12641, pp. 3–19, 2021.
https://doi.org/10.1007/978-3-030-73959-1_1

of the EC vision for AI[2], have identified three components which should be part of trustworthy AI systems - they should be lawful, ethical and robust.

There is an inherent problem though between these three components and the fact that laws and regulations require a human for their interpretation and for decision making. The number of AI applications grows far faster than the number of regulators and governors.

As an example, let us consider the General Data Protection Regulation (GDPR). This legal document aims at regulating data protection over a vast number of applications, among them, one can count almost all websites, but not only. The loss of privacy is of high interest to all of us. Nevertheless, the human regulators can cover only a fraction of possible infringements.

Despite the need for automation in the legal domain, the employment of automated legal reasoning tools is still underrepresented in practice [6] albeit being a relevant and active field of research since the 1980s [2,27,28]. Some examples of such tools and approaches are for courtroom management [1], legal language processing/management [4] and for business compliance [9].

With the exception of [22], there is no application of these methods to the GDPR and similar tasks. While informative, [22] suggests a framework and does not provide a tested solution. the reasons behind that can be found in [6,8], In this paper, one of the recent tools in the domain, the NAI suite [14,15], is applied to article 13 of the GDPR. This article, which is concerned with the transparency of data collection and processing, is first formalized in a way such that its legal meaning is being captured by the machine. Automated reasoning over the formalization is then being demonstrated on several queries which can be used for compliance testing. When combined with the NAI suite public API, tools can be created which can take advantage of this automated compliance checking. Moreover, together with works on natural language processing of legal texts [18], fully automated lawful, ethical and robust trust management systems might become possible.

Discussion of Related Work. The recency of the GDPR means that it features in relatively few works on automation. Among them, the DAPRECO knowledge base [26] is the most extensive one. This knowledge base is a formalization of most articles of the GDPR into formulas of IO logic [16]. On the other hand, there are currently no known tools which allow for reasoning over it. In addition, this knowledge base contains some typos and semantical errors. A discussion about one of them is presented in Sect. 3.2.

A very recent modeling of articles 5 and 6 of the GDPR appears in [17]. This modeling allows automated reasoning via a Prolog interpreter. Using Prolog for the formalization of legal texts is very powerful and was applied to various examples (see for example [27]). Nevertheless, both the formalization process and the usage of this formalization are non trivial and require, if not logic programming skills, at least an understanding of first-order logic. In addition, the direct formalization into a low level logical language might give raise to errors, as is discussed in Sect. 3.2 in the context of the DAPRECO knowledge base.

---

[2] COM(2018)237 and COM(2018)795.

The paper has several contributions. It presents a full formalization of article 13 of the GDPR, which allows for efficient automated reasoning. Since the formalization in the NAI suite is freely available via a public and RESTFull API, it can be immediately integrated into third-party tools which require automation over this article. Second, it demonstrates how fully automated compliance checking can be achieved. Lastly, some errors in previous efforts to formalize the GDPR are discussed and corrected.

In the next section, an introduction to the NAI suite, its theoretical foundations and its graphical user interface is given. The following section describes the extension of the tool and its application to the formalization of article 13. Section 4 describes the support for automated reasoning and gives some examples of compliance checking. A conclusion and possible future work are given last.

2   The NAI Suite

This section is adapted from [15]. The NAI suite integrates theorem proving technology into a usable graphical user interface (GUI) for the computer-assisted formalization of legal texts and applying automated normative reasoning procedures on these artifacts. In particular, NAI includes

1. a legislation editor that graphically supports the formalization of legal texts,
2. means of assessing the quality of entered formalizations, e.g., by automatically conducting consistency checks and assessing logical independence,
3. ready-to-use theorem prover technology for evaluating user-specified queries wrt. a given formalization, and
4. the possibility to share and collaborate, and to experiment with different formalizations and underlying logics.

NAI is realized using a web-based Software-as-a-service architecture, cf. Fig. 1. It comprises a GUI that is implemented as a Javascript browser application, and a NodeJS application on the back-end side which connects to theorem provers, data storage services and relevant middleware. Using this architectural layout, no further software is required from the user perspective for using NAI and its reasoning procedures, as all necessary software is made available on the back end and the computationally heavy tasks are executed on the remote servers only. The results of the different reasoning procedures are sent back to the GUI and displayed to the user. The major components of NAI are described in more detail in the following.

2.1   The Underlying Logic

The logical formalism underlying the NAI framework is based on a universal fragment first-order variant of the deontic logic **DL*** [13], denoted **DL***$_1$. Its syntax is defined as follows. Let V, P and F be disjoint sets of symbols for

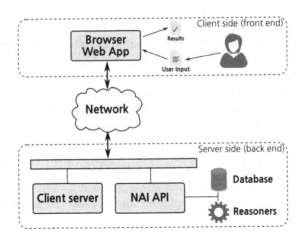

Fig. 1. Software-as-a-service architecture of the NAI reasoning framework. The front end software runs in the user's browser and connects to the remote site, and its different services, via a well-defined API through the network. Data flow is indicated by arrows.

variables, predicate symbols (of some arity) and function symbols (of some arity), respectively. $\mathbf{DL}^*_1$ formulas ϕ, ψ are given by:

$$\phi, \psi ::= p(t_1, \ldots, t_n) \mid \neg\phi \mid \phi \wedge \psi \mid \phi \vee \psi \mid \phi \Rightarrow \psi$$
$$\mid \mathsf{Id}\,\phi \mid \mathsf{Ob}\,\phi \mid \mathsf{Pm}\,\phi \mid \mathsf{Fb}\,\phi$$
$$\mid \phi \Rightarrow_{\mathsf{Ob}} \psi \mid \phi \Rightarrow_{\mathsf{Pm}} \psi \mid \phi \Rightarrow_{\mathsf{Fb}} \psi$$

where $p \in P$ is a predicate symbol of arity $n \geq 0$ and the t_i, $1 \leq i \leq n$, are terms. Terms are freely generated by the function symbols from F and variables from V.

$\mathbf{DL}^*_1$ extends Standard Deontic Logic (SDL) with the normative concepts of ideal and contrary-to-duty obligations, and contains predicate symbols, the standard logical connectives, and the normative operators of obligation (Ob), permission (Pm), prohibition (Fb), their conditional counter-parts, and ideality (Id). Free variables are implicitly universally quantified at top-level.

This logic is expressive enough to capture many interesting normative structures. For details on its expressivity and its semantics, we refer to previous work [13].

2.2   The Reasoning Module

The NAI suite supports formalizing legal texts and applying various logical operations on them. These operations include consistency checks (non-derivability of falsum), logical independence analysis as well as the creation of user queries that can automatically be assessed for (non-)validity. After formalization, the formal representation of the legal text is stored in a general and expressive machine-readable format in NAI. This format aims at generalizing from concrete logical formalisms that are used for evaluating the logical properties of the legal document's formal representation.

There exist many different logical formalisms that have been discussed for capturing normative reasoning and extensions of it. Since the discussion of such formalisms is still ongoing, and the choice of the concrete logic underlying the reasoning process strongly influences the results of all procedures, NAI uses a two-step procedure to employ automated reasoning tools. NAI stores only the general format, as mentioned above, as result of the formalization process. Once a user then chooses a certain logic for conducting the logical analysis, NAI will automatically translate the general format into the specific logic resp. the concrete input format of the employed automated reasoning system. Currently, NAI supports the $\mathbf{DL^*}_1$ logic from Sect. 2.1 and the QMLTP format [25]; however, the architecture of NAI is designed in such a way that further formalisms can easily be supported.

The choice in favor of $\mathbf{DL^*}_1$ is primarily motivated by the fact that it can be effectively automated using a shallow semantical embedding into normal (bi-) modal logic [13]. This enables the use of readily available reasoning systems for such logics; in contrast, there are few to none automated reasoning systems available for normative logics (with the exception of [7]). In NAI, we use the MleanCoP prover [21] for first-order multi-modal logics as it is currently one of the most effective systems and it returns proof certificates which can be independently assessed for correctness [20]. It is also possible to use various different tools for automated reasoning in parallel (where applicable). This is of increasing importance once multiple different logical formalisms are supported.

2.3   The Annotation Editor

The annotation editor of NAI is one of its central components. Using the editor, users can create formalizations of legal documents that can subsequently used for formal legal reasoning. The general functionality of the editor is described in the following.

One of the main ideas of the NAI editor is to hide the underlying logical details and technical reasoning input and outputs from the user. We consider this essential, as the primary target audience of the NAI suite are not necessarily logicians and it could greatly decrease the usability of the tool if a solid knowledge about formal logic was required. This is realized by letting the user annotate legal texts and queries graphically and by allowing the user to access the different reasoning functionalities by simply clicking buttons that are integrated into the GUI. Note that the user can still inspect the logical formulae that result from the annotation process and also input these formulae directly. However, this feature is considered advanced and not the primary approach put forward by NAI.

The formalization proceeds as follows: The user selects some text from the legal document and annotates it, either as a term or as a composite (complex) statement. In the first case, a name for that term is computed automatically, but it can also be chosen freely. Different terms are displayed as different colors in the text. In the latter case, the user needs to choose among the different possibilities, which correspond to either logical connectives or higher-level sentence structures called macros. The composite annotations are displayed as a box around the text and can be done recursively. An example of an annotation result is displayed in Fig. 2.

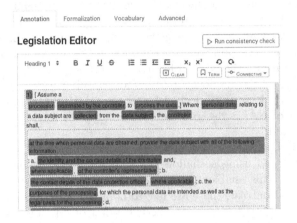

Fig. 2. Article 13, par 1: full annotation

The editor also features direct access to the consistency check and logical independence check procedures (as buttons). When such a button is clicked, the current state of the formalization will be translated and sent to the back-end provers, which determine whether it is consistent resp. logically independent.

User queries are also created using such an editor. In addition to the steps sketched above, users may declare a text passage as *goal* using a dedicated annotation button, whose contents are again annotated as usual. If the query is executed, the back-end provers will try to prove (or refute) that the goal logically follows from the remaining annotations and the underlying legislation.

2.4 The Application Programming Interface (API)

All the reasoning features of NAI can also be accessed by third-party applications. The NAI suite exposes a RESTful (Representational state transfer) API which allows (external) applications to run consistency checks, checks for independence as well as queries and use the result for further processing. The exposure of NAI's REST API is particularly interesting for external legal applications that want to make use of the already formalized legal documents hosted by NAI. A simple example of such an application is a tax counseling web site which advises its visitors using legal reasoning over a formalization of the relevant tax law done in the NAI suite.

3   Formalizing GDPR Article 13

An essential element in the compliance checking of privacy policies and data collection procedures, article 13[3] of the GDPR is concerned with their transparency. This article contains 4 paragraphs, where the first two contain each 6 subsections. The third paragraph extends and modify the second one while the last states a situation in which the three previous paragraphs do not hold.

This section describes the formalization of this article using the NAI suite and the extensions to the suite which were implemented in order to support this formalization. While all necessary information is contained in the paper, the reader is still invited to follow this section and the one immediately after while simultaneously looking at the formalization in the tool itself. The formalization and queries which resulted from this work can be freely accessed via the NAI suite web application on a demo account. No registration is needed and no information (such as IP addresses) is recorded[4].

3.1   Annotating Paragraph 1

The NAI suite, as described in the previous section, requires us first to create a new legislation and then copy the original text into the editor pane. The first paragraph describes a situation in which a controller is obliged to communicate different information to the data subject, according to different conditions. Although not explicitly written, this paragraph also talks about processors and the processing of the data itself, as well as of its collection. In order to formalize the article, we must make these elements explicit in the text. We therefore add this information in brackets ('[',']') as can be seen in Fig. 3a.

Given the explicit text of the paragraph, we are ready to annotate it. The first step of every formalization using the NAI suite is to point out all the legal terms used in the legal text. Those terms correspond to the colorful annotations in the editor. There are many relations between the different legal terms. For example, the personal data of the data subject is being collected and processed and is subject to the supervision of a Data Privacy Officer (DPO). Such complex relations require an expressive language such as fist-order logic, which is used in the annotations of the article.

As an example of term annotations, one can consider the phrases "data subject" and "personal data", for which the following first-order terms were assigned (respectively): `data_subject(Subject)` and `personal_data(Data, Subject)`. As described in Sect. 2, words starting with a lower-case letter are considered as constants while those starting with a capital letter are considered as variables which are quantified over the whole logical expression. An example of this step can be seen in Fig. 4a.

The full list of annotated legal terms can be found on the "Vocabulary" tab in the legislation editor. An example of this tab can be seen in Fig. 3b.

---

[3] https://eur-lex.europa.eu/eli/reg/2016/679/oj.

[4] Please login to https://nai.uni.lu using the email address: gdpr@nai.lu and password: nai. Please note that this account is write protected and cannot be changed.

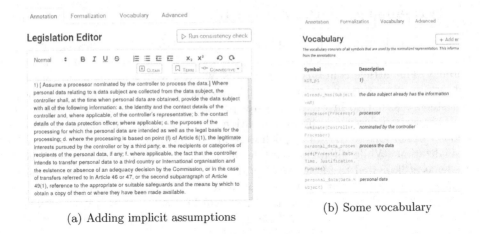

(a) Adding implicit assumptions

(b) Some vocabulary

Fig. 3. Article 13, par. 1

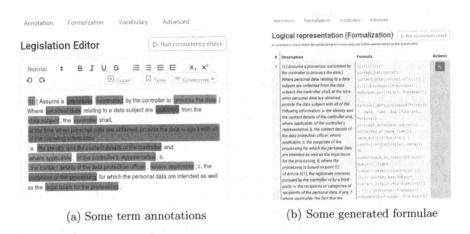

(a) Some term annotations

(b) Some generated formulae

Fig. 4. Article 13, par. 1

Once all legal terms are annotated, we can proceed with annotating the relationships between them as well. The NAI suite supports two kinds of such annotations. The basic connectives cover logical and Deontical annotations. The macros cover all annotations which do not fall within the first group and which normally correspond to certain sentence structures. Connectives of both groups can be found under the "Connectives" tab in the editor. All the connectives within these groups are used for annotating other, already existing, annotations.

The structure of the paragraph is the following. A set of conditions for the whole paragraph are followed by an obligation to communicate information. The precise information to communicate then follows in each of the items, possibly with some further conditions. Such a sentence structure is beyond most logics. In particular, it is not supported by the logic DL*, which is currently used by the NAI suite. A correct formalization of this sentence will consist therefore of a conjunction of obligations, each with its own set of conditions, which are formed by combining the general conditions of the paragraph with the specific condition of each item.

In order for the annotation process to be as simple as possible, we need to avoid major changes to the original text. We need therefore to be able to annotate the original text such that the target structure mentioned above is generated.

The NAI suite supports such a sentence structure via the "Multi-obligation Macro". This macro accepts an annotation denoting the general conditions and a second annotation denoting the additional obligations and their specific conditions. When applied, the macro generates a conjunction of obligations, one for each of the annotated obligations and with the general conditions as well as the specific ones. We therefore annotate the whole paragraph 1 with this annotation.

We now proceed with annotating the conditions and obligations. First, we use the "And" connective to annotate all the general conditions, such as the existence of a process and a controller, etc. We then proceed by using the "And" connective to annotate all the obligations. Each obligation can have one of three forms. A simple obligation contains just a term. The macro will convert this obligation into a conditional obligation where the conditions are all the general ones from the first conjunction. The more complex obligations are either "If/Then" and "Always/If".

The difference between these two connectives is syntactical only. While in "If/Then", the conditions are specified by the first annotation and the conclusion with the second, the order is reversed in "Always/If". By using one of these two annotations for the differed obligations, the macro will know to add the additional, specific conditions to the conditions of each resulted obligation. An example of the fully annotated text can be seen in Fig. 2.

The automatically generated annotation of the first item of paragraph 1 can be seen in Fig. 5.

Once annotating the text has finished and the user clicks the "Save" button, the tool generates representation of the formalization in the logic $\mathbf{DL}^*_1$. The formulae are accessible via the "Formalization" tab. An example can be seen in Fig. 4b.

```
IF-THEN-OB(AND(processor(Processor),nominate(Controller,
Processor),personal_data_processed(Processor,Data,Time,
Justification,Purpose),personal_data(Data,Subject),
collected_at(Data,Time0),data_subject(Subject),
controller(Controller, Data)),communicate_at_time(Controller,
Subject,Time0,contact_details(Controller)))
```

Fig. 5. Automatically generated annotation of item 1 in paragraph 1

The specific annotations can be seen by hovering with the mouse over the relevant parts of the text.

The annotation of paragraph 2 is similar.

3.2   Annotating Paragraph 3

Paragraph 3 is relatively short syntactically but complex semantically. It expands on paragraph 2 and places further conditions and obligations. While paragraph 2 describes the obligations in case of the first data processing, paragraph 3 describes those in all subsequent ones.

The annotation of this paragraph makes use of two additional macros. The "Labeling" macro supports naming previous annotations while the "Copying" macro uses such labels in order to copy previous annotations and modify them.

The modification which is required for this paragraph is the addition of the conditions involving further processing. In addition, the macro makes sure to apply all the obligations from paragraph 2 to the additional processing instead of to the original one. Lastly, the macro adds the additional obligation for the controller to communicate the purpose of this additional processing as well.

Facilitating Correct Formalizations. There is a further interesting issue which relates to this paragraph. Clearly, its annotation is far from trivial and is error prone. Still, by using macros and annotations, the chance of error occurring is reduced since there is a clear connection between the text itself and its annotation. This is not the case when the paragraph is translated into a logical formula manually. As an example, consider the DAPRECO formalization of the GDPR [26]. As mentioned in the introduction to this paper, this ambitious knowledge base contains a manual translation of almost all articles of the GDPR.

Nevertheless, if we focus on the translation of this paragraph[5], we can see several errors. First, the translation does not mention at all the fact that all of the required information mentioned in paragraph 2 is required here as well. Even more important though, there is no distinction between the two processing events of the data, except in the name of the variable used to denote them. There is a relation between the times of the two occurrences but it is defined as "greater or equal". Clearly, this formalization will always apply to any processing, whether first or not, since one can substitute for the universally quantified variables the same processing and the same time.

Such an error is not easy to spot, when one translates regulations manually. Using macro annotations makes errors easier to spot and avoid due to several reasons. First, annotating the original text makes the formalization closer to the text, than when replacing this text with another, which is closer to the end formula. Second, the well known software engineering principle - Don't Repeat Yourself (DRY) - is applicable also here. If we manually expand paragraph 1, for example, we obtain at least 6 different new sentences of very similar content. The same goes with duplicating all the requirements of paragraph 2 in paragraph 3. The same benefits of using this principle in software engineering apply also here. For example, any update or change to the repeated information needs to

---

[5] Please search for the text "statements51Formula" in https://raw.githubusercontent. com/dapreco/daprecokb/master/gdpr/rioKB_GDPR.xml, of a version no later than 11/2019.

be done only once and therefore, the chances of typos and mistakes are reduced. Last, it should be noted that the formalization process is far from being trivial. For example, the process of formalizing just article 13 took the author almost a day. Automating as much of this process by the use of macros has saved some time and as a consequence, reduced the change of making an error.

On the other hand, when using annotations and macros, we could more easily spot this and use a correct annotation.

3.3   Annotating Paragraph 4

The last paragraph in the article has a standard legal form. Its purpose is to set exceptional circumstances in which other paragraphs do not hold. In our example, none of the obligations in the previous paragraphs should hold in case the data subject already has the required information.

In the previous subsection, we have seen a utility macro for labeling annotations. This macro is handy here as well as we will need to be able to refer to other annotations, in order to apply a macro for exceptional circumstances.

The "Exception" macro takes the labels of other annotations and apply to them the negation of a further condition. In this case, the negated condition is that the data subject does not already has the required information.

4   Automated GDPR Compliant Checking

The previous section listed some of the technical issues we face, as well as their solution, when trying to correctly formalize complex legal documents. Section 2 has described several automated deduction based tools, which can be used for checking the correctness of the formalization. Nevertheless, the main usage of automated deduction within the NAI suite is for allowing the computer to answer questions and make legal deductions. Given a correctly formalized legislation, NAI can currently answer Yes/No questions. This is done by employing the state-of-the-art theorem prover MleanCoP [21], which in turn tries to build a formal proof that the question logically follows from the formalization and assumptions. Since this process is incomplete, some negative answers cannot be given. The NAI suite displays a warning in this case.

The main expected usage of this feature is by third-party tools, which will use the deduction engine of the NAI suite over an already formalized legislation in order to answer arbitrary questions. For example, the queries we are going to see in this section might be constructed automatically by such a third-party tool and sent, via the API, to the NAI suite for compliance checking.

Nevertheless, the NAI suite also supports the possibility of writing queries directly in the tool. This feature is mainly used for testing and as a support tool for lawyers and jurists. Similarly, this feature can be used in order to demonstrate automatic reasoning over the article.

The example queries in this section are all about the compliance of certain sentences from possible privacy policies. There are various ways for checking compliance and some are mentioned in [22]. In this section, compliance is being checked by asking if something is permitted. In all the examples, we will ask if a sentence appearing in the privacy policy can be considered as permitted according to the law. This gives raise to at least two interpretations of permissions, weak permissions allow something in case it is not explicitly forbidden by law while strong permissions allow something in case it is explicitly permitted [10]. Both can be obtained by using the correct formalizations but the more straightforward, at least with regard to automated reasoning and in the absence of meta-logical operators such as negation-as-failure, is the strong permission. We will therefore take permission to mean strong permission in this section. These questions can be found and executed on the "Queries" menu of the tool.

In order to best illustrate how the tool can be used for compliance checking, a specific scenario is chosen. We assume that the privacy policy contains a sentence about a possible future use of the subject data which was not considered when the data was collected. The policy then describes the time frame in which the purpose of this use will be communicated to the subject. We distinguish three different time frames and discuss for each how automated reasoning can provide an answer for compliance.

Time Frame 1: Within 24 h After the Additional Processing. In order to create a query to this affect, one must first build the whole scenario. In our case, it contains information about data, data subject, controller, the first processor and the second processor. For the reader who is following the demo account on nai.uni.lu, this information appears within brackets for all the compliance queries. Figures 6 and 7 shows the annotation and generated formalization of this query, respectively.

We are now in a position to ask our specific yes/no question: "Is it compliant to have in the policy: We will update you about the purpose of the processing within 24 h after the time of processing"? The way we formalize this question as a compliance test is as follows: "Is it permitted by article 13 of the GDPR to communicate this information to the data subject within 24 h after the time of processing"?

The above query and assumptions, as well as the formalization of the GDPR are then being translated into multi-modal first-order logic and sent to the MleanCoP prover. The prover will find a proof only if the above normative question can be derived. Clearly, this time frame is beyond that allowed to the controller to communicate this information and indeed, the theorem prover will answer "No" to the question.

In Fig. 6, one can see the result of executing the query displayed above the annotation, as well as the result of running a consistency check.

The reader might note that this question concerns time and that time computations require numerical operators such as "greater than", etc. The logic currently in use does not support such operations out of the box and they need to be included in the formalization. The formalization gives us the certain time of each of the processings as well as the time of the collection of data. We additionally use temporal sentences such as before, after, at and

Fig. 6. Annotation of first compliance query

within. In this case, paragraph 3 of the article obliges the controller to notify the subject any time before the second processing takes place. We ask a question about a time frame which is within 24 h after this processing took place. For the compliance test to be accurate, we must add logical expressions associating the terms "before" and "within" correctly, such as $\forall X, Y, Z, Action :$ $before(Action, Z) \wedge earlier(X, Y) \wedge earlier(Y, Z) \Rightarrow within(Action, X, Y).$

We add this formula to the formalization and click "Execute query". The NAI Suite answers "No". We conclude that the above sentence which appears in a privacy policy is not compliant with the law.

Time Frame 2: Anytime Before the Additional Processing. This query is much easier as it asks for permission of something which is already an obligation. We expect the tool to answer "Yes" and indeed it does. Therefore, having the sentence above is compliant with the law.

Time Frame 3: At the Moment of Collecting the Data. This is a more interesting query which depends again on some temporal reasoning. In this case, we need to say that if something is permitted before time Z and that time X is earlier than time Z, then it is also permitted in time X. Nevertheless, the tool answers "Yes" even without us adding a logical expression of the above.

The reason for that is the following. The interpretation which was given by the author to paragraph 2 of the article is that it holds for any processing, whether it is the first, second or later. At the same time, paragraph 3 holds for any processing except the first one. Therefore, it seems that both paragraphs apply to any processing except the first, while for the first processing, only paragraph 2 applies. This might be a simplistic view of the law, not taking into

Fig. 7. Automatically generated assumptions of the first compliance query

account different legal interpretations such as those which consider paragraph 3 as "lex specialis" to paragraph 2 and therefore exclude the subject of paragraph 3 from paragraph 2. For the normative reasoning done by the tool to be correct, a "correct" legal interpretation must be used. This discussion about the "correct" legal interpretation of the GDPR is beyond the scope of this paper and we take paragraph 3 to be "lex posterior" to paragraph 2.

Still, whether because of our legal interpretation of because of the addition of the temporal expressions, the tool answers "Yes". It is indeed compliant with the law to communicate to the subject the purpose of the second processing already at the time of collecting the data.

5   Conclusion and Future Work

Automated reasoning over legal texts in general, and the GDPR in particular, is advantageous. Automatizing reasoning over the GDPR can support lawful, ethical and robust data privacy governing as well as compliance checking.

This paper has presented a formalization of article 13 of the GDPR. The article was first annotated using the NAI suite. The logical interpretation of the article was then automatically extracted. Several examples of queries over this formalization were then presented. The real potential though is by connecting various third-party tools to the NAI suite API. This will allow the creation of tools for supporting the work of controllers, data privacy officers, regulators and auditors, to name a few.

This work can be extended to include more articles of the GDPR as well as relevant case law. At the same time, web applications can be created based on the formalization to support the work of various people, as discussed in the previous paragraph.

Currently, the NAI suite supports an expressive Deontic first-order language. This language is rich enough to describe many scenarios which appear in legal texts. Nevertheless, more work is required in order to capture all such scenarios. Among those features with the highest priority, we list support for exceptions, temporal sentences and arithmetic. In Sect. 3.3, one possible direction for addressing exceptions was given. Other possible solutions for these issues already exist in the form of tools such as non-monotonic reasoners [11], temporal provers [29] and SMT solvers [5]. The current approach investigated in NAI is to use logic programming for Deontic reasoning [12].

On the level of usability, the tool currently does not give any information as to why a query is counter-satisfiable. The user needs to look on the vocabulary in order to determine possible reasons. Integrating a model finder, such as Nitpick [3], will help "debugging" formalizations and enriching the query language.

A crucial element of any legal formalization tool is the ability to use relevant vocabulary (contract law, privacy law, etc.). The current approach of NAI of using terms to denote this vocabulary will be soon replaced with an method for choosing entities from a privacy law ontology, such as PrOnto [23], GDPRtEXT [24] and PrivOnto [19].

NAI's graphical user interface (GUI) aims at being intuitive and easy to use and tries to hide the underline complexities of the logics involved. A continuously updated list of new features can be found on the GUI's development website[6].

References

1. Aucher, G., Berbinau, J., Morin, M.L.: Principles for a judgement editor based on binary decision diagrams. IfCoLog J. Log. Appl. **6**(5), 781–815 (2019)
2. Biagioli, C., Mariani, P., Tiscornia, D.: Esplex: a rule and conceptual model for representing statutes. In: Proceedings of the 1st International Conference on Artificial Intelligence and Law, pp. 240–251. ACM (1987)
3. Blanchette, J.C., Nipkow, T.: Nitpick: a counterexample generator for higher-order logic based on a relational model finder. In: Kaufmann, M., Paulson, L.C. (eds.) ITP 2010. LNCS, vol. 6172, pp. 131–146. Springer, Heidelberg (2010). https://doi.org/10.1007/978-3-642-14052-5_11
4. Boella, G., Di Caro, L., Humphreys, L., Robaldo, L., Rossi, P., van der Torre, L.: Eunomos, a legal document and knowledge management system for the web to provide relevant, reliable and up-to-date information on the law. Artif. Intell. Law **24**(3), 245–283 (2016)
5. Bouton, T., Caminha B. de Oliveira, D., Déharbe, D., Fontaine, P.: veriT: an open, trustable and efficient SMT-solver. In: Schmidt, R.A. (ed.) CADE 2009. LNCS (LNAI), vol. 5663, pp. 151–156. Springer, Heidelberg (2009). https://doi.org/10.1007/978-3-642-02959-2_12

---

[6] https://github.com/normativeai/frontend/issues.

6. de Bruin, H., Prakken, H., Svensson, J.S.: The use of legal knowledge-based systems in public administration: what can go wrong? In: Evaluation of Legal Reasoning and Problem-Solving Systems, pp. 14–16 (2003)
7. Governatori, G., Shek, S.: Regorous: a business process compliance checker. In: Proceedings of the 14th International Conference on Artificial Intelligence and Law, pp. 245–246. ACM (2013)
8. Groothuis, M.M., Svensson, J.S.: Expert system support and juridical quality. In: Proceedings of JURIX, vol. 110. IOS Press, Amsterdam (2000)
9. Hashmi, M., Governatori, G.: Norms modeling constructs of business process compliance management frameworks: a conceptual evaluation. Artif. Intell. Law **26**(3), 251–305 (2018). https://doi.org/10.1007/s10506-017-9215-8
10. Henrik, G., Wright, V.: Norm and action, a logical enquiry (1963)
11. Kifer, M.: Nonmonotonic reasoning in FLORA-2. In: Baral, C., Greco, G., Leone, N., Terracina, G. (eds.) LPNMR 2005. LNCS (LNAI), vol. 3662, pp. 1–12. Springer, Heidelberg (2005). https://doi.org/10.1007/11546207_1
12. Kowalski, R., Satoh, K.: Obligation as optimal goal satisfaction. J. Philos. Logic **47**(4), 579–609 (2018)
13. Libal, T., Pascucci, M.: Automated reasoning in normative detachment structures with ideal conditions. In: Proceedings of the Seventeenth International Conference on Artificial Intelligence and Law, pp. 63–72. ACM (2019)
14. Libal, T., Steen, A.: The NAI suite - drafting and reasoning over legal texts. In: JURIX (2019, to appear)
15. Libal, T., Steen, A.: NAI: the normative reasoner. In: ICAIL, pp. 262–263. ACM (2019)
16. Makinson, D., Van Der Torre, L.: Input/output logics. J. Philos. Logic **29**(4), 383–408 (2000)
17. de Montety, C., Antignac, T., Slim, C.: GDPR modelling for log-based compliance checking. In: Meng, W., Cofta, P., Jensen, C.D., Grandison, T. (eds.) IFIPTM 2019. IAICT, vol. 563, pp. 1–18. Springer, Cham (2019). https://doi.org/10.1007/978-3-030-33716-2_1
18. Nanda, R., et al.: Concept recognition in European and national law. In: JURIX, pp. 193–198 (2017)
19. Oltramari, A., et al.: PrivOnto: a semantic framework for the analysis of privacy policies. Semant. Web **9**(2), 185–203 (2018)
20. Otten, J.: Implementing connection calculi for first-order modal logics. In: IWIL@ LPAR, pp. 18–32 (2012)
21. Otten, J.: MleanCoP: a connection prover for first-order modal logic. In: Demri, S., Kapur, D., Weidenbach, C. (eds.) IJCAR 2014. LNCS (LNAI), vol. 8562, pp. 269–276. Springer, Cham (2014). https://doi.org/10.1007/978-3-319-08587-6_20
22. Palmirani, M., Governatori, G.: Modelling legal knowledge for GDPR compliance checking. In: JURIX, pp. 101–110 (2018)
23. Palmirani, M., Martoni, M., Rossi, A., Bartolini, C., Robaldo, L.: PrOnto: privacy ontology for legal reasoning. In: Kő, A., Francesconi, E. (eds.) EGOVIS 2018. LNCS, vol. 11032, pp. 139–152. Springer, Cham (2018). https://doi.org/10.1007/978-3-319-98349-3_11
24. Pandit, H.J., Fatema, K., O'Sullivan, D., Lewis, D.: GDPRtEXT - GDPR as a linked data resource. In: Gangemi, A., et al. (eds.) ESWC 2018. LNCS, vol. 10843, pp. 481–495. Springer, Cham (2018). https://doi.org/10.1007/978-3-319-93417-4_31
25. Raths, T., Otten, J.: The QMLTP library: Benchmarking theorem provers for modal logics. Technical report, University of Potsdam (2011)

26. Robaldo, L., Bartolini, C., Palmirani, M., Rossi, A., Martoni, M., Lenzini, G.: Formalizing GDPR provisions in reified I/O logic: the DAPRECO knowledge base. J. Logic Lang. Inf. **29**, 401–449 (2020)

27. Sergot, M.J., Sadri, F., Kowalski, R.A., Kriwaczek, F., Hammond, P., Cory, H.T.: The British nationality act as a logic program. Commun. ACM **29**(5), 370–386 (1986)

28. Stamper, R.: LEGOL: modelling legal rules by computer. Computer Science and Law, pp. 45–71 (1980)

29. Suda, M., Weidenbach, C.: A PLTL-prover based on labelled superposition with partial model guidance. In: Gramlich, B., Miller, D., Sattler, U. (eds.) IJCAR 2012. LNCS (LNAI), vol. 7364, pp. 537–543. Springer, Heidelberg (2012). https://doi.org/10.1007/978-3-642-31365-3_42

Underestimation Bias and Underfitting in Machine Learning

Pádraig Cunningham[1(✉)] and Sarah Jane Delany[2]

[1] University College Dublin, Dublin, Ireland
padraig.cunningham@ucd.ie
[2] Technological University Dublin, Dublin, Ireland
sarahjane.delany@tudublin.ie

Abstract. Often, what is termed algorithmic bias in machine learning will be due to historic bias in the training data. But sometimes the bias may be introduced (or at least exacerbated) by the algorithm itself. The ways in which algorithms can actually accentuate bias has not received a lot of attention with researchers focusing directly on methods to eliminate bias - no matter the source. In this paper we report on initial research to understand the factors that contribute to bias in classification algorithms. We believe this is important because underestimation bias is inextricably tied to regularization, i.e. measures to address overfitting can accentuate bias.

Keywords: Machine Learning · Algorithmic bias

1 Introduction

Research on bias in Machine Learning (ML) has focused on two issues; how to measure bias and how to ensure fairness [12]. In this paper we examine the contribution of the classifier algorithm to bias. An algorithm would be biased if it were more inclined to award desirable outcomes to one side of a sensitive category. The desirable outcome could be a loan or a job, the category might be gender or race. It is clear that there are two main sources of bias in classification [10]:

- **Negative Legacy**: the bias is there in the training data, either due to poor sampling, incorrect labeling or discriminatory practices in the past.
- **Underestimation**: the classifier under-predicts an infrequent outcome for the minority group. This can occur when the classifier *underfits* the data, thereby focusing on strong signals in the data and missing more subtle phenomena.

In most cases the data (negative legacy) rather than the algorithm itself is the root of the problem. This question is neatly sidestepped in most fairness research by focusing on fair outcomes no matter what is the source of the problem.

We argue that it is useful to explore the extent to which algorithms accentuate bias because this issue is inextricably tied to regularisation, a central issue in ML.

© Springer Nature Switzerland AG 2021
F. Heintz et al. (Eds.): TAILOR 2020, LNAI 12641, pp. 20–31, 2021.
https://doi.org/10.1007/978-3-030-73959-1_2

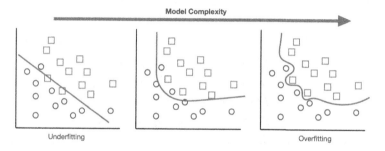

Fig. 1. The relationship between model fitting and model complexity. The fitted model is shown as a grey line that separates two classes in the data (red circles and green squares). Overfitted models can fit to noise in the training data while underfitted models miss a lot of the detail. (Color figure online)

In developing ML models a key concern is to avoid overfitting. Overfitting occurs when the model fits to noise in the training data, thus reducing generalisation performance (see Fig. 1). Regularisation controls the complexity of the model in order to reduce the propensity to overfit. The way regularisation is achieved depends on the model. The complexity of decision trees can be controlled by limiting the number of nodes in the tree. Overfitting in neural networks can be managed by limiting the magnitude of the weights. In this paper we discuss models at the other end of the complexity spectrum that underfit the training data. We show that underestimation bias can occur with underfitted models.

2 Background

Before proceeding to the evaluation it is worth providing some background on the key concepts discussed in this paper. In the next section we provide some definitions relating to regularisation. In Sect. 2.2 we review some relevant research on bias and fairness in ML. Section 2.3 introduces the concept of Illusory Correlation and discusses its relevance to algorithmic bias.

2.1 Regularisation

Regularisation is a term from Statistics that refers to policies and strategies to prevent overfitting. In training a supervised ML model, the objective it to achieve good generalisation performance on unseen data. This can be assessed by holding back some test data from the training process and using it to get an assessment of generalisation performance. The relative performance on these training and test sets provides some insight on underfitting and overfitting [8]:

– **Underfitting** occurs when a model does not capture the detail of the phenomenon; these models will have some errors on the training data (see Fig. 1).

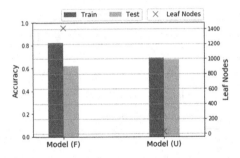

Fig. 2. A demonstration of underfitting Model(U) and overfitting Model(F) on the Recidivism task presented in Sect. 3.2.

– **Overfitting** occurs when the model fits too closely to the training data picking up detail that does not generalise to unseen data. An overfitted model will have low error on the training data but higher error on test data.

Controlling overfitting is one of the central concerns in ML. It is difficult because it depends on the interplay between the volume of data available and the *capacity* of the model. If the training data provides comprehensive coverage of the phenomenon then overfitting is not a problem – it need only be an issue when the training data is not comprehensive. The capacity of the model refers to its expressive power; low capacity models will underfit while high capacity models can overfit. Figure 2 shows examples of under and overfitting on the Recidivism task described in Sect. 3.2. In this case the model is a decision tree and the capacity is managed by controlling the number of leaf nodes. Limiting the number of leaf nodes to 30 results in an underfitted model whereas the overfitted model has been allowed to extend to 1413 leaf nodes. The overfitted model has good performance on the training data but does not generalise well. The underfitted model has better performance on the test (unseen) data.

2.2 Bias and Fairness

The connection between regularisation and bias arises from the context in which bias occurs. Consider a scenario where the desirable classification outcome is the minority class (e.g. job offer) and the sensitive feature represents groups in the population where minority groups may have low *base rates* for the desirable outcome [1]. So samples representing good outcomes for minority groups are scarce. Excessive regularisation causes the model to ignore or under-represent these data.

We are not aware of any research on bias in ML that explores the relationship between underestimation and regularisation. This issue has received some attention [1,10] but it is not specifically explored. Instead research has addressed algorithmic interventions that ensure fairness as an outcome [2,12,14,15].

Fundamental to all research on bias in ML are the measures to quantify bias. We define Y to be the outcome (class variable) and $Y = 1$ is the 'desirable' outcome. $\hat{Y} = 1$ indicates that the classifier has predicted the desirable outcome. S is a 'sensitive' feature and $S \neq 1$ is the minority group (e.g. non-white). In this notation the Calders Verwer *discrimination score* [2] is:

$$\text{CV} \leftarrow P[\hat{Y} = 1 | S = 1] - P[\hat{Y} = 1 | S \neq 1] \tag{1}$$

If there is no discrimination, this score should be zero.

In contrast the *disparate impact* (DI_S) definition of unfairness [7] is a ratio rather than a difference:

$$\text{DI}_S \leftarrow \frac{P[\hat{Y} = 1 | S \neq 1]}{P[\hat{Y} = 1 | S = 1]} < \tau \tag{2}$$

$\tau = 0.8$ is the 80% rule, i.e. outcomes for the minority should be within 80% of those for the majority.

For our evaluations we define an *underestimation score* (US_S) in line with DI_S that quantifies the underestimation effect described above:

$$\text{US}_S \leftarrow \frac{P[\hat{Y} = 1 | S \neq 1]}{P[Y = 1 | S \neq 1]} \tag{3}$$

If $\text{US}_S < 1$ the classifier is predicting fewer desirable outcomes than are present in the training data.

2.3 Illusory Correlation

Algorithmic bias due to underestimation is similar in some respects to the concept of Illusory Correlation in Psychology [3]. With Illusory Correlation people associate the frequent class with the majority group and the rare class with the minority, the infrequent class is overestimated for the minority group [5]. For instance, if the infrequent class is antisocial behaviour, the incidence will be over-associated with the minority. If the frequent class is a good credit rating, it will be over-associated with the majority. This over-estimation also happens for the frequent class in ML. However, the impact for the infrequent class and the minority feature is the opposite; the algorithm will likely accentuate the under-representation. In ML, the infrequent class outcome will be underestimated for the minority feature.

In Fig. 3 we see the similarities and differences between Illusory Correlation and ML bias. For the majority feature and the frequent class the behaviour is the same, the association is accentuated. However, the impact on the infrequent side of the classification is different, the ML bias is always *towards* the frequent class. This is a problem if the infrequent outcome is the desirable one (e.g. loan approval, job offer). This difference is probably due to the different underlying mechanisms in humans and computers. Hamilton and Gifford [9] argue that Illusory Correlation is due to cognitive mechanisms that produce distortions in judgement and contribute to the formation of stereotypes. Whereas we argue here that underestimation results from a combination of poor data coverage and restricted model capacity.

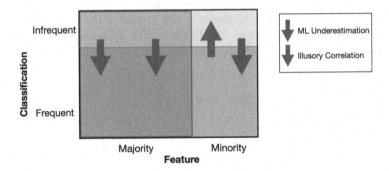

Fig. 3. The relationship between Illusory Correlation and ML Underestimation. Illusory Correlation accentuates the frequent class for the majority and the infrequent class for the minority. With ML Underestimation the bias is all towards the Frequent outcome.

3   Evaluation

We present preliminary results on three binary classification datasets from the UCI repository[1]. We also include an analysis on an anonymised and reduced version of the *ProPublica* Recidivism dataset [6,11]. Our analysis is based on the same set of seven features as used in the study by Dressel and Farid [6]. The UCI datasets are Adult, Wholesale Customers and User Knowledge Modelling (see Table 1).

We use the Adult and Recidivism datasets to demonstrate the relationship between underestimation and regularisation (Sect. 3.2) and then we explore this in more detail in the other two datasets. In this second part of the evaluation, in order to control the propensity for bias, we introduce a sensitive binary feature S with $S \neq 0$ representing the sensitive minority. To show bias due to underestimation we set $P[S \neq 1|Y = 1] = 0.15$ and $P[S \neq 1|Y \neq 1] = 0.3$, i.e. the sensitive group is under-represented in the desirable class. We also report baseline results with the incidence of $S \neq 1$ balanced with the sensitive group occurring 30% of the time in both classes. We are interested in uncovering situations where this

Table 1. The datasets used in the evaluation. For consistency, the Positive outcome is the minority class in all datasets.

Dataset	Samples	Features	% Positive	Train:Test
Adult	48,842	14	25%	2:1
Recidivism	7,214	7	45%	2:1
Knowledge	403	5	26%	1:2
Wholesale	440	7	32%	1:1

---

[1] archive.ics.uci.edu/ml/.

under-representation is accentuated by the classifier. In Sect. 3.3 we look at the untuned performance of seven classifiers from scikit-learn. In Sect. 3.4 we look at the impact of regularisation on neural net performance. In the next section we provide a more formal account of our bias measures.

3.1 Evaluation Measures

If a binary classifier is biased this will show up as a mismatch between the predicted positives P′ and the actual positives P (see Table 2). This is likely to happen when the training data is significantly imbalanced resulting in predictions that underestimate the overall minority class [4]. From this perspective, bias is

Table 2. Confusion matrix for binary classification.

		Predicted		
		Pos	Neg	
Actual	Pos	TP	FN	P
	Neg	FP	TN	N
		P′	N′	

independent of accuracy so whether predictions are correct or not (True or False) is not relevant. So the minority class bias is effectively an underestimation at a class level, i.e.:

$$\text{US} \leftarrow \frac{\text{TP+FP}}{\text{TP+FN}} = \frac{\text{P}'}{\text{P}} \qquad (4)$$

When the classifier is biased away from the positive class, P′ < P this US score is less than 1. The US_S score defined in Eq. 3 measures the same fraction, but for samples where the sensitive feature $S \neq 1$.

$$\text{US}_S \leftarrow \frac{\text{P}'_{S \neq 1}}{\text{P}_{S \neq 1}} \qquad (5)$$

While bias can be considered independently of accuracy, there is an important interplay between bias and accuracy. So the final evaluation measure we consider is the overall accuracy:

$$\text{Acc} \leftarrow \frac{\text{TP+TN}}{\text{TP+FN+FP+FN}} \qquad (6)$$

3.2 Underestimation in Action

We use the Adult and Recidivism datasets to show the impact of underestimation. In Table 3 we see that in the Adult dataset Females with salaries greater than 50K account for just 4% of cases and in the Recidivism dataset Caucasians are relatively underrepresented among repeat offenders. We will see that this under-representation is accentuated by the classifiers.

Table 3. Summary statistics for the Adult and Recidivism datasets. In both cases a feature/class combination is significantly underrepresented in the data. Key feature-specific percentages are shown in red, for instance 11% of females are in the > 50K salary category.

Adult	Gender		
	Male	Female	Totals
< 50k	47%	29%	76%
> 50k	20% (30%)	4% (11%)	24%
Totals	67%	33%	100%

(Salary, rows)

Recidivism	Caucasian		
	No	Yes	Totals
No	34%	21%	55%
Yes	32%(48%)	13%(39%)	45%
Totals	66%	34%	100%

(Reoffend, rows)

Adult Dataset: This dataset is much studied in research on bias in ML because there is clear evidence of Negative Legacy [2]. At 33%, females are underrepresented in the dataset. This under-representation is worse in the > 50K salary category where only 1/6 are female.

(a)

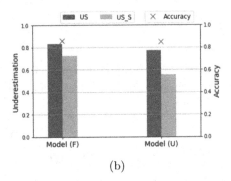

(b)

Fig. 4. A demonstration of model bias and underestimation on the Adult dataset. (a) 24% of all cases and 11% of Females have Salary > 50K. Both models underestimate these outcomes with the underfitted model Model (U) underestimating most. (b) Both models have similar accuracies and both underestimate overall (US). The underestimation for Females (US_S) is worse and is worst in the underfitted model Model (U).

To illustrate underestimation we use a gradient boosting classifier [13]. We build two classifiers, one with just 5 trees (Model (U)) and one with 50 (Model (F)). Both models have good accuracy, 85% and 86% respectively. Figure 4(a) shows the actual incidence of Salary > 50 overall and for females. It also shows the predicted incidence by the two models. We can see that both models underestimate the probability of the Salary > 50 class overall. On the right in Fig. 4(a) we can see that this underestimation is exacerbated for females. This underestimation is worse in the underfitted model. The actual occurrence of salaries > 50K for females is 11% in the data, the underfitted model is predicting 6%. The extent of this underestimation is quantified in Fig. 4(b).

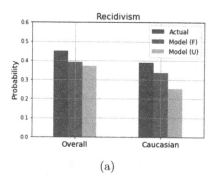
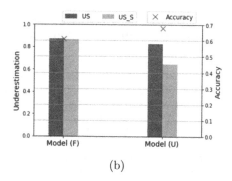

(a)   (b)

Fig. 5. A demonstration of bias and underestimation on the Recidivism dataset. (a) 46% of all cases and 38% of Caucasians are recidivists. Both models underestimate these outcomes with the underfitted model Model (U) underestimating most. (b) The underfitted model has better generalisation accuracy. Both models underestimate overall (US) with the underfitted model underestimating more for Caucasians (US_S).

So underestimation is influenced by three things, underfitting, minority class and minority features. The underfitted model does a poor job of modelling the minority feature (female) in the minority class (>50K). This is not that easy to fix because it is often desirable not to allow ML models overfit the training data.

Recidivism Dataset: We use the decision tree classifier from scikit-learn[2] to demonstrate underestimation on the Recidivism dataset. In this case we control overfitting by constraining the size of the tree. The underfitted model (Model (U)) has 30 leaf nodes and the other model (Model (F)) has 1349 leaves. The picture here is similar but in this case the underfitted model has better accuracy (Fig. 5). This accuracy comes at the price of increased underestimation. The underestimation is particularly bad for the minority feature with the level of recidivism for Caucasians significantly underestimated. As reported in other analyses [6,11] the input features do not provide a strong signal for predicting recidivism. So the fitted model does not generalise well to unseen data. On the other hand the model that is forced to underfit generalises better but fails to capture the Caucasian recidivism pattern.

3.3 Baseline Performance of Classifiers

We move on now to look at the impact of a synthetic minority feature injected into the other two datasets. This synthetic feature is set up to be biased (negative legacy) $P[S \neq 1|Y = 1] = 0.15$ and $P[S \neq 1|Y \neq 1] = 0.3$. We test to see if this bias is accentuated (i.e. $US_S < 0$) for seven popular classifiers available in scikit-learn. For this assessment, the default parameters for the classifiers are used. There are two exceptions to this; the number of iterations for Logistic

---
[2] scikit-learn.org.

Regression and the Neural Network were increased to get rid of convergence warnings. For the results shown in Fig. 6 the main findings are:

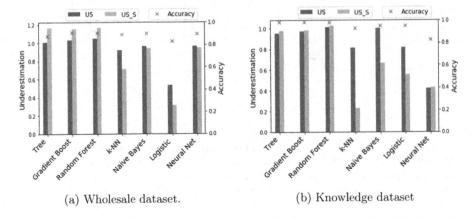

(a) Wholesale dataset.   (b) Knowledge dataset

Fig. 6. The varying impact of underestimation across multiple classifiers. A sensitive feature S $\neq$ 1 has been added to both datasets (15% in the desirable class and 30% in the majority class. With the exception of the three tree-based classifiers, underestimation is exacerbated for this sensitive feature (US_S).

- The tree-based classifiers (Decision Tree, Gradient Boost & Random Forest) all perform very well showing no bias (or a positive bias), both overall (US) and when we filter for the sensitive feature(US$_S$).
- The other classifiers (k-Nearest Neighbour, Naive Bayes, Logistic Regression & Neural Network) all show bias (underestimation), overall and even more so in the context of the sensitive feature.
- The accentuation effect is evident for the four classifiers that show bias, i.e. they predict even less than 15% of the desirable class for the sensitive feature.

This base-line performance by the tree based classifiers is very impressive. However, it is important to emphasise that the performance of the other methods can be improved significantly by parameter tuning – as would be normal in configuring an ML system. Finally, it should not be inferred that tree-based methods are likely to be free of underestimation problems. In particular, the Decision Tree implementation in scikit-learn provides a number of mechanisms for regularisation that may introduce underestimation as a side effect.

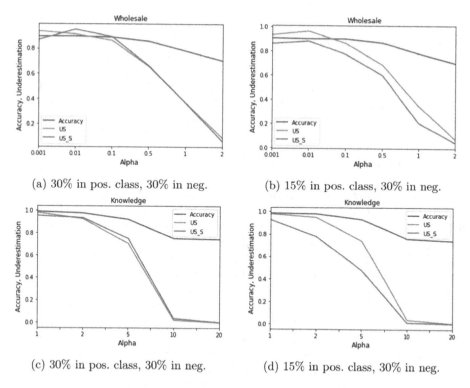

Fig. 7. The impact of underfitting on bias. A synthetic sensitive attribute has been added, it is underrepresented in the plots on the right (15% compared with 30%). Higher values of Alpha result in underfitting. Furthermore, when the sensitive attribute is underrepresented in the desirable class (b) and (d) the bias is exacerbated.

3.4   Impact of Underfitting

The standard practice in training a classifier is to ensure against overfitting in order to get good generalisation performance. Kamishima *et al.* [10] argue that bias due to underestimation arises when a classifier underfits the phenomenon being learned. This will happen when the data available is limited and samples covering the sensitive feature and the desirable class are scarce.

The scikit-learn (see Footnote 2) neural network implementation provides an α parameter to control overfitting. It works by providing control over the size of the weights in the model. Constraining the weights reduces the potential for overfitting. The plots in Fig. 7 show how underestimation varies with this α – high values cause underfitting. These plots show Accuracy and Underestimation for different values of α. For the plots on the left (Fig. 7(a) and (c)) the incidence of the sensitive feature is the same in both the positive and negative class (30%). For the plots on the right ((b) and (d)) the sensitive feature is underrepresented (15%) in the positive class.

In Fig. 7(a) and (c) we see that high values of α (i.e. underfitting) result in significant bias. When the base rates for the minority group in the positive and negative classes are the same the US and US_S rates are more or less the same.

When the prevalence of the sensitive group in the desirable class is lower ((b) and (d)) the bias is exacerbated. It is important to emphasise that a good US_S score simply means that underestimation is not present. There may still be bias against the minority group (i.e. poor CV or DI_S scores).

4 Conclusions and Future Work

In contrast to what Illusory Correlation tells us about how humans perceive things, underestimation occurs in ML classifiers because they are inclined to over-predict common phenomena and under-predict things that are rare in the training data. We have shown, on two illustrative datasets, Adult and Recidivism, how the impact of under-representation in data leads to underestimation of the classifiers built on that data. We believe classifier bias due to underestimation is worthy of research because of its close interaction with regularisation. We have demonstrated this interaction on two datasets where we vary the levels of under-representation and regularisation showing the impact on underestimation. Underfitting data with an under-represented feature in the desirable class leads to increased underestimation or bias of the classifiers.

We are now exploring how sensitive underestimation is to distribution variations in the class label and the sensitive feature. Our next step is to develop strategies to mitigate underestimation.

Acknowledgements. This work was funded by Science Foundation Ireland through the SFI Centre for Research Training in Machine Learning (Grant No. 18/CRT/6183).

References

1. Barocas, S., Hardt, M., Narayanan, A.: Fairness and Machine Learning (2019). http://www.fairmlbook.org
2. Calders, T., Verwer, S.: Three naive Bayes approaches for discrimination-free classification. Data Min. Knowl. Disc. **21**(2), 277–292 (2010). https://doi.org/10.1007/s10618-010-0190-x
3. Chapman, L.J., Chapman, J.P.: Illusory correlation as an obstacle to the use of valid psychodiagnostic signs. J. Abnorm. Psychol. **74**(3), 271 (1969)
4. Chawla, N.V., Lazarevic, A., Hall, L.O., Bowyer, K.W.: SMOTEBoost: improving prediction of the minority class in boosting. In: Lavrač, N., Gamberger, D., Todorovski, L., Blockeel, H. (eds.) PKDD 2003. LNCS (LNAI), vol. 2838, pp. 107–119. Springer, Heidelberg (2003). https://doi.org/10.1007/978-3-540-39804-2_12
5. Costello, F., Watts, P.: The rationality of illusory correlation. Psychol. Rev. **126**(3), 437 (2019)
6. Dressel, J., Farid, H.: The accuracy, fairness, and limits of predicting recidivism. Sci. Adv. **4**(1), eaao5580 (2018)

7. Feldman, M., Friedler, S.A., Moeller, J., Scheidegger, C., Venkatasubramanian, S.: Certifying and removing disparate impact. In: Proceedings of the 21th ACM SIGKDD International Conference on Knowledge Discovery and Data Mining, pp. 259–268 (2015)

8. Goodfellow, I., Bengio, Y., Courville, A.: Deep Learning. MIT Press (2016). http://www.deeplearningbook.org

9. Hamilton, D.L., Gifford, R.K.: Illusory correlation in interpersonal perception: a cognitive basis of stereotypic judgments. J. Exp. Soc. Psychol. **12**(4), 392–407 (1976)

10. Kamishima, T., Akaho, S., Asoh, H., Sakuma, J.: Fairness-aware classifier with prejudice remover regularizer. In: Flach, P.A., De Bie, T., Cristianini, N. (eds.) ECML PKDD 2012. LNCS (LNAI), vol. 7524, pp. 35–50. Springer, Heidelberg (2012). https://doi.org/10.1007/978-3-642-33486-3_3

11. Larson, J., Mattu, S., Kirchner, L., Angwin, J.: How we analyzed the COMPAS recidivism algorithm. ProPublica 9 (2016)

12. Menon, A.K., Williamson, R.C.: The cost of fairness in binary classification. In: Conference on Fairness, Accountability and Transparency, pp. 107–118 (2018)

13. Prokhorenkova, L., Gusev, G., Vorobev, A., Dorogush, A.V., Gulin, A.: CatBoost: unbiased boosting with categorical features. In: Advances in Neural Information Processing Systems, pp. 6638–6648 (2018)

14. Zemel, R., Wu, Y., Swersky, K., Pitassi, T., Dwork, C.: Learning fair representations. In: International Conference on Machine Learning, pp. 325–333 (2013)

15. Zhang, Y., Zhou, L.: Fairness assessment for artificial intelligence in financial industry. arXiv preprint arXiv:1912.07211 (2019)

Consensus for Collaborative Creation of Risk Maps for COVID-19

M. Rebollo[(✉)], C. Carrascosa, and A. Palomares

VRAIn - Valencian Research Institute for Artificial Intelligence,
Universitat Politècnica de València, Camino de Vera S/N, 46022 Valencia, Spain
{mrebollo,ccarrasc,apaloma}@vrain.upv.es

Abstract. The rapid spread of COVID-19 has demonstrated the need for accurate information to contain its spread. Technological solutions are a complement that can help citizens to be informed about the risk in their environment. Although measures such as contact traceability have been successful in some countries, their use raises some societal concerns.

The current challenge is how to track people infected by coronaviruses that can spread the disease. How can this be done while maintaining privacy? This paper proposes a variation of the consensus processes in networks to collaboratively build a risk map by sharing information with trusted contacts. These contacts are the people we would notify of being infected: close relatives, colleagues at work, or friends. The information spreads in an aggregate way through the network. When the process converges, each participant has the risk value calculated for the different zones.

The structure of the connections among close contacts generates a network that allows the process to work correctly with barely 20% of the population involved, instead of the values estimated for the tracking apps, which need 60% participation.

Keywords: Consensus · Agreement · Complex network · COVID · Risk map · Collaboration

1 Introduction

Imagine that you feel under the weather, you call the health services, and when they test, you are positive for COVID-19.

One of the first things to do when you confirm the infection with COVID-19 is to review who you have been in contact with to warn them of the risk. In this way, they can isolate themselves and consult with health services. You will usually notify your immediate family, the people who live with you, and those you see regularly. You should also tell your closest friends and work colleagues with whom you have a close relationship. In the end, it is a handful of people you trust who have some information about you (they know where you live) and with whom you would share your health status concerning this disease.

© Springer Nature Switzerland AG 2021
F. Heintz et al. (Eds.): TAILOR 2020, LNAI 12641, pp. 32–48, 2021.
https://doi.org/10.1007/978-3-030-73959-1_3

The rapid spread of COVID-19 has demonstrated the need for accurate information to contain its diffusion. The current challenge is to track people infected with coronaviruses that can spread the disease. Although technological solutions such as contact-tracing have been successful in some countries, they raise resistance in society due to privacy concerns [18]. The European Data Protection Board has published a guideline for the governments to use this kind of technology, guaranteeing privacy and proper access to the data [16]. The solutions currently being considered fall into two main groups: (1) personalized tracking of users, (2) private tracking of contacts. These groups correspond to the two waves of technological responses in Europe to the COVID-19 pandemic [8].

User Tracking. They use two sources of information: (i) data provided by telecommunication companies, which know precisely the position of the terminals, or (ii) the location provided by users from their own volition via GPS

- advantage: precise information is available on the movements of people and their contacts, known or unknown, allowing the tracking and control of people
- drawback: a threat to privacy

Private Tracking of Contacts. Every time two mobiles are nearby, they exchange an encrypted key via Bluetooth (BT). These keys remain stored in the device or at centralized servers.

- advantage: some privacy is maintained
- drawback: the administration does not receive global data or statistics. Moreover, the information is available a posteriori, which makes prevention difficult (it prevents further propagation, but not contagion since direct contact is still produced)

Most of the governments have recommended using the second type of applications, advising against proposals based on the geolocation of individuals. Nevertheless, even contact tracking has vulnerabilities that allow hacking the system and generate undesirable results [3]. Besides the problems regarding privacy, there are other ethical issues to consider, including treating the data in post-pandemic scenarios [7,11].

Simko et al. [15] made a series of surveys over 100 participants to analyze their opinion about contact-tracking applications and privacy. Since the first part finished when some European countries were under different forms of lock-downs, it is a relevant study, and contact-tracking apps were not available yet. Between the first and the second study, appeared several proposals, such as the ones made by Apple and Google [1,2], the Massachusetts Institute of Technology (MIT) [13], the University of Washington (UW) [5], PEPP-PT [12], Inria [4], WeTrace [19], and DP3T [17]. The study shows that people are more comfortable using an existing mapping application that adds tracking for COVID-19 instead of using new apps, with reservations even if they provide 'perfect' privacy. One of the main concerns is related to sharing data, preferring that Google or organizations such as the UN develop the application. In general, participants manifest a lack of trust in how their governments would use the citizens' location data. They thought that it was unlikely that their government would erase the data after the crisis and also that they would use it for other purposes. Common to both studies was the following trend: mixed feeling about using proximity tracking for the contacts and negative towards using any other data source.

Therefore, how can this be done while maintaining privacy? Alternatively, at least, allowing citizens to control when and with whom they share the health data. This work proposes a third type: a process of **dissemination in local environments**, in exchanging information with known and trusted contacts only. It can be considered a variant of private tracking of contacts.

The main difference is that the purpose is not to share private data but to calculate aggregate information. In this case, the risk index of a geographical area. Although the first exchange of information contains an individual's data, this is shared with trusted contacts. It is also handled internally by the process, as discussed in Section. The obtained result is an infection risk value for each region in which the study area is divided. The risk value is calculated from the distributed aggregation of risk factors of the people who live or work in them. In this way, any citizen has a map available to make decisions about mobility within their area and make personal decisions to maintain their safety and isolate themselves as they deem necessary.

- advantage: (i) privacy is maintained, (ii) the administration obtains aggregated information at the time, and (iii) the citizenry and the administration have the same data (transparency)
- drawback: the first exchange contains the data of only one node (in case someones hacks it and retrieve the information), and a critical mass is necessary

Throughout the day, we have contact with various people in different places: home, transport, work, or leisure. In each place we relate in different degrees (see Fig. 1): closer (B, E F G) or farther (C,D,H,I). Private tracking of contacts via BT is useful for detecting risk in contact with unknown people and isolating those who have been in contact with the infectious agent to control the disease's spread. The consensus process is useful to identify persons already infected or at risk in the immediate environment. A second potential is to provide aggregated statistical information to the health services [6].

This paper proposes a variation of the consensus processes in networks [9]. Consensus processes in networks are information dissemination processes that allow calculating the value of a function in a distributed way in a network, exchanging information only with direct neighbors, and without global knowledge of the structure, size, values, or other network characteristics. Each node uses only its data and its direct neighbors' information to recalculate the function's value iteratively and propagate it through its neighbors. This process converges to a final single value for the calculated function.

Despite the focus on SARS-Cov-2 dissemination, the approach presented in this paper has general applicability as a tool for monitoring disease spread processes using people as citizen sensors. As it is a decentralized application based

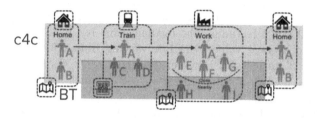

Fig. 1. Integration of BT's anonymous user tracking with a local broadcast application for close contacts (c4c) Image adapted from Ferreti et al. [6]

on a simple mechanism, it is relatively easy to adapt it to other situations, even in environments not related to infectious diseases. It can be seen as a tool that encourages citizen participation to aggregate very heterogeneous information: measures of air, noise or light pollution, energy consumption, or socio-economic indicators.

The rest of the paper is structured as follows. Section 3 explains how citizens can collaboratively create risk maps using a consensus process with their close contacts. Section 4 shows the results over a municipality of 5,000 inhabitants. Finally, Sect. 5 closes the paper with the conclusions of this work.

2 Review of Contact Tracing Apps

States have put their efforts into creating mobile applications to track the spread of the SARS-Cov-2 over the population. The MIT Technology Review [10] has been collecting the different proposals. Previous to this work's publication, there were 43 registered apps (last check, July 2020). Table 1 summarizes their characteristics. There are initiatives in the five continents, but most of the countries belong to Asia and Europe since they were the firsts places where COVID-19 appeared (Fig. 2).

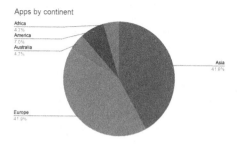

Fig. 2. Distribution of the tracing apps by continent

The population that uses the applications varies from 9,000 inhabitants in Cyprus to 100,000,000 in India. The median value is 1,613,500. Regarding the penetration, the average value is 11.1%, varying from 0.3% in cases such as Malaysia to 38.5% in Iceland. However, the data is not Gaussian. The median is 4.9%, and the median absolute deviation 4.2%, which gives a more accurate view of the actual penetration.

The Bluetooth technology is the solution that most countries have chosen (Fig. 3), with 72% of the apps. Moreover, almost half of them use the API provided by Google and Apple. Despite the recommendation to avoid location services, 36% of the apps use it.

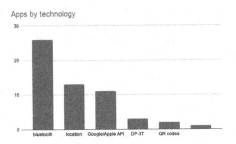

Fig. 3. Technology used by the different proposals

In Fig. 4, we can see that privacy concerns have been considered in general. The proportion of the characteristics that somehow preserve privacy is 80-20, except the voluntary (present in the 90% of the apps). On the other hand, the decentralized-centralized balance and transparency are only a 60-40.

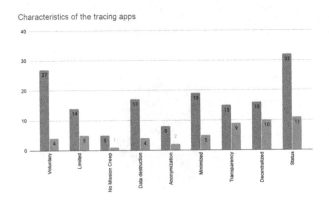

Fig. 4. Characteristics present in the available solutions

The apps' usage is not extended enough despite the efforts to develop technological solutions to track the propagation of COVID-19. This problem appears even with people follow recommendations to keep their privacy at reasonable levels. That is why we propose a third method that can work with the penetration obtained with current applications.

3   Collaborative Risk Map Generation

3.1   Consensus Adaption to Counting

The following formulation governs the consensus process: let $G = (V, E)$ be a non-directed network formed by a set of vertices V and a set of links $E \subseteq V \times V$ where $(i, j) \in E$ if there is a link between the nodes i and j. We denote by N_i the set formed by the neighbors of i. A vector $x = (x_1, \ldots, x_n)^T$ contains the initial values of the variables associated with each node. Olfati–Saber and Murray [9] propose an algorithm whose iterative application converges to the mean value of x.

$$x_i(t + 1) = x_i(t) + \varepsilon \sum_{j \in N_i} [x_j(t) - x_i(t)] \tag{1}$$

The convergence of this method is guaranteed. Without losing generality, it can be extended reach a consensus over m independent variables just, considering $x_i = (x_i^1, \ldots, x_i^m) \in \mathbb{R}^m$.

The consensus process converges to the average of the initial values. With a proper initialization, we can use this result to count the number of nodes and determine the size of the network. Let's init the values of $x_i(0)$ as follows: we choose one node, for example $i = 1$ and

$$\begin{cases} x_1(0) = 1 \\ x_i(0) = 0 \ \forall i \neq 1 \end{cases}$$

One key property on consensus is the conservation of the sum along the iterations. That is, $\sum_i x_i(0) = \sum_i x_i(t) \ \forall t \leq 0$. By executing until convergence Eq. 1, we obtain $x_i(t) = \frac{1}{n} \sum_i x_i(t) = \frac{1}{n} \sum_i x_i(0) = \frac{1}{n} 1$. Therefore, the size of the network is

$$n = \frac{1}{x_i(t)}. \tag{2}$$

Combining both considerations, it is possible to define a distributed mechanism to determine the preferences of a group, implement a distributed voting platform or, as in our case, calculate the cumulated risk value in different areas that constitute a town.

Each node contains a vector $x_i = (x_i^1, \ldots, x_i^m) \in \mathbb{R}^m$. Only one component $x_i^k = 1$ and all the rest $x_i^j = 0$, $j \neq k$. Note that, as only one component is

Table 1. Tracing apps in the world. **Dep:** deployer, government (gov), private (priv), academic (acad) and NGO, **Pen:** penetration, **Tech:** technology bluetooth (BT), location, GPS, Google/Apple API (G/A), QR codes, **Min:** Minimized data, **Transp:** transparency, **Central:** centralized (C) or decentralized (D) data storage, **Status:** launched or in development (Source: MIT Technology Review[10])

Name	Loc	Cont	Dep	Users	Pen	Tech	Vol	Lim	No Mis	DD	Anon	Min	Transp	Central	Status
Algeria's App	Algeria	Africa													launch
COVIDSafe	Australia	Oceania	gov	5,300,000	21.2%	BT	Y	Y	Y	Y		Y	N	C	launch
Stopp Corona	Austria	Europe	ngo			BT G/A	Y	Y	Y	Y		Y	Y	D	launch
BeAware	Bahrain	Asia	gov		25.0%	BT loc		Y							launch
ViruSafe	Bulgaria	Europe	g+p	55,000	0.8%	loc	Y	Y		Y		Y	Y	C	launch
COVID Alert	Canada	America	priv			BT G/A	Y	Y		Y		Y	Y	D	dev
Chinese health code system	China	Asia	gov			loc, Data mining	N	N	N	N		N	N	C	launch
CovTracer	Cyprus	Europe	acad	9,000	0.8%	loc, GPS	Y	N		Y		Y	Y		launch
eRouska	Czech	Europe	gov	160,000	1.5%	BT	Y	N		Y	Y	Y	Y		launch
Smittestop	Denmark	Europe	priv			BT G/A	Y	Y		Y	Y	Y		D	launch
Estonia's App	Estonia	Europe	priv			BT DP-3T, G/A	Y	Y			Y	Y		D	dev
CareFiji	Fiji	Asia													dev
Ketju	Finland	Europe	g+ps			BT DP-3T	Y			Y	Y	Y	Y	D	dev
StopCovid	France	Europe	acad	1,800,000	2.7%	BT	Y							C	dev
Corona-Warn-App	Germany	Europe	priv			BT G/A	Y				Y	Y	N	D	dev
GH COVID-19 Tracker	Ghana	Africa	gov			loc	Y						N		launch
Beat Covid Gibraltar	Gibraltar	Europe													dev
Rakning C-19	Iceland	Europe	gov	140,000	38.5%	loc	Y	Y		Y		Y	Y	C D	launch
Aarogya Setu	India	Asia	gov	100,000,000	7.4%	BT loc	N	N		Y		N	Y	C	launch
PeduliLindungi	Indonesia	Asia	priv	19,000,000	0.7%		Y			Y					launch
Mask.ir	Iran	Asia	acad	4,000,000	4.9%	loc	Y						N		launch
HSE Covid-19 App	Ireland	Europe	gov			BT G/A	Y			Y		Y		D	launch
HaMagen	Israel	Asia	gov	2,000,000	22.5%	loc	Y	Y		Y		Y	Y	D	launch
Immuni	Italy	Europe	priv	2,200,000	3.6%	BT G/A	Y	Y		Y	Y	Y	Y	D	dev
COCOA	Japan	Asia	gov	2,700,000	2.0%	G/A	Y			Y				D	launch
Shlonik	Kuwait	Asia				loc				Y	N				launch
MyTrace	Malaysia	Asia	gov	100,000	0.3%	BT G/A	Y			N	Y	N		D	launch
CovidRadar	Mexico	America	gov			BT	Y				N	N	N		launch
NZ COVID Tracer	New Zealand	Oceania	gov	573,000	11.8%	BT QR									launch

(continued)

Table 1. (*continued*)

Name	Loc	Cont	Dep	Users	Pen	Tech	Vol	Lim	No Mis	DD	Anon	Min	Transp	Central	Status
StopKorona	North Macedonia	Europe	priv			BT	Y	Y		Y	Y		Y	D	launch
Smittestopp	Norway	Europe	gov	1,427,000	26.6%	BT loc	Y	Y	Y	Y			N	C	launch
ProteGO	Poland	Europe	gov	41,665	0.1%	BT	Y			Y		Y	Y	D	launch
Ehteraz	Qatar	Asia	gov			BT loc	N			N		Y	N	C	launch
Tawakkalna	Saudi Arabia	Asia	gov												launch
Tabaud	Saudi Arabia	Asia	gov												launch
Trace Together	Singapore	Asia	gov	2,000,000	35.5%	BT BlueTrace	Y	Y		Y		Y	Y	C	launch
Swiss Contact Tracing App	Switzerland	Europe	acad			BT DP-3T, G/A	Y	Y	Y	Y		Y		D	dev
MorChana	Thailand	Asia				QR	Y								launch
E7mi	Tunisia	Asia				BT									launch
Hayat Eve Sığar	Turkey	Asia	gov			BT loc	N	N		N		Y	N	C	launch
TraceCovid	UAE	America	gov			BT	Y	N				Y		D	launch
NHS COVID-19 App	UK	Europe	gov			BT G/A	Y	N	Y			Y	Y	D	dev
BlueZone	Vietnam	Asia													launch

Table 2. Configuration of $x_i(0)$ for counting. Nodes 1 to 6 mark with 1 the chosen option and the rest of the vector remains with zeros. An extra node x_0 is included, filled to zeros, and it is the only one that inits the auxiliary variable as one to count the number of participants in the process.

	x_i^1	x_i^2	x_i^3	y_i
x_0	0	0	0	1
x_1	1	0	0	0
x_2	0	1	0	0
x_3	1	0	0	0
x_4	0	0	1	0
x_5	0	0	1	0
x_6	1	0	0	0
Total	3	1	2	

different from zero, $\sum_i x_i^k$ is the number of nodes that have chosen option k, and $\sum_i \sum_j x_i^j = n$.

We extend the vote vector with an additional element that we use to determine the network's size.

$$(x_i|y_i) = (x_i^1, \ldots, x_i^m \mid y_i) \tag{3}$$

and, initially, $y_i = 0 \; \forall i$. Without losing generality, we can introduce an additional node in the network whose initial values are

$$(x_0|y_0) = (\underbrace{0, \ldots, 0}_{m} \mid 1) \tag{4}$$

This node does not affect the result since it does modify the values of any component of x_i. When the consensus process converges, each node calculates how many participants have chosen each option, dividing the final vector x_i by the value obtained in the last column y_i (see Eq. 2) to determine the overall result, as shown in Eq. 5.

$$\frac{x_i(t)}{y_i(t)} = \frac{(\langle x^1 \rangle, \ldots, \langle x^m \rangle)}{1/n} = (n\langle x^1 \rangle, \ldots, n\langle x^m \rangle)$$
$$= (\sum_j x_j^1, \ldots, \sum_j x_j^m) \tag{5}$$

Table 2 shows an example of the initialization of a network with six nodes. The nodes choose between 3 options, being the choice of each one $x(0) = (1, 2, 1, 3, 3, 1)$. Therefore, $(x_1|y_1) = (1, 0, 0|0)$, $(x_2|y_2) = (0, 1, 0|0)$, $(x_3|y_3) = (1, 0, 0|0)$, and so on.

We can see in Fig. 5 the evolution of the consensus process over each one of the components of the vector x_i. The network converges to the total result

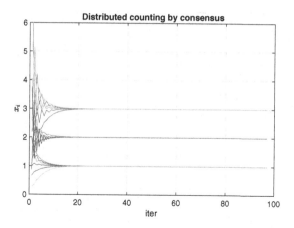

Fig. 5. Evolution of the consensus process for calculating the result of a distributed count. Random network with $n = 6$ nodes and $m = 3$ options. The options are $x(0) = (1, 2, 1, 3, 3, 1)$, which gives a result of $(3, 1, 2)$.

$x_i(t) = (1/2, 1/6, 1/3 \mid 1/6)$, and applying Eq. 5 each node obtains the total counting

$$x_i(t) = \left(\frac{1/2}{1/6}, \frac{1/6}{1/6}, \frac{1/3}{1/6}\right) = (3, 1, 2) \tag{6}$$

3.2 Map Generation

The goal is to create a citizen network in an area: town, region, department, province, state, or any other administrative division. Inhabitants share a risk index that measures their probability of being infected by COVID-19 to create a common risk map for the selected area. The map is divided into smaller zones, big enough to avoid reidentification and guarantee privacy, but small enough to obtain a detailed view of the infection's state along the area.

In our case, we have chosen the census districts from the National Institute of Statistics (INE) of Spain. The sizes of the districts are homogeneous, having between 900 and 3,000 inhabitants each one. It is easily scalable, aggregating the information in bigger administrative units. Moreover, they never provide statistics with less than 100 persons to avoid reidentification.

The risk in a census district depends on the risk index (RI) of all the people that live in it. Each person obtains the RI with data from different sources: medical symptoms, symptoms of the close contacts (neighbors in the network), age, family situation, and habitability conditions.[1]

---

[1] In this work, we use the mean risk as an aggregate function, but it can consider many others changing the consensus function, such as the geometric mean.

Algorithm 1. Risk map creation executed in each node

1: calculate $ri_i(t)$
2: $x_i(t) = (0, \ldots, ri_i(t), \ldots, 0 \mid 0)$,
3: **repeat**
4:     send $x_i(t)$ to all $j \in Ni$
5:     receive all $x_j(t)$ from all $j \in Ni$
6:     $x(t+1) = x_i(t) + \varepsilon \sum_{j \in N_i} (x_j(t) - x_i(t))$
7: **until** the system converge
8: $R = \frac{x_i(t)}{y_i(t)}$

Notation

- ri_i: risk index of node i, $i = 1, \ldots, n$
- $cd_i = k$: census district in which i lives, $k = 1, \ldots, m$
- $x_i = (x_i^1 \ldots, x_i^m \mid y_i)$: vector with the risk map values in node i
- N_i: direct contacts of node i
- $R = (ri_1, \ldots, ri_n)$: complete risk map

Let us assume an extra node representing an administrative unit, such as the town hall, acts as the x_0 node. Algorithm 1 describes the complete process.

Some important remarks related to the process are:

1. N_i is a set of trustful contacts
2. the first exchange is the only moment in which vectors contain individual values: the risk and the district of i. We assume that there are no privacy concerns since the node would share this information with N_i
3. in the following exchanges, the vectors received $x_j(t)$ contains aggregated information. As N_j remains unknown for i, it is impossible to track back the data.

It is a successive refinement mechanism: there is a map available at any time, and the longer the algorithm executes, the more accurate are the risk values calculated by the algorithm (see Fig. 7). The final map obtained R is the same one that would obtain a centralized process with all the risk indexes available.

4   Results

As an application example, we have chosen Albaida, a town of 4,881 inhabitants in the province of Valencia (Spain). The National Institute of Statistics divides the municipality into six zones. The population that lives in each area is publicly available. The network has as many nodes as inhabitants. We generate two coordinates for each node: one for their home address and another for their working address. They are random coordinates following the density distribution of the census districts.

To simulate the spread of the COVID-19, we use an SEIR model, where each person can be in one of these states:

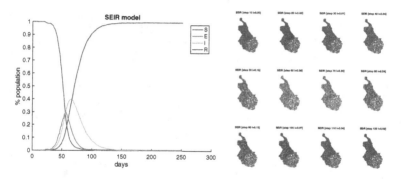

Fig. 6. SEIR model for COVID-19 over a population $\approx 5,000$. At $t = 1$, there is only one infected person $|I| = 1$. (Left) Evolution of the populations (Right) Snapshots of the spread of the disease within the municipality

- Susceptible (S): a person that has not the disease and can be infected
- Exposed (E): someone that has been in contact with an infected person. He or she cannot infect others yet
- Infected (I): someone with symptoms that can infect other people
- Recovered (R): people cured that is immune to the disease

The SEIR model parameters follow the findings shown in the literature that has analyzed the COVID-19 propagation [20]. Particularly, the incubation time is 7 days, so $\beta = 1/7$, the probability of infection $\sigma = 0.1$ and the recovery time is 15 days, so $\gamma = 1/15$ (Fig. 6). The purpose of the model is not to predict or model precisely the behavior of the disease among the population. The model provides the consensus process with different scenarios to check the accurateness of the risk maps.

People start at their home location. They move to their corresponding working place, where they interact with the other persons at a specific contact range (20 m). Nodes update their state according to the epidemic model, and they go back to their home locations. A new infection stage is performed at home since, in COVID-19, some researches demonstrate the family to be a strong transmission source. Once completed the update, a new cycle begins (Fig. 7).

To create the contact network, we have analyzed the network formed by the users that follow the Twitter account of the town hall of Albaida. The degree of that network follows a power-law distribution of parameter $\alpha = -1.7$. To model the entire population's contact network, we have generated a preferential attachment network following the same distribution (Fig. 8, left). As a potential application would bound the number of closer contacts, we choose a subset of the potential links. A reasonable limit is 15 contacts, five of each type (family, colleagues, and friends). The degree of network obtained with this procedure follows a Weibull distribution with parameters rs $\alpha = 13.4$ and $\gamma = 0.48$ with a 95% confidence interval (Fig. 8, right). It is important to remark that it is not a random network despite the distribution of the degree.

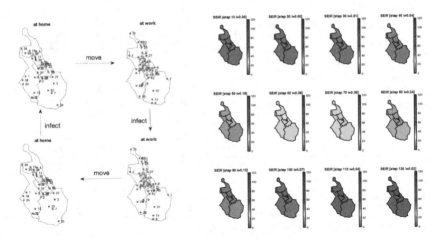

Fig. 7. (Left) The population moves alternatively between the home and the working location. Carriers can infect other people in both places. The cycle consists of a sequence movement → infection → movement → infection. (Right) Evolution of the risk map

Over this scenario, the inhabitants can determine the risk map of their town every day. We assume that no additional measures, such as social distancing or limitations of movements, are taken. As an example, let us consider the situation on day 60.

Each node has a vector of six components, one for each census district $x_i = (x_i^1, \ldots, x_i^6 \mid 0)$. Let be ri_i the risk index of i and $cd_i = k$ the census district i lives in. $x_i^k = ri_i$ and the rest $x_i^l = 0$, $l \neq k$.

All the nodes execute the process detailed in Algorithm 1. The evolution appears in Fig. 9. Each node shares their data with their neighbors, who are bounded in $1 \leq N_i \leq 16$ (see Fig. 8, right). The process begins marking the census district with its own RI, and while the consensus is executing, the map

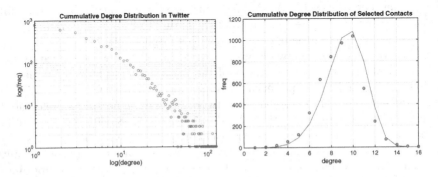

Fig. 8. Cumulated degree distribution of the networks (Left) Twitter relations in Albaida with a power-law with $\alpha = -1.7$ (Right) Random selection of contacts following a Weibull distribution with parameters $\alpha = 13.4$, $\gamma = 0.48$.

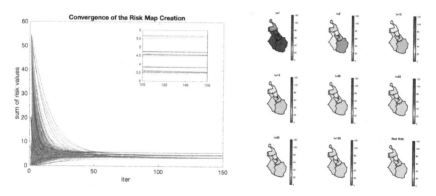

Fig. 9. Evolution of the consensus in the creation of a risk map. (Left) Convergence of the process. The plot shows the sum of the risk values obtained for each node. (Right) Evolution of the map calculated for one random node. The two last plots are the final map calculated at $t = 150$ and the real risk map

refines, including the values propagated through the network. When the values converge and the process finish, each node has a copy of the risk map. Figure 9 (right), the two last maps are the definitive map calculated by consensus and the real risk map calculated in a centralized way. After 30 iterations, the map is a good approximation for the selected node. After 50 iterations, all the nodes are near convergence.

A problem with tracking applications is that they need a large percentage of the population to use them. Some works suggest that tracking applications need at least 60% of penetration to be effective [14]. In our case, the main problem for this solution to work is that we require a strongly connected network. Without this condition, isolated communities appear in the network, and each one arrives at a different risk map, none of them precise (especially for small and sparse groups).

Due to the characteristics of the network that allow considering it a random network, we can assume that the giant component appears when the number of links is $m \approx n \log(n)$. In a network of $n = 5,000$ nodes we need $m = 42,500$ links. In our case, the network has around 42,800 links, and it fulfills this condition.

This property is general, and it does not depend on the size of the network. The proportion of nodes among the total population is the same. Figure 10 compares the giant component formation with different network sizes: 100, 1 000, 10 000 and 100 000 nodes. All cases follow a similar curve. With 20% of the possible installations, between 85% and 90% of the nodes are connected in the giant component. Therefore, we can create the map with the risk index of the 85%-90% of the nodes, and we can consider it a good enough approximation. With 40% of participants, more than 95% of the nodes connected.

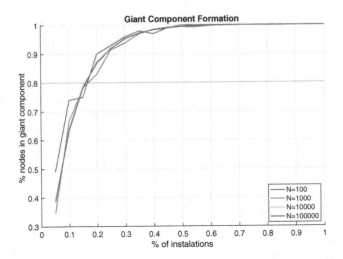

Fig. 10. The formation of the giant component network is independent of the size of the network. The 80% of the network is strongly connected with less than the 20% of the population using an application to create the risk maps.

5   Conclusions

Technology can be an essential ally to control the transmission of COVID-19. Nevertheless, concerns about privacy and the possible use of the data after the pandemic has passed difficult the implantation of technological solutions.

This work proposes an alternative for users to create risk maps collaboratively. This approach executes a consensus process that uses local information and data from the direct neighbors to calculate the value of a shared function. In our case, the values are the risk index of the different districts that form the town. Close contacts (family, colleagues, and friends) define the relationships in the network, whom we warned about being infected. The data exchanged is an aggregation, and it is not possible to reidentify the personal information. At the end of the process, all the participants obtain the same copy of the complete risk map.

This proposal solves the problem of the high participation that contact tracking apps need. With 20% of the population involved, almost 90% of the participants connected in a giant component, and the consensus obtains a sufficiently accurate approximation of the risk map.

Nevertheless, the risk measure has uncertainty, and its communication can cause non-desired effects that the public administration should address and mitigate.

– discrimination: accusations, prejudices, or bullying to contacts with low or medium risk but without confirmation of the infection. Sadly, some of these behaviors have appeared already. Although they are the exception, they can be a big problem for people that suffer from them.

- boycott to commerces and stores inside districts marked as risky. In this case, administrations should take measures to minimize the impact: subventions or ensuring that health measures are guaranteed.
- deviation of the risk of infection to clean, proper districts when the movement of the population changes because potential risks (similar to traffic jam evolution, when drivers avoid jammed roads, and they propagate the congestion)
- barriers of access to technology for groups that, because of age, social exclusion, or digital competence, cannot access the application. This situation is particularly problematic since these are some of the groups more unprotected and with higher risk.

References

1. Apple, Google: Exposure notifications: Using technology to help public health authorities fight covid-19 (2020). https://www.google.com/covid19/exposurenotifications/. Accessed 01 June 2020
2. Apple, Google: Privacy-preserving contact tracing (2020). https://www.apple.com/covid19/contacttracing. Accessed 01 June 2020
3. Bonnetain, X., et al.: Anonymous tracing, a dangerous oxymoron, a risk analysis for non-specialists (2020). https://risques-tracage.fr. Accessed 01 June 2020
4. Castelluccia, C., et al.: ROBERT: ROBust and privacy-presERving proximity Tracing, May 2020. https://hal.inria.fr/hal-02611265/file/ROBERT-v1.1.pdf
5. Chan, J., et al.: PACT: Privacy sensitive protocols and mechanisms for mobile contact tracing (2020). arXiv:2004.03544 [cs.CR]
6. Ferretti, L., et al.: Quantifying SARS-CoV-2 transmission suggests epidemic control with digital contact tracing. Science 368(6491), eabb6936 (2020)
7. Global Health Ethics Unit: The COVID-19 pandemic: two waves of technological responses in the European Union. Technical report WHO/2019-nCoV/Ethics_Contact_tracing_apps/2020.1, World Health Organization (2020). https://apps.who.int/iris/rest/bitstreams/1278803/retrieve
8. Klonowska, K.: The COVID-19 pandemic: two waves of technological responses in the European Union (2020). https://hcss.nl/sites/default/files/files/reports/COVID-19
9. Olfati-Saber, R., Fax, J.A., Murray, R.M.: Consensus and cooperation in networked multi-agent systems. Proc. IEEE 95(1), 215–233 (2007)
10. O'Neill, P.H., Ryan-Mosley, T., Johnson, B.: A flood of coronavirus apps are tracking us. Now it's time to keep track of them (2020). https://www.technologyreview.com/2020/05/07/1000961/launching-mittr-covid-tracing-tracker/. Accessed 07 May 2020
11. Parker, M.J., Fraser, C., Abeler-Dörner, L., Bonsall, D.: Ethics of instantaneous contact tracing using mobile phone apps in the control of the COVID-19 pandemic. J. Med. Ethics 46, 106314 (2020)
12. Pan-European privacy-preserving proximity tracing (2020). https://www.pepp-pt.org/. Accessed 01 June 2020
13. Rivest, R.L., Weitzner, D.J., Ivers, L.C., Soibelman, I., Zissman, M.A.: PACT: private automated contact tracing. pact.mit.edu. Accessed 01 June 2020
14. Hinch, R.: Effective configurations of a digital contact tracing app: a report to NHSX. University of Oxford, 16 April 2020

15. Simko, L., Calo, R., Roesner, F., Kohno, T.: Covid-19 contact tracing and privacy: studying opinion and preferences (2020). arXiv:2005.06056 [cs.CR]
16. The European Data Protection Board: Guidelines 04/2020 on the use of location data and contact tracing tools in the context of the COVID-19 outbreak (2020). https://edpb.europa.eu/our-work-tools/our-documents/usmernenia/guidelines-042020-use-location-data-and-contact-tracing_en. Accessed 01 June 2020
17. Troncoso, C., et al.: Decentralized privacy-preserving proximity tracing, April 2020. https://github.com/DP-3T/documents/blob/master/DP3T
18. Vinuesa, R., Theodorou, A., Battaglini, M., Dignum, V.: A socio-technical framework for digital contact tracing (2020). arXiv:2005.08370 [cs.CY]
19. WeTrace: Privacy-preserving bluetooth covid-19 contract tracing application (2020). https://wetrace.ch/. Accessed 01 June 2020
20. Yang, Z., et al.: Modified SEIR and AI prediction of the epidemics trend of COVID-19 in China under public health interventions. J. Thorac. Dis. **12**(3), 165 (2020)

Guided-LORE: Improving LORE with a Focused Search of Neighbours

Najlaa Maaroof[1(✉)] (ID), Antonio Moreno[1] (ID), Aida Valls[1] (ID),
and Mohammed Jabreel[1,2] (ID)

[1] ITAKA-Intelligent Technologies for Advanced Knowledge Acquisition,
Universitat Rovira i Virgili, Tarragona, Spain
najlaamaaroofwahib.al-ziyadi@urv.cat
[2] Department of Computer Science, Hodeidah University, Hodeidah, Yemen

Abstract. In the last years many Machine Learning-based systems have achieved an extraordinary performance in a wide range of fields, especially Natural Language Processing and Computer Vision. The construction of appropriate and meaningful explanations for the decisions of those systems, which are in may cases considered black boxes, is a hot research topic. Most of the state-of-the-art explanation systems in the field rely on generating synthetic instances to test them on the black box, analyse the results and build an interpretable model, which is then used to provide an understandable explanation. In this paper we focus on this generation process and propose *Guided-LORE*, a variant of the well-known LORE method. We conceptualise the problem of neighbourhood generation as a search and solve it using the Uniform Cost Search algorithm. The experimental results on four datasets reveal the effectiveness of our method when compared with the most relevant related works.

Keywords: Explainable AI · LORE · Neighbourhood generation

1 Introduction

The past decades have witnessed a tremendous growth in the volume, complexity and diversity of available data. Such growth has led to the development of highly successful Machine Learning (ML)-based systems in many different domains, including problems as diverse as the identification of the feelings of users from their posts or the prediction of the evolution of the condition of a patient [4]. However, in most cases, high precision is not enough to convince the public to trust the decisions of ML-based systems. When a decision is taken or suggested by an automated system, it is essential for practical, social, and increasingly legal reasons to justify that decision to users, developers or regulators. For example, a doctor or a patient may want to know the reason for the suggestion of a certain treatment, or a customer of a bank may demand why his/her loan application was rejected. Another example in which interpretability

© Springer Nature Switzerland AG 2021
F. Heintz et al. (Eds.): TAILOR 2020, LNAI 12641, pp. 49–62, 2021.
https://doi.org/10.1007/978-3-030-73959-1_4

may be useful is the understanding of the own ML system. Machine learning specialists need to understand the behaviour of the systems they develop to improve their performance, make sure that decisions are taken for the right reasons, and address drawbacks or bias that might appear.

Furthermore, many applications in different domains like biology [14], economic forecasting [11], or energy require that models are interpretable as explanations help to bridge the gap between domain experts and ML specialists. When a domain experts need to make an important decision, learning from data can improve their results or support them in their decision making process. Thus, it is necessary that they understand and trust the model [3,8,15,19], i.e., systems provide users with a rationale for why a decision was taken using a piece of data, or they show counter-factual knowledge of what would happen if the circumstances were different. In addition to that, interpretable ML models allow healthcare experts to make reasonable and data-driven decisions to provide personalised choices that can ultimately lead to a higher quality of service in healthcare. In summary, there is an increasing need of developing algorithms that are able to interpret the decisions taken by ML-based systems and to generate 'domain-level' knowledge that is closer to experts' activities.

In the literature we can find a variety of ways to address the problem of ML explanation. The naive solution is to use directly so-called "interpretable" models such as decision trees, rules [10,22], additive models [5], or sparse linear models [21]. Unlike other models that are considered to be black boxes such as neural networks or random forests with thousands of trees, we can directly inspect the components of the interpretable models— e.g. an activated path in a decision tree, or the weight of a specific feature in a linear model. Thus, as long as the model is accurate for a task and uses a reasonably small number of internal components, such approaches provide beneficial insights. However, it has been shown that such models are limited in terms of their learning curve.

Explainability mechanisms for complex ML models can be model-dependent or model-agnostic. The former ones analyse the internal structure of the model (e.g. the weights inside a neural network) to try to explain how the solution is computed. The idea of the latter approaches, in which we are going to focus on this paper, is to extract post-hoc explanations by treating the original model as a black box. Most of them generate, in some way, a set of inputs, analyse the answers provided by the black box to them, and then construct a more simple model form which an explanation can be inferred [1,6,9,16,20].

Model-agnostic methods can try to build local or global models. Local models explain a single prediction (local explanation) whereas global models try to explain the entire model behaviour (global explanation) [13]. Although it is useful, in some scenarios, to understand the global logic of a black box model, we are going to focus on the generation of a local explanation for the classification of each instance individually.

One of the most popular methods to obtain a local model is *Local Interpretable Model-agnostic Explanations (LIME)* [16]. It provides local explanations for a prediction of a classifier by fitting a linear regression model locally around the data point of which the prediction is to be explained. Despite its popularity, one of the criticisms of LIME is that it does not provide a counter-factual explanation. Moreover, it does not measure the fidelity of its regression coefficients, which may lead to giving a false explanation.

Another well-known local model-agnostic explainability method in the literature is *LORE (Local Rule-Based Explanations)* [7]. This method generates a set of neighbours of the input point, obtains the result of the black box system for each of them, and then it builds a decision tree on these results. The explanation obtained by the LORE method is composed of two parts: the activated path, i.e., the rule used to produce the decision, and a set of counter-factual rules which represent the minimal number of changes in the feature values of the instance that would change the conclusion of the system.

The main difference between LORE and LIME is the neighbourhood generation procedure. In the LIME method, a set of points is generated by sampling points randomly from the same distribution of the instance to be explained. In contrast, the LORE method employs a genetic algorithm to perform a focused generation procedure to explore the decision boundary in the neighbourhood of the data point. Unlike the instances generated by LIME, which are very distant from one another, the ones generated by the LORE method form a dense and compact neighbourhood [7]. This can be attributed to the genetic-based instance generation of the LORE method.

However, we argue that there are several drawbacks in the neighbourhood generation procedure in both LIME and LORE. First, the generated instances may contain features with values that are out-of-bounds. For example, in some cases, we may find that the value of the "age" feature is negative. Second, the generation process is not knowledge-driven and it misses the context (in particular, the characteristics of the features). For example, in some cases, it could be more beneficial to keep some features unchangeable (e.g. gender), or to allow only positive changes to some features (e.g. age).

Hence, as the neighbourhood generation step plays an essential role in producing a robust explanation, in this article we propose *Guided-LORE*, a variant of LORE in which neighbourhood generation is formalised as a search problem and solved using Uniform Cost Search. Given a black box model b and a specific instance x with an outcome y given by b, our goal is to make a focused analysis of the neighbourhood of x, trying to find the closest "frontier" between the class of x and other classes. Following the main idea of LORE, in *Guided-LORE* the generated samples are used to train a decision tree and generate an explanation for the output of the black box model. The obtained explanation is composed of an activated rule and a set of counter-factual rules. Several experiments have been conducted to evaluate the proposed method and compare it to LIME and LORE. The experimental results show the effectiveness of the proposed method.

The rest of this article is structured as follows. Section 2 provides an overview of the related works. Section 3 explains the proposed neighbourhood generation procedure. In Sect. 4 we describe the experimental setup and discuss the obtained results. Finally, in Sect. 5, we conclude the work and list some points for future work.

2 Related Work

As stated in the previous section, the need for interpretable Machine Learning models has increased at a very high rate, due to the availability of ever-larger datasets and its use in computer-based decision support systems. Thus, even though the research on interpretable models has a long history [2,3,15,18], in the last five years there has been an impressive number of articles in the topic of ML. Some of the most relevant ones, in the context of the work described in this paper, are commented in this section.

LIME [16], already mentioned in the introduction, is independent of the type of data and the black box to be explained. Given a black-box model b, an instance x, and a predicted class y produced by b on x, LIME constructs a simple linear model that approximates b's input-output behaviour to explain why b predicts y, based on some neighbours of x in the feature space that are generated randomly and centered on x. This approach is becoming a growingly popular method, and we can find now LIME implementations in multiple popular packages, including Python, R and SAS.

An extension of *LIME*, proposed by the same authors, is *Anchors* [17]. In this work the authors remarked that *LIME* does not measure its fidelity and, hence, the local behaviour of an extremely non-linear model may lead to poor linear approximations. So, they were motivated to work on a new model-agnostic method, *Anchors*, based on if-then rules. This method highlights the part of the input that is sufficient for the classifier to make the prediction, making explanations more intuitive and easy to understand.

The method *SHAP* [12] produces an explanation of the prediction of the output of a black box for an instance x by estimating the contribution of each feature to that prediction. These contributions are obtained by computing the Shapley Values from coalitional game theory. Hence, the features' value act as players in a coalition. Each player can be formed by an individual feature or a subset of features. Based on that, the Shapley values can show the distribution of the payout, i.e., the prediction, among the features. The same authors have proposed some variants like *KernelSHAP* (a kernel-based estimation approach for Shapley values inspired by local surrogate models) and *TreeSHAP* (which can estimate tree-based models efficiently).

The approach that is more related to our work, as mentioned in the introduction, is *LORE* [7], which constructs a decision tree c based on a synthetic neighbourhood of the input point generated by a genetic algorithm. Then, an explanation e, composed of a decision rule and a set of counterfactual rules, is extracted from the logic of c. The counterfactual rules explain the smallest changes in the instance's features that would lead to a different outcome.

In the next section we propose a new way to generate the neighbours of the input point in *LORE*, so that we can find the individuals closest to this point for which the black box changes (rather than using an unguided genetic procedure), so that we find the closest decision boundaries and we can make a more accurate local explanation.

3   Proposed Method

We propose a variant of LORE, *Guided-LORE*, to build local explanations of complex black box predictors. The main steps of our system are shown in Algorithm 1. Given an instance x_i and its outcome y_i, produced by a black box system b, the objective is to generate an explanation towards the decision of b. First, we use the uniform-cost search algorithm, described later in Algorithm 2, to generate two sets of instances. The first one, D^+, is called the *positive set*, and it contains a set of instances that are close to x_i and belong to the same class. The second one, D^-, is the *negative set*, and it contains examples that are close to x_i but have a different class.

As it will be seen later, a neighbour of a point p will be generated by making a small positive or negative change in the value of a feature of p. In that way, we will be making an exhaustive search of all possible points in the locality of x_i.

We obtain the set D^- by looking at an auxiliary set T, and finding the closest example to x_i , x^-, that has a different label than y_i (this is the aim of the procedure $FindDiffExample$ in line 3). T can be the training set used to train the black-box model, if we have access to it, or any other dataset that is from the same distribution. Once we get x^-, we pass it to Algorithm 2 to generate the *negative set*.

Algorithm 1: Guided-LORE

> **input**   : x_i: an instance to explain, T: an auxiliary set, b: a black-box model, L: maximum level of exploration, and KB: knowledge base.
> **output:** E: the explanation of the decision of b on x

1   $y_i \longleftarrow b(x_i)$;
2   $D^+ \longleftarrow GetNeighbours(x_i, y_i, b, L, KB)$;
3   $x^-, y^- \longleftarrow FindDiffExample(x_i, y_i, b, T)$;
4   $D^- \longleftarrow GetNeighbours(x^-, y^-, b, L, KB)$;
5   $D \longleftarrow D^+ \cup D^-$;
6   $t \longleftarrow BuildTree(D)$;
7   $r = (p \to y) \longleftarrow ExtractRule(x_i, t)$;
8   $\Theta \longleftarrow ExtractCounterfactuals(x_i, r, t)$;
9   $E \longleftarrow (r, \Theta)$;

As soon as we get the two sets, we merge them to get the final set D. The standard LORE process is then used to train a decision tree t, which is employed to produce the explanation (the rule used by the decision tree to classify x_i and the set of counterfactual rules of the decision tree that produce a different outcome). It is worth mentioning that the *Guided-LORE* generation method labels the generated neighbours on-the-fly. Thus, in the GetNeighbours procedure each generated instance is assigned a label obtained from the black-box model. The next subsection explains in more detail the proposed generation method.

3.1   Neighbours Generation

The problem of generating neighbours is conceptualised as a search problem. The idea is to explore the neighbourhood space of a point x_0 by applying a Uniform Cost search based on the Heterogeneous Value Difference Metric (HVDM, [23]), using some knowledge (KB) about the attributes (the maximum and minimum values, and the step to be employed to modify the value in the attribute positively or negatively).

The neighbourhood generation procedure, *GetNeighbours*, is described in Algorithm 2. We start by formalising the problem as a search and then we explain the steps of Algorithm 2.

The neighbours generation problem can be formulated as a search problem as follows:

- **State Space**: the set of all possible examples S. If F is the set of features and Y is the set of labels in our problem, then we can define $S = \{(x_i, y_i) | x_{i,f} \in range(f), y \in Y, f \in F\}$. The range of a feature f depends on its type. We consider three types of features: nominal, numerical and ordinal.
- **Initial State**: (x_0, y_0), where x_0 is the instance of which we want to generate its neighbours and y_0 is the label of this instance calculated by the black box model.
- **Actions**: All the possible actions that can be made to obtain a neighbour of an instance by modifying the value of a single attribute (feature). Each feature can be associated to one or more actions. Each action leverages some domain knowledge about the feature, contained in the KB parameter. In our case we define three types of actions: *forward, backward* and *choose*. The first two action types are used with the numerical and the ordinal features. The knowledge that we have about each of these attributes is the range (minimum and maximum values), and a *step* value, which is used to generate the closest neighbours of an instance after adding/substracting this step from the value of the attribute of the instance. In the case of the nominal features we consider the *choose* action, which generates a neighbour of an instance by changing the value of the nominal feature by another one. The knowledge that we have in KB about these attributes is the set of allowed values.
- **Transition Model**: returns a new instance in which the value of the feature $f \in F$ is incremented by *step* if the action is *forward*, decremented by *step* if the action is *backward* or chosen from the set of possible values if the action is *choose*.
- **Goal Test**: This condition checks, for each generated individual, if, according to the black box, it has the same label as x_0, y_0. If that is the case, we will generate the neighbours of the individual in the same way (i.e. applying one positive/negative change in the value of a single attribute); otherwise, we have found an individual close to x_0 that belongs to another class; thus, we have reached a boundary of y_0, and we will not continue the search from that instance.
- **Path Cost**: The path cost of each step is calculated by measuring the HVDM distance between the generated example and x_0.

Algorithm 2: Guided Neighbours Generator

---

    input : An example x_0, its output y_0, a black-box model B, the maximum level of exploration L, and a knowledge-base KB.

    output: The set of neighbours, N.

1 initialization;

2 $root \longleftarrow node(x_i, NULL, 0)$;

3 $root.label = y_0 \longleftarrow B(x_0)$;

4 $q \longleftarrow [root]$;

5 $N \longleftarrow []$;

6 **while** *Not need to stop* **do**

7 | $n \longleftarrow head[q]$;

8 | **if** *n.label! = root.label or n.level > L* **then**

9 | | continue;

10 | **else**

11 | | **foreach** *feature $f \in KB$* **do**

12 | | | **if** *f is Nominal* **then**

13 | | | | // chose action

14 | | | | $x_c \longleftarrow copy(n.x)$;

15 | | | | $x_c[f] \longleftarrow choose(KB[f][range])$ $n_c \longleftarrow node(x_c, n, n.level + 1)$;

16 | | | | $n_c.label \longleftarrow B(x_c)$;

17 | | | | $n_c.d \longleftarrow distance(x_c, x_0)$;

18 | | | | add n_c to q and N;

19 | | | **else**

20 | | | | $step \longleftarrow KB[f][[step]$;

21 | | | | $max\_value \longleftarrow KB[f][max]$;

22 | | | | $min\_value \longleftarrow KB[f][min]$;

23 | | | | **if** *n.x[f] + step ≤ max_value* **then**

24 | | | | | // forward action

25 | | | | | $x_l \longleftarrow copy(n.x)$;

26 | | | | | $x_l[f] \longleftarrow n.x[f] + step$;

27 | | | | | $n_l \longleftarrow node(x_l, n, n.level + 1)$;

28 | | | | | $n_l.label \longleftarrow B(x_l)$;

29 | | | | | $n_l.d \longleftarrow distance(x_l, x_0)$;

30 | | | | | add n_l to q and N;

31 | | | | **end**

32 | | | | **if** *n.x[f] − step ≥ min_value* **then**

33 | | | | | // backward action

34 | | | | | $x_r \longleftarrow copy(n.x)$;

35 | | | | | $x_r[f] \longleftarrow n.r[f] − step$;

36 | | | | | $n_r \longleftarrow node(x_r, n, n.level + 1)$;

37 | | | | | $n_r.label \longleftarrow B(x_r)$;

38 | | | | | $n_r.d \longleftarrow distance(x_r, x_0)$;

39 | | | | | add n_r to q and N;

40 | | | | **end**

41 | | | **end**

42 | | **end**

43 | **end**

44 **end**

Algorithm 2 shows the generation of the closest neighbours of an instance x_0. The search tree starts from this instance, and the available actions to move from one instance to another are applied. Each action only changes one feature by taking its value and adding some positive/negative quantity (forward/backward action) or replacing it by another value (choose action). So, in the neighbours in the first level of the tree, one feature will be changed whilst the rest remain the same. In this case, if we have, for example, five numerical features and five nominal features, we will get a maximum of fifteen neighbours (each value of a nominal feature can be changed, and the value of each numerical feature can be increased or decreased, if the new value is still in the range of the feature). If the outcome of the black box model changes in one of these nodes, then it is a leaf of the tree, and we do not expand that node further. Otherwise, we expand that node. Consequently, on the second level, we would have changes in two attributes or double changes in the same attribute, and so on. The node to be expanded in each step is the one that has the shortest path cost to the initial one, x_0. The generation process is terminated when there are no more nodes to be expanded (all the leaves have led to changes in the initial classification) or when all the nodes at the maximum level of exploration L have been expanded.

3.2 Explanation Extraction

In this step we use the generated neighbours D to train a decision tree t, which mimics the behaviour of the black model b locally on D. Hence, we can extract the explanation of its decision towards x_i and use it to explain the decision of b. Following the idea of the LORE method [7], the extracted explanation is formed by a tuple (r, Θ). Here, r is the decision rule, that can be naturally derived from a root-leaf path in t. To extract the counter-factual rules, i.e., Θ, we look for all paths in t leading to a decision $\hat{y} \neq y_i$ and choose the ones with the minimum number of conditions not satisfied by x_i.

4 Experiments and Results

We evaluated the effectiveness of *Guided-LORE* by comparing it with LIME and LORE, arguably two of the most popular explanation methods at the moment. We used three publicly available datasets: adult, german and compas. The first two datasets are available in the well-known UCI Machine Learning Repository. The adult dataset includes 48,842 records and 14 attributes. The german dataset is composed by 1,000 individuals, which are classified as "good" or "bad" creditors according to 20 categorical and numerical features. The compas dataset from ProPublica, that contains 1000 instances, was used by the COMPAS algorithm for scoring the risk of defendants (Low, Medium and High). In this final experiment we followed the work in LORE and considered a binary classification version with the two classes "Low-Medium" and "High". In addition to that, we compared our method with LORE on a private dataset with 9 features for the assessment of risk of developing diabetic retinopathy (DR) for diabetic patients.

In the case of the diabetic retinopathy risk assessment problem we directly used our fuzzy random forest-based system, called Retiprogram, that is currently being used in the Hospital de Sant Joan in Reus(Tarragona). Considering the public datasets, we followed the experimental setup described in [7] to make the comparisons fair. We randomly split each dataset into a training set with 80% instances, and a test set, i.e. the set of instances for which the black-box decision has to be explained, with 20% instances. We used the former to train the black box predictors, whereas the latter was used to evaluate the systems. The black-box predictors used in the test were the following: a Support Vector Machine (SVM) with RBF kernel, a Random Forest classifier (RF) with 100 trees, and a Neural Network (NN) with two layers (the first one has 100 neurons and the last one has one neuron) and the *lbfg* solver. Table 1 shows the number of training and testing examples used in the test for each data set.

Table 1. Datasets employed in the evaluation.

	Train	Test	Total
Adult	39,074	9768	48,842
Compas	800	200	1,000
German	8,000	2,000	10,000
Diabetic Retinopathy	1,212	1,111	2,323

4.1 Evaluation Metrics

We used the following metrics to evaluate the effectiveness of *Guided-LORE*.

- **hit**: this metric computes the accuracy between the output of the decision tree t and the black-box model b for the testing instances. It returns 1 if $t(x)$ is equal to $b(x)$ and 0 otherwise.
- **fidelity**: this metric measures to which extent the decision tree can accurately reproduce the black-box predictor. It answers the question of how good is the decision tree at mimicking the behaviour of the black-box by comparing its predictions and the ones of the black-box on the instances D.
- **l-fidelity**: it is similar to the *fidelity*; however, it is computed on the set of instances covered by the decision rule in a local explanation for x. It is used to measure to what extent a decision rule is good at mimicking the black-box model.
- **c-hit**: this metric compares the predictions of the decision tree and the black-box model on a counterfactual instance of x that is extracted from the counterfactual rules in a local explanation of x.
- **cl-fidelity**: it is also similar to the *fidelity*; however, it is computed on the set of instances covered by the the counterfactual rules in a local explanation for x.

4.2   Results and Discussion

Table 2 shows the results of *Guided-LORE*, LIME and LORE on the three public
datasets. Specifically, it reports the mean and standard deviation of the *hit* score
of each black-box model. It may be seen that *Guided-LORE* outperforms LORE
and LIME. In most of the cases it obtains the best *hit* score and, in those cases
where LORE or LIME is better, it shows a very close performance to them. In
the case of the Random Forest black-box model, *Guided-LORE* gives the best
performance with the three datasets, and the worst one is LIME. Thus, it seems
that decision trees can effectively mimic the performance of random forests more
than linear regression models. Our method gives the best score for the three
black-boxes with the Compass dataset. In the case of the NN black-box model,
LIME gives the best performance, and LORE is the worst one. *Guided-LORE*
and LIME show a similar performance with the German data set.

Table 2. The comparison of the three evaluated systems on the hit score.

Method	BlackBox	Datasets		
		Compass	German	Adult
A. Guided-LORE	SVM	**1.0 ± 0.0**	**1.0 ± 0.0**	0.96 ± 0.2
	NN	**1.0 ± 0.0**	0.99 ± 0.01	0.94 ± 0.2
	RF	**1.0 ± 0.0**	**0.98 ± 0.1**	**0.91 ± 0.3**
B. LORE	SVM	0.99 ± 0.1	**1.0 ± 0.0**	**0.98 ± 0.1**
	NN	0.98 ± 0.1	0.98 ± 0.1	0.91 ± 0.3
	RF	0.94 ± 0.2	0.92 ± 0.2	0.90 ± 0.3
C. LIME	SVM	0.82 ± 0.4	0.96 ± 0.1	**0.98 ± 0.1**
	NN	0.90 ± 0.3	**1.0 ± 0.0**	**0.98 ± 0.1**
	RF	0.82 ± 0.6	0.88 ± 0.3	0.82 ± 0.4

In Fig. 1 and Table 3, we compare the performance of *Guided-LORE* with
LORE, as they share the same extraction explanation process. The values in
Table 3 report the evaluation results of the application of these two methods
on the DR dataset and the FRF black-box model. The reported results reveal
that *Guided-LORE* outperforms LORE in all the metrics. Such finding can be
ascribed to the fact that as the backbone of the generation function of LORE is a
genetic algorithm, it may tend to generate very similar examples to the original
instance by making only small changes. In a classical numerical feature space,
such small differences may be relevant enough. However, when we deal with
fuzzy-based models, the transformation from the classical numerical space to the
fuzzy feature space may remove these differences and lead to almost identical
instances. In that case, we lose the diversity in the generated neighbours. For
example, LORE (or even LIME) may generate an instance that only differs from
the original one by changing the age from being 55 to 55.5. Such an example is

likely to be identical to the original one in the fuzzy feature space. In our case, as we propose a guided generation process, we avoid this problem by generating examples that are different but close to the original one, in terms of both the classical and fuzzy feature spaces.

Table 3. Guided-LORE vs LORE.

	hit	fidelity	l-fidelity	c-hit	cl-fidelity
Guided-LORE	**0.996 ± 0.06**	**0.991 ± 0.04**	**0.989 ± 0.07**	**0.795 ± 0.4**	**0.836 ± 0.32**
LORE	0.963 ± 0.18	0.953 ± 0.03	0.943 ± 0.18	0.765 ± 0.4	0.789 ± 0.31

Figure 1 shows the box-plots of the *fidelity*, *l-fidelity* and *cl-fidelity* measures for *Guided-LORE* and LORE. The former has the highest mean and median values for the three measures, and the lowest variability. Concerning the outliers, both *Guided-LORE* and LORE show similar performance. Such findings confirm our claim that *Guided-LORE* performs a focused analysis of the neighbourhood of the initial individual x, trying to find the closest "frontier" between the class of x and the other classes and as a result produces a decision boundary that is clear and simple. Figure 2 shows a multi-dimensional scaling of the neighbourhood of a sample instance from the DR dataset generated by the two methods. In general, the neighbours generated by *Guided-LORE* are more separable, more compact and denser than the ones generated by LORE. Considering that we are interested in searching the boundary of the predicted class in the state space, we can find that the decision boundary is clear.

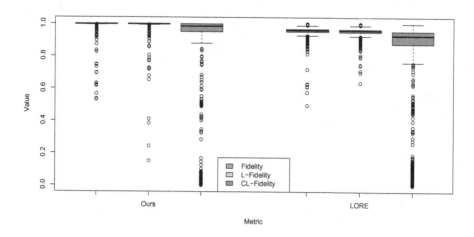

Fig. 1. Comparing the neighbourhood generation method in Guided-LORE and LORE

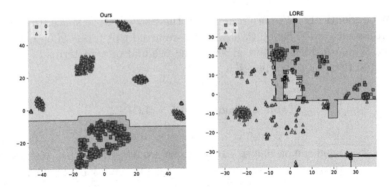

Fig. 2. Decision boundaries of the neighbours generated for an instance using *Guided-LORE* (left) and LORE (right).

5   Conclusion

We have proposed a variant of *LORE*, *Guided-LORE*, to explain the decisions of black-box classifiers. The critical component of our method is the generation of neighbours of the point for which the explanation has to be made. We proposed to formulate it as a search problem and we have used the uniform cost search to find the closest neighbours for which a change in the predicted class appears. This method can generate neighbours that are compact, dense and have a simple and straightforward decision boundary. The experimental results show the effectiveness of our method, that outperforms the state-of-the-art methods of *LIME* and *LORE* in several metrics. In the future work our main target is to develop explanation methods for fuzzy-based black-box models, such as fuzzy random forests, so we plan to adapt the proposed method to work directly on the fuzzy space. We also plan to apply the proposed method on different problem domains such as Computer Vision and Natural Language Processing and try to make it work not only on tabular data but also on different data types.

Acknowledgements. The authors would like to thank the support of the FIS project PI18/00169 (Fondos FEDER) and the URV grant 2018-PFR-B2-61. The first author is supported by a URV Martí Franquès predoctoral grant.

References

1. Baehrens, D., Schroeter, T., Harmeling, S., Kawanabe, M., Hansen, K., Müller, K.R.: How to explain individual classification decisions. J. Mach. Learn. Res. **11**, 1803–1831 (2010)
2. Briand, L.C., Brasili, V., Hetmanski, C.J.: Developing interpretable models with optimized set reduction for identifying high-risk software components. IEEE Trans. Softw. Eng. **19**(11), 1028–1044 (1993)

3. Carroll, J.B.: An analytical solution for approximating simple structure in factor analysis. Psychometrika **18**(1), 23–38 (1953)

4. Caruana, R., Lou, Y., Gehrke, J., Koch, P., Sturm, M., Elhadad, N.: Intelligible models for healthcare: predicting pneumonia risk and hospital 30-day readmission. In: Proceedings of the 21th ACM SIGKDD International Conference on Knowledge Discovery and Data Mining, pp. 1721–1730. KDD 2015, Association for Computing Machinery, New York, NY, USA (2015)

5. Caruana, R., Lou, Y., Gehrke, J., Koch, P., Sturm, M., Elhadad, N.: Intelligible models for healthcare: predicting pneumonia risk and hospital 30-day readmission. In: Proceedings of the 21th ACM SIGKDD International Conference on Knowledge Discovery and Data Mining, pp. 1721–1730 (2015)

6. Craven, M., Shavlik, J.: Extracting tree-structured representations of trained networks. Adv. Neural. Inf. Process. Syst. **8**, 24–30 (1995)

7. Guidotti, R., Monreale, A., Ruggieri, S., Pedreschi, D., Turini, F., Giannotti, F.: Local rule-based explanations of black box decision systems. arXiv preprint arXiv:1805.10820 (2018)

8. Guillaume, S.: Designing fuzzy inference systems from data: an interpretability-oriented review. IEEE Trans. Fuzzy Syst. **9**(3), 426–443 (2001)

9. Krause, J., Perer, A., Ng, K.: Interacting with predictions: visual inspection of black-box machine learning models. In: Proceedings of the 2016 CHI Conference on Human Factors in Computing Systems, pp. 5686–5697 (2016)

10. Letham, B., Rudin, C., McCormick, T.H., Madigan, D., et al.: Interpretable classifiers using rules and Bayesian analysis: building a better stroke prediction model. Ann. Appl. Stat. **9**(3), 1350–1371 (2015)

11. Lin, J., Keogh, E., Wei, L., Lonardi, S.: Experiencing sax: a novel symbolic representation of time series. Data Min. Knowl. Discov. **15**(2), 107–144 (2007)

12. Lundberg, S.M., Lee, S.I.: A unified approach to interpreting model predictions. In: Advances in Neural Information Processing Systems, pp. 4765–4774 (2017)

13. Molnar, C.: Interpretable Machine Learning. Lulu. com (2020)

14. Qian, L., Zheng, H., Zhou, H., Qin, R., Li, J.: Classification of time seriesgene expression in clinical studies via integration of biological network. PLoS ONE **8**(3), e58383 (2013)

15. Revelle, W., Rocklin, T.: Very simple structure: an alternative procedure for estimating the optimal number of interpretable factors. Multivar. Behav. Res. **14**(4), 403–414 (1979)

16. Ribeiro, M.T., Singh, S., Guestrin, C.: Why should I trust you?: explaining the predictions of any classifier. In: Proceedings of the 22nd ACM SIGKDD International Conference on Knowledge Discovery and Data Mining, pp. 1135–1144. ACM (2016)

17. Ribeiro, M.T., Singh, S., Guestrin, C.: Anchors: high-precision model-agnostic explanations. AAAI **18**, 1527–1535 (2018)

18. Ridgeway, G., Madigan, D., Richardson, T., O'Kane, J.: Interpretable boosted naïve bayes classification. In: KDD, pp. 101–104 (1998)

19. Schielzeth, H.: Simple means to improve the interpretability of regression coefficients. Methods Ecol. Evol. **1**(2), 103–113 (2010)

20. Strumbelj, E., Kononenko, I.: An efficient explanation of individual classifications using game theory. J. Mach. Learn. Res. **11**, 1–18 (2010)

21. Ustun, B., Rudin, C.: Supersparse linear integer models for optimized medical scoring systems. Mach. Learn. **102**(3), 349–391 (2015). https://doi.org/10.1007/s10994-015-5528-6
22. Wang, F., Rudin, C.: Falling rule lists. In: Artificial Intelligence and Statistics, pp. 1013–1022 (2015)
23. Wilson, D.R., Martinez, T.R.: Improved heterogeneous distance functions. J. Artif. Intell. Res. **6**, 1–34 (1997)

Interactive Natural Language Technology for Explainable Artificial Intelligence

Jose M. Alonso[1]([✉])[iD], Senén Barro[1][iD], Alberto Bugarín[1][iD],
Kees van Deemter[2][iD], Claire Gardent[3][iD], Albert Gatt[4][iD], Ehud Reiter[5][iD],
Carles Sierra[6][iD], Mariët Theune[7][iD], Nava Tintarev[8][iD], Hitoshi Yano[9][iD],
and Katarzyna Budzynska[10][iD]

[1] Centro Singular de Investigación en Tecnoloxías Intelixentes (CiTIUS),
Universidade de Santiago de Compostela, Santiago de Compostela, Spain
{josemaria.alonso.moral,senen.barro,alberto.bugarin.diz}@usc.es
[2] Universiteit Utrecht, Utrecht, Netherlands
c.j.vandeemter@uu.nl
[3] Lorraine Research Laboratory in Computer Science and its Applications (LORIA),
Centre National de la Recherche Scientifique (CNRS), Nancy, France
claire.gardent@loria.fr
[4] Institute of Linguistics and Language Technology, University of Malta (UM),
Msida, Malta
albert.gatt@um.edu.mt
[5] Department of Computing Science, University of Aberdeen (UNIABDN),
Aberdeen, Scotland
e.reiter@abdn.ac.uk
[6] Artificial Intelligence Research Institute (IIIA), Spanish National Research Council
(CSIC), Bellaterra, Spain
sierra@iiia.csic.es
[7] Human Media Interaction, Universiteit Twente (UTWENTE),
Enschede, Netherlands
m.theune@utwente.nl
[8] Department of Software Technology, Technische Universiteit Delft (TU Delft),
Delft, Netherlands
n.tintarev@tudelft.nl
[9] MINSAIT, INDRA, Madrid, Spain
hyano@minsait.com
[10] Laboratory of The New Ethos, Warsaw University of Technology, Warsaw, Poland
Katarzyna.Budzynska@pw.edu.pl

Abstract. We have defined an interdisciplinary program for training a new generation of researchers who will be ready to leverage the use of Artificial Intelligence (AI)-based models and techniques even by non-expert users. The final goal is to make AI self-explaining and thus contribute to translating knowledge into products and services for economic and social benefit, with the support of Explainable AI systems. Moreover, our focus is on the automatic generation of interactive explanations

Supported by the European Union's Horizon 2020 research and innovation programme under the Marie Skłodowska-Curie grant agreement No 860621.

F. Heintz et al. (Eds.): TAILOR 2020, LNAI 12641, pp. 63–70, 2021.
https://doi.org/10.1007/978-3-030-73959-1_5

in natural language, the preferred modality among humans, with visualization as a complementary modality.

Keywords: Explainable Artificial Intelligence · Trustworthiness · Multi-modal explanations · Argumentative conversational agents · Human-centered modeling · Human-machine persuasive interaction

1   Introduction

According to Polanyi's paradox [25], humans know more than they can explain, mainly due to the huge amount of implicit knowledge they unconsciously acquire through culture, heritage, etc. The same applies to Artificial Intelligence (AI)-based systems, which are increasingly learnt from data. However, as EU laws also specify, humans have a right to explanation of decisions affecting them, no matter who (or what AI-based system) makes such decisions [23].

In addition, it is worth noting that the European Commission identified AI as the most strategic technology of the 21st century [10] and eXplainable AI (XAI for short) has fast become a fruitful research area. In particular, CLAIRE[1], a Confederation of Laboratories for AI Research in Europe, emphasizes "the need of building trustworthy AI that is beneficial to people through fairness, transparency and explainability". In addition, TAILOR[2], one of four AI networks in the H2020 program ICT-48 "Towards a vibrant European network of AI excellence centres", has the purpose of developing the scientific foundations for Trustworthy AI in Europe. Moreover, Explainable Human-centred AI is highlighted as one of the five key research areas to consider and it is present in five out of the eight pilot experiments to be developed in the H2020 AI4EU project[3] that is funded by call ICT-26 2018.

However, even though XAI systems are likely to make their impact felt in the near future, there is a lack of experts to develop fundamentals of XAI, i.e., researchers ready to develop and to maintain the new generation of AI-based systems that are expected to surround us soon. This is mainly due to the inherently multidisciplinary character of this field of research, with XAI researchers and practitioners coming from very heterogeneous fields. Moreover, it is hard to find XAI experts with a holistic view as well as sufficient breadth and depth in all related topics. Therefore, the H2020-MSCA-ITN project "Interactive Natural Language Technology for Explainable Artificial Intelligence" (NL4XAI[4]) is developing an outstanding training program, deployed across scientific lead institutions and industry partners, with the aim of training 11 creative, entrepreneurial and innovative Early-Stage Researchers (ESRs) who are learning how to develop trustworthy self-explanatory XAI systems. NL4XAI is

---

[1] https://claire-ai.org/.
[2] https://liu.se/en/research/tailor.
[3] https://www.ai4eu.eu/.
[4] https://nl4xai.eu/.

the first European training network with a focus on Natural Language (NL) and XAI. In the NL4XAI program, ESRs are trained in the fundamentals of AI, along with Computational Linguistics, Argumentation and Human-Machine Interaction Technologies for the generation of interactive explanations in NL as a complement to visualization tools.

In this position paper, we describe how the NL4XAI project contributes to strengthening European innovation capacity in the XAI research area. The rest of the manuscript is organized as follows. Section 2 introduces the research objectives in the NL4XAI project. Section 3 sketches the training program for ESRs. Finally, Sect. 4 provides readers with final remarks.

2 Research Challenges for Early-Stage Researchers

The NL4XAI training program covers four main research objectives:

- **Designing and developing human-centred XAI models.** This objective is addressed by four ESRs who face the challenges of (1) explaining current AI algorithms (paying special attention to the explanation of decision trees and fuzzy rule-based systems [2–5], logical formulas [20], counterfactual facts [32,33], knowledge representation and reasoning, temporal and causal relations in Bayesian networks [18,24,29], and black-box machine learning algorithms [15,19] such as deep neural networks [17]); and (2) generating new self-explanatory AI algorithms. Explanations in NL, adapted to user background and preferences, will be communicated mainly through multi-modal (e.g., graphical and textual modalities) via interactive interfaces to be designed as a result of achieving the next three objectives.
- **Enhancing NL Technologies for XAI.** This objective refers to the need to go deeper with the generation of explanations in NL, as humans naturally do. Two ESRs focus on the study of NL technologies, regarding both NL processing (NLP) and NL generation (NLG) [16,22]; but paying special attention to the grounding of symbolic representations in multi-modal information, and to text production and verbalization in both data-driven/neural and knowledge-based systems [11]. Such systems can be end-to-end or modular [12,21], in the latter case incorporating well-understood NLG sub-tasks such as content determination, lexicalization, linguistic realization, etc. A promising format for NL explanations is in the form of a narrative or story, which is known to aid human comprehension [13,36].
- **Exploiting Argumentation Technology for XAI.** This objective deals with analyzing advantages and drawbacks of current argumentation technology in the context of XAI [6,26,30]. Two ESRs address the challenge of how to organize naturally the discourse history in either narrative/story or dialogue, in terms of standard and customized argumentation schemes [35]; with the focus on designing argumentation-based multi-agent recommender systems [34] that are expected to be self-explainable, non-biased and trustworthy [7].

– **Developing Interactive Interfaces for XAI**. This objective refers to the communication layer between XAI systems and humans [1]. Three ESRs research multi-modal interfaces [31] (i.e., with the goal to generate explanations based on textual and non-verbal information such as graphics/diagrams, but also gestures by embodied conversational agents) associated to virtual assistants in different application domains (e.g., e-Health); with an emphasis on how to convey non-biased, effective and persuasive explanations through verbal and non-verbal interaction between XAI systems and humans [28].

3   Training Program

Each ESR has a principal supervisor in his/her host institution, a secondary supervisor in another institution of the NL4XAI consortium, and a secondment supervisor (inter-sectoral secondments, i.e., from academic to non-academic partners and vice versa). We have defined the following 11 cutting-edge research projects to be executed in three years: (1) explaining black-box models in terms of grey-box twin models; (2) from grey-box models to explainable models; (3) explaining Bayesian Networks; (4) explaining logical formulas; (5) multi-modal semantic grounding and model transparency; (6) explainable models for text production; (7) argumentation-based multi-agent recommender system; (8) customized interactive argumentation schemes for XAI; (9) personalized explanations by virtual characters; (10) interactions to mitigate human biases; and (11) explaining contracts and documentation of assets for companies.

Each single project is developed by an ESR with the guidance of his/her supervisors. Nevertheless, all ESRs contribute to create the framework depicted in Fig. 1, where ESRs are grouped in agreement with their research challenges. They all share a common open source software repository and collaborate in solving practical use cases posed by the companies involved in the project, regarding varied applications domains such as e-Health, education or telecommunications. Moreover, ESRs will do significant experimental work with human participants to inform and evaluate their algorithms. Accordingly, they will follow the Ethics guidelines for Trustworthy AI issued by the High-Level Expert Group on AI set up by the European Commission [8,9]. This will lead to generalizable methodologies and guidelines for generating and evaluating explanations.

The work developed by each ESR will end up with the publication of a PhD dissertation. Expected results are publications in top journals and conferences, but also additional resources such as open source software. Accordingly, each ESR has a personal career development plan with three main goals: (1) to develop the knowledge and skills required for performing high-quality doctoral research; (2) to develop transferable skills to enhance their personal effectiveness, leadership, management skills, research support, career and personal development, technology transfer and entrepreneurship, ethics and languages; and (3) to acquire ample insights in generating language and interactive solutions for XAI. To fulfil these training goals, the NL4XAI project includes a variety of network-wide training courses, motivating interactions at multiple levels (local,

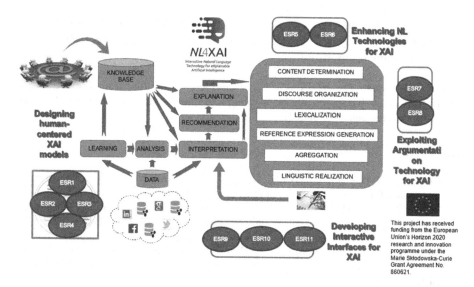

Fig. 1. NL4XAI framework for generating interactive explanations.

network-global) and at different depths (basics-general, specialisation-specific). All in all, we promote that ESRs collaborate actively during training activities and secondments (regarding both online and in person events).

4 Final Remarks

With the aim of generating narrative explanations in NL, we have identified the following major challenges [27] that will be jointly addressed by all ESRs:

- **Evaluation**: Develop "cheap but reliable" ways of estimating scrutability, trust, etc. Fair universal evaluation metrics and protocols supported by statistics for XAI are missing. Correlation among data-driven metrics and both intrinsic and extrinsic human evaluation needs to be studied.
- **Data Quality**: Develop techniques to let users know how results are influenced by data issues. Research on data bias is particularly encouraged.
- **Explanation effectiveness:** Develop models that make explicit how the effectiveness of an explanation depends on such factors as: the domain, the user, the context, the degree of interactivity, the level of precision and detail of the explanation, as well as on many concrete presentational choices involving the form and content of the explanation.

Finally, we note that ESRs will pay attention not only to technical but also to ethical and legal issues due to the worldwide social impact of XAI [8,9]. For example, Floridi et al. [14] defined an ethical framework for AI in which the concept of "explicability" captures the need for transparency and for accountability with reference to both "intelligibility" and "explainability". The interested reader is referred to the NL4XAI website for further insights on the development of this challenging project where the interplay between XAI and NL technologies leverages European innovation capacity.

Acknowledgment. The NL4XAI project has received funding from the European Union's Horizon 2020 research and innovation programme under the Marie Skłodowska-Curie Grant Agreement No. 860621.

References

1. Abdul, A., Vermeulen, J., Wang, D., Lim, B.Y., Kankanhalli, M.: Trends and trajectories for explainable, accountable and intelligible systems: an HCI research agenda. In: Proceedings of the CHI Conference on Human Factors in Computing Systems. ACM, New York (2018). https://doi.org/10.1145/3173574.3174156
2. Alonso, J.M., Bugarín, A.: ExpliClas: automatic generation of explanations in natural language for Weka classifiers. In: Proceedings of the IEEE International Conference on Fuzzy Systems (FUZZ-IEEE) (2019). https://doi.org/10.1109/FUZZ-IEEE.2019.8859018
3. Alonso, J.M., Castiello, C., Magdalena, L., Mencar, C.: Explainable Fuzzy Systems - Paving the Way from Interpretable Fuzzy Systems to Explainable AI Systems. Studies in Computational Intelligence. Springer (2021). https://doi.org/10.1007/978-3-030-71098-9
4. Alonso, J.M., Ramos-Soto, A., Reiter, E., van Deemter, K.: An exploratory study on the benefits of using natural language for explaining fuzzy rule-based systems. In: Proceedings of the IEEE International Conference on Fuzzy Systems (2017). https://doi.org/10.1109/FUZZ-IEEE.2017.8015489
5. Alonso, J.M., Toja-Alamancos, J., Bugarín, A.: Experimental study on generating multi-modal explanations of black-box classifiers in terms of gray-box classifiers. In: Proceedings of the IEEE World Congress on Computational Intelligence (2020). https://doi.org/10.1109/FUZZ48607.2020.9177770
6. Budzynska, K., Villata, S.: Argument mining. IEEE Intell. Inform. Bull. **17**, 1–7 (2016)
7. Demollin, M., Shaheen, Q., Budzynska, K., Sierra, C.: Argumentation theoretical frameworks for explainable artificial intelligence. In: Proceedings of the Workshop on Interactive Natural Language Technology for Explainable Artificial Intelligence (NL4XAI) at the International Conference on Natural Language Generation (INLG). Dublin, Ireland (2020). https://www.aclweb.org/anthology/2020.nl4xai-1.10/
8. EU High Level Expert Group on AI: AI Ethics Guidelines for Trustworthy AI. Technical report, European Commission, Brussels, Belgium (2019). https://doi.org/10.2759/346720
9. EU High Level Expert Group on AI: The assessment list for trustworthy artificial intelligence (ALTAI) for self assessment. Technical report, European Commission, Brussels, Belgium (2019). https://doi.org/10.2759/002360
10. European Commission: Artificial Intelligence for Europe. Technical report, European Commission, Brussels, Belgium (2018). https://ec.europa.eu/digital-single-market/en/news/communicationartificial-intelligence-europe. Communication from the Commission to the European Parliament, the European Council, the Council, the European Economic and Social Committee and the Committee of the Regions (SWD(2018) 137 final)

11. Faille, J., Gatt, A., Gardent, C.: The natural language pipeline, neural text generation and explainability. In: Proceedings of the Workshop on Interactive Natural Language Technology for Explainable Artificial Intelligence (NL4XAI) at the International Conference on Natural Language Generation (INLG), Dublin, Ireland (2020). https://www.aclweb.org/anthology/2020.nl4xai-1.5/

12. Ferreira, T.C., van der Lee, C., van Miltenburg, E., Krahmer, E.: Neural data-to-text generation: a comparison between pipeline and end-to-end architectures. In: Proceedings of the Conference on Empirical Methods in Natural Language Processing (EMNLP), Hong Kong, pp. 552–562. Association for Computational Linguistics (2019). https://doi.org/10.18653/v1/D19-1052

13. Fisher, W.R.: Human Communication as Narration: Toward a Philosophy of Reason, Value, and Action. University of South Carolina Press, Columbia (1989)

14. Floridi, L., et al.: AI4People - an ethical framework for a good AI society: opportunities, risks, principles, and recommendations. Minds Mach. **28**(4), 689–707 (2018). https://doi.org/10.1007/s11023-018-9482-5

15. Forrest, J., Sripada, S., Pang, W., Coghill, G.: Towards making NLG a voice for interpretable machine learning. In: Proceedings of the International Conference on Natural Language Generation (INLG), The Netherlands, pp. 177–182. Association for Computational Linguistics, Tilburg University (2018). https://doi.org/10.18653/v1/W18-6522

16. Gatt, A., Krahmer, E.: Survey of the state of the art in natural language generation: core tasks, applications and evaluation. J. Artif. Intell. Res. **61**, 65–170 (2018). https://doi.org/10.1613/jair.5477

17. Guidotti, R., Monreale, A., Ruggieri, S., Turini, F., Giannotti, F., Pedreschi, D.: A survey of methods for explaining black box models. ACM Comput. Surv. **51**(5), 93:1–93:42 (2018). https://doi.org/10.1145/3236009

18. Hennessy, C., Bugarin, A., Reiter, E.: Explaining Bayesian Networks in natural language: state of the art and challenges. In: Proceedings of the Workshop on Interactive Natural Language Technology for Explainable Artificial Intelligence (NL4XAI) at the International Conference on Natural Language Generation (INLG), Dublin, Ireland (2020). https://www.aclweb.org/anthology/2020.nl4xai-1.7/

19. Mariotti, E., Alonso, J.M., Gatt, A.: Towards harnessing natural language generation to explain black-box models. In: Proceedings of the Workshop on Interactive Natural Language Technology for Explainable Artificial Intelligence (NL4XAI) at the International Conference on Natural Language Generation (INLG), Dublin, Ireland (2020). https://www.aclweb.org/anthology/2020.nl4xai-1.6/

20. Mayn, A., van Deemter, K.: Towards generating effective explanations of logical formulas: challenges and strategies. In: Proceedings of the Workshop on Interactive Natural Language Technology for Explainable Artificial Intelligence (NL4XAI) at the International Conference on Natural Language Generation (INLG), Dublin, Ireland (2020). https://www.aclweb.org/anthology/2020.nl4xai-1.9/

21. Moryossef, A., Goldberg, Y., Dagan, I.: Improving quality and efficiency in plan-based neural data-to-text generation. In: Proceedings of the International Conference on Natural Language Generation (INLG), Tokyo, Japan, pp. 377–382. Association for Computational Linguistics (2019). https://doi.org/10.18653/v1/w19-8645

22. Narayan, S., Gardent, C.: Deep learning approaches to text production. In: Synthesis Lectures on Human Language Technologies, vol. 13, no. 1, pp. 1–199 (2020)

23. Parliament and Council of the European Union: General data protection regulation (GDPR) (2016). http://data.europa.eu/eli/reg/2016/679/oj

24. Pereira-Fariña, M., Bugarín, A.: Content determination for natural language descriptions of predictive Bayesian Networks. In: Proceedings of the Conference of the European Society for Fuzzy Logic and Technology (EUSFLAT), pp. 784–791. Atlantis Press (2019)

25. Polanyi, M.: The Tacit Dimension. Doubleday & Company Inc., New York (1966)

26. Rago, A., Cocarascu, O., Toni, F.: Argumentation-based recommendations: fantastic explanations and how to find them. In: Proceedings of the International Joint Conference on Artificial Intelligence (IJCAI), pp. 1949–1955 (2018). https://doi.org/10.24963/ijcai.2018/269

27. Reiter, E.: Natural language generation challenges for explainable AI. In: Proceedings of the Workshop on Interactive Natural Language Technology for Explainable Artificial Intelligence (NL4XAI), pp. 3–7. Association for Computational Linguistics (2019). https://doi.org/10.18653/v1/W19-8402

28. Rieger, A., Theune, M., Tintarev, N.: Toward natural language mitigation strategies for cognitive biases in recommender systems. In: Proceedings of the Workshop on Interactive Natural Language Technology for Explainable Artificial Intelligence (NL4XAI) at the International Conference on Natural Language Generation (INLG), Dublin, Ireland (2020). https://www.aclweb.org/anthology/2020.nl4xai-1.11/

29. Sevilla, J.: Explaining data using causal Bayesian Networks. In: Proceedings of the Workshop on Interactive Natural Language Technology for Explainable Artificial Intelligence (NL4XAI) at the International Conference on Natural Language Generation (INLG), Dublin, Ireland (2020). https://www.aclweb.org/anthology/2020.nl4xai-1.8/

30. Sierra, C., de Mántaras, R.L., Simoff, S.J.: The argumentative mediator. In: Proceedings of the European Conference on Multi-Agent Systems (EUMAS) and the International Conference on Agreement Technologies (AT), Valencia, Spain, pp. 439–454 (2016). https://doi.org/10.1007/978-3-319-59294-7_36

31. Stent, A., Bangalore, S.: Natural Language Generation in Interactive Systems. Cambridge University Press, Cambridge (2014)

32. Stepin, I., Alonso, J.M., Catala, A., Pereira, M.: Generation and evaluation of factual and counterfactual explanations for decision trees and fuzzy rule-based classifiers. In: Proceedings of the IEEE World Congress on Computational Intelligence (2020). https://doi.org/10.1109/FUZZ48607.2020.9177629

33. Stepin, I., Alonso, J.M., Catala, A., Pereira-Fariña, M.: A survey of contrastive and counterfactual explanation generation methods for explainable artificial intelligence. IEEE Access 9, 11974–12001 (2021). https://doi.org/10.1109/ACCESS.2021.3051315

34. Tintarev, N., Masthoff, J.: Explaining recommendations: design and evaluation. In: Ricci, F., Rokach, L., Shapira, B. (eds.) Recommender Systems Handbook, pp. 353–382. Springer, Boston, MA (2015). https://doi.org/10.1007/978-1-4899-7637-6_10

35. Walton, D., Reed, C., Macagno, F.: Argumentation Schemes. Cambridge University Press, Cambridge (2008)

36. Williams, S., Reiter, E.: Generating basic skills reports for low-skilled readers. Nat. Lang. Eng. 14, 495–535 (2008). https://doi.org/10.1017/S1351324908004725

Hybrid AI: The Way Forward in AI by Developing Four Dimensions

Albert Huizing[1(✉)] , Cor Veenman[1,2] , Mark Neerincx[1,3] , and Judith Dijk[1]

[1] TNO, The Hague, The Netherlands
albert.huizing@tno.nl
[2] LIACS, Leiden University, Leiden, The Netherlands
[3] Delft University of Technology, Delft, The Netherlands

Abstract. In recent years, AI based on deep learning has achieved tremendous success in specialized tasks such as speech recognition, machine translation, and the detection of tumors in medical images. Despite these successes there are also some clear signs of the limitations of the current state-of-the-art in AI. For example, biases in AI-enabled face recognition and predictive policing have shown that prejudice in AI systems is a real problem that must be solved. In this position paper, we argue that current AI needs to be developed along four dimensions to become more generally applicable and trustworthy: environment, purpose, collaboration, and governance. Hybrid AI offers the potential for advancements along these four dimensions by combining two different paradigms in AI: knowledge-based reasoning and optimization, and data-driven machine learning.

Keywords: Hybrid AI · Machine learning · Reasoning

1 Introduction

Recent breakthroughs in Artificial Intelligence (AI) based on deep learning have allowed machines to perform at the same level as (or even surpass) humans in specialized tasks such as image classification, speech recognition, and machine translation. These breakthroughs are enabled by the tremendous growth in computational power, the availability of large annotated datasets, and new efficient machine learning algorithms. Most of the recent successes in AI can be attributed to supervised deep learning which is a machine learning approach that uses large labelled training sets and a gradient-based backpropagation algorithm to adapt millions of parameters in a deep neural network. The availability of big data and enormous computing power provided by modern graphical processing units are major contributors to this success.

Despite these successes there are also some disturbing signs of undesirable behavior of AI. For example, unwanted biases in algorithms for face recognition and fraud detection have shown that prejudice and bias in AI systems is a real problem that needs to be solved [1, 2]. Furthermore, accidents with self-driving cars indicate that AI cannot yet be trusted to operate autonomously in safety-critical applications [3].

© Springer Nature Switzerland AG 2021
F. Heintz et al. (Eds.): TAILOR 2020, LNAI 12641, pp. 71–76, 2021.
https://doi.org/10.1007/978-3-030-73959-1_6

The purpose of this position paper is to argue that AI needs to be enhanced along four dimensions to become more general purpose and trustworthy and that hybrid AI can enable these enhancements. In Sect. 2 we introduce the four dimensions: environment, purpose, collaboration, and governance. Section 3 briefly describes a hybrid AI approach and Sect. 4 gives conclusions.

2 Four Dimensions of AI

For AI to become more effective and accepted in society, there is a need for future AI to improve from the current state-of-the art. Fig. 1 shows these needs along four dimensions: (i) environment (ii) purpose, (iii) collaboration, and (iv) governance. For the near future we foresee a need for AI to evolve from operations in a controlled environment to operations in an open world, from special purpose tasks to more general purpose problem solving, from a stand-alone system to a team of humans and AI, and from applications where the governance of the AI can be permissive to applications where governance needs to be strict with respect to compliance with laws, ethical norms, and societal values. The AI challenges that emerge from these needs are discussed in more detail in the next sections.

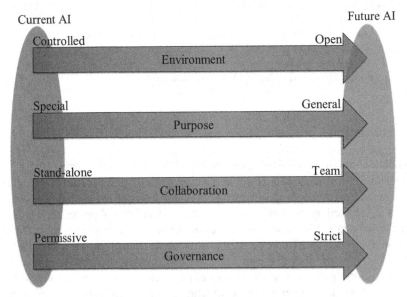

Fig. 1. The need for AI enhancements along four dimensions.

2.1 Environment

When AI was introduced in the second half of the 20th century, it demonstrated considerable success in solving problems that were previously unattainable by computers.

This first generation of AI used knowledge representations such as heuristics, rules and ontologies, and deductive reasoning to solve problems such as search and planning. However, it soon became clear that knowledge-based AI could only solve well-defined problems in carefully controlled environments where uncertainty is minimal and explicit knowledge instead of intuition mostly defines the solution to the problem.

Machine learning techniques such as support vector machines and deep neural networks use large labelled data sets to solve problems. Machine learning does not depend on explicit knowledge representations thereby reducing the need for scarce domain experts and broadening the range of environments in which it can operate. Moreover, it can discover new knowledge embedded in the data that would not be available to human experts. Uncertainty in the environment can also be handled better by machine learning than knowledge-based reasoning methods because it exploits the diversity and fluctuations in the training data to achieve statistically impressive results even when numerous potentially correlated parameters are involved. There are however still significant problems when using machine learning in open environments: e.g. environments with rare but important events, adverse conditions, and unforeseen situations. In these environments there is often few data or no data at all available for training. This scarcity of labelled training data is a big challenge for machine learning which restricts the applications in which AI can be deployed effectively and safely. For example, the danger of relying on machine learning in safety-critical applications such as an Advanced Driver Assist System (ADAS) is vividly illustrated by a recent experiment where a digit on a traffic sign was slightly modified [4]. The interpretation of the image of the traffic sign by the ADAS was 85 mph instead of 35 mph. Clearly, such an error could cause major problems and lethal accidents. In summary, AI faces challenges in an open environment in the identification and characterization of *unforeseen situations*, a *lack of training data* and acting effectively and *safely* in unknown situations. Potential solutions for these challenges include compositional reasoning and simulation models based on *domain knowledge* to generate training data for rare events [5].

2.2 Purpose

AI using deep neural networks can currently outperform humans on specialized tasks such as the detection of tumors in medical images after being extensively trained on large labelled image sets [6]. However, if the purpose of the task changes slightly, for example from localization of a tumor to segmentation of a medical image, the loss function that encodes the purpose of the task and the neural network architecture must be redesigned, and the network must be retrained again. Approaches such as transfer learning can address this problem by reusing parts of a network that has been trained on large publicly available databases such as ImageNet. However, there are often significant differences between images used in different domains. For example, in medical images variations in local textures are used to detect tumors while in natural image datasets there is generally a global subject present [7]. Significant progress has been achieved with transfer learning using homogeneous data sets in decision support systems. Considerably more challenging are applications that involve heterogeneous data sources and planning and control of effectors such as in mobile robots [8].

Instead of designing a specific loss function for each task and tuning task-specific parameters until the machine learning algorithm performs satisfactorily, it would be useful to have a more general-purpose approach in which the problem to be solved can be described at a higher abstraction level. The challenge for general-purpose AI is to offer a user the flexibility to conduct a variety of tasks according to user preferences, ethics, and societal values, while avoiding a detailed specification by the user of how the AI should carry out these tasks [9]. To decide which course of action is best in the current situation, the AI needs a *world model and domain knowledge* to assess the impact of different actions [10].

2.3 Collaboration

Current AI mainly interacts in a pre-determined way with humans (and other systems) in their environment and acts like a smart stand-alone tool that is employed to solve specific problems. This predetermined interaction and fixed task allocation between humans and a smart AI tool helps to manage expectations and assure safety, but it also limits the effectiveness of combined human intelligence and artificial intelligence in complex and dynamic environments. Effective collaboration between humans and AI demands mutual understanding of each other's abilities and shortcomings. Currently, a proper level of mutual understanding and anticipation is lacking. Consequently, there is a need for AI that learns (1) to understand and interpret human abilities [11], and (2) to self-improving forms of collaboration [12].

Another aspect that limits the use of machine learning in collaborative systems is the black box nature of deep neural networks. Even for machine learning experts it is hard to understand how a deep neural network arrives at its conclusions. An explanation to an expert or user of how and why the AI arrived at certain conclusions is a challenge that has been widely recognized [13]. Such an explanation capability is supported by *symbolic communication in terms of domain knowledge that humans understand* [14].

2.4 Governance

Machine learning software behaves differently from conventional software in the sense that decisions are based on training data and not on rules and control flows engineered by humans. This has the advantage that less effort is needed to develop the software. Furthermore, novel solutions may be found to problems that have eluded scientists and software engineers. However, the disadvantage is that there is less (or no) awareness of unwanted biases in the data set. For some applications such as machine translation and recommender systems, the impact of biases is limited, and governance is permissive because humans can correct or compensate for mistakes. However, in many AI applications a stricter governance is needed because the tolerance for errors and biased decisions is low. A well-known example of biased decision-making is AI-based photo-categorization software that labels images of people with a dark skin as gorillas [16].

Fairness, i.e. decisions that are free of unwanted biases, is one of the pillars of the responsible use of AI. Fairness is sometimes in conflict with the accuracy of decisions that is also desired for a responsible use of AI. Most deep learning algorithms can achieve a high accuracy only by having access to large data sets. Individuals and organizations sometimes contribute willingly to large data sets to reap the benefits of useful machine learning applications. In case of sensitive data, however, most individuals and organizations are reluctant to disclose these data. A possible solution for this dilemma is federated learning and secure multiparty computation that enable machine learning methods to learn from confidential data without disclosure of the data [17]. The final element of responsible use of AI addressed in this paper is that decision making also needs to be transparent. A lack of transparency leads to distrust and potentially to rejection of AI in society. However, transparency can also be at odds with the confidential treatment of data on which decisions are based. The challenge for AI is to conduct a *trade-off between these conflicting objectives* that depends on the context.

3   Hybrid Artificial Intelligence

The challenges for AI along four dimensions that have been identified in the previous section include the lack of data in unforeseen situations, the availability of a world model, symbolic communication with a human, and trade-offs between conflicting criteria. We argue that these challenges can be addressed with a hybrid AI approach that integrates data-driven machine learning with domain knowledge, optimization, and reasoning. Clearly, extensive research is needed to discover ways to achieve this since there are several machine learning paradigms and many ways to represent and reason with knowledge [18, 19]. This exploratory research of hybrid AI methods and techniques needs to be supported with use cases and experiments in the real-world to avoid the pitfalls of current AI methods that work well in controlled laboratory environments but fail in applications that are ethically sensitive or safety-critical.

4   Conclusions

In this position paper, we have argued that to make the next steps in AI, it needs to be developed along four dimensions: environment, purpose, collaboration, and governance. With respect to its operational environment, AI needs to improve from controlled environments to open environments where unpredictable situations can occur. General-purpose AI can conduct new tasks without the time and investment that is needed to retrain or redesign special-purpose AI. To make human-machine teams more effective, AI should not be operating as a stand-alone tool but act as a collaborative partner. Finally, AI needs to move from applications where errors have minor consequences and governance is permissive to a much wider range of applications where privacy, ethics, safety and security are very important and AI governance needs to be strict. We have also reasoned in this paper that hybrid AI which combines knowledge-based methods, and data-driven machine learning can address the challenges to improve AI along those dimensions.

Acknowledgements. This position paper was funded by the TNO Early Research Program Hybrid AI.

References

1. Grother, P., Ngan, M., Hanaoka, K.: Face Recognition Vendor Test (FRVT) Part 3: Demographic Effects, NISTIR 8280. NIST (2019)
2. Hunt, M.: Automated welfare fraud detection system contravenes international law. Dutch court rules, Global Government Forum (2020). https://www.globalgovernmentforum.com/
3. Banerjee, S., Jha, S., Cyriac, J., Kalbarczyk, Z., Iyer, R.: Hands off the wheel in autonomous vehicles? A systems perspective on over a million miles of field data. In: Proceedings 48th Annual IEEE/IFIP International Conference on Dependable Systems and Networks (DSN), Luxembourg City, pp. 586–597 (2018)
4. Povolny S., Trivedi, S.: Model Hacking ADAS to Pave Safer Roads for Autonomous Vehicles. https://www.mcafee.com/blogs/other-blogs/mcafee-labs/model-hacking-adas-to-pave-safer-roads-for-autonomous-vehicles/. Accessed 23 Nov 2020
5. Lake, B., Ullman, T., Tenenbaum, J., Gershman, S.: Building machines that learn and think like people. Behav. Brain Sci. **40**, E253 (2016)
6. McKinney, S., Sieniek, M., Godbole, V., Godwin, J., Antropova, N., et al.: International evaluation of an AI system for breast cancer screening. Nature **577**, 89–94 (2020)
7. Raghu, M., Zhang, C., Brain, G., Kleinberg, J., Bengio, S.: Transfusion: understanding transfer learning for medical imaging. In: Advances in Neural Information Processing Systems, vol. 32 (2019)
8. Weiss, K., Khoshgoftaar, T.M., Wang, D.: A survey of transfer learning. J. Big Data **3**(1), 1–40 (2016). https://doi.org/10.1186/s40537-016-0043-6
9. Werkhoven, P., Kester, L., Neerincx, M.: Telling autonomous systems what to do. In: Proceedings of the 36th European Conference on Cognitive Ergonomics, New York, NY (2018)
10. Elands, P., Huizing, A., Kester, L., Peeters, M., Oggero, S.: Governing ethical and effective behaviour of intelligent systems. Militaire Spectator **188**(6), 303–313 (2019)
11. van Diggelen, J., Neerincx, M., Peeters, M., Schraagen, J.: Developing effective and resilient human-agent teamwork using team design patterns. IEEE Intell. Syst. **34**(2), 15–24, (2019)
12. Neerincx, M., et al.: Socio-cognitive engineering of a robotic partner for child's diabetes self-management. In: Front. Robot. AI **6**,118 (2019)
13. Adadi, A., Berrada, M.: Peeking inside the black-box: a survey on explainable artificial intelligence (XAI). IEEE Access **6**, 52138–52160 (2018)
14. van der Aalst, W.M.P., Bichler, M., Heinzl, A.: Responsible data science. Bus. Inf. Syst. Eng. **59**(5), 311–313 (2017). https://doi.org/10.1007/s12599-017-0487-z
15. Islam, S., Eberle, W., Ghafoor, S., Siraj, A., Rogers, M.: Domain knowledge aided explainable artificial intelligence for intrusion detection and response. In: AAAI Spring Symposium: Combining Machine Learning with Knowledge Engineering (2020)
16. Simonite, T.: When It Comes to Gorillas, Google Photos Remains Blind (2018). https://www.wired.com/story/when-it-comes-to-gorillas-google-photos-remains-blind/
17. Sangers, A., et al.: Secure multiparty PageRank algorithm for collaborative fraud detection. In: Goldberg, I., Moore, T. (eds.) FC 2019. LNCS, vol. 11598, pp. 605–623. Springer, Cham (2019). https://doi.org/10.1007/978-3-030-32101-7_35
18. von Rueden, L., Mayer, S., Garcke, J., Bauckhage, C., Schuecker, J.: Informed machine learning – towards a taxonomy of explicit integration of knowledge into machine learning. arXiv:1903.12394 (2019)
19. Elisa Celis, L., Huang, L., Keswani, V., Vishnoi, N.K.: Classification with fairness constraints: a meta-algorithm with provable guarantees. In: Proceedings of the Conference on Fairness, Accountability, and Transparency (2019)

Towards Certifying Trustworthy Machine Learning Systems

Roland H. C. Yap[✉]

School of Computing, National University of Singapore, Singapore, Singapore
ryap@comp.nus.edu.sg

Abstract. Machine Learning (ML) is increasingly deployed in complex application domains replacing human-decision making. While ML has been surprisingly successful, there are fundamental concerns in wide scale deployment without humans in the loop. A critical question is the trustworthiness of such ML systems. Although there is research towards making ML systems more trustworthy, there remain many challenges. In this position paper, we discuss the challenges and limitations of current proposals. We focus on a more adversarial approach, borrowing ideas from certification of security software with the Common Criteria. While it is unclear how to get strong trustworthy assurances for ML systems, we believe this approach can further increase the level of trust.

1 Introduction

Machine Learning (ML) has emerged as a promising technology for solving complex problems which have traditionally been the domain of humans. Until recently it was thought that computer Go could not beat human experts. Yet the AlphaGo program won against the world's top players demonstrating the superiority of AI Go playing [15]. ML has been shown to be successful in a range of complex tasks such as image, face and speech recognition, autonomous driving, recommendation systems, question answering, medical diagnosis, etc. Naturally, this has led to the rapid adoption of ML in these domains. We use the term *ML system* to encompass software and services where ML forms the core techniques for solving "complex tasks".

Technology replacing or augmenting humans is not a new phenomenon. However, the use of ML in complex domains affecting humans warrants more care—deployed ML systems do not seem to give much by way of guarantees. Concerns raised by both non-experts as well as the Computer Science and ML research community indicate that there is an underlying basis that the deployment of ML is "special" and different. Kumar [12] questions "irrational exuberance". Obermeyer et al. [14] highlighted biased results in a widely-used health risk prediction tool used in the United States. While ML techniques have been successful, many aspects of their use are not well understood, indeed, they are the

This research was supported by Google under the "Democratizing AI and Building Trust In the Technology" project and grant R-726-000-006-646.

F. Heintz et al. (Eds.): TAILOR 2020, LNAI 12641, pp. 77–82, 2021.
https://doi.org/10.1007/978-3-030-73959-1_7

focus of (evolving) research. This position paper is not intended to show in detail how to certify if an ML system is trustworthy, rather, we propose the basics of a workable practical framework taking into account adversarial issues by adapting a simplification of Common Criteria used in certifying IT/security software. The goal is that users (and public) can have a reasonable belief in a certification process to engender trust in the ML system.

1.1 Related Work

Related work and proposals focus more on data and declarations of the ML system from the developers perspective. Datasheets [8] proposes a fact sheet to document how the data is created and used, to give accountability and transparency, analogous to datasheets for electronic parts. "Data statements" [4] is a related proposal focusing on NLP systems. Qualitative and quantitative descriptions of the data as an analog to a nutritional label is proposed in [9]. Model Cards [13] extends the declaration idea to the learning model adding details relevant to trust such as declarations of the intended use, metrics for the learning model and ethical considerations. FactSheets [2] is a more comprehensive effort to combine these kinds of declarations together. However, while such declarations are useful towards transparency and accountability of the ML system, they do not capture all aspects needed to establish trustworthiness. They are also limited from a certification perspective focusing on data and learning models.

2 Challenges

We first ask if trustworthiness of an ML system is any different from that of any other software system. There are similarities from a general software perspective but also differences. We remark that despite decades of research, fully verified systems where one can have a high degree of trust are the exception rather than the norm. An example of the effort needed for verification is the seL4 microkernel—the formal verification [11] requires ~480K lines of Isabelle proof and specifications for ~10K lines of microkernel code. In this position paper, we focus on the differences between ML systems and typical software when it comes to trustworthy assurances:

Formal Specification. The ML system may not have a well defined/formal specification of its functionality. Consider an ML system for facial recognition in airports. The intended specification might informally be: "recognize specific faces". However, what should the formal specification be and its relationship to the intended specification? Does one even exist?

In contrast, in existing software systems where a high degree of trust is needed, such as microkernels (e.g. seL4), power plants, aircraft flight control, etc., the task and specifications can be sufficiently well understood to have formal specifications at a usable level for (machine) verification. Correctness of the ML system should be with respect to its specification. However, in practice, a usable formal specification may not be known.

Non-Functional Requirements. Apart from basic functional requirements, the ML system will have other requirements arising from the ML systems interacting with humans such as: fairness, privacy, security (covering the ML component and general software security) and safety. These requirements factor into the evaluating trustworthiness as they concern interactions and effects of the ML system on humans and the system's environment.

Verification Limitations. Ideally, to satisfy the functional and other requirements, we should verify the code together with the claims made by the ML system. However, we saw that verification alone is challenging.

The other requirements also pose challenges, we discuss some below. While data privacy has been studied with differential privacy [6] which is usually considered as a robust approach, applying it can be challenging [10]. Security will need to address adversarial attacks on the learning component but defenses have been shown to be weak and generating adversarial examples may not be difficult [3]. Fairness is a complex issue with numerous definitions of fairness but no consensus on which ones should be used. For instance, various measures of fairness can have incompatible assumptions [7].

3   Towards Trustworthy ML Certification

We use trustworthiness of an ML system to mean how users can reasonably be convinced to trust the ML system. We propose that the question of trustworthiness be decomposed into two parts: (i) is the system developed to be trustworthy?; and (ii) can we be (reasonably) convinced that the system is trustworthy? Answering the first question requires looking into the details of the ML system—what is disclosed on its workings and development. We propose the second question be addressed by a certification process taking into account an adversarial perspective. As discussed, the ideal goal of a provably correct trustworthy ML system will be very challenging for software developers. Instead, we propose a more workable approach that recognizes the tradeoffs while attempting to increase trustworthiness.

Transparency is typically used as one step to increase trust, i.e. disclosing details about the data, processes used, learning models, usage, etc. The proposals discussed in Sect. 1.1 are mainly about disclosure and transparency and help with the first question. However, the second question concerning trust, verification and security is not addressed by those proposals. Disclosure alone is not sufficient to engender trust—any claims, including code, needs a way of believing in its validity. For example, FactSheets proposes the following question in the disclosure:

> *Are you aware of possible examples of bias, ethical issues, or other safety risks as a result of using the service?*

But the developers could simply answer "No" to this question. What is needed is a process to check the information and its implication on the ML system.

Since there is no strong technical solution (yet) to the challenges in Sect. 2, we propose a process-based framework where users/public can rely on a certification process to gain confidence that an ML system is trustworthy. We propose to learn from frameworks which have been used to certify software, namely, Common Criteria (CC).[1] However, CC is complex and the challenges here further complicate the certification. Rather than replicate CC, we employ some of its ideas. Furthermore, the CC process is often considered time consuming and expensive, requiring working within a ISO/TEC standard. For the emerging questions on how to make ML systems trustworthy, we believe that a simple and lightweight framework provides useful assurances.

Care should be taken not to simply trust the developers.[2] A trusted third party is proposed to certify that the ML system is trustworthy, which we call the *evaluator*.[3] For simplicity, we will omit the certification body which certifies the report of the evaluator as it is only useful when there are standards and laws governing the certification of trustworthy ML systems. In CC, the rigor and detail of the evaluation is quantified into an Evaluation Assurance Level (EAL), from EAL1 (basic) to EAL7 (highest). We do not propose specific EALs but they can cover from simplest (least trusted) to formally verified (most trusted). As a simplification, the EALs could cover: (i) basic disclosure (this level means that one has full faith in the developers' disclosure); (ii) claims are tested for processes disclosed; (iii) active testing which is analogous to penetration testing in a software security context, e.g. constructing/testing adversarial examples, testing privacy leaks in black box models, etc.; and (iv) formal verification of the code and required properties, e.g. correctness of code if we are looking at the specification. The evaluator may have different degrees of access to different components of the ML system. For example, the learning component may be evaluated as: white-box (full access including data, code, and running system); black-box (access limited to interactions with the running ML system); or grey-box (in between). This will naturally affect the EAL, with greater access allowing a higher EAL. The evaluator plays the role of an adversary against the ML system to see if it meets the desired properties.[4] Depending on the EAL, the evaluator may also perform formal modelling and verification. The evaluation results should be detailed enough to be checked by interested parties.

Certification Process. We divide the certification of the ML system into: (i) certifying basic system components; and (ii) certifying desired properties. The basic system components are what is covered by a disclosure, similar to

---

[1] The Common Criteria is a well defined process and standard (ISO/IEC 15408) for evaluation of the functional and assurance requirements of IT/security software.

[2] The U.S. House Committee investigation into the Boeing 737 Max flight control system found weaknesses given compliance processes were delegated to Boeing [1].

[3] In CC, there is further step, the evaluator's work is sent to another trusted third party, the *certification body*, to give an official certificate for the evaluator's work.

[4] An attack model is needed to capture potential malicious users of the ML system who try to exploit the system.

FactSheets, such as: data, algorithms, machine learning model, training & evaluation, explainability features, and intended usage together with applications. Evaluation should take into account: (i) completeness of the disclosure (is anything missing?); (ii) are there flaws in the data, techniques, processes used such as biases; and (iii) testing of the components of the ML system including the training and evaluation. At the minimum, it should be feasible to reproduce or replicate the claims of the developers. Ideally assumptions should be disclosed and should be analyzed for any weaknesses, e.g. if the training dataset is small, it may not be representative of the population. Assumptions with weaknesses should be qualified. Explainability features should be tested whether they give the claimed explanation. Ethical issues should be disclosed—it may be simpler to identify the kinds of public good which arises from the ML system. This allows an evaluation of positive and negative benefits of the system to help increase trust and delineate the risk-benefit tradeoffs.

Properties such as from Sect. 2 also need to be certified. As the specification may be informal, evaluating correctness is closer to traditional software testing, i.e. checking inputs and outputs. Since fairness is complex, one approach is to evaluate what the fairness goals of the ML system should be and how it is achieved. Privacy assurances need the use of privacy mechanisms, i.e. differential privacy. We remark that anonymization will likely not suffice. There may be privacy laws, e.g. the European GDPR, and terms of service to be considered. Care has to be taken to employ a broad perspective—not fall into the trap of defining a specific property with a narrow definition which then follows from the implementation, but will not meet a reasonable interpretation of the property.

ML systems may be used where safety is required, e.g. safety critical systems. Disclosure should detail safety risks and compliance with regulations. Evaluation should analyze the risks in the context of the system usage and check that the ML system has safety mechanisms. Where there is a formal safety model, model checking techniques could be applied to analyse failure modes. Security evaluation will include software security, in this case, vulnerability assessment and penetration testing could be applied together with the kinds of security assessments used in CC. Evaluating the learning component should include adversarial examples for higher EAL levels. As many defences against adversarial examples may not be robust, the use of techniques which use provable approaches [5] will be better regarded in the evaluation.

The evaluator will consider to what level the different components and properties can be evaluated. Evaluating also the tradeoffs from cost and requirements on the disclosure detail and system access. Different EALs can be chosen, however, the evaluation should consider how the different levels affect the trustworthiness of the ML system as a whole. The proposed certification framework can be quite involved but given that there can be considerable risks if one of the depended upon property fails, this seems to be a reasonable cost-benefit assessment. We leave open the possibility that the evaluator is not a third party but rather the system developers. In such a case, the trustworthiness criteria and EAL may need to be more stringent.

4   Conclusion

ML systems are increasingly being deployed but such systems may not be trustworthy, e.g. the health prediction algorithm in [14]. We propose elements of a practical framework which can be used to help establish trust in ML systems at different levels. It might be the case that an evaluation shows the deployed system to be not yet trustworthy. Weakness or lack thereof found by the evaluation will give a clearer picture of how much we can trust the ML system.

References

1. https://transportation.house.gov/committee-activity/boeing-737-max-investigat ion (2020)
2. Arnold, M., et al.: FactSheets: increasing trust in AI services through supplier's declarations of conformity. IBM J. Res. Dev. **63**(4/5), 1–13 (2019)
3. Athalye, A., Carlini, N., Wagner, D.A.: Obfuscated gradients give a false sense of security: circumventing defenses to adversarial examples. In: International Conference on Machine Learning (2018)
4. Bender, E.M., Friedman, B.: Data statements for natural language processing: toward mitigating system bias and enabling better science. Trans. Assoc. Comput. Linguist. **6**, 587–604 (2018)
5. Carlini, N., et al.: On evaluating adversarial robustness. https://arxiv.org/abs/ 1902.06705 (2019)
6. Dwork, C., Roth, A.: The algorithmic foundations of differential privacy. Found. Trends Theor. Comput. Sci. **9**(3–4), 211–407 (2014)
7. Friedler, S.A., Scheidegger, C., Venkatasubramanian, S.: On the (im)possibility of fairness (2016). http://arxiv.org/abs/1609.07236
8. Gebru, T., et al.: Datasheets for datasets. In: Workshop on Fairness, Accountability, and Transparency in Machine Learning (2018)
9. Holland, S., Hosny, A., Newman, S., Joseph, J., Chmielinski, K.: The dataset nutrition label: a framework to drive higher data quality standards. https://arxiv.org/ abs/1805.03677 (2018)
10. Kifer, D., Machanavajjhala, A.: No free lunch in data privacy. In: ACM SIGMOD International Conference on Management of Data (2011)
11. Klein, G., et al.: Comprehensive formal verification of an OS microkernel. ACM Trans. Comput. Syst. **32**(1), 1–70 (2014)
12. Kumar, V.: Irrational Exuberance and the 'FATE' of Technology. BLOG@CACM, 20 August (2018)
13. Mitchell, M., et al.: Model cards for model reporting. In: Conference on Fairness, Accountability, and Transparency (2019)
14. Obermeyer, Z., Powers, B., Vogeli, C., Mullainathan, S.: Dissecting racial bias in an algorithm used to manage the health of populations. Science **366**(6464), 447–453 (2019)
15. Silver, D., et al.: Mastering the game of go without human knowledge. Nature **550**, 354–359 (2017)

Lab Conditions for Research
on Explainable Automated Decisions

Christel Baier[1], Maria Christakis[3], Timo P. Gros[2], David Groß[1],
Stefan Gumhold[1], Holger Hermanns[2,4], Jörg Hoffmann[2(✉)],
and Michaela Klauck[2]

[1] Technische Universität Dresden, Dresden, Germany
[2] Saarland University, Saarland Informatics Campus, Saarbrücken, Germany
`hoffmann@cs.uni-saarland.de`
[3] Max Planck Institute for Software Systems,
Kaiserslautern and Saarbrücken, Germany
[4] Institute of Intelligent Software, Guangzhou, China

Abstract. Artificial neural networks are being proposed for automated
decision making under uncertainty in many visionary contexts, including high-stake tasks such as navigating autonomous cars through dense
traffic. Against this background, it is imperative that the decision making entities meet central societal desiderata regarding dependability, perspicuity, explainability, and robustness. Decision making problems under
uncertainty are typically captured formally as variations of Markov decision processes (MDPs). This paper discusses a set of natural and easy-to-
control abstractions, based on the Racetrack benchmarks and extensions
thereof, that altogether connect the autonomous driving challenge to
the modelling world of MDPs. This is then used to study the dependability and robustness of NN-based decision entities, which in turn are
based on state-of-the-art NN learning techniques. We argue that this
approach can be regarded as providing laboratory conditions for a systematic, structured and extensible comparative analysis of NN behavior,
of NN learning performance, as well as of NN verification and analysis
techniques.

1 Introduction

The field of automated driving – especially in its fully automated form, often
referred to as autonomous driving – is considered a grand and worthwhile challenge to tackle. In light of the importance and safety criticality of the application, it is imperative that the core technical components meet societal desiderata regarding dependability, perspicuity, explainability, and trust. The process

Authors are listed alphabetically. This work was partially supported by the German Research Foundation (DFG) under grant No. 389792660, as part of TRR 248,
see https://perspicuous-computing.science, by the ERC Advanced Investigators Grant
695614 (POWVER), and by the Key-Area Research and Development Program
Grant 2018B010107004 of Guangdong Province.

F. Heintz et al. (Eds.): TAILOR 2020, LNAI 12641, pp. 83–90, 2021.
https://doi.org/10.1007/978-3-030-73959-1_8

of automated driving can be broken down into three stages [22]. The first stage deals with machine perception based on the sensor data collected, followed by a stage on intention recognition, behavior prediction and risk assessment. The last stage is about risk-aware behavioral decisions, the planning of the trajectory to be driven and the effectuation and control of the resulting behavior. Many areas of computer science are in demand here: machine learning, numerics, cyber-physical systems and, last but not least, verification and validation. Across all the three stages, artificial neural networks are being experimented with, and tremendous progress is being reported especially in areas relating to the first and second stage [2,4,8,19–21,24].

In formal terms, the interface between the second and third stage can be viewed as a (albeit dauntingly large) Markov decision process (MDP) [18] spanned by a multitude of continuous and discrete dimensions, in which probability annotations reflect the outcomes of risk assessments carried out before. Of course, it is practically infeasible to capture all the precise details of a real vehicle navigating through dense traffic in a single MDP model, and thus it is common practice to instead work on more abstract representations. Typical abstractions are (i) discretization of the continuity of time, space, speed, acceleration and the like, (ii) linearization of non-linearities, and (iii) abstraction from irrelevant details (such as the temperature of the fuel in the vehicle tank) – all that in order to arrive at a model of feasible size. The quality of the abstraction process and the properties of the resulting model are major components in the overall trust we can place on the resulting decision making entity.

In this realm, this paper reports on orchestrated ongoing efforts that aim at systematizing research on (i) the process of abstraction and concretization, and (ii) reproducibility and explainability of decision making entities for automated driving based on neural networks. In a nutshell, we consider the third stage of the automated driving challenge in which a neural network takes the task of risk-aware maneuvering of the vehicle, but in a two-dimensional grid world consisting of blocked and free grid cells, which are observable in full from a bird's-eye view, i.e., without ego-perspective. Furthermore, in a first step, we do not consider moving obstacles, weather or road conditions and resource consumption.

What results after all these abstractions is the problem of navigating a vehicle on a gridded 2D-track from start to goal, as instructed by a neural network and subject to probabilistic disturbances of the vehicle control. This problem family, known as the Racetrack [3] in the AI community is arguably very far away from the true challenges of automated driving, but (i) it provides a common formal ground for basic studies on NN behavioral properties (as we will highlight below), (ii) it is easily scalable, (iii) it is extensible in a natural manner, namely by undoing some of the abstractions listed above (which we are doing already), and (iv) it is made available to the scientific community together with a collection of supporting tools. These four properties are at the core of what we want to advocate with this paper, namely a bottom-up approach to explainability in autonomous driving, providing laboratory conditions for a systematic, structured and extensible analysis. In what follows, we provide a survey of orchestrated ongoing efforts that revolve around the Racetrack case. All infrastructure, documentation, tools, and examples covered in this paper or otherwise related to Racetrack are made available at https://racetrack.perspicuous-computing.science.

2 Racetrack Lab Environment

This section gives a brief overview of the basic model considered and then reviews ongoing work relating to it. The Racetrack evolved from a pen and paper game [10] and is a well known benchmark in AI autonomous decision making contexts [3,5,14,16,17]. In Racetrack, a vehicle needs to drive on a 2D-track (grey) from start cells (green) to goal cells (blue), the track being delimited by walls (red) as depicted in Fig. 1. The vehicle can change acceleration in unit steps in nine directions spanned by the x- and y-dimensions $[-1, 0, 1]$.

The natural abstraction of the autonomous driving challenge in this simplified setting is the task of finding a policy that manages to reach the goal with a probability as high as possible and crashes as rarely as possible. Probabilities enter the picture by imperfect acceleration modelling slippery road conditions.

We use Racetrack as our lab environment to study various aspects of machine-learnt entities that are supposed to solve the task. These aspects include quantitative evaluations of effectiveness, safety, quality, explainability and verifiability. We will review our work in the remainder of this section. The overarching assumption

Fig. 1. A Racetrack [3]. (Color figure online)

is that a neural network has been trained by state-of-the-art machine learning techniques for the very purpose of navigating the map as well as possible, and is then put into our lab environment. Beyond that, we also briefly discuss how the lab can be inserted into the machine learning pipeline for the purpose of better learning performance.

2.1 Deep Statistical Model Checking

To enable a deep inspection of the behavior induced by a neural network we developed an evaluation methodology called *Deep Statistical Model Checking* (DSMC) [12]. Concretely, we considered the default Racetrack use case in which the neural network has been trained on the task of reaching the goal with a probability as high as

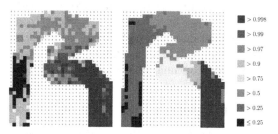

Fig. 2. Effect of expected (left) and more slippery (right) road conditions [12].

possible while crashing as rarely as possible. After training, the NN represents a policy taking the crucial steering decisions when driving on the map. This policy can be considered as determinizer of the MDP modelling the Racetrack. For the resulting stochastic process, we harvested state-of-the-art statistical model

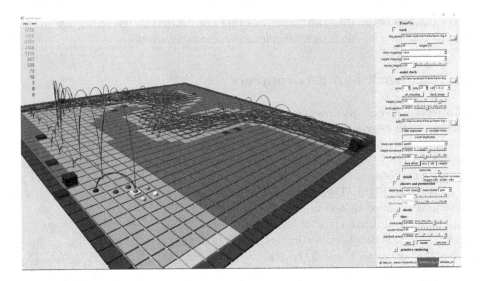

Fig. 3. *TraceVis* in action [11].

checking [6,23] techniques to study the detailed behavior of the net. More concretely, we treat the NN as a black box to resolve the nondeterminism in the given MDP of the model. The NN gets a description of the current state and returns the action to apply next. The statistical analysis of the resulting Markov chain and thereby of the NN properties gives insights in the quality of the NN, not only for the whole task but also for specific regions of the Racetrack.

An impression is given in Fig. 2, where simple heat maps visualize the chance to safely reach the goal if starting in each of the cells along the track. On the left, the lab model agrees exactly with the model used for training the net, while on the right, it is used in a lab model with a drastically increased probability for the acceleration decision to not take effect (modelling a far more slippery road).

This brief example demonstrates how DSMC enables the inspection of risky driving behavior induced by the NN. Such information can be used to retrain the net in a certain area of the map to improve quality or to see if the net prefers a specific route over an equivalent one. In a nutshell, DSMC provides a scalable verification method of NNs. For small case instances, standard probabilistic model checking can be used, too, for instance to compare the NN behavior with the provably optimal policy, see for more details [12].

2.2   Trajectory Visualization of NN-Induced Behavior

TraceVis [11] is a visualization tool tailored to evaluations in Racetrack-like 2D environments, exploiting advanced 3D visualization technology for data representation and interactive evaluation. In a nutshell, trajectories are mapped to tubes that can be optionally bent to arcs in order to show the discrete nature of stepping, probabilistic information is mapped to a bar chart embedded in the Racetrack or to color, and time can be mapped to a height offset or animation along exploration steps. To reduce visual clutter, segments are aggregated and whole trajectories are clustered by outcome, i.e., final goal or crash position. *TraceVis* offers multiple views for different inspection purposes, including (i) interactive context visualization of the probabilities induced, (ii) visualization of the velocity distribution aggregated from all trajectories, with the possibility to animate particular aspects as a function of time, and (iii) convenient support for hierarchical navigation through the available clusters of information in an intuitive manner, while still allowing views on individual trajectories. An impression of the UI of the *TraceVis* tool can be found in Fig. 3.

These interactive visualization techniques provide rich support for a detailed inspection of the data space, for the purpose of investigating, for instance, which map positions come with a considerable crash risk, or for what crashes the dominating reason is a bad policy decision taken by the controlling NN, relative to the scenario-intrinsic noise. With these overarching functionalities *TraceVis* offers support for analyzing and verifying neural networks' behavior for quality assurance and learning pipeline assessment in a more detailed and informative way than the raw data and simple heat maps provided in the DSMC work [12].

TraceVis is implemented as a plugin for the CGV-Framework [13], and as such, it is easily extensible to support other dimensions of the autonomous driving challenge.

2.3   Safety Verification for NNs in the Loop

State-of-the-art program analyses are not yet able to effectively verify safety properties of heterogeneous systems, that is, of systems with components implemented using different technologies. This shortcoming becomes especially apparent in programs invoking neural networks – despite their acclaimed role as innovation drivers across many application domains.

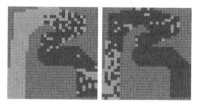

Fig. 4. Effect of training quality on verifiability, for a moderately trained (left) and a well trained (right) NN [7].

We have lately [7] embarked on the verification of system-level safety properties for systems characterized by interacting programs and neural networks. This has been carried out in the lab environment of the Racetrack. The main difference to DSMC is that this work does not consider the net in isolation, but instead takes into consideration the controller program querying the net. Our technique, which is based on abstract interpretation, tightly integrates a program and a neural-network analysis that communicate with each other. For the example case considered, we have for instance studied the dependency between the quality of the NN and the possibility to verify its safety, as illustrated in Fig. 4, where a green cell indicates that it is verifiable that a goal is eventually reached, and red encodes that no property can be verified.

With this work, we address the growing number of heterogeneous software systems and the critical challenge this poses for existing program analyses. Our approach to verifying safety properties of heterogeneous systems symbiotically combines existing program and neural-network analysis techniques. As a result, we are able to effectively prove non-trivial system properties of programs that invoke neural networks.

3   Discussion: Racetrack in the Wild

This paper has discussed several works concentrating on the most basic version of Racetrack. They are supported by a joint software infrastructure, aspects of which are presented in more detail in individual papers. The entirety of the tool infrastructure is available at https://racetrack.perspicuous-computing.science. This web portal presents example tracks to generate Racetrack benchmarks of different sizes and levels of difficulty. Furthermore, it provides demonstrations and explanations how to use the tool infrastructure to

- generate Racetrack versions with different features
- train neural networks on a Racetrack
- perform automated safety verification on a Racetrack
- perform deep statistical model checking on a Racetrack
- explore the resulting behavior with TraceVis.

Beyond this benchmarking infrastructure, what we advocate is a bottom-up approach to autonomous driving (and potentially to other high-stake sequential decision making problems in a similar manner), starting with Racetrack and working upwards to more realism. This endeavor essentially consists in *undoing* the simplifications inherent in the Racetrack benchmark: (i) consideration of resource consumption, (ii) varying road/weather conditions, (iii) moving obstacles, i.e., traffic, (iv) fine discretization, (v) continuous dynamics, (vi) ego-perspective, and (vii) incomplete information. Racetrack can readily be extended with all of these aspects, slowly moving towards a lab environment that encompasses more of the real automated driving challenge. We advocate this as a research road map.

At this point, we are already busy with activities (i)–(iii) of the road map. The basic Racetrack scenario has been extended with different road conditions (tarmac, sand and ice), different engine types that influence maximal speed and acceleration, as well as with tanks of different size, such that the fuel consumption has to be taken into account while driving. Racetrack variants with all these features have been considered in a feature-oriented evaluation study, combined with a hierarchy of different notions of suitability [1]. We are furthermore developing a Lanechange use case, which adds traffic and comes with a switch from a full-observer view, like in Racetrack, to the ego-perspective, where the vehicle has in its view only a certain area to the front, the sides and back. The vehicle here drives on a road with multiple lanes and other traffic participants that move with different speeds in the same direction [9,15]. The aim is to navigate the road effectively, changing lanes to overtake slow traffic, while avoiding accidents. We have developed initial test-case generation methods, adapting fuzzing methods to identify MDP states (traffic situations) that are themselves safe, but on which the neural network policy leads to unsafe behavior.

Overall, we believe that Racetrack, while in itself a toy example, can form the basis of a workable research agenda towards dependability, perspicuity, explainability and robustness of neural networks in autonomous driving. We hope that the infrastructure and research agenda we provide will be useful for AI research in this direction.

References

1. Baier, C., Dubslaff, C., Hermanns, H., Klauck, M., Klüppelholz, S., Köhl, M.A.: Components in probabilistic systems: suitable by construction. In: Margaria, T., Steffen, B. (eds.) ISoLA 2020. LNCS, vol. 12476, pp. 240–261. Springer, Cham (2020). https://doi.org/10.1007/978-3-030-61362-4_13
2. Barnaghi, P., Ganz, F., Henson, C., Sheth, A.: Computing perception from sensor data. In: SENSORS, 2012 IEEE, pp. 1–4. IEEE (2012)
3. Barto, A.G., Bradtke, S.J., Singh, S.P.: Learning to act using real-time dynamic programming. Artif. Intell. **72**(1–2), 81–138 (1995). https://doi.org/10.1016/0004-3702(94)00011-O
4. Berndt, H., Emmert, J., Dietmayer, K.: Continuous driver intention recognition with hidden Markov models. In: 11th International IEEE Conference on Intelligent Transportation Systems, ITSC 2008, Beijing, China, 12–15 October 2008, pp. 1189–1194. IEEE (2008). https://doi.org/10.1109/ITSC.2008.4732630
5. Bonet, B., Geffner, H.: Labeled RTDP: improving the convergence of real-time dynamic programming. In: Giunchiglia, E., Muscettola, N., Nau, D.S. (eds.) Proceedings of the Thirteenth International Conference on Automated Planning and Scheduling (ICAPS 2003), Trento, Italy, 9–13 June 2003, pp. 12–21. AAAI (2003). http://www.aaai.org/Library/ICAPS/2003/icaps03-002.php
6. Budde, C.E., D'Argenio, P.R., Hartmanns, A., Sedwards, S.: A statistical model checker for nondeterminism and rare events. In: Beyer, D., Huisman, M. (eds.) TACAS 2018. LNCS, vol. 10806, pp. 340–358. Springer, Cham (2018). https://doi.org/10.1007/978-3-319-89963-3_20
7. Christakis, M., et al.: Automated Safety Verification of Programs Invoking Neural Networks (2020). Submitted for publication
8. Dietmayer, K.: Predicting of machine perception for automated driving. In: Maurer, M., Gerdes, J.C., Lenz, B., Winner, H. (eds.) Autonomous Driving, pp. 407–424. Springer, Heidelberg (2016). https://doi.org/10.1007/978-3-662-48847-8_20
9. Faqeh, R., et al.: Towards dynamic dependable systems through evidence-based continuous certification. In: Margaria, T., Steffen, B. (eds.) ISoLA 2020. LNCS, vol. 12477, pp. 416–439. Springer, Cham (2020). https://doi.org/10.1007/978-3-030-61470-6_25
10. Gardner, M.: Mathematical games. Sci. Am. **229**, 118–121 (1973)
11. Gros, T.P., Groß, D., Gumhold, S., Hoffmann, J., Klauck, M., Steinmetz, M.: TraceVis: towards visualization for deep statistical model checking. In: Proceedings of the 9th International Symposium on Leveraging Applications of Formal Methods, Verification and Validation. From Verification to Explanation (2020)
12. Gros, T.P., Hermanns, H., Hoffmann, J., Klauck, M., Steinmetz, M.: Deep statistical model checking. In: Gotsman, A., Sokolova, A. (eds.) FORTE 2020. LNCS, vol. 12136, pp. 96–114. Springer, Cham (2020). https://doi.org/10.1007/978-3-030-50086-3_6

13. Gumhold, S.: The computer graphics and visualization framework. https://github. com/sgumhold/cgv. Accessed 18 May 2020
14. McMahan, H.B., Gordon, G.J.: Fast exact planning in Markov decision processes. In: Biundo, S., Myers, K.L., Rajan, K. (eds.) Proceedings of the Fifteenth International Conference on Automated Planning and Scheduling (ICAPS 2005), 5–10 June 2005, Monterey, California, USA, pp. 151–160. AAAI (2005). http://www. aaai.org/Library/ICAPS/2005/icaps05-016.php
15. Meresht, V.B., De, A., Singla, A., Gomez-Rodriguez, M.: Learning to switch between machines and humans. CoRR abs/2002.04258 (2020). https://arxiv.org/ abs/2002.04258
16. Pineda, L.E., Lu, Y., Zilberstein, S., Goldman, C.V.: Fault-tolerant planning under uncertainty. In: Rossi, F. (ed.) IJCAI 2013, Proceedings of the 23rd International Joint Conference on Artificial Intelligence, Beijing, China, 3–9 August 2013, pp. 2350–2356. IJCAI/AAAI (2013). http://www.aaai.org/ocs/index.php/IJCAI/ IJCAI13/paper/view/6819
17. Pineda, L.E., Zilberstein, S.: Planning under uncertainty using reduced models: revisiting determinization. In: Chien, S.A., Do, M.B., Fern, A., Ruml, W. (eds.) Proceedings of the Twenty-Fourth International Conference on Automated Planning and Scheduling, ICAPS 2014, Portsmouth, New Hampshire, USA, 21–26 June 2014. AAAI (2014). http://www.aaai.org/ocs/index.php/ICAPS/ICAPS14/ paper/view/7920
18. Puterman, M.L.: Markov decision processes: discrete stochastic dynamic programming. In: Wiley Series in Probability and Statistics. Wiley (1994). https://doi.org/ 10.1002/9780470316887
19. Sadri, F.: Logic-based approaches to intention recognition. In: Handbook of Research on Ambient Intelligence and Smart Environments: Trends and Perspectives, pp. 346–375. IGI Global (2011)
20. Strickland, M., Fainekos, G.E., Amor, H.B.: Deep predictive models for collision risk assessment in autonomous driving. In: 2018 IEEE International Conference on Robotics and Automation, ICRA 2018, Brisbane, Australia, 21–25 May 2018, pp. 1–8. IEEE (2018). https://doi.org/10.1109/ICRA.2018.8461160
21. Tahboub, K.A.: Intelligent human-machine interaction based on dynamic Bayesian networks probabilistic intention recognition. J. Intell. Robotic Syst. 45(1), 31–52 (2006). https://doi.org/10.1007/s10846-005-9018-0
22. Wissenschaftsrat: Perspektiven der Informatik in Deutschland, October 2020. https://www.wissenschaftsrat.de/download/2020/8675-20.pdf
23. Younes, H.L.S., Simmons, R.G.: Probabilistic verification of discrete event systems using acceptance sampling. In: Brinksma, E., Larsen, K.G. (eds.) CAV 2002. LNCS, vol. 2404, pp. 223–235. Springer, Heidelberg (2002). https://doi.org/10.1007/3-540-45657-0_17
24. Yu, M., Vasudevan, R., Johnson-Roberson, M.: Risk assessment and planning with bidirectional reachability for autonomous driving. In: 2020 IEEE International Conference on Robotics and Automation, ICRA 2020, Paris, France, 31 May–31 August 2020, pp. 5363–5369. IEEE (2020). https://doi.org/10.1109/ICRA40945. 2020.9197491

Paradigms

Assessment of Manifold Unfolding in Trained Deep Neural Network Classifiers

Štefan Pócoš, Iveta Bečková, Tomáš Kuzma, and Igor Farkaš[✉]

Faculty of Mathematics, Physics and Informatics, Comenius University in Bratislava,
Bratislava, Slovak Republic
igor.farkas@fmph.uniba.sk

Abstract. Research on explainable artificial intelligence has progressed remarkably in the last years. In the subfield of deep learning, considerable effort has been invested to the understanding of deep classifiers that have proven successful in case of various benchmark datasets. Within the methods focusing on geometry-based understanding of the trained models, an interesting, *manifold disentanglement hypothesis* has been proposed. This hypothesis, supported by quantitative evidence, suggests that the class distributions become gradually reorganized over the hidden layers towards lower inherent dimensionality and hence easier separability. In this work, we extend our results, concerning four datasets of low and medium complexity, and using three different assessment methods that provide robust consistent support for manifold untangling. In particular, our quantitative analysis supports the hypothesis that the data manifold becomes flattened, and the class distributions become better separable towards higher layers.

Keywords: Deep classifiers · Manifold unfolding · Class distributions

1 Introduction

Deep neural networks, albeit data greedy, have proven successful in learning various complex, mostly supervised end-to-end tasks [13]. On the other hand, these black-box models are primary candidates for the need to apply to them techniques, allowing the users to understand the functioning of the trained model [14]. Poorly understood functionality of models can have serious consequences, as for example the sensitivity to adversarial examples (explained and investigated in [5,18]), bad generalisation and overall low credibility of used models.

Research towards explainable AI (XAI) has progressed considerably in the last years and has become widely acknowledged as a crucial feature for the practical deployment of AI models (for an extensive overview, see e.g. [1,4,19]). Within XAI focusing on deep learning, various analytical or visualization methods have been proposed trying to shed light on models' behaviour and the internal causal processes [10,11,15].

© Springer Nature Switzerland AG 2021
F. Heintz et al. (Eds.): TAILOR 2020, LNAI 12641, pp. 93–103, 2021.
https://doi.org/10.1007/978-3-030-73959-1_9

One of the research goals in this direction is to understand the neuron activations in trained deep classifiers, typically from a layer-based perspective. The function of a deep neural network mathematically corresponds to a cascade of smooth nonlinear transformations, each composed of a linear mapping (mediated by the complete matrix of individual neuron weights) and a subsequent nonlinearity (activation function). This lends itself to an interpretation allowing us to examine the process of classifying an input from a manifold perspective. *The manifold untangling hypothesis* [2], supported by quantitative evidence, suggests that the process of mapping the inputs across layers can be interpreted as the flattening of manifold-shaped data in high-dimensional spaces (hidden layers). The data is often assumed to lie on a *low-dimensional manifold* that becomes eventually partitioned in the output space where the final layer has one neuron for each class, and the classification is determined by which neuron has the largest activation [12]. This process of manifold disentangling may be tightly related to the aforementioned problem of adversarial examples, as they were studied in the context of their distances to (input data) manifolds (for details, see [3,17]).

In [7] we proposed a method to assess the extent of the class separation effect by testing several measures based on the *embedding complexity* of the internal representations, of which the t-distributed stochastic neighbour embedding (t-SNE) turned out to be the most suitable method. Using t-SNE we then demonstrated the validity of the disentanglement hypothesis by measuring embedding complexity, classification accuracy and their relation on a sample of image classification datasets. The process was observed to be very robust, occurring for various activation functions and regardless of the number of hidden layers.

In this work we extend our work in two ways, by adding two more datasets into computational analysis and by adding two methods that help shed light on the manifold untangling hypothesis.

2   Datasets

To study the process of untangling class manifolds, datasets of medium complexity are required. The complexity should be high enough so that the problem cannot be solved in the input space by a simple classifier, but a complex transformation, such as by an artificial neural network, is necessary. However, at the same time, the untransformed or partially transformed inputs cannot be inscrutable to available embedding methods as to remain interpretable. These restrictions led us to select four suitable datasets, all inadvertently being visual tasks.

In [7] we tested MNIST and SVHN datasets. MNIST [8] is a basic well-known dataset for optical character recognition (handwritten grayscale digits). The SVHN (Street View House Numbers dataset) is a more challenging task for digit recognition, which adds colour, distracting surroundings, blurring and oblique perspectives. In this work, we add two more datasets of moderate complexity: F(ashion)-MNIST and CIFAR-10. F-MNIST [20] is a dataset of a higher complexity compared to MNIST. It consists of 60 000 training and 10 000 testing images in ten classes. Data are 28×28 grayscale images of clothing or accessories. Some examples:

The CIFAR-10 [6] dataset provides a variety of 32×32 colour images with medium difficulty of classification. As in previous cases, the dataset consists of exclusive 10 classes, but here they depict animals or vehicles. Training and testing subsets contain 50 000 and 10 000 images, respectively. A few random examples:

3   Models

Following [7], we employ simple (deep) feed-forward networks that are minimally powerful enough to satisfactorily classify the selected datasets. By default, we use fully-connected layers of 100 neurons and use the same activation function at each hidden layer. In [7] we tested four activation functions: logistic sigmoid, hyperbolic tangent, softsign, and rectified linear units (ReLU). Of these, ReLU worked best for t-SNE, so we only focus on it henceforth.

For evaluation of CIFAR-10 we use a more complex architecture to get satisfactory classification accuracy. The architecture consists of 1-to-4 VGG [16] type blocks (two convolutional layers followed by pooling) and a fully-connected hidden layer of 100 neurons before the output layer. In order to achieve higher accuracy, we also use dropout.

The final classification layer has a neuron for each class with a *softmax* activation. All of these networks can be satisfactorily trained within 100 epochs using a simple stochastic gradient descent with momentum.

4 Method

To assess the progress of the manifold disentanglement process we measure the *embedding complexity*, i.e. how difficult it is to embed the activation vectors for a balanced sample of training inputs to a lower dimensional space. For the purpose of visualization, we use 2D (or 3D) output space. In [7] we examined several popular embedding methods (in order of increasing sophistication): PCA, LLE, MDS, Isomap and t-SNE [9], of which the last one turned out to be the most useful. Here, we hence only use t-distributed Stochastic Neighbour Embedding, a popular non-linear embedding method, which is based on preserving the *stochastic neighbourhood* of elements. This stands in contrast to more conventional methods which usually use a fixed neighbourhood, either using an adjustable parameter of the algorithm (e.g. k nearest neighbours in LLE or Isomap), or optimized to satisfy an internal condition, or factor all data points into consideration (e.g. MDS or PCA). The disparity between the distributions of probabilities in the input and output spaces in t-SNE is quantified by *KL-divergence* and the desired embedding is then produced by minimizing this divergence with respect to the placement of points in the output space.

5 Results

We train five independent networks (or runs) for one to seven layers on F-MNIST and one to four VGG blocks on CIFAR-10. For F-MNIST dataset the increasing number of layers did not improve the accuracy ($\sim$88%) but in case of CIFAR-10 the accuracy increased from 71% (using one block) to 82% (using four blocks). We then sample activations of each hidden neuron for 100 randomly selected input samples for each of the 10 input classes, yielding 1000 activation vectors for each layer. In each independent run, we then embed those activations into two dimensions using t-SNE and measure the resulting KL-divergence as the hardness score. For a quantitative overview, we plot the result of all runs into a single bar chart, with the averaged value shown as the bold line and individual runs as translucent overlapping rectangles (this is an alternate version of a boxplot, which puts the greatest emphasis on the mean value).

The phenomenon of decreasing KL-divergence is also visible in a more complex (convolutional) network, trained on CIFAR-10. KL-divergence scores for progressive layers of a chosen network are depicted in Fig. 1. As in the case of simpler networks, after using t-SNE we observe clustering of data which belongs to the same class. Moving to higher layers, individual clusters become more discernible and separable. The t-SNE visualization of layer activations in a 4-block VGG network in Fig. 2 illustrates the unfolding process at several stages.

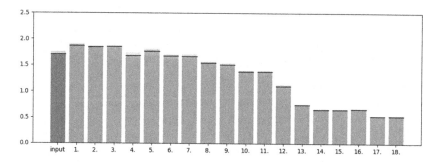

Fig. 1. KL-divergence on a 4-block VGG-type network, trained on CIFAR-10.

Figure 3 confirms the intuition that the model benefits from the higher number of layers.

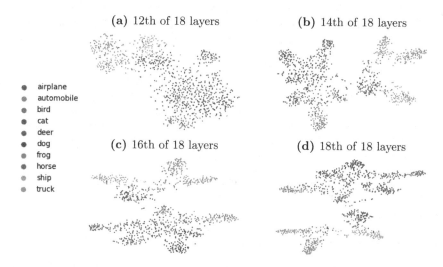

Fig. 2. t-SNE visualisation of activations on a 4-block VGG-type network trained on CIFAR-10. The higher (deeper) the layer, the clearer clusters are obtained.

The idea of measuring the KL-divergence after manifold disentanglement using t-SNE to two dimensions can be extended to three or more dimensions. Since t-SNE is computationally demanding, we additionally test only embedding to three dimensions. The results show that embeddings to three dimensions have preserved more of the original structure, as they have lower KL-divergence scores. Figure 4 provides a comparison of KL-divergence scores for a randomly chosen network trained on F-MNIST dataset, whereas in Fig. 5 we can find an example of 2D and 3D embeddings on the same network.

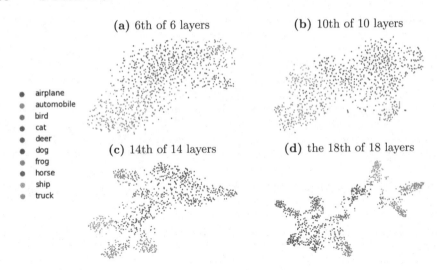

Fig. 3. t-SNE visualisation of classes on 1-to-4 block VGG-type network performed on the last hidden layer. It is evident that more blocks are beneficial for better unfolding of the classes, which leads to higher classification rate.

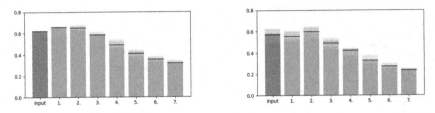

Fig. 4. KL-divergence scores for t-SNE embedding into two (left) and three (right) dimensions on a 7-layer network trained on F-MNIST.

5.1   Assessing Class Distributions

Another way to assess manifold disentanglement is to measure the complexity (in terms of data distribution) of the manifolds themselves. This can be done by performing the singular value decomposition (SVD) and evaluating, how many eigenvalues (and their corresponding principal components) explain 95% of variance in the given data, in this case per-class activations on hidden layers. We chose to not perform this testing on models trained on CIFAR-10, as the number of neurons on hidden layers varies rapidly, due to the use of convolution and pooling. Thus, the results are harder to interpret, since the changes of hidden-layer dimensionality might also contribute to the change of manifold complexity.

(a) 2D embedding   (b) 3D embedding

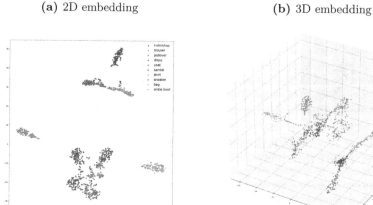

Fig. 5. Examples of t-SNE embeddings of activations (on the 7th layer) into various dimensions on a feed-forward network with 7 hidden layers trained on F-MNIST.

The other three datasets provided the following observations. Models trained on MNIST and SVHN datasets show the same trend, regardless the class or the number of hidden layers. In case of MNIST, complexity of manifolds decreases through the network. In case of SVHN it increases rapidly through first 2 layers, then slowly decreases (as shown in Fig. 6). This difference between MNIST and SVHN might be caused by the different input size (784 vs. 3072), but also different task complexity with SVHN being much more demanding, thus resulting in a lower classification accuracy. The models trained on F-MNIST are slightly different and it is possible to observe two distinct behaviours dependent on the class, shown in Fig. 7. Classes 'trouser', 'sandal', 'sneaker', 'bag' and 'ankle-boot' show the same trend as in case of MNIST and complexity monotonically decreases. Classes 't-shirt/top', 'pullover', 'dress', 'coat' and 'shirt' are similar to SVHN and complexity initially rises and decreases afterwards. This seemingly correlates with per-class classification accuracy (Fig. 8) and even t-SNE embedding of the model activations, as classes 'trouser', 'sandal', 'sneaker', 'bag' and 'ankle-boot' are classified with a higher accuracy and also form clusters easier than the remaining classes. These observations show possible correlation between model accuracy and the development of activation complexity, offering interesting ideas for future research.

5.2   Assessing Class Separation

Finally, we support manifold disentanglement hypothesis by appreciating the degree of class separability. We do this by monitoring the inter-class and intra-class distances between activation vectors on hidden layers of the trained networks. Let us denote the hidden neuron activations (of j-th sample) belonging to a class k as x_j^k, where $k = 1, 2, ..., K$. Let N be the number of all samples,

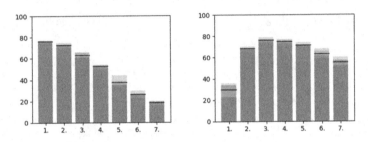

Fig. 6. Number of eigenvalues explaining 95% of variance through the hidden layers for class 5 from MNIST (left) and class 7 from SVHN (right).

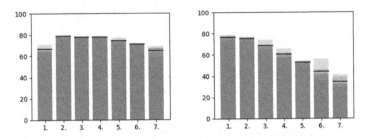

Fig. 7. Number of eigenvalues explaining 95 % of variance through the hidden layers for classes 'pullover' (left) and 'sandal' (right) from F-MNIST.

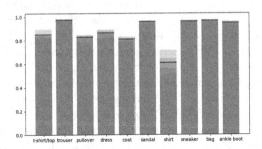

Fig. 8. Per-class accuracy of a model with 7 hidden layers trained on F-MNIST.

and N^k be the number of samples belonging to class k. Let c^k be the centroid of k-th class and C the arithmetic mean of all samples. The mean inter-class distance is defined as a mean squared (Euclidean) distance of class centroids from C and the mean intra-class distance as an average of squared distances of all class samples from the corresponding class centroid, i.e.

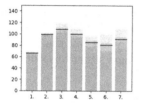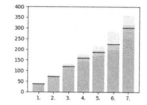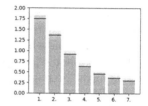

Fig. 9. Intra-class (left), inter-class (middle) and the ratio (right) of mean distances computed from the internal activation vectors on a model with 7 hidden layers trained on F-MNIST.

$$Dist_{\text{Inter}} = \frac{1}{K} \sum_{k=1}^{K} \|c^k - C\|^2 \qquad Dist_{\text{Intra}} = \frac{1}{K} \sum_{k=1}^{K} \frac{1}{N^k} \sum_{j=1}^{N^k} \|x_j^k - c^k\|^2 \qquad (1)$$

For this task, we chose a model with 7 hidden layers, trained on F-MNIST[1]. This dataset uses classes with an equal number of samples, so there is no need to perform the weighted average while evaluating average distances. At the same time, all hidden layers have the same dimensionality, which allows consistent comparisons across layers.

Results depicted in Fig. 9 reveal that the mean intra-class distance changes non-monotonically, at smaller magnitudes, but the inter-class distance grows steadily, dominating the trend. Thus, their decreasing ratio indicates that the classes become gradually unfolded, hence allowing their better separation on higher layers, which supports the manifold disentanglement hypothesis.

6   Conclusion

In this paper, we extend our results focused on visual and computational analysis of trained deep neural network classifiers. The qualitative and quantitative results related to four chosen datasets of simple and medium complexity point towards the data manifold unfolding process that explains geometric changes in the data distribution. This drives the formation of high-dimensional activation vectors that step-by-step, given the available number of hidden layers, appear to contribute to better separability of classes. This process is typically associated with a gradual decrease of the inherent manifold dimensionality, which is quantified by the quality of (decreasing) complexity embedding into 2D (or 3D), as measured by KL divergence of t-SNE visualization method. This robust process has consistently been confirmed by three different methods we used in this paper. At the same time, these may motivate further research, for instance, what is the relationship between manifold unfolding and the network accuracy, or where are the adversarial examples situated relatively to the manifolds of each layer. Another topic worth exploring is the relationship between manifolds with

---

[1] For the same reason as in SVD, we did not analyse CIFAR-10 dataset.

low KL-divergence scores and their class separability in trained networks. Our work provides evidence that these measures might correlate, however, there may exist configurations where the KL-divergence is sufficiently low but the individual classes are not separated well. For that reason, in some situations different methods might be required.

Acknowledgment. This research was partially supported by TAILOR, a project funded by EU Horizon 2020 research and innovation programme under GA No 952215, and by national projects VEGA 1/0796/18 and KEGA 042UK-4/2019.

References

1. Barredo Arrieta, A., et al.: Explainable Artificial Intelligence (XAI): concepts, taxonomies, opportunities and challenges toward responsible AI. Inf. Fusion **58**, 82–115 (2020)
2. Brahma, P.P., Wu, D., She, Y.: Why deep learning works: a manifold disentanglement perspective. IEEE Trans. Neural Netw. Learn. Syst. **10**(27), 1997–2008 (2016)
3. Gilmer, J., et al.: Adversarial spheres (2018). arXiv:1801.02774 [cs.CV]
4. Gilpin, L.H., Bau, D., Yuan, B.Z., Bajwa, A., Specter, M., Kagal, L.: Explaining explanations: an overview of interpretability of machine learning. In: International Conference on Neural Information Processing, pp. 378–385 (2020)
5. Goodfellow, I., Shlens, J., Szegedy, C.: Explaining and harnessing adversarial examples. In: International Conference on Learning Representations (2015)
6. Krizhevsky, A.: Learning multiple layers of features from tiny images. Technical report TR-2009, University of Toronto (2009)
7. Kuzma, T., Farkaš, I.: Embedding complexity of learned representations in neural networks. In: Tetko, I.V., Kůrková, V., Karpov, P., Theis, F. (eds.) ICANN 2019. LNCS, vol. 11728, pp. 518–528. Springer, Cham (2019). https://doi.org/10.1007/978-3-030-30484-3_42
8. LeCun, Y., Cortes, C.: MNIST handwritten digit database (2010). http://yann.lecun.com/exdb/mnist/
9. van der Maaten, L., Hinton, G.: Visualizing data using t-SNE. J. Mach. Learn. Res. **9**, 2579–2605 (2008)
10. Montavon, G., Samek, W., Müller, K.R.: Methods for interpreting and understanding deep neural networks. Digit. Signal Process. **73**, 1–15 (2018)
11. Montúfar, G.F., Pascanu, R., Cho, K., Bengio, Y.: On the number of linear regions of deep neural networks. In: Advances in Neural Information Processing Systems, pp. 2924–2932 (2014)
12. Recanatesi, S., Farrell, M., Advani, M., Moore, T., Lajoie, G., Shea-Brown, E.: Dimensionality compression and expansion in deep neural networks (2019). arXiv:1906.00443 [cs.LG]
13. Schmidhuber, J.: Deep learning in neural networks: an overview. Neural Netw. **61**, 85–117 (2015)
14. Schubbach, A.: Judging machines: philosophical aspects of deep learning. Synthese (2019). https://doi.org/10.1007/s11229-019-02167-z
15. Schulz, A., Hinder, F., Hammer, B.: DeepView: visualizing classification boundaries of deep neural networks as scatter plots using discriminative dimensionality reduction. In: Proceedings of the 29th International Joint Conference on Artificial Intelligence, pp. 2305–2311 (2020)

16. Simonyan, K., Zisserman, A.: Very deep convolutional networks for large scale image recognition. In: International Conference on Learning Representations (2015)
17. Stutz, D., Hein, M., Schiele, B.: Disentangling adversarial robustness and generalization (2019). arXiv:1812.00740 [cs.CV]
18. Szegedy, C., et al.: Intriguing properties of neural networks. In: International Conference on Learning Representations (2014)
19. Vilone, G., Longo, L.: Explainable artificial intelligence: a systematic review (2020). arXiv:2006.00093 [cs.AI]
20. Xiao, H., Rasul, K., Vollgraf, R.: Fashion-MNIST: a novel image dataset for benchmarking machine learning algorithms (2017). arXiv:1708.07747 [cs.LG]

Towards Utilitarian Combinatorial Assignment with Deep Neural Networks and Heuristic Algorithms

Fredrik Präntare[✉], Mattias Tiger, David Bergström, Herman Appelgren, and Fredrik Heintz

Linköping University, 581 83 Linköping, Sweden
{fredrik.prantare,mattias.tiger,david.bergstrom,herman.appelgren,
fredrik.heintz}@liu.se

Abstract. This paper presents preliminary work on using deep neural networks to guide general-purpose heuristic algorithms for performing utilitarian combinatorial assignment. In more detail, we use deep learning in an attempt to produce heuristics that can be used together with e.g., search algorithms to generate feasible solutions of higher quality more quickly. Our results indicate that our approach could be a promising future method for constructing such heuristics.

Keywords: Combinatorial assignment · Heuristic algorithms · Deep learning

1 Introduction

A major problem in computer science is that of designing cost-effective, scalable *assignment* algorithms that seek to find a *maximum weight matching* between the elements of sets. We consider a highly challenging problem of this type—namely *utilitarian combinatorial assignment* (UCA), in which indivisible elements (e.g., items) have to be distributed in bundles (i.e., partitioned) among a set of other elements (e.g., agents) to maximize a notion of aggregated value. This is a central problem in both artificial intelligence, operations research, and algorithmic game theory; with applications in optimal task allocation [9], winner determination for auctions [13], and team formation [11].

However, UCA is computationally hard. The state-of-the-art can only compute solutions to problems with severely limited input sizes—and due to Sandholm [12], we expect that no polynomial-time approximation algorithm exists

This work was partially supported by the Wallenberg AI, Autonomous Systems and Software Program (WASP) funded by the Knut and Alice Wallenberg Foundation, and by grants from the National Graduate School in Computer Science (CUGS), Sweden, Excellence Center at Linköping-Lund for Information Technology (ELLIIT), TAILOR funded by EU Horizon 2020 research and innovation programme (GA 952215), and Knut and Alice Wallenberg Foundation (KAW 2019.0350).

© Springer Nature Switzerland AG 2021
F. Heintz et al. (Eds.): TAILOR 2020, LNAI 12641, pp. 104–111, 2021.
https://doi.org/10.1007/978-3-030-73959-1_10

that can find a feasible solution with a provably good worst-case ratio. With this in mind, it is interesting to investigate if and how low-complexity algorithms can generate feasible solutions of high-enough quality for problems with large-scale inputs and limited computation budgets. In this paper, we present preliminary theoretical and experimental foundations for using function approximation algorithms (e.g., neural networks) together with heuristic algorithms to solve UCA problems.

2 Related Work

The only UCA algorithm in the literature is an optimal branch-and-bound algorithm [10,11]. Although this algorithm greatly outperforms industry-grade solvers like CPLEX in difficult benchmarks, it can only solve fairly small problems.

Furthermore, a plethora of heuristic algorithms [3–5,16,19] have been developed for the closely related *characteristic function game coalition structure generation* (CSG) problem, in which we seek to find an (unordered) utilitarian partitioning of a set of agents. However, due to the CSG problem's "unordered nature", all of these methods are unsuitable for UCA unless e.g., they are redesigned from the ground up.

Apart from this, there has been considerable work in developing algorithms for the *winner determination problem* (WDP) [1,12,13]—in which the goal is to assign a subset of the elements to alternatives called *bidders* in a way that maximizes an auctioneer's profit. WDP differs from UCA in that the value function is not given in an exhaustive manner, but instead as a list (often constrained in size) of explicit "bids" that reveal how much the bidders value different bundles of items.

Moreover, heuristic search with a learned heuristic function has in recent years achieved super-human performance in playing many difficult games. A key problem in solving games with massive state spaces is to have a sufficiently good approximation (heuristic) of the value of a sub-tree in any given state. Recent progress within the deep learning field with *multi-layered (deep) neural networks* has made learning such an approximation possible in a number of settings [8,17].

Using a previously learned heuristic function in heuristic search is an approach of integrating machine learning and combinatorial optimization (CO), and it is categorized as *machine learning alongside optimization algorithms* [2]. Another category is *end-to-end learning*, in which machine learning is leveraged to learn a function that outputs solutions to CO problems directly. While, the end-to-end approach has been applied to graph-based problems such as the *traveling salesman problem* [6] and the *propositional satisfiability problem* [15], the learned heuristic-based approach remain both a dominating and more fruitful approach [14,18].

3 Problem Description

The UCA problem that we investigate is defined as the following optimization problem:

Input: A set of elements $A = \{a_1, ..., a_n\}$, a set of alternatives $T = \{t_1, ..., t_m\}$, and a function $v : 2^A \times T \mapsto \mathbb{R}$ that maps a value to every possible pairing of a bundle $C \subseteq A$ to an alternative $t \in T$.

Output: A *combinatorial assignment* (Definition 1) $\langle C_1, ..., C_m \rangle$ over A that maximizes $\sum_{i=1}^{m} v(C_i, t_i)$.

Definition 1. $S = \langle C_1, ..., C_m \rangle$ *is a* combinatorial assignment *over* A *if* $C_i \cap C_j = \emptyset$ *for all* $i \neq j$, *and* $\bigcup_{i=1}^{m} C_i = A$.

Note that there are applications for which it is realistic (or even preferred) to have the value function given in this type of fashion. Examples of this include the strategy game *Europa Universalis 4*, where it is given by the game's programmers to enforce a certain behaviour from its game-playing agents [11]. Other such examples include when it can be defined concisely but e.g., not given as an explicit list due to the problem's size, such as in winner determination for combinatorial auctions [13], or when the value function is a result of machine (e.g., reinforcement) learning.

Moreover, we use $V(S) = \sum_{i=1}^{m} v(C_i, t_i)$ to denote the value of a *partial assignment* (Definition 2) $S = \langle C_1, ..., C_m \rangle$, and define $||S|| = \sum_{i=1}^{m} |C_i|$. The terms *solution* and *combinatorial assignment* are used interchangeably, and we often omit "over A" for brevity. We also use Π_A for the set of all combinatorial assignments over A, and define $\Pi_A^m = \{S \in \Pi_A : |S| = m\}$. We say that a solution S^* is *optimal* if and only if $V(S^*) = \max_{S \in \Pi_A^m} V(S)$.

Definition 2. *If S is a combinatorial assignment over some $A' \subseteq A$, we say that S is a* partial assignment *over* A.

(Note that we are intentionally using a non-strict inclusion in Definition 2 for practical reasons. Consequently, a combinatorial assignment is also a partial assignment over the same agent set.)

Now, to formally express our approach to UCA, first let $\langle a'_1, ..., a'_n \rangle$ be any permutation of A, and define the following recurrence:

$$V^*(S) = \begin{cases} V(S) & \text{if } ||S|| = n \\ \max_{S' \in \Delta(S, a'_{||S||+1})} V^*(S') & \text{otherwise} \end{cases} \tag{1}$$

where $\Delta(\langle C_1, ..., C_m \rangle, a) = \{\langle C_1 \cup \{a\}, ..., C_m \rangle, ..., \langle C_1, ..., C_m \cup \{a\} \rangle\}$, and S is a combinatorial assignment over $\{a'_1, ..., a'_{||S||}\}$. As a consequence of Theorem 1, UCA boils down to computing recurrence (1). Against this background, in this paper, we investigate approximating V^*, in a dynamic programming fashion, using neural networks together with heuristic methods with the goal to find better solutions quicker.

Theorem 1. $V^*(S) = \max_{S \in \Pi_A^m} V(S)$ *if $S = \langle C_1, ..., C_m \rangle$ is a partial assignment over A with $C_i = \emptyset$ for $i = 1, ..., m$.*

Proof. This result follows in a straightforward fashion by induction. $\square$

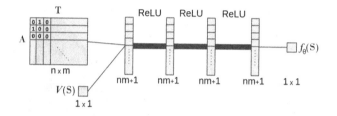

Fig. 1. Our multi-layered neural network architecture.

4   Heuristic Function Model and Training

We approximate (1) with a fully connected *deep neural network* (DNN) $f_\theta(S)$ with parameters θ, where S is a partial assignment. Our DNN has three hidden layers using *ReLU* [8] activation functions. Each hidden layer has width $mn + 1$. The input is a $m \times n$ *binary assignment-matrix* representation of S, and a scalar with the partial assignment's value $V(S)$. See Fig. 1 for a visual depiction of our architecture.

Our training procedure incorporates generating a data set $\mathcal{D}$ that consists of pairs $\langle S, V^*(S) \rangle$, with randomized partial assignments $S \in \Pi_{A_i}^m$, where $A_i \subset A$ is a uniformly drawn subset from A with $|A_i| = i$, for $i = n - 1, \ldots, n - \kappa$, where $\kappa \in \{1, ..., n\}$ is a hyperparameter. In our experiments, $\mathcal{D}$ consists of exactly 10^4 such pairs for every i. Note that it is only tractable to compute V^* if κ is kept small, since in such cases we only have to search a tree with depth κ and branching factor m to compute the real value of V^*. For this reason, we used $\kappa \leq 10$ in our benchmarks. θ is optimized over the training data using stochastic optimization to minimize:

$$\mathbb{E}_{\langle S, V^*(S) \rangle \sim \mathcal{D}} \big[V^*(S) - f_\theta(S) \big]. \tag{2}$$

The data set is split 90%/10% into a training set and a test set. The stochastic optimizer Adam [7] is used for minimizing (2) over the training set. The hyperparameters *learning rate* and *mini-batch size* are optimized using grid search over the test set. In our subsequent experiments, the same V is used as the one used for generating $\mathcal{D}$ by storing the value function's values.

5   Experiments

We use the problem set distributions *NPD* (3) and *TRAP* (4) for generating difficult problem instances for evaluating our method. NPD is one of the more difficult standardized problem instances for optimal solvers [11], and it is defined as follows:

$$v(C, t) \sim \mathcal{N}(\mu, \sigma^2), \tag{3}$$

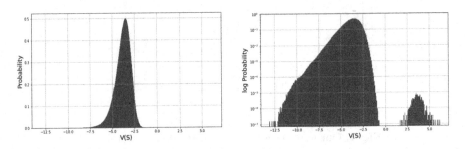

Fig. 2. Empirical estimation of $P(V(S))$ for TRAP from 10^8 samples.

for $C \subseteq A$ and $t \in T$. TRAP is introduced by us in this paper, and it is defined with:

$$v(C,t) \sim \mathcal{N}(\tau(C), \sigma^2), \tag{4}$$

for all $C \subseteq A$ and $t \in T$, where:

$$\tau(C) = \delta \begin{cases} |C| - |C|^2, & 0 \le |C| < \tau \\ |C| - |C|^2 + |C|^{(2+\epsilon)}, & \tau \le |C| \end{cases}$$

for all $C \subseteq A$. τ is defined to make it difficult for general-purpose greedy algorithms that work on an element-to-element basis to find good solutions by providing a "trap". This is because when $\epsilon > 0$, they may get stuck in (potentially arbitrarily bad) local optima, since for TRAP, the value $V(S)$ of a partial assignment S typically provides little information about $V^*(S)$. In contrast, for NPD, $V(S)$ can often be a relatively accurate estimation for $V^*(S)$. It is thus interesting to deduce whether our learned heuristic can overcome this problem, and consequently outperform greedy approximations.

We used $n = 20$, $m = 10$, $\mu = 1$, $\sigma = 0.1$, $\delta = 0.1$, $\tau = n/2$ and $\epsilon = 0.1$ in our experiments. n and m are chosen to be small enough for exact methods to be tractable.

To give an idea of how difficult it is to find good solutions for TRAP, we plot an empirical estimation of it in Fig. 2, generated using 10^8 draws with (4). The probability of drawing a combinatorial assignment $S \in \Pi_A^m$ at random with a value larger than zero, i.e., $P(V(S) > 0)$, is approximately 7.43×10^{-6} (only 743 samples found). This was computed using Monte Carlo integration with 10^8 samples.

5.1   Training Evaluation

For NPD, Fig. 3 shows that our neural network generalizes from the 1–5 unassigned elements case to 6–10 unassigned elements with only a slight degradation in prediction error variance (figures to the left). We also see that the predictions are slightly worse for predicting higher assignment values than lower ones, but that the performance is fairly evenly balanced otherwise.

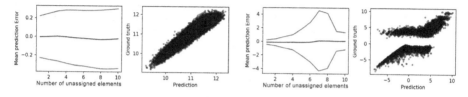

Fig. 3. Neural network results for NPD (left) and TRAP (right). The left figure of each pair shows the mean prediction error and 2 std., as a function of the number of unassigned elements of the partial assignment. The right shows the predicted value compared to the true value.

Similar figures for TRAP are also shown in Fig. 3. Here, the prediction error variance is very high around 5–7 unassigned elements. In the right-most figure, we see that the neural network has problems predicting assignment values close to TRAP's "jump" (i.e., $|C| = \tau$). However, outside of value ranges close to the jump, the prediction performance is decent, if not with as high precision as for NPD. Note that TRAP is trained for 1–10 unassigned elements, so no generalization is evaluated in this experiment.

Despite the seemingly large prediction error variance we find that the neural network has a narrower prediction distribution than an uninformed guess. More so for NPD than TRAP, but even a slightly better prediction than random is helpful as a heuristic. This is especially true for TRAP-like distributions, since for them, we previously had no better alternative. Moreover, the prediction errors' distributions are seemingly unbiased.

5.2   Benchmarks

The result of each experiment in the following benchmarks was produced by computing the average of the resulting values from 5 generated problem sets per experiment. In these benchmarks, the goal is to give an indication how well our neural networks perform compared to more naïve approaches for estimating the optimal assignment's value (and thus their suitability when integrated in a heuristic). These estimation methods are coupled with a standard greedy algorithm to draw samples from the search space. We use the following baseline estimations: 1) *current-value* estimation, which uses the partial assignment's value (so that each evaluation becomes a greedily found local optimum); and 2) a random approach, which is a worst-case baseline based on a random estimation (so that each evaluation is a uniformly drawn sample from the search space). The best solution drawn over a number of samples is then stored and plotted in Fig. 4. The 95% confidence interval is also plotted. The results show that our neural network is able to overcome some problems element-to-element-based heuristics may face with TRAP. For NPD, it performs almost identical to the current-value greedy approach.

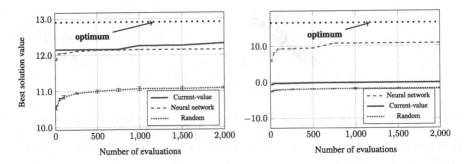

Fig. 4. The best solution values obtained by the different heuristics when using a greedy algorithm for NPD (left) and TRAP (right) problem sets with 20 elements and 10 alternatives.

6 Conclusions

We have made the first theoretical and experimental foundations for using deep neural networks together with heuristic algorithms to solve utilitarian combinatorial assignment problems. Albeit much remains to be explored and tested (including generalization, difficulty, what is learned, etc.etera), our preliminary results and simple function approximator show that using neural networks together with heuristic algorithms could be a promising future method for finding high-quality combinatorial assignments.

References

1. Andersson, A., Tenhunen, M., Ygge, F.: Integer programming for combinatorial auction winner determination. In: Proceedings Fourth International Conference on MultiAgent Systems, pp. 39–46. IEEE (2000)
2. Bengio, Y., Lodi, A., Prouvost, A.: Machine learning for combinatorial optimization: a methodological tour d'horizon. arXiv preprint arXiv:1811.06128 (2018)
3. Di Mauro, N., Basile, T.M.A., Ferilli, S., Esposito, F.: Coalition structure generation with GRASP. In: Dicheva, D., Dochev, D. (eds.) AIMSA 2010. LNCS (LNAI), vol. 6304, pp. 111–120. Springer, Heidelberg (2010). https://doi.org/10.1007/978-3-642-15431-7_12
4. Farinelli, A., Bicego, M., Bistaffa, F., Ramchurn, S.D.: A hierarchical clustering approach to large-scale near-optimal coalition formation with quality guarantees. Eng. Appl. Artif. Intell. **59**, 170–185 (2017)
5. Keinänen, H.: Simulated annealing for multi-agent coalition formation. In: Håkansson, A., Nguyen, N.T., Hartung, R.L., Howlett, R.J., Jain, L.C. (eds.) KES-AMSTA 2009. LNCS (LNAI), vol. 5559, pp. 30–39. Springer, Heidelberg (2009). https://doi.org/10.1007/978-3-642-01665-3_4
6. Khalil, E., Dai, H., Zhang, Y., Dilkina, B., Song, L.: Learning combinatorial optimization algorithms over graphs. In: Advances in Neural Information Processing Systems, pp. 6348–6358 (2017)
7. Kingma, D.P., Ba, J.: Adam: a method for stochastic optimization. arXiv preprint arXiv:1412.6980 (2014)

8. LeCun, Y., Bengio, Y., Hinton, G.: Deep learning. Nature **521**(7553), 436–444 (2015)
9. Präntare, F.: Simultaneous coalition formation and task assignment in a real-time strategy game. In: Master thesis (2017)
10. Präntare, F., Heintz, F.: An anytime algorithm for simultaneous coalition structure generation and assignment. In: Miller, T., Oren, N., Sakurai, Y., Noda, I., Savarimuthu, B.T.R., Cao Son, T. (eds.) PRIMA 2018. LNCS (LNAI), vol. 11224, pp. 158–174. Springer, Cham (2018). https://doi.org/10.1007/978-3-030-03098-8_10
11. Präntare, F., Heintz, F.: An anytime algorithm for optimal simultaneous coalition structure generation and assignment. Auton. Agents Multi-Agent Syst. **34**(1), 1–31 (2020)
12. Sandholm, T.: Algorithm for optimal winner determination in combinatorial auctions. Artif. Intell. **135**(1–2), 1–54 (2002)
13. Sandholm, T., Suri, S., Gilpin, A., Levine, D.: Winner determination in combinatorial auction generalizations. In: Proceedings of the First International Joint Conference on Autonomous Agents and Multiagent Systems: Part 1, pp. 69–76 (2002)
14. Schrittwieser, J., et al.: Mastering atari, go, chess and shogi by planning with a learned model. arXiv preprint arXiv:1911.08265 (2019)
15. Selsam, D., Lamm, M., Bünz, B., Liang, P., de Moura, L., Dill, D.L.: Learning a SAT solver from single-bit supervision. arXiv preprint arXiv:1802.03685 (2018)
16. Sen, S., Dutta, P.S.: Searching for optimal coalition structures. In: Proceedings Fourth International Conference on MultiAgent Systems, pp. 287–292. IEEE (2000)
17. Silver, D., et al.: Mastering the game of go with deep neural networks and tree search. Nature **529**(7587), 484 (2016)
18. Silver, D., et al.: A general reinforcement learning algorithm that masters chess, shogi, and go through self-play. Science **362**(6419), 1140–1144 (2018)
19. Yeh, C., Sugawara, T.: Solving coalition structure generation problem with double-layered ant colony optimization. In: 5th IIAI International Congress on Advanced Applied Informatics (IIAI-AAI), pp. 65–70. IEEE (2016)

An Analysis of Regularized Approaches for Constrained Machine Learning

Michele Lombardi[(✉)], Federico Baldo, Andrea Borghesi, and Michela Milano

University of Bologna, Bologna, Italy
{michele.lombardi2,federico.baldo2,andrea.borghesi3,
michela.milano}@unibo.it

1 Context

Regularization-based approaches for injecting constraints in Machine Learning (ML) were introduced (see e.g. [2,5,8,9]) to improve a predictive model via domain knowledge. Given the recent interest in ethical and trustworthy AI, however, several works are resorting to these approaches for enforcing desired properties over a ML model (e.g. fairness [1,10]). Regularized approaches for constraint injection solve, in an exact or approximate fashion, a problem in the form:

$$\arg \min_{w \in W}\{L(y) + \lambda^\top C(y)\} \quad \text{with: } y = f(\mathbf{x}; w) \tag{1}$$

where L is a loss function and f is the model to be trained, with parameter vector w from space W. The notation $f(\mathbf{x}; w)$ refers to the model output for the whole training set $\mathbf{x}$. The regularization function C denotes a vector of (non-negative) constraint violation metrics for m constraints, while $\lambda \geq 0$ is a vector of non-negative *multipliers*. For instance, in a regression problem we may desire a specific output ordering for two input vectors in the training set. A viable regularizer may be:

$$C(y) \equiv \max(0, y_i - y_j) \tag{2}$$

the term is zero iff the constraint $y_i \leq y_j$ is satisfied. For obtaining balanced predictions in a binary classification problem, we may use instead:

$$C(y) \equiv \left| \sum_{i=1}^{n} y_i - \frac{n}{2} \right| \tag{3}$$

where y_i is the binary output associated to one of the two classes. If n is even, the term is 0 for perfectly balanced classifications.

When regularized methods are used to enforce constraints, *a typical approach consists in adjusting the λ vector until a suitable compromise between accuracy and constraint satisfaction is reached* (e.g. a discrimination index becomes sufficiently low). This approach enables the use of traditional training algorithms, at the cost of having to search over the space of possible multipliers. Though the method is known to work well in many practical cases, the process has been subject to little general analysis, one exception being a proof by counter example in

© Springer Nature Switzerland AG 2021
F. Heintz et al. (Eds.): TAILOR 2020, LNAI 12641, pp. 112–119, 2021.
https://doi.org/10.1007/978-3-030-73959-1_11

[4] that demonstrates how regularization-based approaches can be structurally sub-optimal. With this note, we aim to make a preliminary step in the characterization of the formal properties of the described approach, providing a more systematic overview of their strengths and potential weaknesses. We will concentrate on constrained ML problems, providing a perspective that is not typically considered, as most of the research in this area focus, in general, on duality theory and convex optimization.

2   Analysis

Regularized approaches for constraint injection are strongly related to the concept of duality in optimization, and indeed many of the results presented in this note are rooted in duality theory. Despite this, we opted here for an analysis based on first principles, as it provides a more direct path toward our main results and minimizes the number of needed assumptions, thus rendering this note mostly self-contained.

It will be convenient to reformulate Eq. (1) by embedding the ML model structure in the L and C functions:

$$\mathbf{PR}(\lambda) : \ \arg\min_{w \in W}\{L(w) + \lambda^\top C(w)\} \tag{4}$$

where with some abuse of notation $L(w)$ refers to $L(f(\mathbf{x}; w))$, and the same holds for for $C(w)$. This approach enables a uniform treatment of convex and non-convex models or functions. We are interested in the relation between the unconstrained PR formulation and the following constrained training problem:

$$\mathbf{PC}(\theta) : \ \arg\min_{w \in W}\{L(w) \mid C(w) \le \theta\} \tag{5}$$

where θ is a vector of thresholds for the constraint violation indices. In ethical or trustworthy AI applications, PC will be the most natural problem formulation.

We wish to understand *the viability of solving PC indirectly, by adjusting the λ vector and solving the unconstrained problem PR*, as depicted in Algorithm 1, where line 2 refers to any form of search over the multiplier space. Ideally, the algorithm should be equivalent to solving the PC formulation directly. For this to be true, solving $PR(\lambda)$ should have a chance to yield assignments that are optimal for the constrained problem. Moreover, an optimum of $PC(\theta)$ should always be attainable in this fashion. Additional properties may enable more efficient search. The main goal of our note is characterizing Algorithm 1.

2.1   Regularized and Constrained Optima

The relation between the PR and PC formulations are tied to the properties of their optimal solutions. An optimal PC solution w_c^* satisfies:

$$\mathbf{opt_c}(\mathbf{w}^*, \theta) : \ L(w) \ge L(w^*) \quad \forall w \in W \mid C(w) \le \theta \tag{6}$$

Algorithm 1. PR4PC(θ)

1: **for** $\lambda \in (\mathbb{R}^+)^m$ **do**
2:    Optimize PR to find w^*
3:    **if** $C(w^*) \leq \theta$ **then**
4:       Store $w^*, L(w^*)$
5: Pick the stored solution with the smallest $L(w^*)$

---

while for an optimal solution w_r^* of PR with multipliers λ we have:

$$\mathbf{opt_r(w^*, \lambda)} : \ L(w) + \lambda^\top C(w) \geq L(w^*) + \lambda^\top C(w^*) \quad \forall w \in W \qquad (7)$$

The definitions apply also to local optima, by swapping W with some neighborhood of w_c^* and w_r^*. We can now provide the following result:

Theorem 1. *An optimal solution w^* for PR is also optimal for PC, for a threshold equal to $C(w^*)$, i.e.:*

$$opt_r(w^*, \lambda) \Rightarrow opt_c(w^*, C(w^*)) \qquad (8)$$

Proof (by contradiction). Let us assume that w^* is an optimal solution for PR but not optimal for PC, i.e. that there is a feasible $w' \in W$ such that:

$$L(w') < L(w^*) \qquad (9)$$

Since w^* is optimal for PR, we have that:

$$L(w') \geq L(w^*) + \lambda^\top (C(w^*) - C(w')) \qquad (10)$$

Since w' is feasible for $\theta = C(w^*)$, we have that its violation vector cannot be greater than that of w^*. Formally, we have that $C(w') \leq C(w^*)$, or equivalently $C(w^*) - C(w') \geq 0$. Therefore Eq. (10) contradicts Eq. (9), thus proving the original point. The same reasoning applies to local optima. $\qquad\square$

Theorem 1 shows that solving PR(λ) *always results in an optimum for the constrained formulation*, albeit for a threshold $\theta = C(w^*)$ that cannot be a priori chosen. The statement is true even for non-convex loss, regularizer, and model structure. This is a powerful result, which provides a strong motivation for Algorithm 1.

A case of special interests involves regularizers that encapsulate the threshold θ in their definitions, i.e. whose value is 0 iff the constraint is satisfied to the desired degree. Our two expressions from Eq. (2) and Eq. (3) both belong to this class, while any regularizer can be made to satisfy the property via the substitution:

$$C'(w) \equiv \max (0, C(w) - \theta) \qquad (11)$$

Under these assumptions, any multiplier vector that manages to bring down to zero the regularizer value will also provide an optimum for the original constraint problem: this is actually the mechanism behind penalty methods for continuous optimization [3].

Crucially, however, Theorem 1 does not imply that a multiplier vector capable of reaching the desired constraint violation threshold is guaranteed to exist. We will tackle this question in Theorem 3, but first we will focus on monotonicity properties that are commonly exploited to simplify search in Algorithm 1.

2.2   Monotonicity

We will start by introducing a lemma that relates changes in the multiplier vector λ to changes in the constraint violation metrics $C(w)$.

Lemma 1. *Given a multiplier vector λ and the corresponding PR solution w, adjusting the vector by a quantity δ leads to a PR solution w' such that $\delta C(w) \leq C(w')$. Formally:*

$$opt_r(w, \lambda), opt_r(w', \lambda + \delta) \Rightarrow \delta C(w') \leq \delta C(w) \tag{12}$$

Proof. Due to the optimality of w for multiplier λ, we have that:

$$L(w) + \lambda C(w) \leq L(w') + \lambda C(w') \tag{13}$$

Due to the optimality of λ' we have that:

$$L(w') + (\lambda + \delta)C(w') \leq L(w) + (\lambda + \delta)C(w) \tag{14}$$

Now, from Eq. (13) we know we can replace $L(w') + \lambda C(w')$ with $L(w) + \lambda C(w)$ and still get a valid inequality:

$$L(w) + \lambda C(w) + \delta C(w') \leq L(w) + \lambda C(w) + \delta C(w) \tag{15}$$

which by cancellation leads to the main result.   □

Lemma 1 has several implications. Most notably:

Theorem 2. *If every component of a multiplier vector λ is increased by the same positive quantity δ, then the total degree of constraint violation in the PR solution cannot increase:*

$$opt_r(w, \lambda), opt_r(w', \lambda + \delta), \delta \in \mathbb{R}^+ \Rightarrow \|C(w')\| \leq \|C(w)\| \tag{16}$$

The proof stems directly from Lemma 1. This is a powerful result, and the second main mechanism behind penalty methods. Indeed, it can be proved [3] that if a solution w' with a strictly lower constraint violation exists (and the loss function is bounded), then using a large enough δ will guarantee that $\|C(w')\| < \|C(w)\|$.

In other words, *as long as δ is a scalar*, line 2 in Algorithm 1 can be implemented via a simple approach such as binary search or gradient descent. If we wish to update each component of the multiplier vector individually, then Theorem 2 will not hold at each step, but it can still be eventually satisfied by properly choosing the multiplier update scheme, e.g. as in [6,7].

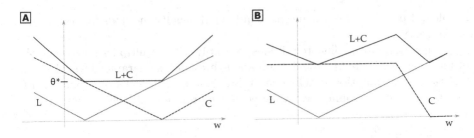

Fig. 1. Multiple Optima in Convex (A) and Non-Convex (B) Regularized Problems

The main drawback of Lemma 1 is that it assumes global optimality for the solutions of the regularized problem PR. Global optimality is attainable only in very specific cases (e.g. convex loss, regularizer, and model) or by using an exact solution approach (which may be computationally expensive). Failing this, the lemma will not hold, in the worst case requiring exhaustive search on the multiplier space. Additionally, relying on local optima will lead to suboptimal solutions, and using stochastic training algorithm will make the whole approach subject to uncertainty.

2.3 Unattainable Constrained Optima

Further issues arise when the regularized problem $PR(\lambda)$ has multiple equivalent optima. In the fully convex case, this may happen if the multiplier values generate plateaus (see Fig. 1A, where $\lambda = 1$). In the non-convex case, there may be separate optima with the same value for the regularized loss, but different trade-offs between loss and constraint violation: this is depicted in Fig. 1B. It may happen that different constrained optima are associated to the same multiplier, *and to no other multiplier.* In Fig. 1A, for example, the multiplier $\lambda = 1$ is associated to all optimal solutions of $PC(\theta)$ with $\theta \leq \theta^*$; no other multiplier is associated to the same solutions. Unless some kind of tie breaking technique is employed, this situation makes specific constrained optima impossible to reach.

The situation we have just described represents a degenerate case, and can still be handled via tie-breaking techniques. However, there exists the possibility that unattainable constrained optima arise under more general (and less manageable) circumstances. Specifically, we will now proceed to investigate whether an optimum of the constrained formulation may be associated to no multiplier value. We have that:

Theorem 3. *An optimal solution w^* for PC is optimal for PR iff there exists a multiplier vector λ that satisfies:*

$$\max_{\substack{w \in W, \\ C_j(w) > C_j(w^*)}} R(w, \lambda) \leq \lambda_j \leq \min_{\substack{w \in W, \\ C_j(w) < C_j(w^*)}} R(w, \lambda) \tag{17}$$

with:

$$R(w, \lambda) = -\frac{\Delta L(w, w^*) + \lambda_{\bar{j}}^\top \Delta C_{\bar{j}}(w, w^*)}{\Delta C_j(w, w^*)} \tag{18}$$

In the theorem, we refer with $\Delta C(w, w^*)$ to the difference $C(w) - C(w^*)$ and with $\Delta L(w, w^*)$ to the difference $L(w) - L(w^*)$. Moreover, $\bar{j}$ refers to the set of all multiplier indices, except for j. Intuitively, every assignment for which constraint j has a lower degree of violation than in w^* enforces an upper bound on λ_j; every assignment for which the violation is higher enforces a lower bound.

Proof. Let w^* be a PC optimum for some threshold θ; this implies that w^* is also optimal for a tightened threshold, i.e. for $\theta = C(w^*)$. We therefore have:

$$L(w) \geq L(w^*) \quad \forall w \in W, C(w) \leq C(w^*) \tag{19}$$

We are interested in the conditions for w^* to be optimal for the regularized formulation, for some multiplier vector λ. This is true iff:

$$L(w) + \lambda^\top C(w) \geq L(w^*) + \lambda^\top C(w^*) \quad \forall w \in W \tag{20}$$

which can rewritten as:

$$\lambda^\top \Delta C(w, w^*) + \Delta L(w, w^*) \geq 0 \quad \forall w \in W \tag{21}$$

If $\Delta C(w, w^*) = 0$, then Eq. (21) is trivially satisfied for every multiplier vector, due to Eq. (19). Otherwise, at least some component in $\Delta C(w, w^*)$ will be non-null, so that we can write:

$$\lambda_j \Delta C_j(w, w^*) + \lambda_{\bar{j}}^\top \Delta C_{\bar{j}}(w, w^*) + \Delta L(w, w^*) \geq 0 \tag{22}$$

If $\Delta C_j(w, w^*) < 0$, we get:

$$\lambda_j \leq -\frac{\Delta L(w, w^*) + \lambda_{\bar{j}}^\top \Delta C_{\bar{j}}(w, w^*)}{\Delta C_j(w, w^*)} \quad \forall w \in W \mid C_j(w) < C_j(w^*) \tag{23}$$

I.e. a series of upper bounds for λ_j. If $\Delta C_j(w, w^*) > 0$, we get:

$$\lambda_j \geq -\frac{\Delta L(w, w^*) + \lambda_{\bar{j}}^\top \Delta C_{\bar{j}}(w, w^*)}{\Delta C_j(w, w^*)} \quad \forall w \in W \mid C_j(w) > C_j(w^*) \tag{24}$$

I.e. a series of lower bounds on λ_j. From these the original result is obtained. $\square$

The main consequence of Theorem 3 is that the reported system of inequalities may actually admit no solution, meaning that *some constrained optima may be unattainable* via Algorithm 1. This is the case for the optimum w^* (for threshold θ^*) in the simple example from Fig. 2, since any multiplier value will result in an unbounded regularized problem. This is a potentially serious limitation of regularized methods: the actual severity of the issue will depend on the specific properties of the loss, regularizer, and ML model being considered.

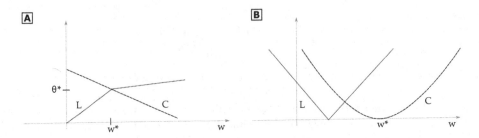

Fig. 2. (A) Unattainable Constrained Optimum; (B) Numerical Issues for w^*

Theorem 3 highlights another issue of regularized approaches, arising when assignments with constraint violations arbitrarily close to $C(w^*)$ exist. The denominator in Eq. (18) becomes vanishingly small: this may result in arbitrarily high lower bounds or arbitrarily small upper bounds. Reaching a specific optimum for the constrained problem may require *extremely high or extremely low multipliers*, which may cause numerical issues at training time. An example is depicted in Fig. 2B, where a regularizer with vanishing gradient and a loss with non-vanishing gradient are combined – the constrained optimum w^* is reached via Algorithm 1 only for $\lambda \to \infty$.

3   Conclusions

Combining the ML and optimization paradigms is a research avenue still under ongoing exploration by the AI community, with advancements towards ethical and trustworthy AI (e.g. by making sub-symbolic models fair and explainable). A possible method to merge these paradigm consists in adding a regularization term to the loss of a learner, to constrain its behaviour. In this note we tackle the issue of finding the right balance between the loss and the regularization term; typically, this search is performed by adjusting a set of multipliers until the desired compromise is reached. The key results of this paper is the formal demonstration that this type of approach *cannot guarantee to find all optimal solutions*. In particular, in the non-convex case there might be optima for the constrained problem that do not correspond to any multiplier value. This result clearly hinders the applicability of regularizer-based methods, at least unless more research effort is devoted to discover new formulations or algorithms.

Besides the ones reported here, one should be wary of pitfalls that are not immediately related to Algorithm 1. Many regularization based approaches for constraint injection, for example, require differentiability of the C function, which is often obtained by making approximations. For instance, in Eq. (3) differentiability does not hold due to the use of binary variables; relaxing the integrally constraint address the issue, but allows to satisfy the constraints by assigning 0.5 to all outputs, i.e. by having completely uncertain, rather than balanced, predictions.

Acknowledgements. This work has been partially supported by European ICT-48–2020 Project TAILOR (g.a. 952215) and EU Horizon 2020 Project StairwAI (g.a. 101017142).

References

1. Aghaei, S., Azizi, M.J., Vayanos, P.: Learning optimal and fair decision trees for non-discriminative decision-making. In: Proceedings of AAAI, pp. 1418–1426 (2019)
2. Borghesi, A., Baldo, F., Lombardi, M., Milano, M.: Injective domain knowledge in neural networks for transprecision computing. In: Nicosia, G., et al. (eds.) LOD 2020. LNCS, vol. 12565, pp. 587–600. Springer, Cham (2020). https://doi.org/10.1007/978-3-030-64583-0_52
3. Boyd, S., Boyd, S.P., Vandenberghe, L.: Convex Optimization. Cambridge University Press, Cambridge (2004)
4. Cotter, A., Jiang, H., et al.: Optimization with non-differentiable constraints with applications to fairness, recall, churn, and other goals. J. Mach. Learn. Res. **20**(172), 1–59 (2019)
5. Diligenti, M., Gori, M., Saccà, C.: Semantic-based regularization for learning and inference. Artif. Intell. **244**, 143–165 (2017)
6. Fioretto, F., Mak, T.W.K., Hentenryck, P.V.: Predicting AC optimal power flows: combining deep learning and lagrangian dual methods. In: The Thirty-Fourth AAAI Conference on Artificial Intelligence, AAAI 2020, The Thirty-Second Innovative Applications of Artificial Intelligence Conference, IAAI 2020, The Tenth AAAI Symposium on Educational Advances in Artificial Intelligence, EAAI 2020, New York, NY, USA, 7–12 February 2020, pp. 630–637. AAAI Press (2020). https://aaai.org/ojs/index.php/AAAI/article/view/5403
7. Fioretto, F., Mak, T.W., et al.: A lagrangian dual framework for deep neural networks with constraints. arXiv preprint arXiv:2001.09394 (2020)
8. Goh, G., Cotter, A., Gupta, M., Friedlander, M.P.: Satisfying real-world goals with dataset constraints. In: Advances in Neural Information Processing Systems, pp. 2415–2423 (2016)
9. Xu, J., Zhang, Z., et al.: A semantic loss function for deep learning with symbolic knowledge. In: Proceedings of the 35th ICML (2018)
10. Zemel, R., Wu, Y., Swersky, K., Pitassi, T., Dwork, C.: Learning fair representations. In: International Conference on Machine Learning, pp. 325–333 (2013)

Acting and Optimizing

Safe Learning and Optimization Techniques: Towards a Survey of the State of the Art

Youngmin Kim[1]([⊠])[iD], Richard Allmendinger[1][iD], and Manuel López-Ibáñez[1,2][iD]

[1] Alliance Manchester Business School, University of Manchester,
Manchester M15 6PB, UK
{youngmin.kim,richard.allmendinger,manuel.lopez-ibanez}@manchester.ac.uk
[2] School of Computer Science, University of Málaga, 29071 Málaga, Spain

Abstract. Safe learning and optimization deals with learning and optimization problems that avoid, as much as possible, the evaluation of non-safe input points, which are solutions, policies, or strategies that cause an irrecoverable loss (e.g., breakage of a machine or equipment, or life threat). Although a comprehensive survey of safe reinforcement learning algorithms was published in 2015, a number of new algorithms have been proposed thereafter, and related works in active learning and in optimization were not considered. This paper reviews those algorithms from a number of domains including reinforcement learning, Gaussian process regression and classification, evolutionary computing, and active learning. We provide the fundamental concepts on which the reviewed algorithms are based and a characterization of the individual algorithms. We conclude by explaining how the algorithms are connected and suggestions for future research.

Keywords: Safe learning · Safe optimization · Markov decision process · Black-box optimization · Expensive optimization

1 Introduction

Standard learning and optimization algorithms are generally concerned with trading off exploration and exploitation of an objective function such that approximation of the objective function is performed efficiently for learning problems, and such that an optimal solution, policy and/or strategy is discovered within as few evaluations as possible for optimization problems. This paper is concerned with learning/optimization problems where the evaluation of *unsafe* solutions imply some significant loss, such as damage of experimental equipment or personal injury.

Safe learning and optimization scenarios typically arise in black-box problems, particularly expensive ones. In *black-box* problems, no explicit mathematical model of the safety constraints is available and the value of the safety constraint function can only be known after a solution has been evaluated. If the

© Springer Nature Switzerland AG 2021
F. Heintz et al. (Eds.): TAILOR 2020, LNAI 12641, pp. 123–139, 2021.
https://doi.org/10.1007/978-3-030-73959-1_12

number of total evaluations is very limited, from ten to a few thousands, due to limited time or available resources, then the problem is also called *expensive*. Such scenarios arise often when the evaluation of a solution requires a simulation [11] or a real-world experiment, as in closed-loop optimization [1,19]. This paper provides an overview of the research carried out in the area of safe learning and optimization, primarily, for black-box and expensive problems.

Algorithms designed for solving expensive (black-box) problems exploit information obtained through a series of expensive evaluations to select the next input point (i.e., solution) for evaluation. In such problems, an evaluation is akin to executing a physical, chemical or biological experiment, and thus, involves the use of resources, such as raw materials, machines, operators, etc. Problems that require time-consuming computer simulations can be seen as another example of expensive problems [1,4,11,23,28]. As mentioned above, in expensive problems, the evaluation of an unsafe solution can lead to a waste of resources, such as damage/loss of equipment, of which we may have limited availability.

A large body of research has been carried out around algorithm design for expensive problems. Arguably, Bayesian optimization (also called surrogate-assisted optimization, meta-model and response surface methods) [12,29] has become the default approach for tackling expensive optimization problems. However, research around non-standard problem features and their implications, such as safety, fairness, and dynamic problem aspects, remains dispersed across the different areas of machine learning, AI and optimization.

García and Fernández [13] provided a survey on safe reinforcement learning (safe RL), including *constrained criterion*-based optimization, which is relevant to this survey. In *constrained criterion*-based optimization, the safe domain of policies (i.e., of input points) is approximated by several constraints. There are several approaches in *constrained criterion*-based optimization. The most typical approach constraints a safety function above a certain threshold. Other approaches evaluate only input points that preserve *ergodicity* [13,21] or ensure that evaluations are only allowed when the expected variance of their output does not exceed a certain threshold [13]. Classical *ergodicity* means that we can get from every state to every other state with positive probability. However, in the context of safe RL, the *ergodicity* assumption differentiates between safe and unsafe states, and the concepts of reachability (an input point is safe only if it can be reached without evaluating any unsafe input points) and returnability (an input point is safe if there is a sequence of transitions via safe input points that reaches any of a given safe state set) are limited to being able to move between safe states only [33–35]; hence, in the remainder of this paper, *ergodicity* refers to this notion from safe RL.

In this paper, we define a safe learning and optimization problem as one subject to one or more safety constraints and/or the preservation of ergodicity as defined above. An input point that violates a safety constraint or ergodicity is deemed *unsafe*. The goal when tackling such problems may be to identify an optimal input point, learn some unknown function, explore a search space or determine the boundaries of the safe input space, while constraining the evaluation of unsafe input points up to a maximum budget, which is often zero if no unsafe evaluations are allowed at all. Thus, we review algorithms that aim to satisfy all safety constraints and/or preserve ergodicity, the latter mostly applies to safe RL algorithms designed for learning tasks. Furthermore, we review several related algorithms in active learning and optimization communities such as Bayesian optimization and evolutionary computing, which were not covered in [13].

The remainder of the paper is organized as follows. In Sect. 2, we propose a general formal definition of safe optimization problems that generalizes many of the formulations found in the literature, and discuss the scope of this survey. Section 3 provides a brief summary of several fundamental concepts related to safe learning and optimization. Section 4 reviews existing safe learning and optimization algorithms that have been proposed after the survey by García and Fernández [13], originating from evolutionary computing, active learning, reinforcement learning and Bayesian optimization. Finally, Sect. 5 discusses links between these algorithms and provides ideas for future research.

2   Problem Statement

This section provides a formal definition of a general safe optimization problem and discusses various special cases.

In a safe optimization problem, we are given an objective function $f\colon \mathbb{R}^m \to \mathbb{R}$ that is typically both black-box and expensive (e.g., costly, time-consuming, resource-intense etc.). The goal is to discover a feasible and safe m-dimensional input point $\mathbf{x} = (x_1, \ldots, x_m) \in \mathbb{R}^m$ that maximizes the objective function $f(\mathbf{x})$ while avoiding the evaluation of *unsafe* input points as much as possible. The objective function may represent reward, efficiency or cost, and input points may represent policies, strategies, states/actions (of an agent/system) or solutions. Formally,

$$
\begin{aligned}
\text{Maximize} \quad & f(\mathbf{x}) & & \mathbf{x} \in \mathbb{R}^m \\
\text{subject to} \quad & g_i(\mathbf{x}) \leq 0 & & i = 1, \ldots, q \\
& s_j(\mathbf{x}) \geq h_j & & j = 1, \ldots, p,
\end{aligned}
\tag{1}
$$

where $g_i(\mathbf{x}) \leq 0$ are q *feasibility constraints*, $s_j(\mathbf{x})$ are p *safety functions* [14] and h_j are p *safety thresholds* (constants). We explicitly separate the safety thresholds from the safety functions since, depending on the application at hand, either the function is black-box [30] or the threshold is unknown *a priori* [26], meaning we only know whether a solution is safe during or after its evaluation. A common special case arises when the safety function is the same as the objective function, that is, there is only one safety constraint ($p = 1$) such that $s_1(\mathbf{x}) = f(\mathbf{x}) \geq h$ [2,30,33].

There is a key difference between (hard and soft) feasibility and safety constraints: Feasibility constraints model aspects that are relevant for an input point solution to be of practical use, such as bounds of instrument settings, physical limitations or design requirements. Depending on the application, an input point that violates a feasibility constraint can or cannot be evaluated (hard vs soft constraints) [20] but if a feasibility constraint is violated by a solution, then this has no serious consequences. On the other hand, evaluating an input point that violates a safety constraint leads to an unsafe situation, e.g., an experimental kit breaks or a human dies. That is, prior to evaluating a solution, an optimizer needs to have as much certainty about its safety status as possible, based either on a continuous measure [18] or binary property of solutions. It is important to note that an input point can be feasible but unsafe, or vice versa.

An input point that violates any safety constraint is *unsafe*. The evaluation of an unsafe input point is counted as a *failure*. Let us assume that a given budget of failures is allowed, $n^{\text{failure}} \in \mathbb{N}_0$. After this budget is consumed, the algorithm has failed and cannot continue. We can distinguish two special cases in the literature. In one case, evaluating *unsafe* input points encountered during the search process is endurable only a limited number of times [2,4,18,23–26]; thus, $n^{\text{failure}} > 0$. When a *failure* represents a relatively innocuous event, such as the crash of an expensive simulation [4,23], a relatively large number of failures may be allowed, but each of them has a cost. However, in other cases, the assumption is that no *unsafe* input point should be evaluated ever ($n^{\text{failure}} = 0$) [6–8,10,30,31,33,35].

In some safe optimization and learning problems, a safety constraint can be violated if the associated safety function $s_j(\mathbf{x})$ cannot be evaluated because the unsafe input point represents an incomplete experiment or expensive simulation [4,23] or physical damage to the input point [2] that prevents measuring the value of the safety function. Thus, it is only known whether the constraint was violated, but not by how much. Within the above definition of safe optimization problem (Eq. 1), such cases are equivalent to the following safety constraint:

$$s'_j(\mathbf{x}) \geq 0 \qquad \text{where} \qquad s'_j(\mathbf{x}) = \begin{cases} s_j(\mathbf{x}) & \text{if } s_j(\mathbf{x}) \geq h_j \text{ (safe)} \\ -1 & \text{if } s_j(\mathbf{x}) < h_j \text{ (unsafe)} \end{cases} \qquad (2)$$

where only the value $s'_j(\mathbf{x})$ is observable, whereas $s_j(\mathbf{x})$ is not directly observable. Moreover, in some contexts [4], the evaluation of an unsafe input point may also prevent the objective function (or feasibility constraints) to be evaluated, even if different from the safety function.

The above optimization model also covers optimal parameter control, if the problem may be modelled as online optimization or multi-arm bandit [7]. Furthermore, the above model can be adapted easily to safe learning and RL. In safe learning, the goal becomes to discover a feasible and safe input point that minimizes the largest amount of uncertainty. Thus, the objective function may represent uncertainty about a performance or safety function. Uncertainty may be measured in different ways, e.g., variance and width of confidence interval. In the particular case of safe RL, a Markov decision process (MDP) is typically used for modelling the problem, such that an agent (e.g., rover or quadrotor) needs to explore the state or state-action space in an uncertain environment [8,33–35]. The sequence of input points (states or state-action pairs) is determined by a transition function, which is often unknown. In this context, a safe input point must also satisfy *ergodicity*, i.e., it needs to satisfy the properties of reachability and returnability to a safe state [33–35]. Here, returnability is allowed to be met in n steps, however, reachability is problem-specific, as we will explain in more detail later. In the context of MDP, the goal may be to optimize a reward function [15, 35] or to find the largest set of safe input points (*safe exploration*) [8, 33, 34]. In either case, the objective function in Eq. (1) may be adapted to reflect those goals.

3   Fundamental Concepts in Safe Learning and Optimization

Safe learning and optimization is a domain that is spread across several research communities, each approaching the problem from a different angle, though there are overlaps in methodologies. This section provides an overview of the main concepts underpinning the different methodologies including Markov decision process (MDP), Gaussian process regression (GPR), Evolutionary algorithm (EA), *safe set operator* (which examines safety of input points based on L-Lipschitz continuity), and *optimistic expander operator* and *optimistic safe set operator* (which is operated based on a safe set established by *safe set operator* followed by naive confidence interval and intersectional confidence interval applied to the operators). In addition, **classifiers**, such as Gaussian process classifier (GPC) [4, 26] and least-squares support vector machine (LS-SVM) [23], have been used for inferring the safety of input points, however, we do not introduce them here for brevity.

We distinguish between function exploration in safe learning and safe **MDP** exploration in RL. In function exploration, the goal is to learn some unknown function, while avoiding unsafe input points. By contrast, in safe MDP exploration, an agent explores the state space of the MDP. Hence, the problem definition includes a reachability constraint, which ensures that safe input points are reachable in one step of the MDP (one-step reachability [33, 35]) or in several steps (n-step reachability [34]), and a returnability constraint, which ensures that the agent can return to any of a given safe state set, usually, in several steps (n-step returnability [8, 33–35]). Details about RL and MDPs can be found in [32].

GPR is a regression method that learns a function using Gaussian processes. GPR can be used for function exploration, exploitation and exploration-exploitation [3, 27]. Following most recent research in safe learning and optimization, we focus here on learning (function exploration) and optimization (function exploration-exploitation) subject to safety constraints, which we denote as safe learning and safe optimization, respectively. Arguably, the majority of safe learning and optimization approaches make use of GPR in one way or the other, primarily to infer (i) an objective function, as generally used in expensive learning/optimization, and/or (ii) safety function(s), which provides information about the likelihood of an input point being safe. For general information about GPR, the reader is referred to [9, 22, 27].

The literature also reports some applications of **Evolutionary Algorithms (EAs)** [5] to safe optimization problems. EAs are heuristic optimization methods inspired by biological evolution. Loosely defined, EAs evolve a population of individuals (solutions) through the application of variation operators (mutation and/or crossover) and selection of the fittest. Naive variation operators involve a great deal of (guided) randomness to generate innovative solutions and thus cover a larger part of the search space. Moreover, naive EAs do not account for the expected mean and uncertainty of a solution before evaluating it, unlike GPR. The combination of being too innovative and unconscious about the safety of a solution prior to evaluation may explain their limited application to problems with safety constraints.

In the literature on safe learning and optimization, two kinds of methods are mostly used for determining the level of safety of input points: L-Lipschitz continuity and classifiers. The concept of **L-Lipschitz continuity** is often used in combination with problems where a known constant safety threshold h is available to the learning/optimization algorithm. An evaluation that yields an output value above the threshold would deem the input point as safe. More formally, given a Lipschitz constant L, the L-Lipschitz continuity assumption is met if

$$d(f(\mathbf{x}), f(\mathbf{x}')) \leq L \cdot d(\mathbf{x}, \mathbf{x}'), \tag{3}$$

where both $\mathbf{x}$ and $\mathbf{x}' \in \mathbb{R}^m$, and $d(\cdot, \cdot)$ denotes the distance between two input points, typically, the Euclidean distance [8]. Then, given a set of safe input points $S \subset \mathbb{R}^m$, an input point $\mathbf{x} \in \mathbb{R}^m$ is deemed safe if $\exists \mathbf{x}' \in S$ such that

$$l(\mathbf{x}') - L \cdot d(\mathbf{x}', \mathbf{x}) \geq h, \tag{4}$$

where $l(\mathbf{x}')$ is the lower bound of the confidence interval for $\mathbf{x}'$, and L is the Lipschitz constant [30]. Using the lower bound makes the above inequality more strict when compared to using the mean or upper bound, thus preventing unsafe evaluations resulting from noisy measurements (i.e., an input point $\mathbf{x}$ that satisfies the above inequality is highly likely to be safe even if a noisy measurement affects its output value). We refer to Eq. (4) as **safe set operator**.

Having derived a set of safe solutions using the safe set operator, next, what is called an **optimistic expander operator** can be used to select input points from that set. The selected points could potentially expand the safe set by helping to classify additional input points (at least one) as safe in the next iteration. That is, an input point $\mathbf{x}$, not known to be safe, may be classified as safe if the following condition is satisfied:

$$u(\mathbf{x}^{\text{safe}}) - L \cdot d(\mathbf{x}^{\text{safe}}, \mathbf{x}) - \epsilon \geq h, \tag{5}$$

where $\epsilon = 0$ and the evaluation of the safe input point $\mathbf{x}^{\text{safe}}$ gives a value equal to $u(\mathbf{x}^{\text{safe}})$, the upper bound of the confidence interval for the safety function of $\mathbf{x}^{\text{safe}}$ [30] (optimistic attitude). The **optimistic expander operator** would select input points that are expected to be safe and also increase the size of the safe set if evaluated. Finally, an **optimistic safe set operator** uses the condition (Eq. 5), but $\mathbf{x}$ can be any input point in $\mathbb{R}^m$ and ϵ is the parameter representing the noise of a safety function, constructs an optimistic safe set consisting of $\mathbf{x}$.

Some algorithms calculate **naive confidence interval** and **intersectional confidence interval** [34], respectively defined as:

$$l_t = \mu_{t-1}(\mathbf{x}) - \beta_t \sigma_{t-1}(\mathbf{x}), \ \ u_t = \mu_{t-1}(\mathbf{x}) + \beta_t \sigma_{t-1}(\mathbf{x}) \tag{6}$$

$$l_t = \max(l_{t-1}, \mu_{t-1}(\mathbf{x}) - \beta_t \sigma_{t-1}(\mathbf{x})), \ \ u_t = \min(u_{t-1}, \mu_{t-1}(\mathbf{x}) + \beta_t \sigma_{t-1}(\mathbf{x})), \tag{7}$$

where β_t is a parameter that determines the width of the confidence interval and σ_{t-1} is the predicted standard deviation at point $\mathbf{x}$ [27] at iteration t of the algorithm.

4   Algorithms

This section provides an overview of existing safe learning and optimization algorithms, and relationships between them (Tables 1 and 2). The tables can be seen as a first attempt of a classification of these algorithms.

Table 1 classifies the safe learning and optimization algorithms according to their aim, either optimization, which is subdivided by the type of method (EA and/or GPR), or learning, which is subdivided into RL or active learning. For each algorithm, the column *Method* shows key features of the algorithm (PSO denotes particle swarm optimization). We notice that most published works use either *L*-Lipschitz continuity or a classifier to infer the safety of input points. VA [18] and GoOSE [34] are methods that augment other algorithms to handle the safety of input points.

Table 2 divides the algorithms by the environment they assume: MDP or non-MDP. For each algorithm, the column *Initial safe seed* shows whether it requires at least one starting input point known to be safe. The column *Safety likelihood* presents the form in which safety of unobserved input points is predicted, either using labels derived from a classifier (safe vs unsafe) or safety constraint(s) (safe set vs the others) (*Label*), probability of safety estimated from a classifier (*Probability*), or none (safety is not inferred: *NI*). As shown in the table, classifiers are used to both predict safety labels of input points and calculate probability of safety. The column *Number of objectives* gives the number of objective functions considered by the algorithm. For example, the number of objectives that GoOSE [34] can handle is problem-specific as the algorithm is augmented onto algorithms that do not have a built-in approach to cope with safety constraints (similar to VA [18]) and thus is driven by the number of objectives that the underlying algorithm is dealing with. The column *Safety constraints* show how many safety constraint(s) can be handled by the algorithm, noticing that some algorithms are limited to a single *safety constraint*. MDP problems additionally include various forms of *ergodicity* as a safety requirement.

4.1   Evolutionary Algorithms (EAs)

Arguably, the evolutionary computation community was one of the first to investigate safety issues as defined in this paper. The work of Kaji et al. [18] in 2009

Table 1. Characterization of existing safe learning and optimization algorithms (part 1).

Discipline	Paper	Year	Algorithm	Method	Comment
Optimization					
EA	Kaji et al. [18]	2009	VA	NNs	VA is a classifier augmented onto other EAs replacing their offspring generation process.
	Allmendinger and Knowles [2]	2011	TGA, RBS and PHC		Various EAs were proposed.
GPR	Sui et al. [30]	2015	SAFEOPT	L-Lipschitz continuity	Inspired several safe algorithms [6,7,10,31,33–35].
	Berkenkamp et al. [7]	2016	Modified SAFEOPT		Lipschitz constant-free model.
	Berkenkamp et al. [6]	2016	SAFEOPT-MC	L-Lipschitz continuity	Multiple safety constraints are dealt with.
	Duivenvoorden et al. [10]	2017	Swarm-based SAFEOPT	PSO	Lipschitz constant-free model.
	Schillinger et al. [24]	2017	SBO		Application of SAL [26] to optimization problem.
	Sui et al. [31]	2018	STAGEOPT	L-Lipschitz continuity	Multiple safety constraints are dealt with. Optimization is performed in two independent processes: learning and optimization stages.
	Bachoc et al. [4]	2020	EFI GPC sign	GPC	A problem-specific GPC was proposed.
GPR with EA	Sacher et al. [23]	2018	EGO-LS-SVM	LS-SVM	GPR is used combined with EA.
Learning					
Reinforcement learning	Turchetta et al. [33]	2016	SAFEMDP	MDP, GPR, L-Lipschitz continuity	Application of SAFEOPT to exploration task.
	Wachi et al. [35]	2018	SAFEEXPOPT-MDP	MDPs, GPR, L-Lipschitz continuity	Extension of SAFEMDP made to maximize cumulative reward while safely exploring the state space.
	Turchetta et al. [34]	2019	GoOSE	GPR, L-Lipschitz continuity	The algorithm is augmented onto other unsafe exploration algorithms.
	Biyik et al. [8]	2019	SEOFUR	MDP, L-Lipschitz continuity	Transition functions are unknown.
Active learning	Schreiter et al. [26]	2015	SAL	GPR, GPC	A problem-specific GPC was introduced.
	Schillinger et al. [25]	2018	SAL	GPR	Application of SAL to high pressure fuel supply system (HPFS).

Table 2. Characterization of existing safe learning and optimization algorithms (part 2).

Environment	Algorithm	Initial safe seed	Safety likelihood	Number of objectives	Safety constraints
Non-MDP	VA [18]	Not required	Label	Single/Multiple	One or multiple
	TGA, RBS, and PHC [2]	Not required	NI	Single	One
	SAFEOPT [30]	Required	Label	Single	One
	Modified SAFEOPT [7]	Required	Label	Single	One
	SAFEOPT-MC [6]	Required	Label	Single	One or multiple
	Swarm-based SAFEOPT [10]	Required	Label	Single	One or multiple
	STAGEOPT [31]	Required	Label	Single	One or multiple
	SAL [26]	Required	Label	Single	One
	SBO [24]	Required	Label	Single	One
	SAL [25]	Required	Label	Single	One
	EGO-LS-SVM [23]	Not required	Probability/Label	Single	One or multiple
	EFI GPC sign [4]	Not required	Probability	Single	One
MDP	SAFEMDP [33]	Required	Label	Single	One *safety constraint* *Ergodicity:* One-step reachability and returnability
	SAFEEXPOPT-MDP [35]	Required	Label	Single	One *safety constraint* *Ergodicity:* One-step reachability and returnability
	SEOFUR [8]	Required	Label	Single	Multiple *safety constraints* *Ergodicity:* Returnability
	GoOSE [34]	Required	Label	Single/Multiple	One *safety constraint* *Ergodicity:* n-step reachability and returnability

introduced the violation avoidance (VA) method, a classification tool that is augmented onto an EA, while the work of Allmendinger and Knowles [2] in 2011 investigated the impact of safety issues on different stochastic optimizers (TGA, RBS, PHC). VA is able to deal with either binary or continuous input variables, while the optimizers considered in [2] assumed binary input variables.

The purpose of the Violation Avoidance (VA) method [18] is to avoid *risky* evaluations by replacing the ordinary offspring generation process of EAs. It applies the nearest neighbors method (NNs) using a weighted distance to decide over the safety of an input point prior to evaluating it. VA assumes the safety label of an input point to be same as the label of the nearest previously evaluated input point.[1]

Allmendinger and Knowles [2] studied reconfigurable, destructible and unreplaceable experimental platforms in closed-loop optimization using EAs. Three types of EAs were investigated varying in the way offspring are generated and the level of collaboration of the individuals in a population. The EAs optimized a single objective function, while avoiding trials that have an output value less than a pre-defined (but unknown to the optimizer) lethal threshold, i.e. the safety threshold (h_j) in Eq. (1). An optimization run was terminated if a predefined number of unsafe input points was evaluated or a maximum number of function evaluations reached. No mechanism was put in place to determine safety of an input point prior to evaluating it, but any evaluated unsafe input point was banned from entering the population as a way to guide the population away from the unsafe region in the search space.

4.2 Algorithms Related to SAFEOPT

Several safe learning and optimization algorithms are based on GPR, L-Lipschitz continuity and set theory. SAFEOPT [30] was the first algorithm of this type, and has inspired others to follow, such as modified SAFEOPT [7], SAFEOPT-MC [6], Swarm-based SAFEOPT [10], STAGEOPT [31], SAFEMDP [33], SAFEEXPOPT-MDP [35], Safe Exploration Optimized For Uncertainty Reduction (SEOFUR [8]) and GoOSE [34].

SAFEOPT [30] was proposed in 2015 for safe optimization aiming to avoid evaluating any *unsafe* input points altogether during the search, i.e., the number of allowed failures is zero. Roughly speaking, the algorithm uses a GP to model the objective function, which together with a known safety threshold is taken as the safety constraint, and the algorithm selects an input point that has the maximum width of confidence interval among those belonging to a *maximizers set* or *expanders set*. The algorithm constructs a safe set using the *safe set operator* (Eq. 4), and to construct the *expanders set* it uses the *optimistic expander operator* (Eq. 5). That is, given an input point deemed to be safe and whose evaluation could potentially help to classify additional input points as safe, then (i) it belongs to the *expanders set* and (ii) the *maximizers set* will comprise input points belonging to the safe set whose upper confidence bound is greater than

---

[1] The notion of risk is considered more formally in SAL [26], discussed in Sect. 4.3.

the greatest lower confidence bound among those calculated for all input points in the safe set. Intuitively speaking, generating *expanders set* and *maximizers set* corresponds to classifying input points in the safe set into (i) *safe set expansion*, which is expected to expand the safe set at the next iteration, and (ii) *safe set exploitation*, which is likely to yield high output value at the current iteration, by evaluating an input point in the set at the current iteration. Generally, whether to expand or exploit is decided at each step of the algorithm. SAFEOPT [30] uses intersectional confidence intervals (Eq. 7), and the same is done by SAFEMDP [33], SAFEEXPOPT-MDP [35], STAGEOPT [31] and GoOSE [34].

In general, algorithms inspired by SAFEOPT [30] share the fundamental structure of SAFEOPT [30]: Constructing the safe set first, and then using it to construct the *expanders set* and *maximizers set*. However, there are some distinctive features between the algorithms. In 2016, three algorithms were proposed: Modified SAFEOPT [7], SAFEOPT-MC [6] and SAFEMDP [33]. Unlike the original SAFEOPT approach [30], the modified SAFEOPT [7] estimates the safe, *maximizers* and *expanders* sets without the specification of a Lipschitz constant. The safe set consists of input points whose lower confidence bound is greater than a safety threshold. To estimate the *expanders* set, the algorithm constructs a GP based on both previously evaluated input points and an artificial data point (with a noiseless measurement of the upper confidence bound) selected from the safe set (as opposed to using previously evaluated input points only as done in the original SAFEOPT approach). SAFEOPT-MC can deal with multiple constraints, and SAFEMDP applies SAFEOPT to RL problems. Swarm-based SAFEOPT [10], proposed in 2017, applies a variant of PSO to SAFEOPT, where multiple independent swarms (sets of input points) are used to construct the *maximizers set* and *expanders set*. The objective function differs across swarms to reflect the different goals when constructing the *maximizers* and *expanders set*. Initialized with initial safe seeds, it updates the safe set only when the input points (also referred to as particles in PSO), found at each run of the PSO, are sufficiently far away from the safe input points in the safe set. Here, input points whose lower confidence bound is greater than a safety threshold are assumed to be safe. The input points in the safe set are used to decide the initial positions of the particles at each iteration. As in typical PSO, the particles move toward new positions by considering their current positions and velocities. In 2018, Sui et al. [31] and Wachi et al. [35] proposed the algorithms STAGEOPT and SAFEEXPOPT-MDP, respectively. STAGEOPT can deal with multiple safety constraints and divides the process in two independent stages: Safe region expansion stage and optimization stage corresponding to *safe set exploration* and *safe set exploitation* [31], respectively. SAFEEXPOPT-MDP is an extension of SAFEMDP (e.g., unsafe set, uncertain set, etc.), and its goal is to maximize the cumulative reward rather than *safe set expansion* (i.e., the safety function is not the objective function). Lastly, in 2019, the RL community proposed the algorithm GoOSE [34], which is augmented onto other unsafe algorithms as a way to control the selection of safe input points.

Algorithms able to handle problems with multiple safety constraints, e.g., SAFEOPT-MC [6] and STAGEOPT [31], model the individual safety constraints, as well as the objective function, using independent GPs. Then, the safe set is the intersection of safe sets estimated from the safety functions, where the *safe set operator* (Eq. 4) is applied to each safety function separately. Now let us remind that the *maximizers set* is used for *safe set exploitation*, meaning this set is constructed based on the objective function values of input points in the current safe set (ignoring information from the safety functions). Since there is one objective function only, the algorithms SAFEOPT and SAFEOPT-MC construct the *maximizers set* using the same approach. However, it is not required for STAGEOPT, as it has its own independent stage devoted for *safe set exploitation*, and optimization is dealt with by input point selection criterion in that stage. Lastly, *optimistic expander operator* (Eq. 5) is applied to each safety constraint, and all of them should be met when including an input point from the safe set into the *expanders set*. However, SAFEOPT-MC and STAGEOPT apply the structure in slightly different ways, e.g., they define Lipschitz constant(s) and safety threshold(s) differently. When SAFEOPT is applied to RL problems [33,35], the set of states allowed to visit is restricted by *ergodicity*. This means that the suggested states should be reachable in one-step and returnable to states in the safe set, established at the previous iteration, in several steps. However, GoOSE [34] applies n-step expansion until convergence of safe set and *expanders set* at each algorithm iteration by applying n-step reachability and returnability. GoOSE is augmented onto an unsafe RL or Bayesian optimization algorithm (i.e., one that is not designed to deal with safety constraints). The unsafe algorithm suggests an input point $\mathbf{x}^*$ that belongs to an *optimistic safe set*. Then, GoOSE evaluates input points from the *expanders set*, until $\mathbf{x}^*$ is inferred to be safe. Otherwise, GoOSE asks for another input point from the unsafe algorithm. In GoOSE, however, additional conditions are used with *optimistic expander operator* for constructing *expanders set*.

SEOFUR [8] is an algorithm for safe exploration of deterministic MDPs with unknown transition functions. Starting from a known safe state set and a list of actions that connect the safe states, and assuming that the unknown transition function is L-Lipschitz continuous over both states and actions, the algorithm tries to efficiently and safely explore the search space. The learned (known) transitions are represented in form of a (deterministic) transition function, while an uncertain transition function is defined to handle unknown states. The uncertain transition function maps each state-action pair to all of its possible outcomes, and if there is a state-action pair whose possible outcomes constitute a subset of the known safe state set, then the state is deemed safe. This problem-specific *safe set expansion* method is repeated at each algorithm iteration until it converges (n-step returnability). The algorithm removes uncertainty as much as possible at each iteration by greedily optimizing an expected uncertainty reduction measure. The paper [8] applies SEOFUR to a simulation problem with safety constraints.

4.3 Safe Learning and Optimization with a Classifier

In addition to the VA method [18] (Sect. 4.1), there are three more algorithms that use a classification method for safety inference of input points: Safe Active Learning (SAL) [26], EGO-LS-SVM [23] and *EFI GPC sign* [4]. In particular, EGO-LS-SVM [23] and *EFI GPC sign* [4] were proposed to avoid simulations from crashing.

SAL [26] is an algorithm for learning a regression model when unknown regions of the input space can be unsafe. SAL builds two GPs to approximate an objective function and a discriminative function, mapped to the unit interval to describe the class (i.e., safe or unsafe) likelihood, for a problem-specific Gaussian Process classifier (GPC). SAL assumes that each evaluated input point $\mathbf{x}$ provides two additional output values: A negative (unsafe) or positive (safe) label $c(\mathbf{x}) \in \{-1, +1\}$ and the value of a black-box, possibly noisy function $h\colon \mathbb{X} \to (-1, 1)$, where $\mathbb{X} \subset \mathbb{R}^m$ for m-dimensional input points. The function $h(\mathbf{x})$ provides a noisy *risk* value for evaluated safe points $\mathbf{x} \in \mathbb{X}$ (i.e., $c(\mathbf{x}) = +1$) close to the unknown boundary of the safe input region, while it provides no useful information for unsafe points, i.e., $c(\mathbf{x}) = -1$. SAL also assumes an upper bound for the expected number of failures. At each iteration, the algorithm selects an input point with the highest conditional variance given previous observations among those expected to be safe according to the GPC. Safe Bayesian Optimization (SBO) [24] is fundamentally the same as SAL with the core difference being that, at each iteration of the algorithm, it selects an input point whose lower confidence bound is the minimum, assuming minimization of the loss function. Another difference between SAL and SBO is that in SBO a standard GP regression, which is trained with discriminative function values only, is used for the discriminative function, while the use of class labels (safe vs unsafe) for training GPC is also an option for SAL. Training a standard GP with discriminative function values only was also the approach adopted in [25], where SAL was applied to safe learning of a high pressure fuel supply system.

EGO-LS-SVM [23] has been designed for safe optimization of complex systems, where simulations are subject to abrupt terminations due to unphysical configurations, ill-posed problems or lack of numerical robustness. That is, it assumes that there is a non-computable sub-domain in the search domain that cannot be expressed by inequality constraints, and thus, applies a binary classifier (least-squares support vector machine or LS-SVM) for this sub-domain. However, the classifier may be used with some inequality constraints that define other non-computable sub-domains. EGO-LS-SVM constructs an independent GP to model an objective function, and assigns observations into the *safe* or *unsafe class*, which represent computable and non-computable input points, respectively. Based on the safety labels attached to the previous observations, LS-SVM predicts the probability that an input point belongs to the safe/unsafe class. The paper [23] also proposed four different selection criteria for the next input point that combine this probability with the augmented expected improvement (AEI) acquisition function [17], which is an input point selection function for Bayesian optimization. Another interesting aspect of the algorithm is that it uses the Covariance Matrix Adaptation Evolutionary Strategy (CMA-ES) [16] to estimate the hyper-parameters of the kernel function for GP regression and for LS-SVM.

Lastly, *EFI GPC sign* [4] was also designed to prevent simulation crashes; thus, it aims to progress an optimization process by efficiently avoiding input points that are likely to fail. In this context, the safety function is binary (safe/unsafe) and a failure implies that the objective function cannot be evaluated. The approach differs from EGO-LS-SVM in that it cannot construct multiple models for safety constraints. *EFI GPC sign* constructs a GP for learning binary inputs, representing safe/unsafe evaluations, that is different from the classical GPC and more appropriate for deterministic safety functions. In addition, GPR is used to model the objective function by keeping only the safe input points. Finally, *EFI GPC sign* selects an input point by considering the probability of non-failure multiplied by the standard expected improvement acquisition function.

5   Discussion and Future Research

In this paper, we reviewed and contextualized 18 algorithms designed for safe learning and optimization.

Two studies in the area of evolutionary computing [2,18] proposed algorithms (VA [18] and modified versions of EAs [2]) designed for safe optimization. In particular, VA [18] is a flexible approach that can be augmented onto other EAs.

Except for SEOFUR [8] and the aforementioned EAs, the other safe learning and optimization algorithms reviewed in this survey are based on GP regression. However, we are able to observe a trend and can divide these algorithms into categories. The first division we observe is that algorithms adopt the L-Lipschitz continuity assumption [6,8,30,31,33–35], use the lower confidence bound [7,10], or apply a classifier to measure the safety of input points [4,23–26]. Interestingly, it was found that modified SAFEOPT [7] and Swarm-based SAFEOPT [10] share a similar structure with algorithms using the L-Lipschitz continuity assumption, but are free from deciding the Lipschitz constant. Furthermore, SEOFUR [8] is based on a method that applies the L-Lipschitz continuity assumption for the problems where transition functions are unknown. Also, while some algorithms [4,7,24–26,30,33–35] deal with one *safety constraint*, others [6,10,23,31] can handle multiple ones. Lastly, while *ergodicity* and *safety constraint*(s) were classified as different concepts applied to distinctive approaches in a previous survey in 2015 [13], we observed that they are used together in SAFEMDP [33], SAFEEXPOPT-MDP [35] and GoOSE [34].

Given the above observations, we envision several open questions for future research. First, how to estimate the Lipschitz constant and safety threshold when these are *a priori* unknown. Second, are there real-world applications that would benefit/require alternative formulations of the problem, such as safety thresholds being a function of the input variables and/or change over time, i.e., use $h_j(\mathbf{x})$,

$h_j(t)$ or $h_j(\mathbf{x}, t)$ instead of a fixed constant h_j. Finally, it is not clear how to apply multiple safety constraints to MDP problems.

Acknowledgements. M. López-Ibáñez is a "Beatriz Galindo" Senior Distinguished Researcher (BEAGAL 18/00053) funded by the Spanish Ministry of Science and Innovation.

References

1. Allmendinger, R.: Tuning evolutionary search for closed-loop optimization. Ph.D. thesis, The University of Manchester, UK (2012)
2. Allmendinger, R., Knowles, J.D.: Evolutionary search in lethal environments. In: International Conference on Evolutionary Computation Theory and Applications, pp. 63–72. SciTePress (2011)
3. Auer, P.: Using confidence bounds for exploitation-exploration trade-offs. J. Mach. Learn. Res. **3**, 397–422 (2002)
4. Bachoc, F., Helbert, C., Picheny, V.: Gaussian process optimization with failures: classification and convergence proof. J. Glob. Optim. **78**, 483–506 (2020). https://doi.org/10.1007/s10898-020-00920-0
5. Bäck, T.: Evolutionary Algorithms in Theory and Practice: Evolution Strategies, Evolutionary Programming, Genetic Algorithms. Oxford University Press, Oxford (1996)
6. Berkenkamp, F., Krause, A., Schoellig, A.P.: Bayesian optimization with safety constraints: safe and automatic parameter tuning in robotics. arXiv preprint arXiv:1602.04450 (2016)
7. Berkenkamp, F., Schoellig, A.P., Krause, A.: Safe controller optimization for quadrotors with Gaussian processes. In: 2016 IEEE International Conference on Robotics and Automation (ICRA), pp. 491–496. IEEE (2016)
8. Bıyık, E., Margoliash, J., Alimo, S.R., Sadigh, D.: Efficient and safe exploration in deterministic Markov decision processes with unknown transition models. In: 2019 American Control Conference (ACC), pp. 1792–1799. IEEE (2019)
9. Brochu, E., Cora, V., de Freitas, N.: A tutorial on Bayesian optimization of expensive cost functions, with application to active user modeling and hierarchical reinforcement learning. arXiv preprint arXiv:1012.2599, December 2010
10. Duivenvoorden, R.R.P.R., Berkenkamp, F., Carion, N., Krause, A., Schoellig, A.P.: Constrained Bayesian optimization with particle swarms for safe adaptive controller tuning. IFAC-PapersOnLine **50**(1), 11800–11807 (2017)
11. Ferrer, J., López-Ibáñez, M., Alba, E.: Reliable simulation-optimization of traffic lights in a real-world city. Appl. Soft Comput. **78**, 697–711 (2019)
12. Forrester, A.I.J., Keane, A.J.: Recent advances in surrogate-based optimization. Prog. Aerosp. Sci. **45**(1–3), 50–79 (2009)
13. García, J., Fernández, F.: A comprehensive survey on safe reinforcement learning. J. Mach. Learn. Res. **16**(1), 1437–1480 (2015)
14. Geibel, P.: Reinforcement learning for MDPs with constraints. In: Fürnkranz, J., Scheffer, T., Spiliopoulou, M. (eds.) ECML 2006. LNCS (LNAI), vol. 4212, pp. 646–653. Springer, Heidelberg (2006). https://doi.org/10.1007/11871842_63
15. Gosavi, A.: Reinforcement learning: a tutorial survey and recent advances. INFORMS J. Comput. **21**(2), 178–192 (2009)

16. Hansen, N., Ostermeier, A.: Completely derandomized self-adaptation in evolution strategies. Evol. Comput. **9**(2), 159–195 (2001)
17. Huang, D., Allen, T.T., Notz, W.I., Zeng, N.: Global optimization of stochastic black-box systems via sequential kriging meta-models. J. Global Optim. **34**(3), 441–466 (2006). https://doi.org/10.1007/s10898-005-2454-3
18. Kaji, H., Ikeda, K., Kita, H.: Avoidance of constraint violation for experiment-based evolutionary multi-objective optimization. In: Proceedings of the 2009 Congress on Evolutionary Computation (CEC 2009), pp. 2756–2763. IEEE Press, Piscataway (2009)
19. Knowles, J.D.: Closed-loop evolutionary multiobjective optimization. IEEE Comput. Intell. Mag. **4**, 77–91 (2009)
20. Likar, B., Kocijan, J.: Predictive control of a gas-liquid separation plant based on a Gaussian process model. Comput. Chem. Eng. **31**(3), 142–152 (2007)
21. Moldovan, T.M., Abbeel, P.: Safe exploration in Markov decision processes. In: Langford, J., Pineau, J. (eds.) Proceedings of the 29th International Conference on Machine Learning, ICML 2012, pp. 1451–1458. Omnipress (2012)
22. Rasmussen, C.E., Williams, C.K.I.: Gaussian Processes for Machine Learning. MIT Press, Cambridge (2006)
23. Sacher, M., et al.: A classification approach to efficient global optimization in presence of non-computable domains. Struct. Multidiscip. Optim. **58**(4), 1537–1557 (2018). https://doi.org/10.1007/s00158-018-1981-8
24. Schillinger, M., Hartmann, B., Skalecki, P., Meister, M., Nguyen-Tuong, D., Nelles, O.: Safe active learning and safe Bayesian optimization for tuning a PI-controller. IFAC-PapersOnLine **50**(1), 5967–5972 (2017)
25. Schillinger, M., et al.: Safe active learning of a high pressure fuel supply system. In: Proceedings of the 9th EUROSIM Congress on Modelling and Simulation, EUROSIM 2016 and the 57th SIMS Conference on Simulation and Modelling SIMS 2016, pp. 286–292, Linköping University Electronic Press (2018)
26. Schreiter, J., Nguyen-Tuong, D., Eberts, M., Bischoff, B., Markert, H., Toussaint, M.: Safe exploration for active learning with Gaussian processes. In: Bifet, A., et al. (eds.) ECML PKDD 2015. LNCS (LNAI), vol. 9286, pp. 133–149. Springer, Cham (2015). https://doi.org/10.1007/978-3-319-23461-8_9
27. Schulz, E., Speekenbrink, M., Krause, A.: A tutorial on Gaussian process regression: modelling, exploring, and exploiting functions. J. Math. Psychol. **85**, 1–16 (2018)
28. Small, B.G., et al.: Efficient discovery of anti-inflammatory small-molecule combinations using evolutionary computing. Nat. Chem. Biol. **7**(12), 902–908 (2011)
29. Snoek, J., Larochelle, H., Adams, R.P.: Practical Bayesian optimization of machine learning algorithms. In: Bartlett, P.L., Pereira, F.C.N., Burges, C.J.C., Bottou, L., Weinberger, K.Q. (eds.) Advances in Neural Information Processing Systems (NIPS 25), pp. 2960–2968. Curran Associates, Red Hook (2012)
30. Sui, Y., Gotovos, A., Burdick, J.W., Krause, A.: Safe exploration for optimization with Gaussian processes. In: Bach, F., Blei, D. (eds.) Proceedings of the 32nd International Conference on Machine Learning, ICML 2015, vol. 37, pp. 997–1005 (2015)
31. Sui, Y., Zhuang, V., Burdick, J.W., Yue, Y.: Stagewise safe Bayesian optimization with Gaussian processes. In: Dy, J.G., Krause, A. (eds.) Proceedings of the 35th International Conference on Machine Learning, ICML 2018. Proceedings of Machine Learning Research, vol. 80, pp. 4788–4796. PMLR (2018)
32. Sutton, R.S., Barto, A.G.: Reinforcement Learning: An Introduction, 2nd edn. MIT Press, Cambridge (2018)

33. Turchetta, M., Berkenkamp, F., Krause, A.: Safe exploration in finite Markov decision processes with Gaussian processes. In: Lee, D.D., Sugiyama, M., Luxburg, U.V., Guyon, I., Garnett, R. (eds.) Advances in Neural Information Processing Systems (NIPS 29), pp. 4312–4320 (2016)
34. Turchetta, M., Berkenkamp, F., Krause, A.: Safe exploration for interactive machine learning. In: Wallach, H.M., Larochelle, H., Beygelzimer, A., d'Alché-Buc, F., Fox, E.B., Garnett, R. (eds.) Advances in Neural Information Processing Systems (NIPS 32), pp. 2887–2897 (2019)
35. Wachi, A., Sui, Y., Yue, Y., Ono, M.: Safe exploration and optimization of constrained MDPs using Gaussian processes. In: McIlraith, S.A., Weinberger, K.Q. (eds.) AAAI Conference on Artificial Intelligence, pp. 6548–6556, AAAI Press, February 2018

A Causal Framework for Understanding Optimisation Algorithms

Alberto Franzin$^{(\boxtimes)}$ and Thomas Stützle

IRIDIA, Université Libre de Bruxelles (ULB), Brussels, Belgium
{afranzin,stuetzle}@ulb.ac.be

1 Introduction

Over the last decades, plenty of exact and non-exact methods have been proposed to tackle NP-hard optimisation problems. Despite the wide success of these methods, however, understanding their behaviour is still an open research question of fundamental interest [2]. Stochastic Local Search (SLS) algorithms mostly provide no guarantees on the running time or the quality of the solution returned [4]. Theoretical analyses of SLS behaviour are limited to specific cases or unrealistic assumptions such as infinite running time. The internal behaviour of branch-and-bound, the basis for state-of-the-art exact algorithms, is chaotic, and therefore it is almost impossible to predict the performance of a solver on a problem instance. Yet, all these algorithms are routinely used with success in countless applications. Thus, the gap between theoretical analyses and practical results is still very large.

In recent years, however, the adoption of rigorous experimental practices led many researchers to develop mathematical and statistical tools to gain insights in algorithmic behaviour. Several works now employ systematic experiments, qualitative comparisons between algorithms, or computational statistical techniques. Data-driven analyses have led to the development of algorithms that leverage the knowledge obtained on data collected on specific problems to make informed decisions during the search process. Automatic algorithm selection and configuration techniques are used to relieve practitioners of the burden of running extensive computational experiments and making unbiased decisions on the choice, respectively, of an algorithm and of a parameter configuration that are likely to perform well on an instance. However, they generate data about the effectiveness of each algorithm or parameter choice in the scenarios considered. This data can not only be used to drive the configuration process, but it can also be used to study algorithmic behaviour.

On the problem side, fitness landscape analyses aim to understand how the solution space of a certain problem instance impacts on the performance of a search algorithm. For example, it is easier for an algorithm to converge to a good solution in a smooth landscape, rather than on a more rugged one with lots of locally optimal solutions with poor quality.

In the literature, however, little work has been done to formally connect these related areas of research. The main issue lies in the difficulty of generalizing the many results obtained for specific problems, instances and algorithms to

© Springer Nature Switzerland AG 2021
F. Heintz et al. (Eds.): TAILOR 2020, LNAI 12641, pp. 140–145, 2021.
https://doi.org/10.1007/978-3-030-73959-1_13

other scenarios. In turn, this difficulty arises from the huge number of options we can choose from, on the stochasticity of the algorithms and instances, and on the computational burden of generating usable information, for example by computing features for a given problem. Algorithm selection usually relies on problem-specific instance features, so insights obtained for e.g. Traveling Salesman Problem (TSP) instances are not easily transferrable to SAT, QAP, or other combinatorial optimisation problems. Algorithm configuration can make an algorithm improve its performance, but current tools do not offer many explanations for their results, and common benchmarks are used mainly to raise the bar. The data generated can help in understanding algorithm performance, but to obtain insights the practitioner still needs to carefully inspect the outcome. Fitness landscape analyses are usually difficult to translate into an algorithm implementation or selection.

In this work, we propose a causal framework to represent the interaction between the entities involved in the resolution of an optimisation problem, and show how several approaches proposed to study algorithmic behaviour can be represented on this framework. With such models we can formally represent a theory or set of beliefs we hold about a certain system. A causal model [6] can be represented as a directed acyclic graph (DAG) whose nodes are the variables of the system under study. The variables can be divided into *exogenous* variables, whose values are determined by reasons external to the model, and *endogenous* variables, whose values are determined only by a subset of the other variables. The arcs encode the causal relationship between the variables, so that the value of an endogenous variable is probabilistically determined by the value of its parent nodes.

2   Causal Models for SLS Algorithms

Causal models provide an appropriate framework for this task, for several reasons. First, they explicitly encode the causality relationships between entities, and in our case such relationships are intuitively clear. In fact, we are convinced that in many works aimed at understanding algorithmic behaviour the authors already implicitly assume such causality relationships. On causal models we can perform inference, that is, estimate some unobserved variables given the value of other observed ones; and this is precisely how we consider the various tasks of algorithm selection and configuration, and several of approaches mentioned above. Causal models can also be used to analyse data collected from different sources and experiments.

While in this work we focus on trajectory-based SLS algorithms for non-constrained combinatorial optimisation problems, our framework can be extended to include other methods and different problem classes. We start from four working hypotheses, each one building on the previous one.

(H1) An Algorithm can be Divided into Basic Components and Parameters. We take a component-based view of SLS algorithms [3,7], that is, we consider an algorithm as a set of basic building blocks, each one possibly coming with a set of parameters, combined together in a certain way.

(H2) Separation Between Algorithm- and Problem-Specific Components. Following (H1), algorithmic blocks are divided in problem-specific and algorithm-specific. Problem-specific components are the parts of a SLS that require specific knowledge of the problem under study, while algorithm-specific components are all the components that define what a SLS is and can be used across different unrelated problems. Thus, a SLS is defined by its algorithmic-specific components and their combination, and an instantiation of a SLS for a problem is the combination of the algorithm-specific components with a set of problem-specific components.

(H3) An Algorithm Operates a Traversal of the Search Space. A SLS works by traversing solutions in a search space. The problem-specific components of a SLS are needed to (i) select one starting point of this traversal, and to (ii) evaluate another solution in the search space, relative to the current one. The separation of the problem-specific components of (H2) can be considered the simulation of an oracle that gives us the desired information about a solution when polled. Thus, we can ideally assume to have complete knowledge of the entire search space, turning any optimisation problem into a search problem for which we do not need additional knowledge on the problem anymore. This assumption lets us bridge the insights we obtain across different problems.

(H4) Identification of Optimal Algorithm Behaviour. For obtaining optimal results on a search space, an algorithm needs to reach an optimal trade-off and alternance of exploration and exploitation behaviour. This optimal behaviour differs for different landscapes, but several different algorithm can, in principle, reach this desired behaviour. In practice, we assume we can identify and configure an algorithm that obtains results that are "good enough" for our purpose.

Starting from these four working hypothesis, we build our causal framework. We consider problems and instances as given inputs to tackle, using an algorithm built starting from the basic components; the efficiency of the algorithm depends also on the computational environment (such as machine power or running time). These factors are the *causes* for the *effects*, the results obtained. What relates the inputs to the results, is how efficiently the algorithm can traverse the search space, that is, how it can efficiently balance diversification and intensification, based on the characteristics of the instance. These characteristics can be represented by the features and the fitness landscape.

The general causal framework representing the theory is shown in Fig. 1. In the general framework each node is actually a macro-node representing a set of nodes, grouped together by their function.

High-Level Entities. I represents the problem instances. P represents the problems. Following (H2), PA is the set of problem-specific components and algorithms (e.g. initial solutions, neighbourhoods, heuristics), and SA the set of algorithm-specific components that compose the search part of the algorithm. Components in PA and SA include both algorithmic functions such as neighbourhoods, acceptance criteria, . . . , but also numerical parameters.

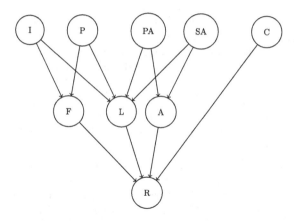

Fig. 1. A generic causal framework representing the interaction between problems, instances, algorithms and results. Arcs represent the causal relationships between the high-level nodes. In a practical application, not all the nodes might be observed, and not all the nodes might be present, depending on the specific instantiation of the problem under study.

A is the set of algorithms that we can use for solving an instance $i_p \in I$ of problem $p \in P$; differently from PA and SA, an algorithm $a \in A$ is an instantiated and fully configured one. The separation of A from its components collected in PA and SA follows from (H1).

C represents the set of computational factors that impact an actual implementation of any algorithm $a \in A$, such as the computational power, running time, random seed, but also quality of the implementation, and any other possible factor affecting the computation.

F contains both the set of instance features, such as the instance size, and the problem-specific features. L represents instead the fitness landscape and the search space features, e.g. the ruggedness or the number of local optima.

Finally, R models the results that can be obtained by an algorithm $a \in A$ on an instance i_p for a problem $p \in P$, under the computational environment specified in C.

Causal Relationships. $\{I, P, PA, SA, C\}$ form the set of exogenous variables, the ones we set when we tackle an optimisation problem; $\{F, L, A, R\}$ are the endogenous variables, whose value depends on other variables, either deterministically or in a probabilistic way.

In F we include features defined solely on the instance itself and by both instance and problem, so we have incoming arcs from I and P. These features do not depend on the algorithm we choose, but are instead properties that arise when we define a specific problem instance.

In L, landscape features arise from the contribution of P and I; their differentiation from L is somewhat arbitrary, but by grouping them into a separate set we reflect in a clear way our working hypothesis (H3) and their "dynamic" characterization with respect to "static" features represented in F. In L we can include probing statistics or other features obtained with a phase of search space traversal by some search algorithm; for them we include arcs from PA and SA to L. Note, however, that the features generated using elements in PA are considered mere properties of the landscape, and not an evaluation of the algorithm (components). Thus, we do not include any arc to F or L from A, as it represents the algorithm used to produce the results, and not from C as we do not assume, in principle, a limitation on the possibility of computing features.

According to (H1) and (H2), an algorithm in A can be instantiated combining components from PA and SA, hence the incoming arcs.

Finally, the results R for an instance in I of a problem in P depend on the performance of an algorithm in A, under the computational environment represented in C; however, following our working hypothesis (H3), once an algorithm from A has been instantiated, it operates on a search space (here represented by L) and can be considered, at that point, unaware of the specific problem that generated F and L. In other words, F and L provide an intermediate (mediator) level of "reasons" that can help us in understanding the performance of A for I under the computational environment specified in C. The relationship here is probabilistic, for the stochastic nature of the algorithms and of the computational environment (hardware faults, etc.) that make effectively impossible to relate deterministically the causes with the results.

At this higher level, we do not need to assume any inter-node connection, that is, the nodes composing the high-level entities are not directly connected to each other, since they are defined either as exogenous variables, or as determined by other entities. Causal and inferential reasoning is as in any causal model [6]. Since there is no edge inside each macro-node, all the flows of information we define on the framework apply also when we "open" the macro-nodes into their constituting nodes.

3   Algorithm Selection and Configuration in the Framework

The main goal of this work is to show how this causal framework can relate several existing approaches, in particular considering them as inference problems. For example, the Algorithm Selection Problem (ASP) requires to find the best algorithm in a portfolio of available ones (in our framework, $a \in A$) for a given set of instances (from I), which are characterized by a set of features (represented in F and L). With (H1) and (H2) we assume that we can instantiate at least one, and possibly more, algorithms from A. Since the selection is made by observing the results R for the alternatives evaluated, we can define ASP as the inference task of finding $a \in A$ given the observed variables in $\{R, F, L, C\}$.

Similarly, the Algorithm Configuration Problem (ACP) requires to find an optimal set of parameters and components (in SA and PA) for a given set of instances (in I) of a problem in P, under computational constraints specified in C. The usual black box formulation of ACP does not make use of any feature, but makes the choice based only on the observed results R. Hence, the ACP can be formulated as the problem of inferring values for the variables in PA, SA given the observed variables in $\{P, I, R, C\}$.

Therefore, we can clearly see the relationship between ASP and ACP. They are both inference tasks on problem and instances, whose outcome depends on the results (in fact, the racing algorithm proposed in 1994 for model selection was subsequently used for configuring algorithms [1]). They instead differ in the practical use, that is, (i) whether we use fully configured algorithms (in A, for ASP) or building blocks (in PA and SA, for ACP), and (ii) if we can observe (and use in the selection or configuration process) some features in F or L. The separation is, however, neither crisp nor immutable. Some configurators can indeed make use of features [5]. By observing any feature in F or L in a configuration or PbO task we open the black box and move towards a selection setting; by allowing the configuration of numerical parameters of the algorithms in a portfolio for a selection task we have the CASH problem [8], instantiated as PA, PA given $\{R, F, L, C\}$.

We have defined a causal framework that models the causal relationships between the entities involved when tackling an optimisation problem. As first examples, we have shown how we can model ACP and ASP as inference tasks. However, several other approaches can be described according to this framework, thus contributing towards an improved ability of understanding and explaning how SLS algorithms work. In future work we are also going to exploit the properties of causal models to tackle other open problems such as transfer learning of configurations across different objective functions.

References

1. Birattari, M., Stützle, T., Paquete, L., Varrentrapp, K.: A racing algorithm for configuring metaheuristics. In: GECCO. Morgan Kaufmann Publishers (2002)
2. Cook, W.: Computing in combinatorial optimization. In: Steffen, B., Woeginger, G. (eds.) Computing and Software Science. LNCS, vol. 10000, pp. 27–47. Springer, Cham (2019). https://doi.org/10.1007/978-3-319-91908-9_3
3. Hoos, H.H.: Programming by optimization. Commun. ACM **55**(2), 70–80 (2012)
4. Hoos, H.H., Stützle, T.: Stochastic Local Search-Foundations and Applications. Morgan Kaufmann Publishers, San Francisco, CA (2005)
5. Hutter, F., Hoos, H.H., Leyton-Brown, K.: Sequential model-based optimization for general algorithm configuration. In: Coello, C.A.C. (ed.) LION 2011. LNCS, vol. 6683, pp. 507–523. Springer, Heidelberg (2011). https://doi.org/10.1007/978-3-642-25566-3_40
6. Pearl, J.: Causality: Models, Reasoning and Inference, 2nd edn. Cambridge University Press, Cambridge (2009)
7. Stützle, T., López-Ibáñez, M.: Automated design of metaheuristic algorithms. In: Gendreau, M., Potvin, J.-Y. (eds.) Handbook of Metaheuristics. ISORMS, vol. 272, pp. 541–579. Springer, Cham (2019). https://doi.org/10.1007/978-3-319-91086-4_17
8. Thornton, C., et al.: Auto-WEKA: combined selection and hyperparameter optimization of classification algorithms. In: SIGKDD. ACM Press (2013)

Uncertainty Quantification and Calibration of Imitation Learning Policy in Autonomous Driving

Farzad Nozarian[1,2]([envelope]) [ID], Christian Müller[1], and Philipp Slusallek[1,2] [ID]

[1] German Research Center for Artificial Intelligence (DFKI), Saarbrücken, Germany
{farzad.nozarian,christian.mueller,philipp.slusallek}@dfki.de
[2] Saarland University (UdS), Saarbrücken, Germany

Abstract. Current state-of-the-art imitation learning policies in autonomous driving, despite having good driving performance, do not consider the uncertainty in their predicted action. Using such an *unleashed* action without considering the degree of confidence in a black-box machine learning system can compromise safety and reliability in safety-critical applications such as autonomous driving. In this paper, we propose three different uncertainty-aware policies, to capture epistemic and aleatoric uncertainty over the continuous control commands. More specifically, we extend a state-of-the-art policy with three common uncertainty estimation methods: heteroscedastic aleatoric, MC-Dropout and Deep Ensembles. To provide accurate and calibrated uncertainty, we further combine our agents with isotonic regression, an existing calibration method in regression task. We benchmark and compare the driving performance of our uncertainty-aware agents in complex urban driving environments. Moreover, we evaluate the quality of predicted uncertainty before and after recalibration. The experimental results show that our Ensemble agent combined with isotonic regression not only provides accurate uncertainty for its predictions but also significantly outperforms the state-of-the-art baseline in driving performance.

Keywords: Uncertainty quantification · Bayesian deep learning · Autonomous driving · Imitation learning

1 Introduction

Imitation learning is one of the promising approaches for solving the Autonomous Driving (AD) problem. In this approach, given a series of states, e.g., sensory information, and actions, e.g., steering angle, generated by an expert driver, a policy or an agent is trained to mimic the expert's actions given the corresponding states. Recently, several methods have been proposed for urban driving environments; however, the focus is mostly on driving performance, and assessing the

This research was supported by the German Federal Ministry for Education and Research (BMB+F) in the project REACT.

F. Heintz et al. (Eds.): TAILOR 2020, LNAI 12641, pp. 146–162, 2021.
https://doi.org/10.1007/978-3-030-73959-1_14

uncertainty of policy is often underappreciated. In fact, to have a reliable, trustworthy and interpretable machine learning model, especially in safety-critical tasks such as AD, quantifying uncertainty is of great importance [13,18,20].

Bayesian Deep Learning (BDL) provides a framework to quantify different types of uncertainty in traditional and Bayesian Neural Networks (BNNs) [10]. The uncertainty is mainly divided into two types. First, the *epistemic* or model uncertainty that represents the uncertainty over network parameters, capturing what the model does not know due to insufficient training dataset or ambiguity in the model itself. Second, *aleatoric* or input uncertainty that represents the inherent noise (e.g. sensor noise) or ambiguity in observations. Aleatoric uncertainty is also divided into two types: *homoscedastic* and *heteroscedastic* uncertainties. While in homoscedastic (task) uncertainty the noise is constant for different inputs of the same task, in heteroscedastic (input-dependent) uncertainty it can vary. Measuring heteroscedastic aleatoric uncertainty is important in AD as sensory inputs can have different levels of noise, for example when weather or lightening conditions change.

Recently, it has been shown that deep Neural Networks (NNs), despite having good performance in many tasks, can surprisingly predict uncalibrated uncertainties [13]. That is, the uncertainty predicted by the network does not match the empirical frequencies of predicted events. For example, in a calibrated object detector, if we have 100 predictions with class "pedestrian" each with 95% confidence, we expect that 95% of those predictions should be classified correctly as pedestrians. In the context of AD, where most of the imitation learning approaches act as a black box, calibrated uncertainties can provide valuable information that improves trustworthiness and interpretability.

In this work, we employ BNNs together with imitation learning to measure the uncertainty of driving policies. More specifically, we extend CILRS [5], one of the state-of-the-art imitation learning baselines, and build three agents with different methods, i.e., heteroscedastic aleatoric uncertainty [10], MC-Dropout [11] and Deep Ensembles [19] to estimate different types of uncertainty over continuous control command outputs. By evaluating the quality of uncertainties in our agents, we find different levels of miscalibration in control commands. Therefore, we employ an uncertainty recalibration method on top of our agents to provide accurate and useful uncertainty. We conduct experiments to evaluate the driving performance of our proposed agents using the recently proposed *NoCrash* benchmark. We further evaluate the quality of uncertainties by calibration plots and Expected Calibration Error (ECE) metric before and after recalibration. To the best of our knowledge, this is the first work that benchmarks and compares agents capturing different types of uncertainty both for driving performance and the quality of uncertainty. We show that our Ensemble agent significantly outperforms the baseline in driving performance while producing calibrated uncertainty when combined with recalibration method.

2   Definitions

In this section, we first summarize the background required to define different types of uncertainty and then we describe the calibration.

2.1   Uncertainty Types

Assume dataset $D = \{\mathbf{X}, \mathbf{Y}\} = \{(\mathbf{x}_i, \mathbf{y}_i)\}_{i=1}^{N}, (\mathbf{x}_i, \mathbf{y}_i) \sim \mathbb{P}$, where $\mathbf{X}, \mathbf{Y}$ and $\mathbb{P}$ represent training inputs, their corresponding outputs and data distribution, respectively. In BNNs, in contrast to traditional neural networks, we consider a distribution over model weights and we aim to compute its posterior, i.e., $p(\theta \mid \mathbf{X}, \mathbf{Y})$. To compute this posterior we can use Bayesian inference by defining the likelihood $p(\mathbf{y} \mid f_\theta(\mathbf{x}))$, where $f_\theta(\mathbf{x})$ is the non-deterministic output of the network, and a prior distribution over weights which is usually considered as Gaussian, e.g., $\theta \sim \mathcal{N}(0, I)$.

In regression, Gaussian likelihood $\mathcal{N}(y; f_\theta(\mathbf{x}), \sigma^2)$ is often used, where σ^2 is the constant observation noise. The predictive posterior distribution is then calculated by averaging over all possible model's parameters:

$$p(\mathbf{y} \mid \mathbf{x}, \mathbf{X}, \mathbf{Y}) = \int p(\mathbf{y} \mid \mathbf{x}, \theta) \, p(\theta \mid \mathbf{X}, \mathbf{Y}) \, d\theta. \tag{1}$$

Computing the exact weights posterior $p(\theta \mid \mathbf{X}, \mathbf{Y})$ is generally interactable for NNs and hence different approximation techniques are used to approximate it with a simple distribution $q_\mathbf{w}(\theta)$ parameterized by $\mathbf{w}$ (e.g., MC-Dropout). The integral (1) thus can be approximated by T Monte Carlo samples from the distribution $q_\mathbf{w}(\theta)$:

$$p(\mathbf{y} \mid \mathbf{x}, \mathbf{X}, \mathbf{Y}) \approx \frac{1}{T} \sum_{i=1}^{T} p(\mathbf{y} \mid \mathbf{x}, \hat{\theta}_i), \quad \hat{\theta}_i \sim q_\mathbf{w}(\theta). \tag{2}$$

For regression tasks, this approximation is the average of T mixture of Gaussians that can be approximated with a single Gaussian with predictive mean and variance as follows [16]:

$$\mathrm{E}(\mathbf{y}) \approx \frac{1}{T} \sum_{1=1}^{T} f_{\hat{\theta}_i}(\mathbf{x}), \tag{3}$$

$$\mathrm{Var}(\mathbf{y}) \approx \sigma^2 + \frac{1}{T} \sum_{i=1}^{T} f_{\hat{\theta}_i}(\mathbf{x})^T f_{\hat{\theta}_i}(\mathbf{x}) - \mathrm{E}(\mathbf{y})^T \mathrm{E}(\mathbf{y}). \tag{4}$$

Here, $\mathrm{Var}(\mathbf{y})$ is considered as the epistemic uncertainty which consists of two parts: the assumed constant inherent noise σ^2 in data and the uncertainty of the model in the prediction.

The constant noise σ^2 or *homoscedastic* aleatoric uncertainty can be tuned by the NN. However, to make it input-dependent, i.e., *heteroscedastic* aleatoric uncertainty, one way is to let the network estimate both the mean and the variance of the Gaussian likelihood, i.e., $\left[\mu_\theta(\mathbf{x}), \sigma_\theta^2(\mathbf{x})\right] = f_\theta(\mathbf{x})$. We can then minimize the negative log-likelihood by plugging in the estimated parameters, i.e., $-\log p(\mathbf{y} \mid \mathbf{x}, \theta) = -\log \mathcal{N}(\mathbf{y}; \mu_\theta(\mathbf{x}), \sigma_\theta^2(\mathbf{x}))$. This results in minimizing the following loss function:

$$\mathcal{L}(\theta) = \frac{1}{N} \sum_{i=1}^{N} \frac{1}{2\sigma_\theta^2(\mathbf{x}_i)} \| \mathbf{y}_i - \mu_\theta(\mathbf{x}_i) \|^2 + \frac{1}{2} \log \sigma_\theta^2(\mathbf{x}_i) . \tag{5}$$

2.2 Uncertainty Calibration

A classification or regression model is said to be calibrated if the probability that the model assigns to an event matches the empirical probability of that event. In regression tasks where $Y \in \mathbb{R}$, by considering $F_i(\mathbf{y})$ as the Cumulative Distribution Function (CDF) targeting y_i, where the network predicts its probability density function $p(y_i \mid \mathbf{x}_i; \theta) = \mathcal{N}(\mu_\theta(\mathbf{x}_i), \sigma_\theta^2(\mathbf{x}_i))$, the perfect calibration is defined by [18] as

$$\mathbb{P}(Y \le F_{\mathbf{X}}^{-1}(p)) = p, \quad \forall p \in [0, 1], \tag{6}$$

where F_i^{-1} is the quantile function, i.e., $F_i^{-1}(p) = inf\{y : p \le F_i(y)\}$.

Same as classification, in regression, we expect that in a calibrated model in 95% of the time the values y_i should fall below their 95% quantile if $p = 95\%$.

3 Related Work

In this section, we first review several methods in uncertainty estimation and their applications. Then we summarize related works for uncertainty calibration and imitation learning in their corresponding subsections.

3.1 Uncertainty Estimation

MC-Dropout [11] is a simple and practical way to approximate the variational inference by training the network with dropout before every weight layer and keeping them activated during test time. This can be interpreted as performing the variational inference where the variational distribution is the Bernoulli distribution. The posterior is approximated by (2) where we perform T stochastic forward passes for each input during test. The weights samples $\hat{\theta}_i \sim q_{\mathbf{w}}(\theta)$ are obtained by applying different dropout masks on model weights during test. Similarly, the mean and variance are approximated using (3) and (4), respectively.

Kendall *et al.* [16] show that both types of uncertainty can be captured on a single model. For regression tasks, for example, this can be simply done by letting the BNN to output μ and σ^2 of the Gaussian. Note that in contrast to heteroscedastic aleatoric that uses maximum likelihood, here, Bayesian inference is used. The posterior is approximated using dropout variational inference similar to MC-Dropout. The network estimates the parameters $\left[\hat{\mu}(\mathbf{x}), \hat{\sigma}^2(\mathbf{x})\right] = f_{\hat{\theta}}(\mathbf{x})$ by sampling from approximate weights distribution $\hat{\theta} \sim q_{\mathbf{w}}(\theta)$. A same loss function as heteroscedastic aleatoric loss (5) is used to tune the network's parameters. The predictive uncertainty is calculated as follows:

$$\text{Var}(\mathbf{y}) \approx \underbrace{\frac{1}{T}\sum_{t=1}^{T}\hat{\sigma}_t^2(\mathbf{x})}_{\text{heteroscedastic uncertainty}} + \underbrace{\frac{1}{T}\sum_{t=1}^{T}\hat{\mu}_t^2(\mathbf{x}) - (\frac{1}{T}\sum_{t=1}^{T}\hat{\mu}_t(\mathbf{x}))^2}_{\text{epistemic uncertainty}}, \quad (7)$$

where T samples from the approximate posterior are drawn and used to estimate $\{\hat{\mu}_t(\mathbf{x}), \hat{\sigma}_t^2(\mathbf{x})\}_{t=1}^{T}$ where $\left[\hat{\mu}_t(\mathbf{x}), \hat{\sigma}_t^2(\mathbf{x})\right] = f_{\hat{\theta}_t}(\mathbf{x})$. Note that this variance, includes both epistemic and heteroscedastic uncertainties as shown in equation.

Deep Ensembles [19] is another easy and scalable way to model both types of uncertainty. In this method, T models with weights $\theta_1, \ldots, \theta_T$, called members of the ensemble, are trained with random initialization and shuffling of the dataset. Similar to heteroscedastic aleatoric, members are trained by maximizing likelihood to predict the Gaussian's parameters. The predictive variance is then calculated similar to (7) with the difference that instead of drawing T sample weights from posterior, here, member's weights $\{\theta_t\}_{t=1}^{T}$ are used. Similar to MC-Dropout this method can be interpreted as approximating the posterior with a distribution where each weight θ_t resembles a sample of $q_{\mathbf{w}}(\theta)$.

Recently, several related works [7,12,14,15] have applied methods mentioned so far for estimating and using uncertainty in low-level computer vision tasks like semantic segmentation, depth estimation, and object detection. For example, [12, 16] use MC-Dropout and Deep Ensembles in semantic segmentation task. They show that the network exhibits high epistemic uncertainty for pixels that are semantically or visually challenging and high aleatoric uncertainty for boundaries of the objects where labels are often inaccurate and noisy. Kendall *et al.* [17] incorporates aleatoric uncertainty in multi-task learning for scene understanding by weighting each task's loss based on its homoscedastic uncertainty. Feng *et al.* [9] model heteroscedastic aleatoric uncertainty on a LiDAR 3D object detector and show that the object detector exhibits high uncertainty for hard objects with high occlusions, truncation, and detection distance, especially when there are fewer points around the objects.

3.2   Uncertainty Calibration

A common way to calibrate the uncertainty is to learn a model that given the uncalibrated uncertainty, predicts its corresponding calibrated uncertainty. Several post-processing methods such as temperature scaling [13] have been introduced based on this approach for classification. Kuleshov *et al.* [18] extend recalibration methods for classification such as Platt scaling [24] to the regression task. The main idea is to estimate the true probability $\mathbb{P}(Y \leq F_{\mathbf{X}}^{-1}(p))$ in (6) from data and learn it by fitting an isotonic regression model.

Feng *et al.* [8] demonstrate that modeling heteroscedastic aleatoric uncertainty directly results in miscalibrated uncertainty for a LiDAR 3D object detector. In fact, we also observe the same phenomenon in our experimental results. To obtain calibrated uncertainties, they use isotonic regression [18] and propose a simple regularization term that encourages the network to predict variances that match the true differences between predicted and true regression targets.

Inspired by [8], in this work we also employ isotonic regression on top of our uncertainty-aware agents to make their uncertainties calibrated. We will discuss our approach in detail in Sect. 4.

3.3   Imitation Learning

Early examples of applying imitation learning in AD [1,21] demonstrate real-world performance for simple tasks such as lane following and obstacle avoidance. Recent works, however, push the boundaries of imitation learning into the complex urban environments. Codevilla *et al.* [4] propose the Conditional Imitation Learning (CIL) approach that conditions the network on high-level navigational commands (e.g., turn left or go straight) to resolve the ambiguity at intersection. Sauer *et al.* [25] extend the affordance learning approach [2] for urban environments by mapping the input video to intermediate representations suitable for urban navigation. Codevilla *et al.* [5] propose CILRS that extends CIL to alleviate the inertia problem where the imitative policy learns a spurious correlation between low speed and no acceleration, resulting in a policy that is unable to restart or stop suddenly in many circumstances. Chen *et al.* [3] decompose the hard problem of urban driving into two phases. In the first phase, given privileged information from the simulator, i.e., a full map of the environment with the position of all traffic participants, a privileged agent is trained to focus on how to imitate perfectly. In the second phase, the privileged agent is used as a teacher to train another vision-based agent that focuses on how to perceive.

We build our uncertainty-aware agents on CILRS, a purely vision-based state-of-the-art baseline that requires no additional privileged information compared to other related works. Note that measuring uncertainty in such a policy is more reasonable than when we have additional inputs. This is because solving the complex problem of driving solely with limited input is a challenging task as it includes more uncertainties and ambiguities that should be captured by the NN.

4   Uncertainty-Aware Agents

In this section, we describe our three uncertainty-aware agents called, Aleatoric, MC-Dropout and Ensemble, to capture heteroscedastic aleatoric uncertainty, epistemic uncertainty and both uncertainties combined. We first describe the architecture of Aleatoric agent and then explain the two other agents based on this agent.

Figure 1 shows the architecture of our Aleatoric agent. The architecture mainly follows the CILRS baseline, except for the conditional module, where

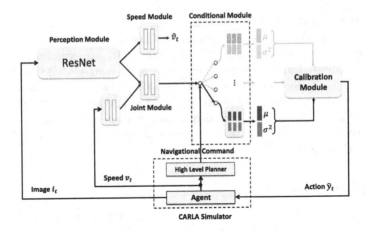

Fig. 1. Our proposed architecture for heteroscedastic Aleatoric agent based on CILRS. The conditional module predicts parameters of Gaussian for control commands. During inference, only one of the branches is activated depending on the navigational command. Disabled branches are shown in gray. The predicted parameters are used by calibration module to produce calibrated confidence level for control commands.

we estimate the uncertainty, and the new recalibration module. Here we only describe our contributions to these modules. For the description of other modules, we refer the reader to the baseline paper [5].

We model each control command c, i.e., steering angle, throttle and brake, independently with a Gaussian distribution and the network predicts their corresponding means and variances. In practice, however, for numerical stability, the network predicts the log variance. The input to each branch is processed by two identical lines of layers (shown in Fig. 1 with red and green colors) that predict means and log variances, i.e., $[\mu_c(\mathbf{x}_t), \log \sigma_c^2(\mathbf{x}_t)] = f_\theta(\mathbf{x}_t), \forall c \in \{steer, throttle, brake\}$. The mean parameters of control commands are then used to form an action $\hat{y}_t$ which is applied on the simulator. Each line contains 3 Fully Connected (FC) layers with 256, 256 and 3 units each. We also apply 50% dropout for the second FC in both lines. Same as the baseline we use ReLU nonlinearities after all hidden layers.

To train the network, the dataset $D = \{(\mathbf{x}_i, n_i, \mathbf{y}_i)\}_{i=1}^N$ is generated by executing an expert policy π^* on the environment that has access to the complete environment state $\mathbf{s}_i$ ($\mathbf{y}_i = \pi^*(\mathbf{s}_i)$), where the $\mathbf{x}_i$ is the observation containing the camera image and the ego vehicle speed, n_i is the navigational command and $\mathbf{y}_i = (y^i_{steer}, y^i_{throttle}, y^i_{brake})$ is the action containing the ground truth values for controls commands (see Sect. 6.1 for more information about the dataset).

We minimize the negative log-likelihood for each control command as follows:

$$\mathcal{L}_c^i(\theta) = exp(-\log \sigma_c^2(\mathbf{x}_i))(y_c^i - \mu_c(\mathbf{x}_i))^2 + \log \sigma_c^2(\mathbf{x}_i). \tag{8}$$

The total multi-loss is then summarized as follows:

$$\mathcal{L}(\theta) = \frac{1}{N} \sum_{i=1}^{N} (\mathcal{L}_v^i(\theta) + \sum_{b=1}^{4} \sum_{c} \mathbb{1}[b = n_i] \cdot \lambda_b \cdot \lambda_c \cdot \mathcal{L}_c^i(\theta)), \qquad (9)$$

where $\mathcal{L}_v^i(\theta)$ is the ℓ_1 loss for speed prediction module, $\mathbb{1}$ indicates an indicator function and λ_b and λ_c are hyperparameters to weight different branches and control commands, respectively.

To have accurate and reliable uncertainties, we consider a recalibration module, that given the predicted means and variances it has learned, maps the predicted CDFs to the empirical CDFs that provide calibrated confidence intervals. To this end, following isotonic regression approach, we estimate the true cumulative distribution $P(Y \leq F_{\mathbf{X}}^{-1}(p))$ empirically from data and separately for each control command. Then we learn a regression model $R_c : [0, 1] \rightarrow [0, 1]$ for each control command that adjusts the uncalibrated confidence $p = F_i(y)$ to calibrated confidence $p' = P(Y \leq F_{\mathbf{X}}^{-1}(p))$.

More formally, given the calibration set $S = \{(\mathbf{x}_i, \mathbf{y}_i)\}_{i=1}^{N}$, we create a recalibration dataset

$$D_c = \{(F_i(y_c^i), \hat{P}(F_i(y_c^i)\}_{i=1}^{N}, \qquad (10)$$

for each control command, where $\hat{P}(p) = |\{y_c^i \,|\, F_i(y_c^i) \leq p, i = 1, \ldots, N\}| \,/N$. In our agents, for each control command, the network predicts the Gaussian parameters from which the CDF probability $p = F_{\mathbf{X}}(Y)$ is obtained. We then learn an isotonic regression model R_c on the recalibration dataset D_c and use it during inference to map the predicted cumulative probability to empirical cumulative probability, i.e., $p' = R(p)$, where p' is the calibrated probability.

We now describe the required changes to build MC-Dropout and Ensemble agents. We approximate the MC-Dropout by considering a dropout layer before the last FC layer of each branch in the conditional module where we predict control commands. Note that in MC-Dropout agent, there is no additional line for estimating the variance. Since the baseline already has a dropout layer before the last FC layer, we simply follow the baseline architecture and training procedure. To sample from the posterior distribution, we keep the last layer dropout activated during inference and perform five stochastic forward passes for each input. We then calculate the predictive mean and epistemic uncertainty by (3) and (4), respectively. The predictive mean is then used as the predicted action $\hat{y}_t$ to apply on the simulator.

We create an ensemble model with five members for our Ensemble agent. Each member has the same architecture as the Aleatoric agent and is trained similarly by minimizing the loss function (9). The final prediction is a uniformly-weighted mixture of Gaussians that is approximated with a single Gaussian whose mean is given by averaging the mean of each member and the variance is calculated by (7) as we described before. Similar to MC-Dropout, the approximated mean is then applied on the simulator as the predicted action $\hat{\mathbf{y}}_t$.

Codevilla *et al.* [5] show that training the baseline agent on the entire dataset degrades the performance due to the bias on common scenarios in dataset. Their best model is thus obtained by training only on a fraction of the dataset, containing 10 h of demonstration. We argue that training several models on different 10-h subsets of dataset would increase the performance as models observe more data diversity without overfitting to common scenarios. Therefore, we train members on different subsets of the training dataset (see Sect. 6.1).

We perform the same recalibration procedure described for Aleatoric agent for the MC-Dropout and Ensemble agents.

5   Evaluation

In this section, we first describe the setup for evaluating the driving performance of our agents. We then explain two methods to visually and quantitatively evaluate the quality of uncertainties provided by our agents.

5.1   Driving Performance Evaluation

To evaluate the performance of the proposed policy under complex urban scenarios we use CARLA 0.8.4 [6] simulator and the recent and realistic NoCrash benchmark [5] that provides better evaluation setup compared to the original CARLA benchmark [6]. Two different towns are available in the benchmark: Town1 with 4 different weather conditions is intended for training and Town2 with 2 additional weather conditions is reserved for testing. Both Town2 and its weather conditions are unseen during the training making a challenging and novel environment to evaluate the generalization of policies.

The benchmark also consists of three different tasks: **Empty** town, **Regular** traffic and **Dense** traffic, with zero, regular and large number of dynamic agents respectively. In each task, the agent is guided by the high-level navigational planner to complete 25 episodes each predefined by a random starting and goal positions in the town. An episode is considered to be successful if the agent can reach the goal position within the time limit and without having a collision with any object. Any infraction that violates traffic rules, e.g., running a red light, is measured but does not result in episode termination. These infraction analyses provide in-depth information about how the policy would work in real situation according to traffic rules. We report the percentage of successfully completed episodes in each task for each agent in Town2 with new weather conditions.

5.2   Uncertainty Evaluation

In order to evaluate the quality of estimated uncertainty we use calibration plot, also called reliability diagram, as a visual tool and ECE as a scalar summary statistic [13]. In regression task, the calibration plot depicts the true frequency of samples in each confidence interval as a function of the predicted fraction of points in that interval. Hence, a perfectly calibrated model plots the identity

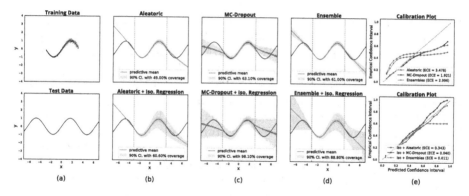

Fig. 2. Capturing different types of uncertainty in a toy regression problem with calibration plots. (a) Training and test datasets. (b) The aleatoric model captures noise in labels but fails to capture epistemic uncertainty. Its recalibrated model still fails to completely calibrate 90% confidence interval. (c) MC-Dropout captures epistemic uncertainty and recalibration improves the quality of uncertainties. (d) Ensemble model captures both types of uncertainty and combined with isotonic regression it provides calibrated uncertainties. (e) Calibration plots show miscalibrated uncertainties for all models. Isotonic regression significantly improves the calibration of all models.

function. To visualize the calibration plot, we divide the range $[0,1]$ into m confidence levels $0 \leq p_1 < \ldots < p_m \leq 1$ and plot $\{(p_j, \hat{p}_j)\}_{j=1}^{m}$, where $\hat{p}_j = |\{y_i \mid F_i(y_i) \leq p_j, i = 1, \ldots, N\}|/N$. To compare the calibration of different methods with a single scalar summary we use the ECE metric

$$\text{ECE} = \sum_{j=1}^{m} w_j \cdot (p_j - \hat{p}_j)^2 . \tag{11}$$

We define the scalar weights w_j uniformly in our experiments. We plot the calibration curve and calculate ECE metric for each control command separately.

6   Experiments

In this section we first describe the setup for our experiments. We have divided our experiments into two groups: first, experiments with a toy regression problem and second, experiments with the uncertainty-aware agents.

6.1   Experimental Setup

We use the CARLA100 [5] dataset for training all agents, creating the recalibration set and performing uncertainty evaluation. CARLA100 is a dataset of 100 h of expert driving demonstrations.

To reproduce the baseline, as the best model is obtained by training on a subset of 10 h, we randomly subsample 50 h and divide it equally into five subsets.

We then train five baseline models on these subsets with different random seeds. Aleatoric, MC-Dropout and Ensemble members are trained similarly on the same subsets and random seeds. For uncertainty recalibration and evaluation, we use a random subsample of 1 h from CARLA100. To build the recalibration datasets (10), we consider only 1% of this subset as the calibration set and the rest is used for uncertainty evaluation using calibration plots. We initially train all layers except the log variance layers (red line) with the baseline ℓ_1 loss. Then we freeze all layers except the two lines and train the log variance layers and fine-tune the mean layers with loss (9). We use PyTorch [22] for the implementation and experiments. For fitting the isotonic regression models we use the Scikit-learn [23] library. In general, for all other training and architectural configurations we follow the baseline.

For experiments in toy regression problem (Sect. 6.2), we follow the setup in [12]. We create three different toy models similar to our agents: the first heteroscedastic aleatoric model consists of 2 FCs each with 128 units followed by ReLU non-linearities. Two separate FC layers each with one unit are then used to predict the mean and log variance of Gaussian likelihood. The MC-Dropout model has 2 FCs with 128 units followed by ReLU non-linearities and dropouts (p = 0.2). The last FC with one unit predicts the output. During inference we keep the dropouts activated and sample the posterior by performing 64 stochastic forward passes for each input. Similarly, we make an ensemble model with 64 members each with the same architecture as the aleatoric model. The predictive mean and variance for the models are estimated as described for our agents.

6.2 Toy Regression Problem

We present our results on an illustrative toy regression problem to gain insights into how different uncertainty estimation approaches capture uncertainty and to show the effect of recalibration. We then evaluate the quality of uncertainties using calibration plots and ECEs.

Figure 2 shows the training and test sets (separated with the vertical dashed lines), our three toy models with their corresponding calibration curves and ECE metrics before and after calibration for 90% confidence interval. The dataset follows Gaussian distribution where the mean and variance are represented by a solid black line and shaded gray region, respectively. The predictive mean and its 90% confidence interval is represented by the solid blue line and shaded red regions, respectively. We use test set for uncertainty evaluation. We expect models to expose different levels of aleatoric uncertainty for the gray shaded regions due to the different levels of noise in labels (vertical axis). For out of training regions, we expect models to expose high epistemic uncertainty.

The aleatoric model is capable of capturing different levels of noise in training set correctly. However, in test regions the predictions are highly overconfident. This results in miscalibration. The isotonic regression in the second row partially improves the model calibration by widening the uncertainty and covering more data points from the test region, but still fails to fully calibrate the 90% confidence interval. MC-Dropout model, on the other hand, is capable of capturing the epistemic uncertainty and indeed it exposes increased uncertainty for the test set as expected. However, it fails to accurately capture the aleatoric uncertainty, especially for regions of training set where there is less noise. Overall, compared to the aleatoric model it shows a better calibration, but similar to the aleatoric model, it is still highly uncalibrated for the 90% confidence interval. The isotonic regression makes the model more calibrated for this confidence interval. However, to cover more data points in test set, it exaggerates the uncertainties and makes them much wider, in a way that it covers almost all data points. The Ensemble model can clearly capture both types of uncertainty: very sharp and accurate for the training set, but overconfident for the test set. Similar to other models it quantifies miscalibrated uncertainties. However, combined with isotonic regression, it covers 88.8% of the points making it almost calibrated.

Figure 2(e) shows the overall calibration results of all models before and after recalibration. Before recalibration, all models provide uncalibrated uncertainties. More specifically, MC-Dropout and Ensemble are highly overconfident for samples with more than 50% confidence and underconfident for samples less than 50% confidence. After calibration, both MC-Dropout and Ensemble become almost calibrated. The aleatoric model, however, remains uncalibrated for confidence levels more than 60% since it does not capture epistemic uncertainty.

6.3   Uncertainty-Aware Agents

In this subsection, we first benchmark the driving performance of our agents with the CILRS baseline. Then we compare the quality of uncertainty in our agents before and after recalibration and finally, we show situations where agents exhibit high uncertainty and how recalibration affects the predicted uncertainty.

Driving Performance. In CILRS, authors reported the results for each task by training models with different seeds and taking the best result among all seeds. Thus, their results are hard to reproduce because of the high variance on initialization (random seed) and choice of training subset. Moreover, there are no fixed 10-h training set and random seed defined by authors to yield the best models. Instead, for each agent, here we report the results by *averaging* over five models trained on different 10-h subsets with different seeds. This makes the results more reliable and realistic as they are less dependent on the choice of training subset or random seeds.

Table 1 shows the percentage of successfully completed episodes in each task in the new town (Town2) and new weather conditions. The mean and standard deviation for all agents except Ensemble are given by benchmarking all five mentioned models once. For Ensemble agent, we benchmark it three times.

Results show that our Ensemble agent significantly outperforms the baseline and two other agents in all tasks. By training members of Ensemble on different subsets of data we can simply benefit from more data without overfitting to common samples and increase the independence and diversity of the members. The members thus can vote for control commands more independently based on their diverse learned experience to handle complex situations better.

Table 1. Driving performance results.

Task	Baseline CILRS	Our Agents Aleatoric	MC-Dropout	Ensemble
Empty	54 ± 11	52 ± 22	42 ± 16	**83** ± 1
Regular	42 ± 6	40 ± 15	34 ± 16	**60** ± 2
Dense	13 ± 6	16 ± 9	17 ± 7	**34** ± 8

Aleatoric agent performs slightly better than the baseline for Dense task, however, it underperformes the baseline by a small margin for Empty and Regular tasks. Similarly, MC-Dropout agent improves the driving performance for Dense task, and performs worse than the baseline in Empty and Regular tasks. One reason that can explain this drop in performance is that the weight posterior is not approximated well. This is due to the fact that we use last layer dropout and we draw relatively low number of samples. One can perhaps increase the performance by applying dropout on all weights and drawing more samples during inference, however it comes at the cost of training a higher capacity model that requires more data and increased training and inference time.

Uncertainty Evaluation. Figure 3, first row, shows the calibration plots for all agents and control commands. In general, all agents estimate miscalibrated uncertainties for control commands. Both Ensemble and Aleatoric agents show the same pattern of miscalibration by estimating highly conservative uncertainties. This shows that the Ensemble agent is mostly influenced by aleatoric uncertainty in this task. In contrast, MC-Dropout agent tends to estimate

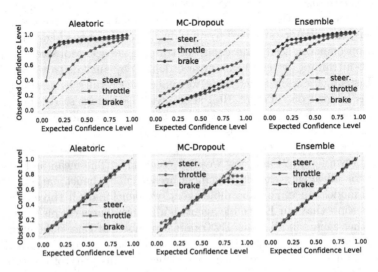

Fig. 3. Calibration plots comparing the quality of uncertainty for different control commands by our agents before (first row) and after (second row) calibration.

Table 2. Comparison of ECEs between agents and control commands before and after recalibration. The best ECE values across agents are shown in bold.

	Control Commands			
Agents	Steering Angle	Throttle	Brake	Mean
Aleatoric	**0.6088**	3.4431	4.2789	2.7770
MC-Dropout	2.3578	**0.5248**	**1.7476**	**1.5434**
Ensemble	1.3100	3.2402	4.2443	2.9315
Aleatoric+Iso.	0.0114	**0.0017**	0.0037	0.0056
MC-Dropout+Iso.	0.0274	0.0932	0.1898	0.1034
Ensemble+Iso.	**0.0014**	0.0029	**0.0031**	**0.0025**

overconfident uncertainties especially for steering angle and throttle. Table 2, first row, summarizes the calibration plots by their corresponding ECEs. While Aleatoric agent provides better uncertainties for steering angle, MC-Dropout considerably outperforms other agents in throttle and brake. Averaged over all commands, MC-Dropout demonstrates better calibration than other agents.

Recalibration Evaluation. Figure 3, second row, shows the calibration plots after recalibration. The recalibration significantly improves the quality of uncertainties by adjusting them according to their empirical probabilities. While both Aleatoric and Ensemble agents show the same pattern of well-calibration, recalibration fails to completely calibrate the MC-Dropout agent. This shows that capturing aleatoric uncertainty is crucial for the recalibration process. Table 2, second row, better shows that the Ensemble agent combined with isotonic regression has the lowest averaged ECE among all agents.

Fig. 4. Front facing camera inputs showing the cases for which the network exposes high aleatoric (first row) and epistemic (second row) uncertainty for steering angle predictions in Ensemble agent.

Fig. 5. The uncertainty of steering angle before (left) and after (right) calibration. The shaded green area represents the 90% confidence interval and the red dashed line and the blue line show the ground truth and the predictive mean, respectively.

Qualitative Analysis. To gain some intuition about the captured uncertainties in control commands, we visualize the samples with high uncertainty for the steering angle. Figure 4 shows samples with high aleatoric (first row) and epistemic (second row) uncertainty for steering angle predictions in Ensemble agent.

It turns out that when the agent is at an intersection or approaching it, we have increased uncertainty for both types. There are two reasons that can explain this phenomenon. First, the proportion of such cases in the dataset is considerably low, as the agent is often driving in a straight road. This can increase model uncertainty at intersections where the model has seen a fewer number of such samples during training. Second, due to the multimodality of steering angle distribution, we have different steering angles for similar inputs. This can increase the aleatoric uncertainty as it captures the noise in the labels.

Figure 5 shows the effect of recalibration on a sample with high uncertainty for the steering angle in Ensemble agent. We observe that recalibration makes the conservative and wide uncertainties over predictions sharp and useful. This holds for all other confidence levels as the Ensemble agent estimates conservative uncertainties for all confidence levels and recalibration makes them well-calibrated.

7   Conclusion

In this paper, we studied estimating different types of uncertainty in control commands for an imitation learning baseline in autonomous driving. We developed three agents based on aleatoric, MC-Dropout, and Deep Ensembles uncertainty estimation methods and compared them in terms of driving performance and the quality of uncertainty. We also adapted an existing calibration method on top of our policies to adjust the predicted uncertainty based on its corresponding empirical uncertainty. Experimental results show that the post-processing recalibration significantly improves the quality of uncertainty. More importantly, our Ensemble agent significantly outperforms the baseline in terms of driving performance while producing well-calibrated uncertainty when combined with the calibration method. Our quantitative results reveal that our policy shows high uncertainty for steering angle predictions at intersections, suggesting that an improved policy can be designed by resolving the ambiguities in these situations. In future work, we would like to investigate different ways to directly incorporate the predicted uncertainty of actions into the decision-making process such that the policy avoids actions with high uncertainty.

References

1. Bojarski, M., et al.: End to end learning for self-driving cars. arXiv preprint arXiv:1604.07316 (2016)
2. Chen, C., Seff, A., Kornhauser, A., Xiao, J.: Deepdriving: learning affordance for direct perception in autonomous driving. In: Proceedings of the IEEE International Conference on Computer Vision, pp. 2722–2730 (2015). https://doi.org/10.1109/ICCV.2015.312
3. Chen, D., Zhou, B., Koltun, V., Krähenbühl, P.: Learning by cheating. In: Conference on Robot Learning, pp. 66–75. PMLR (2020)
4. Codevilla, F., Müller, M., López, A., Koltun, V., Dosovitskiy, A.: End-to-end driving via conditional imitation learning. In: 2018 IEEE International Conference on Robotics and Automation (ICRA), pp. 1–9. IEEE (2018). https://doi.org/10.1109/ICRA.2018.8460487
5. Codevilla, F., Santana, E., López, A.M., Gaidon, A.: Exploring the limitations of behavior cloning for autonomous driving. In: Proceedings of the IEEE International Conference on Computer Vision, pp. 9329–9338 (2019). https://doi.org/10.1109/iccv.2019.00942
6. Dosovitskiy, A., Ros, G., Codevilla, F., Lopez, A., Koltun, V.: Carla: an open urban driving simulator. arXiv preprint arXiv:1711.03938 (2017)
7. Feng, D., Rosenbaum, L., Dietmayer, K.: Towards safe autonomous driving: capture uncertainty in the deep neural network for lidar 3d vehicle detection. In: 2018 21st International Conference on Intelligent Transportation Systems (ITSC), pp. 3266–3273. IEEE (2018). https://doi.org/10.1109/ITSC.2018.8569814
8. Feng, D., Rosenbaum, L., Glaeser, C., Timm, F., Dietmayer, K.: Can we trust you? On calibration of a probabilistic object detector for autonomous driving. arXiv preprint arXiv:1909.12358 (2019)
9. Feng, D., Rosenbaum, L., Timm, F., Dietmayer, K.: Leveraging heteroscedastic aleatoric uncertainties for robust real-time lidar 3D object detection. In: 2019 IEEE Intelligent Vehicles Symposium (IV), pp. 1280–1287. IEEE (2019). https://doi.org/10.1109/IVS.2019.8814046
10. Gal, Y.: Uncertainty in Deep Learning. University of Cambridge, Cambridge, vol. 1, p. 3 (2016)
11. Gal, Y., Ghahramani, Z.: Dropout as a Bayesian approximation: representing model uncertainty in deep learning. In: International Conference on Machine Learning, pp. 1050–1059 (2016)
12. Guafsson, F.K., Danelljan, M., Schon, T.B.: Evaluating scalable Bayesian deep learning methods for robust computer vision. In: Proceedings of the IEEE/CVF Conference on Computer Vision and Pattern Recognition Workshops, pp. 318–319 (2020). https://doi.org/10.1109/CVPRW50498.2020.00167
13. Guo, C., Pleiss, G., Sun, Y., Weinberger, K.Q.: On calibration of modern neural networks. In: Proceedings of the 34th International Conference on Machine Learning, vol. 70, pp. 1321–1330. ICML 2017, JMLR (2017)

14. Harakeh, A., Smart, M., Waslander, S.L.: BayesOD: a Bayesian approach for uncertainty estimation in deep object detectors. In: 2020 IEEE International Conference on Robotics and Automation (ICRA), pp. 87–93. IEEE (2020)
15. He, Y., Zhu, C., Wang, J., Savvides, M., Zhang, X.: Bounding box regression with uncertainty for accurate object detection. In: Proceedings of the IEEE Conference on Computer Vision and Pattern Recognition, pp. 2888–2897 (2019). https://doi.org/10.1109/CVPR.2019.00300
16. Kendall, A., Gal, Y.: What uncertainties do we need in Bayesian deep learning for computer vision? In: Advances in Neural Information Processing Systems, pp. 5574–5584 (2017)
17. Kendall, A., Gal, Y., Cipolla, R.: Multi-task learning using uncertainty to weigh losses for scene geometry and semantics. In: Proceedings of the IEEE Conference on Computer Vision and Pattern Recognition, pp. 7482–7491 (2018)
18. Kuleshov, V., Fenner, N., Ermon, S.: Accurate uncertainties for deep learning using calibrated regression. In: Dy, J., Krause, A. (eds.) Proceedings of the 35th International Conference on Machine Learning. Proceedings of Machine Learning Research, Sockholmsmässan, Stockholm, Sweden, vol. 80, pp. 2796–2804. PMLR, 10–15 July 2018. http://proceedings.mlr.press/v80/kuleshov18a.html
19. Lakshminarayanan, B., Pritzel, A., Blundell, C.: Simple and scalable predictive uncertainty estimation using deep ensembles. In: Advances in Neural Information Processing Systems, pp. 6402–6413 (2017)
20. McAllister, R., et al.: Concrete problems for autonomous vehicle safety: Advantages of bayesian deep learning. In: Proceedings of the Twenty-Sixth International Joint Conference on Artificial Intelligence, IJCAI 2017, pp. 4745–4753 (2017). https://doi.org/10.24963/ijcai.2017/661
21. Muller, U., Ben, J., Cosatto, E., Flepp, B., Cun, Y.L.: Off-road obstacle avoidance through end-to-end learning. In: Advances in Neural Information Processing Systems, pp. 739–746 (2006)
22. Paszke, A., et al.: Pytorch: an imperative style, high-performance deep learning library. In: Wallach, H., Larochelle, H., Beygelzimer, A., d'Alché-Buc, F., Fox, E., Garnett, R. (eds.) Advances in Neural Information Processing Systems, vol. 32, pp. 8024–8035. Curran Associates, Inc. (2019). http://papers.neurips.cc/paper/9015-pytorch-an-imperative-style-high-performance-deep-learning-library.pdf
23. Pedregosa, F., et al.: Scikit-learn: machine learning in Python. J. Mach. Learn. Res. **12**, 2825–2830 (2011)
24. Platt, J., et al.: Probabilistic outputs for support vector machines and comparisons to regularized likelihood methods. Adv. Large Margin Classifiers **10**(3), 61–74 (1999)
25. Sauer, A., Savinov, N., Geiger, A.: Conditional affordance learning for driving in urban environments. In: Conference on Robot Learning, pp. 237–252 (2018)

Synthesising Reinforcement Learning Policies Through Set-Valued Inductive Rule Learning

Youri Coppens[1,2]([✉]) [iD], Denis Steckelmacher[1] [iD], Catholijn M. Jonker[3,4] [iD], and Ann Nowé[1] [iD]

[1] Vrije Universiteit Brussel, Brussels, Belgium
yocoppen@ai.vub.ac.be
[2] Université Libre de Bruxelles, Brussels, Belgium
[3] Delft University of Technology, Delft, The Netherlands
[4] Leiden Institute of Advanced Computer Science (LIACS), Leiden, The Netherlands

Abstract. Today's advanced Reinforcement Learning algorithms produce black-box policies, that are often difficult to interpret and trust for a person. We introduce a policy distilling algorithm, building on the CN2 rule mining algorithm, that distills the policy into a rule-based decision system. At the core of our approach is the fact that an RL process does not just learn a policy, a mapping from states to actions, but also produces extra meta-information, such as action values indicating the quality of alternative actions. This meta-information can indicate whether more than one action is near-optimal for a certain state. We extend CN2 to make it able to leverage knowledge about equally-good actions to distill the policy into fewer rules, increasing its interpretability by a person. Then, to ensure that the rules explain a valid, non-degenerate policy, we introduce a refinement algorithm that fine-tunes the rules to obtain good performance when executed in the environment. We demonstrate the applicability of our algorithm on the Mario AI benchmark, a complex task that requires modern reinforcement learning algorithms including neural networks. The explanations we produce capture the learned policy in only a few rules, that allow a person to understand what the black-box agent learned. Source code: https://gitlab.ai.vub.ac.be/yocoppen/svcn2.

Keywords: Reinforcement Learning · Inductive rule learning · Explainable AI · Policy distillation

1 Introduction

Reinforcement Learning (RL) is a machine learning technique that learns from experience, rather than data that has been collected offline. By interacting with its environment, an intelligent agent learns to adapt its actions to show the desired behaviour. This environment is in general stochastic and its dynamics unknown to the agent.

© Springer Nature Switzerland AG 2021
F. Heintz et al. (Eds.): TAILOR 2020, LNAI 12641, pp. 163–179, 2021.
https://doi.org/10.1007/978-3-030-73959-1_15

RL is particularly useful in settings without a model of the environment, or when the environment is hard to model. RL is also interesting when an accurate simulation model can be built, but solving that model to obtain a decision or control strategy is hard. Telecommunication applications such as routing, load balancing and call admission control are examples where RL has proven its worth as a machine learning technique. RL has unfortunately one crucial weakness which may prevent it from being applied in future critical applications: the control policies learned by the agent, especially using modern algorithms including neural networks, are black boxes that are hard to interpret. This shortcoming could prove a major obstacle to the adoption of RL. For example, the new EU privacy regulation, more specifically Article 22 of the General Data Protection Regulation (GDPR), requires that all AI with an impact on human lives needs to be accountable, which, for an RL agent, means that it must be possible to tell the user why the agent took a particular action in a state. Interpretability of machine learning based models is therefore crucial, as it forms the basis for other concerns such as accountability, that subsumes the justification of the decisions taken. Assume that RL is used to synthesise a prevention strategy for a dangerous infection disease. The agent should learn what regulations and procedures people should follow, while optimally allocating a budget, such as vaccines, medication or closed-school days. While this scenario is plausible, see [14], will a black-box strategy be accepted? The above observation brings us to the following key question: Wouldn't it make more sense to use RL to explore possible strategies and simulate the potential effects on our society, before we would decide to implement such a strategy? However, this requires that the strategies found by RL algorithms are presented in a human-understandable format.

Explainable AI, reviewed in [17], is not new. Even in the early days of Expert Systems, many approaches have been proposed to allow to automatically generate explanations and to reflect on the reasoning being used, see e.g. [16]. Recently, explainability has been put more prominently on the agenda in the Machine Learning (ML) community as well [19]. The massive success of the black-box ML-techniques has culminated in many applications that display powerful results, but provide poor insight into how they find their conclusion. Over the last three years, workshops at major conferences in Machine Learning (e.g. ICML, NeurIPS), Artificial Intelligence (e.g. IJCAI), Human-Computer Interaction (e.g. ACM CHI, ACM IUI) and Planning (e.g. ICAPS) have been held for contributions that increase human interpretability of intelligent systems. At these workshops, initial research related to data mining has been proposed. However, ideas to make RL more explainable are rather limited and often borrowed from existing ML Interpretability literature [2].

In this paper, we present a method that allows the policy learned by a reinforcement learning agent, using modern deep learning methods, to be expressed in a way that is understandable by a person. Our contributions are as follows:

1. We extend the CN2 rule-mining algorithm to make it able to leverage the meta-information of an RL process on equally-good actions. This allows the algorithm to map an RL policy to a simpler and compacter set of rules.

2. We use our extended CN2 algorithm to produce human-understandable rules from a black-box RL policy, and evaluate our method on the Mario benchmark.
3. We introduce a 2-phased method, that produces a first set of rules providing a global view on the policy. Then refines the rules when needed. This refinement is driven by the performance of the rules when used to perform the task, rather than the accuracy when mining the rules.

2   Related Work

Until now, insights in the learnt RL policy were typically limited to showing a typical trace, i.e. an execution of the policy or through analysing and visualising agent reward structures [1]. Relevant efforts to mention are [21], where the authors visualise action versus parameter exploration and [3] that analyses and visualises the usefulness of heuristic information in a state space.

Distillation techniques translate the behaviour from large complex models to simpler surrogate models [10]. While these methods reduce computational overhead and model complexity, the general focus is mostly set on maintaining performance rather than increasing the interpretability through the surrogate model, even in the context of RL policies [20]. In [5], a deep RL policy is distilled into a surrogate soft decision tree model [7], in an effort to gain insights in the RL policy. The surrogate model determines a hierarchy of filters that perform sequential feature extraction from observations. These filters highlight which features are considered important in the decision making. Our work is complementary in the sense that the rules we extract look at the content, i.e. the actual value of the observation features, rather than the importance of a particular feature.

Relational RL (RRL) could be seen as an interpretable RL approach *by design* [25] as it allows to express the policy as well as the quality of the policy using relational expressions. Relational RL requires domain-specific knowledge from the designer, as a set of concepts have to be defined *a priori*. If these concepts are not carefully defined, the expressiveness of the agent is reduced, which may prevent it from learning any good policy. In [27], relational inductive biases have been incorporated into a deep learning process, in an attempt to scale RRL without pre-defined concepts, thus allowing for relevant concepts to emerge. The approach is shown to reveal the high-level plan of the RL strategy, thus identifying subgoals and options that can be generalised. Our work does not consider subgoals and instead focuses on making the actual policy, the mapping from states to actions, transparent to the user.

The paper by Madumal et al. [15] introduces an approach to explain a policy which can either be obtained through model-based RL or planning. It builds upon causal graphs as a means to calculate counterfactuals. As the causal graph is assumed to be given, the symbolic concepts are also defined *a priori*, and have to be carefully chosen, leading to the same vulnerability as Relational RL.

In our approach, we don't want to restrict the policy *a priori*. We allow the RL process to learn complex policies if needed. Recent advances in (deep) function approximation for RL have yielded powerful techniques that learn rich state representations and have advanced state-of-the-art in terms of learning performance in complex environments, see e.g. [18]. However, these techniques obscure a proper understanding of the policy that is being learned.

In the approach we propose, we start from existing state-of-the-art RL techniques and make them more interpretable. Our work performs an *a posteriori* simplification and communication of the strategy. This is realised through a rule-mining approach that exploits the meta-information that is present in the RL learning algorithm. While decision trees are a more commonly adopted interpretable surrogate model that can be visualised in a natural manner, we opted for decision rules, because these have a similar expressiveness while also being more compact and robust. In addition, the use of meta-information, such as which actions are equally good in a state, is more naturally implemented in a rule-mining system, as well as the refinement process we propose. The RL process not only provides us with the best action for a given state, but the probability that an RL actor gives to each of the actions is providing us information on the quality of the sub-optimal actions. Exploiting this meta-information allows to go beyond a mere translation of the policy into a set of rules. As, for instance, knowing that two actions have nearly the same probability in a given state indicates that they are both *equally good*, which allows our rule mining algorithm to chose one action or the other, depending on what leads to the simplest rule set. This exploitation of the meta-information of an RL process also differentiates our work from approaches that translate the RL policy in a set of fuzzy rules, such as [11] and [9].

3   Background

Our work covers several domains of research such as Reinforcement Learning and Inductive Rule Learning.

3.1   Policies Learnt Through Reinforcement Learning

Reinforcement Learning (RL) tackles sequential decision making problems in an interactive setting [23]. An artificial agent learns by operating in an unknown environment, from scratch or boosted by some initial domain knowledge, which actions are optimal over time. Based on the observation of the state of the environment, the agent executes an action of choice which makes the agent transition to a next state. In addition to the new state, the agent will also receive feedback from the environment in the form of a numerical reward. Based on that feedback, the agent will adapt its behaviour into a desired strategy.

Reinforcement learning problems are formally represented as a Markov Decision Process (MDP), a 5-tuple (S, A, T, R, γ), with S and A the sets of states and actions available in the environment. Unknown to the agent are T and R. $T : S \times A \times S \to [0, 1]$ represents the transition probability function, assigning probabilities to a possible transition from state $s \in S$ to another state $s' \in S$, by executing action $a \in A$. $R : S \times A \to \mathbb{R}$ is the environment's reward function, providing the agent with feedback and finally a discount factor $\gamma \in [0,1]$ regulates the agent's preference for immediate rewards over long-term rewards. The agent's goal is to maximise the expected return $\mathbb{E}[G_t]$, where $G_t = \sum_{i=0}^{\infty} \gamma^i R_{t+i}$, the sum of future discounted rewards. Lower values of γ set the preference on immediate reward, whilst higher values result in a more balanced weighing of current and future reward in G_t. The agent learns a policy $\pi : S \times A \to [0,1]$, mapping state-action pairs to probabilities, describing the optimal behaviour strategy.

In value-based RL methods, this policy is implicitly present through the use of a *value function* in combination with an action-selection strategy. The value function $Q(s,a)$ is often represented as the expected return when taking an action a in state s: $Q(s,a) = \mathbb{E}[G_t|S_t = s, A_t = a]$, hence describing which actions are expected to result in more future rewards.

When the Q-values have converged, the highest ranked action is the optimal one, whilst others are granted to be sub-optimal. However, when the Q-values are equal or almost equal, this indicates that there is no clear preference over these actions.

Policy-based algorithms are another family of RL methods. They maintain an explicit policy, or *actor*, often described as a parametric expression π_θ. The policy is optimised iteratively, using methods such as computing and following the gradient of its quality [24], or training it to progressively imitate the greedy policy of a collection of critics [22]. Policy-based methods typically learn a stochastic policy where the difference in probability can be considered to be a proxy for the difference in quality of two alternative actions in a state. The BDPI algorithm [22] that we use in this paper, for instance, learns a policy that associates nearly-equal probability to actions that are of comparable quality, while actions that are clearly worse than the other ones have a probability near 0. In other words, when the probability of two actions in a given state is close to each other, this expresses there is no clear preference of one action over the other action. We exploit this property in our framework in order to find a small and simple set of rules capturing the main elements of the policy.

3.2   Inductive Rule Learning

Inductive rule learning allows us to extract knowledge in a symbolic representation from a set of instances in a supervised manner. The goal of supervised rule induction is the discovery of rules that reflect relevant dependencies between classes and attribute values describing the given data [8]. In our setting, these data instances are state-action pairs drawn from a learned RL policy. More precisely, the instances are pairs of states with *set-valued* actions: for a single instance, a state might be paired with multiple actions.

The set-valued aspect is important to express that two or more actions are high-quality alternatives in a certain state. By supporting the possibility to express this indifference towards which action of that set is selected in the corresponding state, we can create rules with a larger support and as a consequence fewer rules. Regular inductive rule learning is not designed to deal with this set-valued aspect, and therefore we extend this learning paradigm in Sect. 4. Before we introduce our set-valued rule mining, we first summarise the main elements of inductive rule learning and the CN2 algorithm.

Inductive rule learning allows to summarise a set of instances, which might be discrete valued or continuous valued, along with a discrete target class, into a set of rules. The rules are of the form 'IF *Conditions* THEN *c*', where *c* is the class label. Because of their symbolic nature, the resulting model is easy to interpret by humans.

We base our work on CN2 [4], a frequently used rule learning algorithm based on the separate-and-conquer principle, and extend it to support multiple equally-good labels per input. In CN2, rules are iteratively identified through the application of beam search, a heuristic tree search algorithm. The best rule that is identified in this search procedure will be selected as new rule. The consequent (classifying label) of the rule is the majority class of the examples covered by the rule.

The commonly used evaluation heuristic in CN2 is *weighted relative accuracy* (WRA) [13,26], which aims to find a good balance between a large coverage and a high accuracy. Equation 1 describes the WRA of a proposed rule r:

$$\text{WRA}(r) = \frac{\hat{P}(r) + \hat{N}(r)}{P(r) + N(r)} \times \left(\frac{\hat{P}(r)}{\hat{P}(r) + \hat{N}(r)} - \frac{P(r)}{P(r) + N(r)} \right) \quad (1)$$

where $P(r)$ and $N(r)$ represent the number of positive and negative examples in the current training set and $\hat{P}(r)$ and $\hat{N}(r)$ represent the number of positive and negative examples covered by the considered rule r. From hereon, we will drop the parameter r as no confusion is to be expected. Examples are said to be positive when they have the same classification label as the consequent of the rule, otherwise they are considered to be negative. $\hat{P}$ and $\hat{N}$ can be thus considered the true and false positive examples covered by the rule respectively. The first factor in Eq. 1, $\frac{\hat{P} + \hat{N}}{P + N}$, represents the *coverage* of the proposed rule, the rate of examples that satisfy the antecedent, and weighs the second factor of the equation. That factor, $\left(\frac{\hat{P}}{\hat{P} + \hat{N}} - \frac{P}{P + N} \right)$, represents the relative classification accuracy of a rule. It is the difference between the accuracy of the samples covered by the rule and the overall accuracy of the training examples.

The algorithm stops generating rules if there are no other significant rules to be found or an insufficient number of samples remain. These thresholds are expected to be application dependent and are therefore to be determined by the user.

We now introduce the main contribution of this paper, a rule mining algorithm based on CN2 that extends two aspects of it relevant for reinforcement learning applications: allowing states to be mapped to *several* equally-good actions, and ensuring that the distilled policy performs comparably to the original policy.

4   Extending CN2 to Set-Valued Labels

Our main contribution consists of extending two important aspects of CN2, to make it suitable to policy distillation in an explainable reinforcement learning setting:

1. We exploit meta-information generated by the reinforcement learning process to associate *sets* of equally-good actions to each state. By offering choice to the rule miner in which action to map to every state, we potentially (and in practice do) reduce the number of rules needed to cover the original policy.
2. Contrary to classical Supervised Learning settings, the main application domain of CN2, what matters in our setting is not primarily the classification accuracy, but the loss in performance of the distilled policy. In other words, one little misclassification in a particular state can have a big impact on the performance of the policy, but in other states, this misclassification might almost be unnoticeable from a policy performance perspective. We propose a two-step approach that allows to identify those *important* misclassifications, leading to short rule sets that, when executed in the environment, still perform as well as the original policy. This ensures that the explanations we provide with the mined rules correspond to a good policy, and not some over-simplified degenerate policy.

The first point, associating sets of equally-good actions to each state, requires an extension of the CN2 algorithm itself. The second point, and the application of the whole framework to reinforcement learning policy distillation, requires an iterative framework that we present in Sect. 5.

The CN2 algorithm iteratively learns a rule through a beam search procedure. The objective of this step is to search for a rule that on the one hand covers a large number of instances, and on the other hand has a high accuracy. This is steered through the evaluation heuristic, i.e. the weighted relative accuracy (WRA), which makes a distinction between positive and negative examples based on the label of the training sample. In order to deal with the Set-Valued instances, which express an indifference with respect to the actual label chosen by the rule, we adapted the WRA heuristic.

In the regular single-label setting, the sum of positive and negative examples covered by the rule and in the overall training set, $\hat{P} + \hat{N}$ and $P + N$, always corresponds to the number of respective training examples, $\hat{E}$ and E. However, in a multi-label setting this is not necessarily the case, as an instance can be assigned to any of the labels and is thus potentially both a positive and negative example at the same time according to the standard WRA heuristic. The heuristic aims at maximising the correctly classified instances for a rule by assigning the majority class of the covered samples as the class label. In order to deal with the indifference to which instances with multiple class labels are assigned, we propose the following adaptation to the WRA heuristic, described in Eq. 2, where we replace the sum of positive and negative examples covered by

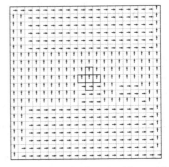

(a) In each cell, the most optimal action(s) to perform are shown by arrows. Notice how some cells in the grid contain two optimal actions leading to the top rightmost goal state. The cross in the middle indicates the muddy states

(b) Distillation of the muddy gridworld policy with standard CN2: Samples provided to CN2 are state-action pairs. When multiple optimal actions exist for a state, an action is selected at random.

Fig. 1. Muddy gridworld environment with its optimal policy, and a distillation of this policy using standard CN2 (no support for equally-good actions).

the rule and in the overall set by the actual number of distinct samples in the set, respectively denoted by E and $\hat{E}$:

$$\text{WRA}_{set} = \frac{\hat{E}}{E} \times \left(\frac{\hat{P}}{\hat{E}} - \frac{P}{E} \right) \qquad (2)$$

This will have the effect that the heuristic will only count the multi-labelled instances as a positive example when the majority class is one of the options, and as a negative example otherwise.

4.1 Impact of Set-Valued Labels on Policy Distillation

Before we discuss our approach on the Mario AI benchmark, we illustrate the effect of our set-valued rule mining heuristic on a simple 20 by 20 discrete-state gridworld problem, where a navigating agent has to walk to the top rightmost cell from any initial position.[1] Actions are up, down, right and left. Near the center of the grid, a couple of cells contain mud. The agent receives a reward of -1 per time-step, -10 when entering a muddy cell.

Figure 1a shows the environment, and the optimal policy learned by a Q-learning agent in this setting. In most cells, two optimal actions exist to navigate to the goal, namely moving upward or to the right. Meaning there are quite a lot of optimal policies in this example. In the cells neighboring the muddy cells however, the agent has learned not to walk towards the muddy parts, but rather

---

[1] Another illustration can be found on pages 8 and 9 of https://www.ida.liu.se/~frehe08/tailor2020/TAILOR_2020_paper_48.pdf.

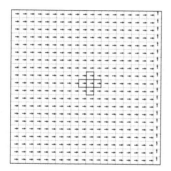

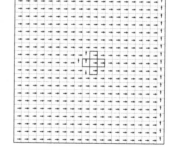

1. IF X<=18 THEN Class=RIGHT
2. IF X=19 THEN Class=UP

(a) An initial distillation of the muddy gridworld policy using our Set-Valued extension of CN2, taking multiple possible actions into account. The rules are simple, but do not yet consider the policy details in the muddy states into account, leading to sub-optimal performance.

1.1 IF X<=18 AND Y=10 AND X>=8 AND
    X<=9 THEN Class=UP
1.2 IF X<=18 AND X>=10 THEN
    Class=RIGHT
1.3 IF X<=18 AND X<=8 THEN
    Class=RIGHT
1.4 IF X<=18 AND Y=11 THEN Class=UP
1.5 IF X<=18 AND Y=9 THEN Class=DOWN
1.6 IF X<=18 THEN Class=RIGHT
  2 IF X=19 THEN Class=UP

(b) Refining the rules shown in (a), as detailed in Section 5, identifies the state near the mud that requires a different action from the surrounding states, leading to optimal behavior.

Fig. 2. Distilled policy with our modified CN2 algorithm, without and with our refinement step.

walk around it. In essence, the general behavior of the agent can be summarized as moving upward or to the right. Hence an acceptable simplified policy would be to first walk to either the upper or right border and then walk straight to the goal. Such a simplified policy would be a desired outcome of the rule mining process, as it provides a first high level view on the policy. This high level policy can be refined, see Sect. 5 below. As explained in that section, this refinement is not driven by increasing the accuracy requirements of the rule-mining algorithm, but rather by improving the performance of the distilled policy.

Figure 1b shows the resulting policy derived from the standard single-labeled CN2 algorithm, using the regular WRA heuristic. As the algorithm expects single labeled data, whenever multiple optimal actions exist for a state, one of these had to be sampled randomly. The resulting rule list covers several sectors in the grid where the agent either moves upward or to the right, eventually ending up in the goal. As standard CN2 cannot take alternative actions into account during the mining process, it cannot distil a simple policy, meaning a policy expressed with few rules, yet having a good performance.

Figure 2a presents the resulting simplified policy of our Set-Valued extension of CN2. Our algorithm can nicely summarize the essence of the policy into two simple rules, making the agent walk to the right border of the grid first, and afterwards walk upwards to the goal. Note that the rule mining process did not capture the avoidance of the muddy cells which is an exceptional region in the environment. However, Fig. 2b shows that the refinement step that we propose in Sect. 5 allows extra rules to be identified, restoring optimal performance of the agent around the muddy region.

Our extension of CN2, able to learn from pairs of states and multiple equally-good labels, is only one component of our explainable reinforcement learning framework. We now fully detail the iterative algorithm that we built on our CN2 extension, that allows a policy to be learned, distilled, evaluated and fine-tuned by the user, to ensure that state-action pairs that are crucial for the performance of the policy are classified correctly.

5   Explaining Policies Through Distillation

In this work, we are using inductive rule mining to translate a deep reinforcement learning policy into a simplified ordered list of rules that reveal the agent's behaviour in the environment. The simplification is performed through a rule-mining approach that exploits the meta-information that is present in the RL learning algorithm, hereby balancing between accuracy and readability.

We extended the implementation of CN2 in the open source data mining framework Orange[2], in order to support multi-label data and incorporated our proposed WRA_{set} heuristic to perform set-valued rule mining. We evaluated our methods on an altered level of the Mario AI benchmark [12]. The goal of the Mario agent is to collect rewarding red coins and avoiding penalising green and blue coins. The action space of the Mario agent is restricted so that it can only press one of the 5 available controller buttons during each step. The agent can also decide not to press any controller button, bringing the total number of actions to 6.

The observations provided to the RL agent are built from a description of the enemies, coins and blocks around the current position of Mario in the environment. We consider a 10 by 10 receptive field, that is, we look at 10 by 10 unit squares in the environment, centred around Mario's current position. Each square can either be empty, or contain a block, enemy or coin. Because every class of enemy, or every colour of a coin, is uniquely identified, each square can take 24 different values (0 being empty, then positive values identifying the kind of object in the square). When producing observations for the agent, we consider this 10 by 10 set of squares that can each take a value among 24, and produced a flattened, one-hot encoded, large observation vector of $10 \times 10 \times 24 = 2400$ entries, with each entry either 0 or 1. Figure 3 illustrates the transformation from a game frame to a receptive field. Because one-hot encoded states can be decoded back to their integer variant (a 10 by 10 grid of integers in our case), and

---

[2] https://github.com/biolab/orange3.

the integers we consider uniquely identify objects in the Mario game that have human-friendly game, any observation passed to the agent can also be described in a human-friendly way, such as *"there is a red coin above Mario"*.

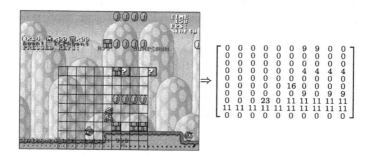

Fig. 3. Transformation from a MarioAI game frame to a 10 by 10 receptive field grid centred around Mario, which is returned by the emulator. Each cell of the grid corresponds to a pixel region about the size of a brick block in the game. The game objects in each of the grid's cells are translated into numerical labels as state representation for the learning agent. Whenever the receptive field ranges out of the game frame, it is padded with zeros (e.g. the bottom row).

As explained above, we propose a two-phased distillation algorithm, to produce meaningful rules from a black-box policy learned with Deep Reinforcement Learning. The first phase produces a list of rules that approximate how the Deep RL policy maps states to actions. These rules capture the general and high-level behaviour of the policy, and produce compact and human-friendly descriptions. However, some of the approximations made by our rule mining algorithm may lead to rules that, if executed in the environment, lead to a significant loss in performance. Because small mistakes in a single state may or may not have an impact on the performance of the agent, increasing the target accuracy of the rule-mining algorithm does not address the problem. Instead, we introduce a second phase, that evaluates the rules in the environment, and corrects small mistakes when they have an impact on the performance of the agent.

5.1   Phase 1: Supervised Post-processing

Our first phase distills a Deep Reinforcement Learning policy into rules, using the rule-mining algorithm that we introduce in Sect. 4:

1. We train a Deep RL agent, that we assume produces a stochastic policy. Q-Values can be mapped to a stochastic policy with Boltzmann exploration;
2. We record multiple trajectories sampled from the policy;
3. We translate the trajectories into a collection of symbolic states and set-valued actions, so that each state can be mapped to several actions if the Deep RL policy gives similar probability to these actions;

4. Our rule-mining algorithm learns rules that cover the state-action pairs identified above.

First, a deep RL agent is trained to control Mario to play a single level. In this paper we realise this through the use of Bootstrapped Dual Policy Iteration (BDPI) [22]. We chose this algorithm because it produces an explicit actor, from which we can obtain action probabilities, and the off-policy actor-critic nature of the algorithm leads to an actor that computes the probability that an action is optimal, instead of a simple number that empirically led to high returns, as Policy Gradient approaches do.

Once a policy has been learnt, a data set is recorded by executing the converged RL policy in the environment for 50 episodes. The data set consists of tuples $(s, \pi(s))$ of state observations and action probabilities for each step of the performed episodes.[3]

Given the data set of states and their corresponding action probabilities, a translation is applied in order to prepare for mining the rules. The numerical values of the state observations are transformed back to their symbolic counterpart, as each value in the observation represents a specific game object in Mario's receptive field. Since the state observation represents a receptive field around Mario, we can assign x, y coordinates to each cell (feature of the state) with the agent in the center.

For each state observation s in the data set, the predicted action distribution $\pi(s)$ is transformed into a set, $\mathcal{L}(s)$. This set denotes which actions are considered suitable to be executed in that particular state. Equation 3 describes this transformation formally. For each state s in the recordings, we take the probability of the best action, i.e. the action with the highest probability, $\max_{a'}(\pi(s, a'))$, and set a proportional threshold, $\tau * \max_{a'} \pi(s, a')$, where $\tau \in (0, 1]$ determines how tolerant we are with respect to sub-optimal actions. Lower values of τ will lead to more actions exceeding the threshold, while high values will put the threshold closer to $\max_{a'}(\pi(s, a'))$. For our experiments we picked a value for $\tau = 90\%$.

$$\forall s \in S : \mathcal{L}(s) = \{a \in A(s) : \pi(s, a) \geq \tau * \max_{a'}(\pi(s, a')) \mid \forall a' \in A(s)\} \qquad (3)$$

Once the symbolic data set is created, we can proceed mining rules with our Set-Valued CN2 algorithm. We explored different settings; providing the rule mining the full state space of the RL as feature space or reducing the feature space to the upper right quadrant of Mario's receptive field, that is the cells in front of Mario. We also performed rule mining including and excluding the inequality (! =) predicate. The reduced feature set, with the excluded inequality predicate provides more interpretable rules, and are listed below. The default parameters of the beam search, expressing the maximal number of conditions per rule, the minimal number of samples to be covered by a rule and the beam

---

[3] Since BDPI is an actor-critic algorithm, we use the actor predictions as output, i.e. probabilities over actions. With value-based algorithms, e.g. DQN [18], one could record the Q-values instead.

width, were put respectively to 5, 20 and 10. Learned rules by Set-Valued CN2 using our WRA_{set} heuristic, that explain the policy our BDPI agent has learned in the Mario environment, are listed below. Note that the rules need to be interpreted sequentially.

```
 1. IF (1, 5)=NULL AND (0, 5)=NULL AND (0, 1)=NULL THEN Class=JUMP
 2. IF (1, 5)=BRICK AND (1, 0)=COIN_RED THEN Class=RIGHT
 3. IF (1, 5)=BRICK AND (2, 4)=COIN_RED THEN Class=RIGHT
 4. IF (4, 2)=NULL AND (0, 4)=NULL THEN Class=JUMP
 5. IF (4, 5)=NULL AND (3, 3)=NULL THEN Class=JUMP
 6. IF (3, 5)=BRICK THEN Class=JUMP
 7. IF (2, 2)=BRICK THEN Class=JUMP
 8. IF (0, 2)=NULL AND (0, 1)=NULL THEN Class=RIGHT
 9. IF (0, 5)=NULL THEN Class=JUMP
10. IF TRUE THEN Class=JUMP
```

The extraction resulted in a list of 10 rules, capturing the agent's behaviour at a high level. In overall, the conditions of the rules focus on empty spaces (NULL) and the presence of bricks or red coins. The second rule, for instance, explains that the policy likes to move to the right when there is a (positive rewarding) red coin in front of Mario. However, a problem with the learned rules is that they over-emphasise jumping, the action that is most often the best one, but that is not enough to finish a Mario level (Mario also has to move right to win). While the rules provide a high-level explanation of the policy followed by the agent, they do not allow the agent to obtain high returns when executed. Our second phase, the refinement, addresses this issue by allowing the rule mining algorithm to produce more refined rules, that lead to better execution performance.

5.2   Phase 2: Refinement

The rules produced by the first phase, described above, are optimised for classification accuracy. However, accuracy is not the main objective in policy distillation, as even high accuracy may still lead to poor performance in the environment. We therefore introduce a second phase, that refines the rules of the first phase based on roll-outs in the reinforcement learning environment. The second phase ensures that good policies are produced by our algorithm:

1. Use the Deep RL policy to perform an episode in the environment, observe the predicted actions step-wise;
2. In each time-step, predict the action that would be chosen by the obtained rules from phase 1 and note which rule was applied for the prediction;
3. When the predicted action of the Deep RL policy and the rules are different, store the observed state together with the action of the Deep RL policy in the training set of the respective rule;
4. Once the episode is finished, we extend each training set with samples from phase 1 that were correctly classified in order to get a balanced data set;

5. Launch a new rule mining process for each balanced training set using Set-Valued CN2 with the respective rule of the first phase as a starting point for the beam search process.

The procedure described above leads to each rule produced during phase 1 to have additional datapoints belonging to them, created when the rules and the black-box policy disagree in some state. By re-running our rule-mining algorithm on these rules, with extra datapoints, overly-general rules that lead to poor performance will be split into additional rules that better capture important actions in important states. If we were to take for example the fourth rule from the resulting rule list in the first phase, one of the resulting refined rules would be:

```
IF (4, 2)=NULL AND (0, 4)=NULL AND (2, 5)!=BRICK AND (0,
3)=NULL AND (1, 2)!=COIN_RED AND (1, 2)!=COIN_BLUE AND (1,
2)!=BORDER_CANNOT_PASS_THROUGH THEN Class=RIGHT
```

This additional rule ensures that the agent sometimes moves right, allowing the level to be finished. Because we keep track of which phase-1 rules are split into phase-2 rules, we are able to show the user a hierarchical view of the rules, with simple and general phase-1 rules that capture the overall policy, and some rules having *children* that identify refinements required for top performance.

Performing this refinement procedure in our example of Mario with the rules obtained from the first phase (listed in Subsect. 5.1), caused a refinement of multiple rules. We executed the refined rule list in the environment for 50 episodes and compared its performance with the performance of the original BDPI policy. Figure 4 shows that the refined rules are capable to reach a performance similar to BDPI, which demonstrates that our algorithms are able to produce intuitive explanations of black-box reinforcement learning policies, while ensuring that the explanations correspond to high-performance policies.

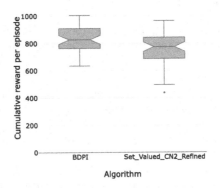

Fig. 4. Box plot comparison of episodic cumulative reward (y-axis) achieved by the refined extracted rules of our Set-Valued CN2 on the Mario environment with the original BDPI agent. 50 episodes were played by both agents (x-axis). The refined rules we obtain after phase 2 have an equivalent performance to the original policy since the box plots highly overlap. A bad-performing agent obtains a score 100 on this environment.

6   Conclusion

In this paper we have proposed an approach to translate a policy trained by a Deep RL algorithm into a set of rules. The set is human-readable, captures the behaviour of the policy, and can be iteratively refined to obtain higher returns if executed in the environment. A key element of our approach is that we associate every state to a *set* of equally-good actions, obtained by looking at the action probabilities predicted by the RL policy. This part of our contributions allows our modified rule mining algorithm to simplify its rule set. By allowing to select one of the almost equally-good actions for a state, the number of generated rules is significantly reduced compared to applying CN2 on the greedy policy. We find the iterative refinements appealing with respect to explainability. The rules of phase one are not altered, but only hierarchically expanded. Thus, the rules of the first phase provide a high-level view and every refinement adds details. Our refinement process is driven by the performance of the rules, measured by their execution in the environment. This prevents us from being dependent on magic numbers (i.e. the setting of the different parameters) of the rule mining algorithm. Furthermore, our method only assumes that the Deep RL algorithm produces a probability distribution over the actions, which can also be retrieved from value-based algorithms by using e.g. a Softmax function over Q-values. Alternatively, Eq. 3 can also be directly applied to Q-values. Finally, in our experiments, the states are semantically meaningful for users. The readability of the rules could however be further improved by using rule simplification or *syntactic sugar*. For example, in the Mario experiment, position (0, 4) could be translated into *right of Mario*. In settings where the features are not semantically meaningful, a double representation could be used as proposed in [6], where states represented in the feature space of the RL agent are grounded in a semantically meaningful representation for users. In future work we will also explore other rule-mining algorithms, as the use of CN2 is not crucial to our approach. What is however important is that the algorithm can handle Set-Valued labels. Therefore, adaptations of bi-clustering or Markov Random fields are appealing for exploiting meta-information of an RL process.

Acknowledgements. This work is supported by the Research Foundation Flanders (FWO) [grant numbers G062819N and 1129319N], the AI Research Program from the Flemish Government (Belgium) and the Francqui Foundation. This work is part of the research program Hybrid Intelligence with project number 024.004.022, which is (partly) financed by the Dutch Ministry of Education, Culture and Science (OCW).

References

1. Agogino, A.K., Tumer, K.: Analyzing and visualizing multiagent rewards in dynamic and stochastic domains. Auton Agents Multi-Agent Syst. **17**(2), 320–338 (2008). https://doi.org/10.1007/s10458-008-9046-9
2. Alharin, A., Doan, T.N., Sartipi, M.: Reinforcement learning interpretation methods: a survey. IEEE Access **8**, 171058–171077 (2020). https://doi.org/10.1109/ACCESS.2020.3023394

3. Brys, T., Nowé, A., Kudenko, D., Taylor, M.E.: Combining multiple correlated reward and shaping signals by measuring confidence. In: Proceedings of the Twenty-Eighth AAAI Conference on Artificial Intelligence, pp. 1687–1693. AAAI Press, Palo Alto (2014)

4. Clark, P., Niblett, T.: The CN2 induction algorithm. Machine Learn. **3**(4), 261–283 (1989). https://doi.org/10.1007/BF00116835

5. Coppens, Y., Efthymiadis, K., Lenaerts, T., Nowé, A.: Distilling deep reinforcement learning policies in soft decision trees. In: Miller, T., Weber, R., Magazzeni, D. (eds.) Proceedings of the IJCAI 2019 Workshop on Explainable Artificial Intelligence, Macau, pp. 1–6 (2019)

6. De Giacomo, G., Iocchi, L., Favorito, M., Patrizi, F.: Restraining Bolts for reinforcement learning agents. In: Proceedings of the Thirty-Fourth AAAI Conference on Artificial Intelligence. vol. 9, pp. 13659–13662. AAAI Press, Palo Alto (2020). https://doi.org/10.1609/aaai.v34i09.7114

7. Frosst, N., Hinton, G.: Distilling a neural network into a soft decision tree. In: Besold, T.R., Kutz, O. (eds.) Proceedings of the First International Workshop on Comprehensibility and Explanation in AI and ML 2017. AI*IA Series, vol. 2071. CEUR Workshop Proceedings, Aachen (2017)

8. Fürnkranz, J., Gamberger, D., Lavrač, N.: Foundations of Rule Learning. Cognitive Technologies. Springer, Heidelberg (2012). https://doi.org/10.1007/978-3-540-75197-7

9. Gevaert, A., Peck, J., Saeys, Y.: Distillation of deep reinforcement learning models using fuzzy inference systems. In: Beuls, K., et al. (eds.) Proceedings of the 31st Benelux Conference on Artificial Intelligence (BNAIC 2019) and the 28th Belgian Dutch Conference on Machine Learning (Benelearn 2019), vol. 2491. CEUR Workshop Proceedings, Aachen (2019)

10. Hinton, G., Vinyals, O., Dean, J.: Distilling the knowledge in a neural network. arXiv e-prints arXiv:1503.02531 (2015)

11. Huang, J., Angelov, P.P., Yin, C.: Interpretable policies for reinforcement learning by empirical fuzzy sets. Eng. Appl. Artif. Intell. **91** (2020). https://doi.org/10.1016/j.engappai.2020.103559

12. Karakovskiy, S., Togelius, J.: The Mario AI benchmark and competitions. IEEE Trans. Comput. Intell. AI Games **4**(1), 55–67 (2012). https://doi.org/10.1109/TCIAIG.2012.2188528

13. Lavrač, N., Flach, P., Zupan, B.: Rule evaluation measures: a unifying view. In: Džeroski, S., Flach, P. (eds.) ILP 1999. LNCS (LNAI), vol. 1634, pp. 174–185. Springer, Heidelberg (1999). https://doi.org/10.1007/3-540-48751-4_17

14. Libin, P.J.K., et al.: Deep reinforcement learning for large-scale epidemic control. In: Dong, Y., Ifrim, G., Mladenić, D., Saunders, C., Van Hoecke, S. (eds.) ECML PKDD 2020. LNCS (LNAI), vol. 12461, pp. 155–170. Springer, Cham (2021). https://doi.org/10.1007/978-3-030-67670-4_10

15. Madumal, P., Miller, T., Sonenberg, L., Vetere, F.: Explainable reinforcement learning through a causal lens. In: Proceedings of the Thirty-Fourth AAAI Conference on Artificial Intelligence, vol. 3, pp. 2493–2500. AAAI Press, Palo Alto (2020). https://doi.org/10.1609/aaai.v34i03.5631

16. Maes, P.: Computational reflection. In: Morik, K. (ed.) GWAI-87 11th German Workshop on Artifical Intelligence. Informatik-Fachberichte, vol. 152, pp. 251–265. Springer, Heidelberg (1987). https://doi.org/10.1007/978-3-642-73005-4_27

17. Miller, T.: Explanation in artificial intelligence: insights from the social sciences. Artif. Intell. **267**, 1–38 (2019). https://doi.org/10.1016/j.artint.2018.07.007

18. Mnih, V., et al.: Human-level control through deep reinforcement learning. Nature **518**(7540), 529–533 (2015). https://doi.org/10.1038/nature14236

19. Molnar, C.: Interpretable Machine Learning. Leanpub, Victoria (2019)

20. Rusu, A.A., et al.: Policy distillation. In: International Conference on Learning Representations (2016). arXiv:1511.06295

21. Rückstieß, T., Sehnke, F., Schaul, T., Wierstra, D., Sun, Y., Schmidhuber, J.: Exploring parameter space in reinforcement learning. Paladyn, J. Behav. Robot. **1**(1), 14–24 (2010). https://doi.org/10.2478/s13230-010-0002-4

22. Steckelmacher, D., Plisnier, H., Roijers, D.M., Nowé, A.: Sample-efficient model-free reinforcement learning with off-policy critics. In: Brefeld, U., Fromont, E., Hotho, A., Knobbe, A., Maathuis, M., Robardet, C. (eds.) ECML PKDD 2019. LNCS (LNAI), vol. 11908, pp. 19–34. Springer, Cham (2020). https://doi.org/10.1007/978-3-030-46133-1_2

23. Sutton, R.S., Barto, A.G.: Reinforcement Learning: An Introduction, 2nd edn. MIT Press, Cambridge (2018)

24. Sutton, R.S., McAllester, D., Singh, S., Mansour, Y.: Policy gradient methods for reinforcement learning with function approximation. In: Neural Information Processing Systems (NIPS), pp. 1057–1063 (2000)

25. Tadepalli, P., Givan, R., Driessens, K.: Relational reinforcement learning: an overview. In: Tadepalli, P., Givan, R., Driessens, K. (eds.) Proceedings of the ICML-2004 Workshop on Relational Reinforcement Learning, Banff, Canada, pp. 1–9 (2004)

26. Todorovski, L., Flach, P., Lavrač, N.: Predictive performance of weighted relative accuracy. In: Zighed, D.A., Komorowski, J., Żytkow, J. (eds.) PKDD 2000. LNCS (LNAI), vol. 1910, pp. 255–264. Springer, Heidelberg (2000). https://doi.org/10.1007/3-540-45372-5_25

27. Zambaldi, V., et al.: Deep reinforcement learning with relational inductive biases. In: International Conference on Learning Representations (2019)

Modelling Agent Policies with Interpretable Imitation Learning

Tom Bewley[✉][iD], Jonathan Lawry[iD], and Arthur Richards[iD]

University of Bristol, Bristol, UK
{tom.bewley,j.lawry,arthur.richards}@bristol.ac.uk

Abstract. As we deploy autonomous agents in safety-critical domains, it becomes important to develop an understanding of their internal mechanisms and representations. We outline an approach to imitation learning for reverse-engineering black box agent policies in MDP environments, yielding simplified, interpretable models in the form of decision trees. As part of this process, we explicitly model and learn agents' latent state representations by selecting from a large space of candidate features constructed from the Markov state. We present initial promising results from an implementation in a multi-agent traffic environment.

Keywords: Explainable artificial intelligence · Interpretability · Imitation learning · Representation learning · Decision tree · Traffic modelling

1 Introduction

Data-driven learning is state-of-the-art in many domains of artificial intelligence (AI), but raw statistical performance is secondary to the trust, understanding and safety of humans. For autonomous agents to be deployed at scale in the real world, people with a range of backgrounds and remits must be equipped with robust mental models of their learning and reasoning. However, modern learning algorithms involve complex feedback loops and lack semantic grounding, rendering them black boxes from a human perspective. The field of explainable artificial intelligence (XAI) [5] has emerged in response to this challenge.

Most work in XAI focuses on developing insight into classification and regression systems trained on static datasets. In this work we consider dynamic problems comprising agents interacting with their environments. We present our approach to interpretable imitation learning (I2L), which aims to model the policy of a black box agent from analysis of its input-output statistics. We call the policy model *interpretable* because it takes the form of a binary decision tree, which is easily decomposed and visualised, and can be used for both factual and

---

Supported by an EPSRC/Thales industrial CASE award in autonomous systems.

F. Heintz et al. (Eds.): TAILOR 2020, LNAI 12641, pp. 180–186, 2021.
https://doi.org/10.1007/978-3-030-73959-1_16

counterfactual explanation [3]. We move beyond most current work in the imitation learning literature by explicitly learning a latent state representation used by the agent as the basis for its decision making. After formalising our approach, we report the initial results of an implementation in a traffic simulator.

2   I2L Framework

Preliminaries. Our I2L approach is applied to agents that operate in Markov Decision Process (MDP) environments. At time t, an agent perceives the current Markov state $s_t \in \mathcal{S}$. We then assume that it maps this state into an intermediate representation $x_t = \phi(s_t)$ then selects an action from the discrete space $\mathcal{A}$ via a deterministic policy function $a_t = \pi(x_t)$. The next Markov state s_{t+1} is a function of both s_t and a_t. Modelling a state-dependent reward function is not necessary for the present work.

Generic Problem Formulation. We adopt the perspective of a passive spectator of the MDP with access to its Markov state and the action taken by the agent at each time step. This allows us to observe a history of N states and actions $\mathcal{H} = [(s_1, a_1), ..., (s_N, a_N)]$ to use as the basis of learning. Our objective is to imitate the agent's behaviour, that is, to reverse-engineer the mapping $s_t \rightarrow a_t$. This effectively requires approximations of both ϕ and π, denoted by ϕ' and π' respectively. The need to infer both the policy and the representation on which this policy is based makes this problem a hybrid of imitation learning and state representation learning [4].

It is essential to constrain the search spaces for ϕ' and π' (Φ and Π respectively) so that they only contain functions that are human-interpretable, meaning that their operation can be understood and predicted via visualisations, natural-language explanations or brief statements of formal logic. This property must be achieved while minimally sacrificing imitation quality or tractability of the I2L problem. Given the history of state-action pairs $\mathcal{H}$, this problem can be formulated as an optimisation over ϕ' and π':

$$\underset{\phi' \in \Phi, \pi' \in \Pi}{\text{argmin}} \left[\sum_{t=1}^{N} \ell\left(\pi'\left(\phi'\left(s_t\right)\right), a_t\right) \right] \quad \text{where } \Phi, \Pi = \text{``interpretable''} \quad (1)$$

and $\ell : \mathcal{A} \times \mathcal{A} \rightarrow \mathbb{R}_{\geq 0}$ is a pairwise loss function over the discrete action space. The schematic in Fig. 1[1] outlines the task at hand.

Space of Representation Functions. As highlighted above, it is important that Φ permits human-interpretable state representations. We achieve this by limiting its codomain to vectors of real-valued features, generated from s_t through recursive application of elementary operations from a finite set $\mathbb{F}$. To

---

[1] Icons from users *Freepik* and *Pixel Perfect* at www.flaticon.com.

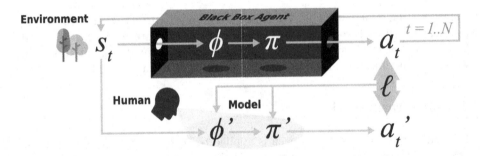

Fig. 1. Generic I2L problem setup. The objective is to minimise the loss between a_t and a'_t $\forall t \in 1..N$, while ensuring ϕ' and π' are comprehensible under human scrutiny.

limit the complexity of Φ, we specify a limit r on the recursion depth. Prior domain knowledge is used to design $\mathbb{F}$, which in turn has a shaping effect on ϕ' without requiring the stronger assumption of which precise features to use. Each feature also has a clear interpretation by virtue of its derivation via canonical operations. In our traffic simulator implementation, $\mathbb{F}$ contains operations to extract a vehicle's speed/position, find the nearest vehicle/junction ahead of/behind a position, and subtract one speed/position from another.

Space of Policy Functions. Π must be similarly limited to functions that are comprehensible to humans while retaining the representational capacity for high-quality imitation. Following prior work [2,6], we achieve this by adopting a decision tree structure. The pairwise loss function ℓ over the action space $\mathcal{A}$ is used to define an impurity measure for greedy tree induction. For a decision node n, let $P_n(a)$ be the proportion of data instances at that node with action value a. We use the following measure of node impurity:

$$I(n) = \sum_{a \in \mathcal{A}} \sum_{a' \in \mathcal{A}} P_n(a) \cdot P_n(a') \cdot \ell(a, a') \tag{2}$$

The popular Gini impurity is a special case of this measure, recovered by defining ℓ such that $\ell(a, a') = 0$ if $a = a'$, and $\ell(a, a') = 1$ otherwise.

Learning Procedure. In general, the joint inference of two unknown functions (in this case ϕ' and π') can be very challenging, but our constraints on Φ and Π allow us to approximately solve Eq. 1 through a sequential procedure:

1. Apply domain knowledge to specify the feature-generating operations $\mathbb{F}$ and recursion depth r. Denote the representation of all valid features ϕ_{all}.
2. Iterating through each state s_t in the observed state-action history $\mathcal{H}$, apply ϕ_{all} to generate a vector of numerical feature values. Store this alongside the corresponding action a_t in a training dataset.

3. Define a pairwise action loss function ℓ and deploy a slightly-modified version of the CART tree induction algorithm [1] to greedily minimise the associated impurity measure (Eq. 2) on the training set. Let the induction process continue until every leaf node is pure, yielding a large, overfitted tree $\mathcal{T}_0$.
4. Prune the tree back using minimal cost complexity pruning (MCCP) [1], whose output is a tree sequence $[\mathcal{T}_0, \mathcal{T}_1, \mathcal{T}_2, ...]$, each a subtree of the last, representing a progressive reduction of $\mathcal{T}_0$ down to its root.
5. Pick a tree from this sequence to use as the policy model π', and define ϕ' as the subset of features from ϕ_{all} used at least once in that tree.

Having a sequence of options for the tree model and associated representation allows us to manage a tradeoff between accuracy on one end, and interpretability (through simplicity) on the other. In the following implementation, we explore the tradeoff by selecting several trees from across the pruning sequence.

3 Implementation with a Traffic Simulator

We implement I2L in a traffic simulator, in which multiple vehicles follow a common policy to navigate a track while avoiding collisions. Five track topologies are shown in Fig. 3 (left). Coloured rectangles are vehicles and red circles are junctions. Since the policy is homogeneous across the population we can analyse the behaviour of all vehicles equally to learn ϕ' and π'.

Target Policies. Instead of learned policies, we use two hand-coded controllers as the targets of I2L. From the perspective of learning these policies remain opaque. For both policies, $\mathcal{A}$ contains five discrete acceleration levels, which determine the vehicle's speed for the next timestep within the limits $[0, v_{max}]$.

- Fully-imitable policy (π_F): a rule set based on six features including the vehicle's speed, distance to the next junction, and separations and speeds relative to other agents approaching that junction. This policy is itself written as a decision tree with 39 leaves, hence can be modelled exactly in principle.
- Partially-imitable policy (π_P): retains some logic from π_F, but considers more nearby vehicles and incorporates a proportional feedback controller. These changes cannot be modelled exactly by a finite decision tree.

Representation. We use a set of eight operations $\mathbb{F}$ which allows the six-feature representation used by π_F (denoted ϕ_F) to be generated. These are:

- pos : $i \to p$ or $j \to p$. Get the position of vehicle i or junction j.
- speed : $i \to v$. Get the speed of vehicle i.
- fj : $i \to j$. Find the next junction in front of vehicle i.
- fa : $i \to i'$ or $j \to i'$. Find the next vehicle in front of vehicle i or junction j.
- ba : $i \to i'$ or $j \to i'$. Find the next vehicle behind vehicle i or junction j.
- twin : $j \to j'$. Flip between the two track positions comprising a junction.

– sep : $(p_1, p_2) \rightarrow s$. Compute the separation between two positions.
– sub : $(v_1, v_2) \rightarrow \Delta$ or $(s_1, s_2) \rightarrow \Delta$. Subtract two speeds or separations.

With $r = 6$, ϕ_{all} has 308 features, including all six in ϕ_F. The vast majority are irrelevant for imitating the target policies, so we face a feature selection problem.

Training. We run simulations with 11 vehicles on all five topologies in Fig. 3 (left). The recorded history $\mathcal{H}$ is converted into a training dataset by applying ϕ_{all} for each vehicle. After rebalancing action classes, our final dataset has a length of 125000. For tree induction, we use the simple loss function $\ell(a, a') = |a - a'|$. For each tree in the sequence output by MCCP, we measure the predictive accuracy on a validation dataset, and consider the number of leaf nodes and features used as heuristics for interpretability. Figure 2 plots these values across the sequence for both targets. We select five pruning levels (in addition to $\mathcal{T}_0$) for evaluation.

Baselines. We also train one tree using only the six features in ϕ_F, and another with an alternative representation $\phi_{\text{naïve}}$, indicative of what might be deemed useful without domain knowledge (radius, angle, normal velocity and heading of nearby agents in egocentric coordinates). Two further baselines use training data from only one track topology (either the smallest topology A or the largest D). This tests the generalisability of single-topology learning. For all baselines, we use the pruned tree with the highest validation accuracy.

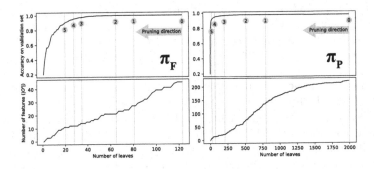

Fig. 2. Validation accuracy and used feature count across the pruning sequences for each target policy. *Note the very different horizontal axis scales*; the unpruned tree for π_P is much larger. Numbered vertical lines indicate trees chosen for evaluation.

4   Results and Discussion

The heat maps in Fig. 3 (right) contain results for two metrics of imitation quality for both π_F and π_P. Each row corresponds to a pruned tree or baseline, and each column indicates the track topology used for testing.

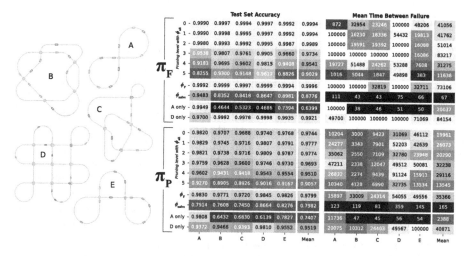

Fig. 3. (Left): the five test topologies used. (Right): results for I2L quality metrics.

Accuracy. This metric is predictive accuracy on a held-out test set. For both π_F and π_P, mean accuracy exceeds 90% for even the smallest prune levels and 95% for the second-smallest. The fact that accuracy for π_P is bounded at around 97.5% reflects the fact that this policy is not a decision tree so cannot be perfectly imitated by one. As expected, providing ϕ_F upfront (thereby removing the representation learning requirement) yields somewhat better accuracy, but it is promising to see that down to prune level 2, performance differs by under 0.25% for both targets. Lacking information about junctions, the tree using $\phi_{\text{naïve}}$ is unable to obtain the same levels of accuracy, demonstrating the importance of choosing the correct representation for imitation. The single-topology training results show that trees generalise well from the large topology D, but poorly from the small topology A. This suggests the latter contains insufficient variety of vehicle arrangements to capture all important aspects of the target policies.

Failure. Here we deploy the models as control policies in the environment and measure the mean time between failures (either collision or 'stalls', when traffic flow grinds to a halt) over 100 episodes of up to 1000 timesteps. A value of 100000 indicates zero failures occurred. While results broadly correlate with accuracy, this metric shows more marked aggregate distinctions between π_F and π_P, and between different test topologies. Nonetheless, there is minimal degradation with pruning down to level 4, with a constant average of just 1-2 failures for π_F, and 3-4 for π_P. In fact, it appears that intermediate pruning levels fail less often than the largest trees. While the reason for this is not immediately clear, it may be that having fewer leaves yields less frequent changes of acceleration and smoother motion. Providing ϕ_F confers no significant benefit over ϕ_{all}, while $\phi_{\text{naïve}}$ and single-topology training on A are utterly unable to perform/generalise well.

5   Conclusion

We have introduced our approach to interpretable imitation learning for black box agent control policies that use intermediate low-dimensional state representations. Our models take the form of decision trees, which select from large vectors of candidate features generated from the Markov state using a set of basic operations. The accuracy-interpretability tradeoff is managed by post-pruning.

Our initial implementation has shown that trees trained by I2L exhibit high predictive accuracy with respect to two hand-coded control policies, and are able to avoid failure conditions for extended periods, even when heavily pruned. It has also highlighted that using a plausible-but-incorrect state representation places a severe limitation on imitation quality, and that learning from data that do not capture the full variation of the environment leads to poor generalisation.

In ongoing follow-up work, we are exploring how our decision tree models can be used to interpret and explain their target policies, and are also implementing I2L with a truly black box policy trained by reinforcement learning.

References

1. Breiman, L., Friedman, J., Olshen, R., Stone, C.: Classification and Regression Trees. Wadsworth & Brooks, Cole Statistics/Probability Series, California (1984)
2. Coppens, Y., Efthymiadis, K., Lenaerts, T., Nowé, A., Miller, T., Weber, R., Magazzeni, D.: Distilling deep reinforcement learning policies in soft decision trees. In: Proceedings of the IJCAI 2019 Workshop on Explainable AI, pp. 1–6 (2019)
3. Guidotti, R., Monreale, A., Giannotti, F., Pedreschi, D., Ruggieri, S., Turini, F.: Factual and counterfactual explanations for black box decision making. IEEE Intell. Syst. (2019)
4. Lesort, T., Díaz-Rodríguez, N., Goudou, J.F., Filliat, D.: State representation learning for control: an overview. Neural Networks **108**, 379–392 (2018)
5. Samek, W., Wiegand, T., Müller, K.R.: Explainable AI: understanding, visualizing and interpreting deep learning models. arXiv:1708.08296 (2017)
6. Turnbull, O., Lawry, J., Lowenberg, M., Richards, A.: A cloned linguistic decision tree controller for real-time path planning in hostile environments. Fuzzy Sets Syst. **293**, 1–29 (2016)

Social

Value-Alignment Equilibrium
in Multiagent Systems

Nieves Montes[(⊠)] and Carles Sierra

Artificial Intelligence Research Institute, IIIA-CSIC, Campus UAB, Bellaterra, Spain
{nmontes,sierra}@iiia.csic.es

Abstract. Value alignment has emerged in recent years as a basic principle to produce beneficial and mindful Artificial Intelligence systems. It mainly states that autonomous entities should behave in a way that is aligned with our human values. In this work, we summarize a previously developed model that considers values as preferences over states of the world and defines alignment between the governing norms and the values. We provide a use-case for this framework with the Iterated Prisoner's Dilemma model, which we use to exemplify the definitions we review. We take advantage of this use-case to introduce new concepts to be integrated with the established framework: alignment equilibrium and Pareto optimal alignment. These are inspired on the classical Nash equilibrium and Pareto optimality, but are designed to account for any value we wish to model in the system.

Keywords: Value alignment · Normative systems · Responsible AI

1 Introduction

In the last decades, research in Artificial Intelligence (AI) has been able to design and deploy increasingly complex systems, from robots and software agents, to recommendation algorithms and social networking apps [10]. Given that nowadays interaction with AI systems happens on a daily basis, a new challenge arises: how to ensure that all these systems, with all their complexity and power, behave in a way that is aligned with our human values. This requirement is referred to as the Value-Alignment Problem (VAP) [16], and is the focus of this work.

In this paper, we summarise a previously developed value alignment model [19] motivated by the assumption that we should be able to prove that any designed system is actually complying with our values [15]. It uses *norms* as the essential tools to supervise and limit autonomous agents' behaviour [11]. More importantly, it provides a precise definition of what it means for a norm to be aligned with a given value. We then provide a use-case based on the benchmark Iterated Prisoner's Dilemma game [3]. Inspired by the concepts of Nash equilibria and Pareto optimality in game theory, we introduce new concepts of value equilibria and optimality that build on top of the formal framework in [19].

© Springer Nature Switzerland AG 2021
F. Heintz et al. (Eds.): TAILOR 2020, LNAI 12641, pp. 189–204, 2021.
https://doi.org/10.1007/978-3-030-73959-1_17

2   Value Alignment Model

2.1   Revision of Our Background Formal Model

In order to introduce the necessary background, we provide a summary of the value alignment model that constitutes the starting point of this paper [19]. Its main underlying assumption is a *consequentialist view of values* [20], which expresses that the worthiness of any value is entirely determined by the outcomes of the actions that it motivates. Values, then, can serve as numerical quantifiers to assess how (un)desirable is a state in the world. In particular, we can use values to compare any two states and decide which of the two is preferred.

In the reviewed framework, the common conception of the world as a labelled transition system [8] is adopted. The world, then, is composed of a set of states S, a set of actions A and a set of transitions $T \subseteq S \times A \times S$. We refer to any transition $(s, a, s') \in T$ with the notation $s \xrightarrow{a} s'$.

Values are conceived as mental constructs [12] that allow agents to decide which state of the world they prefer, according to their most prioritised values. This consideration motivates the following definition:

Definition 1 (from [19]). *A value-based preference* Prf *is a function over pairs of states that indicates how much preferred is one state over another in light of a particular value:* Prf $: S \times S \times G \times V \to [-1, 1]$, *where G is the set of agents and V is the set of values. The notation* $\mathsf{Prf}_v^\alpha(s, s')$ *indicates how much does agent α prefer state s' over state s with respect to value v.*

Value-based preferences, then, are bounded functions between -1 and $+1$. Positive (negative) preference indicates the post-transition state is more (less) desirable than the pre-transition state with respect to a specific value v. Preferences equal to 0 indicate that both states are identically preferred.

Values are held at the agent level. However, very rarely do agents' belief systems consist of a single value [18]. Aggregations over subsets of values and/or agents are also considered in [19]. However, we will not be employing any aggregation functions in this work. The interested reader is referred to the original paper for further details.

Now we have a clear view of the role of values when it comes to evaluating states. However, the states that can arise when letting a multiagent system evolve are dependent upon the *norms* in place, since these are the constructs which govern behaviour and therefore limit the actions that can be taken. Thus, value alignment is conceived as the alignment of a norm (or a set of norms) with respect to a value that is held in high regard. When a set of norms N is incorporated into the world (S, A, T), it is modified into a new, *normative* world (S, A, N, T_N) [1], where $T_N \subseteq T$ is the subset of all the original transitions allowed by N.

To evaluate how well or badly aligned is a norm $n \in N$, the transitions that can happen when this norm is enforced have to be evaluated. A norm is positively (negatively) aligned if it gives rise to transitions that move the system towards more (less) preferred states. However, beyond single transitions, the long-term evolution of the world under the norms in place should be considered. This necessity motivates the following definition:

Definition 2 (from [19]). *A path p in the world $(\mathcal{S}, \mathcal{A}, \mathcal{T})$ is a finite sequence of consecutive transitions $\{s_0 \xrightarrow{a_0} s_1, s_1 \xrightarrow{a_1} s_2, ..., s_i \xrightarrow{a_i} s_{i+1}, ..., s_f \xrightarrow{a_{f-1}} s_f\}$, where $p_F[i] = p_I[i+1]$, and $p_I[i]$ and $p_F[i]$ denote the pre- and post-transition states of the i-th transition.*

Paths are used to evaluate preferences over consecutive transitions, and support the formal definition of value alignment:

Definition 3 (from [19]). *The degree of alignment of norm $n \in N$ with respect to value $v \in V$ in the world $(\mathcal{S}, \mathcal{A}, \mathcal{T})$ for agent $\alpha \in G$ is defined as the accumulated preference over all the paths in the normative world that results from implementing such norm:*

$$\mathsf{Algn}_{n,v}^{\alpha}(\mathcal{S}, \mathcal{A}, \mathcal{T}) = \frac{\sum\limits_{p \in paths} \sum\limits_{d \in [1,|p|]} \mathsf{Prf}_v^{\alpha}(p_I[d], p_F[d])}{\sum\limits_{p \in paths} |p|} \tag{1}$$

where paths *is the set of all paths in the normative world $(\mathcal{S}, \mathcal{A}, \{n\}, \mathcal{T}_n)$, and $|p|$ corresponds to the cardinality of p, i.e. the number of transitions in the path.*

Note that we exclude the possibility of infinite transition systems by considering all paths to be finite.

In this approach, the same exact weight is given to every single transition. Other suggestions are conceivable; for example one may want to consider whether preferences remain approximately stable along the paths or, conversely, there are large surges or sinks. In other fields, it is typical to consider a discount parameter that reduces the weight of transitions that happen into the distant future [17]. We acknowledge the existence of alternative approaches, but leave their exploration for future work.

Another issue to note with Definition 3 is that its notation indicates the alignment for a single agent α with respect to a single value v, since it takes the individual preferences with respect to that one value. However, as previously mentioned, preferences can be aggregated over agents and/or sets of values. Using such aggregated preferences would, consequently, result in alignment for sets of agents and/or with respect to sets of values.

Equation (1) states that alignment should take into account all possible transitions in the normative world. In general, this approach is not efficient, and to solve this issue, Monte Carlo sampling over all possible paths is recommended. Additionally, it is also advisable to keep the length of the paths fixed. These modifications lead to the following reformulation for the alignment:

$$\mathsf{Algn}_{n,v}^{\alpha}(\mathcal{S}, \mathcal{A}, \mathcal{T}) = \frac{\sum\limits_{p \in paths} \sum\limits_{d \in [1,l]} \mathsf{Prf}_v^{\alpha}(p_I[d], p_F[d])}{x \times l} \tag{2}$$

where l is the number of transitions in all paths, and x is the number of sampled paths.

In summary, the approach proposed in [19] provides a formal model to numerically quantify how compliant is a certain normative world designed towards some particular value. Differently to other works related to value alignment [2,7], such a model is separate from the decision-making process of the participating agents and their respective goals, and can hence be applied to any kind of agent and social space architecture.

2.2   Value-Alignment Solution Concepts

In this work, we model agents' interactions as normal-form games. In game theory, a stage game refers to each of the identical rounds played in one iteration. The Nash equilibrium is then defined as the set of players' actions such that no player can obtain a higher profit by unilaterally deviating from it, given the actions of all other players are fixed [14, Chapter 2]. In formal terms, Nash equilibria correspond to action profiles $(a_1^*, ..., a_{|G|}^*)$ such that, for all agents $i \in G$, it holds that:

$$r_i(a_1^*, ..., a_{i-1}^*, a_i^*, a_{i+1}^*, ..., a_{|G|}^*) \geq r_i(a_1^*, ..., a_{i-1}^*, a_i, a_{i+1}^*, ..., a_{|G|}^*) \qquad (3)$$

Nash equilibria may not represent the best option for players in terms of individual revenues, but profiles of joint actions for which no player has an incentive to unilaterally deviate. This solution concept represents *status quo* positions that persist despite not necessarily being the best solutions from a social perspective. In other terms, the Nash equilibria do not necessarily correspond with Pareto optimal outcomes [5], as in the case of the classical Prisoner's Dilemma game.

The concept of stage game Nash equilibrium is not directly applicable in our theoretical framework for two main reasons. First, in general, agents interact repeatedly. And second, we are interested in the alignment with respect to values, not in the game rewards themselves, even if alignments may be computed from rewards. However, Nash-like equilibria situations can be identified when the alignment satisfies an adapted version of Eq. (3). When considering this possibility, the argument a_i^* should not be identified as actions taken by agents in a single round, but rather by the strategies that individuals follow for the whole duration of the game. We conceive individual strategies as separate from norms. While strategies are part of the agents' internal decision process, we understand norms to be externally imposed constraints on the system, whose definition is the responsibility of the model's designer and beyond the control of the participating agents.

Therefore, given a set of norms N governing a multiagent system, agents adopt a particular strategy to play the game. Strategies are functions that take into account the past history of the game to return an action to be performed next [14]. The set of all strategies being played is $E = \{e_1, e_2, ..., e_{|G|}\}$, where e_i is the strategy followed by the i-th agent. Then, we can make the following definition:

Definition 4. *Given a normative system N and an alignment function with respect to the value of choice for agent i* Algn_v^i, *the alignment equilibrium is defined as the tuple of all individual strategies* $\left(e_1^*, ..., e_{|G|}^*\right)$ *such that, for all agents $i \in G$, it holds that:*

$$\mathsf{Algn}^i_{\left(e_1^*, ..., e_{i-1}^*, e_i^*, e_{i+1}^*, ..., e_{|G|}^*\right), v} \geq \mathsf{Algn}^i_{\left(e_1^*, ..., e_{i-1}^*, e_i, e_{i+1}^*, ..., e_{|G|}^*\right), v} \qquad (4)$$

Note that the alignment equilibria depend on the alignment function of choice and the norms constraining the system. Another point to note is that, despite Eq. (4) is stated in terms of alignment with respect to individual agents, a natural extension arises when applied to subsets of agents or even aggregated for the whole society. Additionally, it can also be extended to sets of values.

Another important point is that, unlike the classical Nash equilibrium, whose existence is guaranteed for games played by a finite number of agents following mixed strategies [9], the properties of Eq. (4) have not been explored to the point of establishing conditions for existence. This is left as future work.

It is worth trying to understand the motivation behind Eq. (4). Classical game theory takes the view of trying to maximise one's own reward while minimising risks. The classical Nash equilibrium for a stage game is a possible response to this approach for a game that is played once. Our definition of alignment equilibrium, then, generalises the classical Nash equilibrium to account for games and situations that are presented repeatedly.

More importantly, Eq. (4) allows to examine a game from a different perspective other than that of the individual payoffs r_i, as we can analyse the alignment equilibria with respect to as many values as alignment functions we are able to come up with. Moreover, agents may consider different preferences or may take into account different variables to compute their preferences, and thus Eq. (4) need not be symmetric with respect to agents. By considering the particular instance where a game is played for a path of length one (a single round) and using the actual rewards as preferences, the classical concept of Nash equilibrium can be recovered.

Previously, we have mentioned the concept of Pareto optimality [5]. This solution concept from game theory can also be adapted to the value alignment framework. Classically, an action profile $(a_1^*, ..., a_{|G|}^*)$ is said to lead to a *Pareto optimal outcome* if there is no other profile $(a_1, ..., a_{|G|})$ such that:

$$r_j\left(a_1, ..., a_{|G|}\right) > r_j\left(a_1^*, ..., a_{|G|}^*\right) \text{ for at least one agent } j \in G, \text{ and} \qquad (5)$$

$$r_i\left(a_1, ..., a_{|G|}\right) \geq r_i\left(a_1^*, ..., a_{|G|}^*\right) \text{ for all agents } i \in G \qquad (6)$$

In other words, in classical game theory a Pareto optimal outcome is one where we cannot improve anyone's reward without damaging someone else's.

In a similar fashion to our extension from the classical Nash equilibrium to the alignment equilibrium, we can adapt Pareto optimality to our value alignment framework. Again, we need not consider actions for a single transition, but rather strategies adopted during the whole duration of the game:

Definition 5. *Given a normative system N and an alignment function with respect to the value of choice for agent i Algn^i_v, a tuple of individual strategies $\left(e^*_1, ..., e^*_{|G|}\right)$ is said to lead to a Pareto optimal alignment if there is no other tuple of individual strategies $\left(e_1, ..., e_{|G|}\right)$ such that:*

$$\mathsf{Algn}^j_{\left(e_1,...,e_{|G|}\right),v} > \mathsf{Algn}^j_{\left(e^*_1,...,e^*_{|G|}\right),v} \quad \text{for at least one agent } j \in G, \text{ and} \quad (7)$$

$$\mathsf{Algn}^i_{\left(e_1,...,e_{|G|}\right),v} \geq \mathsf{Algn}^i_{\left(e^*_1,...,e^*_{|G|}\right),v} \quad \text{for all agents } i \in G \quad (8)$$

Therefore, a Pareto optimal alignment corresponds to a situation where no agent can improve its alignment without hurting one or several other agent alignments. The novel concept of Pareto optimal alignment allows us to make the same generalisations than those when moving from the classical Nash equilibrium to the alignment equilibrium. They have been explicitly described previously.

3   Use-Case: Two-Agent Iterated Prisoner's Dilemma

Now, we consider a very simple two-agent system modelled after the benchmark Iterated Prisoner's Dilemma (IPD) game [3], and we use it to illustrate the previously introduced concepts.

Table 1. Outcome matrix for the Prisoner's Dilemma game.

		β	
		Cooperate	Defect
α	Cooperate	$(6,6)$	$(0,9)$
	Defect	$(9,0)$	$(3,3)$

In formal terms, this model consists of an agent set with two members, $G = \{\alpha, \beta\}$; the set of individual actions available to each of them is $\mathcal{A}_i = \{\text{cooperate}, \text{defect}\}$. The transitions between states are characterised by the joint actions that α and β take, hence the set of actions is $\mathcal{A} = \mathcal{A}^2_i = \{(a_\alpha, a_\beta)\}$. The tuple of individual actions (a_α, a_β) determines the outcome of the transition. Such outcomes are tied to rewards agents receive, $r_i(a_\alpha, a_\beta), \forall i \in G$, via the outcome matrix displayed in Table 1.

In this model, the game is played in an iterated way. We characterise states by the agents' wealth, which is defined as the accumulated rewards received since the game started. The states of the world correspond to the tuple of agents' wealth, noted by (x_α, x_β). Initially, both agents start with $(x_\alpha, x_\beta) = (0, 0)$. After agents have chosen their actions (a_α, a_β) and the rewards (r_α, r_β) are determined, the transition $s \to s'$ is completed by updating the values for agents' wealth.

We formally lay out the main features of our model in the following terms:

Definition 6. *We define the Two-Agent Iterative Prisoner's Dilemma (2A-IPD) model as a tuple $(G, \mathcal{S}, \mathcal{A}, \mathcal{T})$, where:*

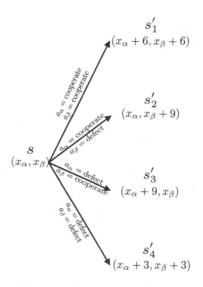

Fig. 1. Labelled transition system representing a single transition of the 2A-IPD model.

- $G = \{\alpha, \beta\}$ *is a set of two agents.*
- $S = \{(x_\alpha, x_\beta)\}$ *is the set of states, composed by the tuples of all possible combinations of agents' wealth.*
- $A = \{(a_\alpha, a_\beta)\}$, *where* $a_i \in \{cooperate, defect\}$, *is the set of joint actions.*
- $T : S \times A \times S$ *is the set of transitions which relate the current state* $s = (x_\alpha, x_\beta)$ *and joint actions* (a_α, a_β) *to the next state* $s' = (x'_\alpha, x'_\beta)$:

$$\forall t \in T, \quad t = (s, (a_\alpha, a_\beta), s') \quad such \ that \quad \begin{cases} x'_\alpha = x_\alpha + r_\alpha(a_\alpha, a_\beta) \\ x'_\beta = x_\beta + r_\beta(a_\alpha, a_\beta) \end{cases} \quad (9)$$

where $r_i(a_\alpha, a_\beta)$ *are the rewards given by the outcome matrix (Table 1).*

A labelled transition system representation for one transition of this model is displayed in Fig. 1.

3.1 Preference Functions

Within this model, we wish to quantify the alignment of different agent behaviours with respect to two apparently opposed values: *equality* and *personal gain*. In [19] some preferences related to these values were already formulated. However, we introduce new ones here that are less sensitive to the numerical choice for the rewards in Table 1.

In order to quantify alignment with respect to equality, we will assess it in each state by making use of the well-known Gini Index (GI) [6]. In our two-agent model, the GI is computed for state s by taking the values of agents' wealth at that particular point in the repeated game, (x_α, x_β). For $|G| = 2$, the Gini Index for our system becomes:

$$\text{GI}(s) = \frac{|x_\alpha - x_\beta|}{2(x_\alpha + x_\beta)} \tag{10}$$

The lower bound for the GI is always 0, indicating perfect equality among all participants. In the case of two agents, the maximum possible value is $\frac{1}{2}$ [4]. Then, in order to map perfect equality (GI = 0) to maximum preference ($+1$) and perfect inequality (GI = $\frac{1}{2}$) to minimum preference (-1), the interval for the Gini Index $[0, \frac{1}{2}]$ is linearly mapped to the interval of definition of preferences $[-1, 1]$. This transformation results in the following definition for the preference function over the value *equality*:

$$\text{Prf}^i_{\text{equality}}(s, s') = 1 - 4 \cdot \text{GI}(s') = 1 - 2 \cdot \frac{|x'_\alpha - x'_\beta|}{x'_\alpha + x'_\beta} \tag{11}$$

where $i = \alpha, \beta$.

There are two important points to be noted about this preference function. First, it is numerically equivalent for both agents, since x'_α and x'_β are interchangeable. It is an intuitive property of the preference with respect to the value *equality* that it should be indeed identical for both agents. Second, $\text{Prf}^i_{\text{equality}}(s, s')$ is a function of only the properties of the system in the post-transition state s'. Hence, states with high (low) equality are (not) preferred regardless of the parity in the previous state s.

The latter property is not a requirement of preference functions. Other formulae could be devised that depend on the increase/decrease of the Gini Index or some other indicator. Since our model starts off from a very peculiar position of perfect equality, we have considered that it is more helpful to monitor the eventual disparity that may arise as the game proceeds, rather than comparing consecutive states.

The other value under consideration, personal gain, is quantified through the following preference function:

$$\text{Prf}^i_{\text{gain}}(s, s') = \begin{cases} -1 & \text{if } x'_i - x_i = 0 \\ -\frac{1}{3} & \text{if } x'_i - x_i = 3 \\ \frac{1}{3} & \text{if } x'_i - x_i = 6 \\ 1 & \text{if } x'_i - x_i = 9 \end{cases} \tag{12}$$

According to this definition, states are preferred with respect to personal gain by ranking the possible rewards in any given transition and mapping them to equally spaced points in the preference interval $[-1, 1]$. This choice is made to reflect the greediness of this value, since the preference is only dependent on immediate gains, regardless of how well off the agent may already be or the circumstances of her peer.

Now, we have the preference functions to evaluate the alignment of the system for the two agents. In order to compute the alignment from preferences, Eq. (2) is employed, with $x = 10,000$ sampled paths of length $l = 10$ (the number of game iterations).

3.2   Individual Strategies

Now that we have encoded values into two different preference functions, our purpose, then, is to find which agent strategies in the 2A-IPD model result in alignment equilibrium and Pareto optimal alignment positions with respect to equality and personal gain. The set of all possible strategies for a single agent is a vast space of logical formulae, dictating whether past actions should be taken into account to decide the future action, how far back to look and many other considerations. In order to work with the alignment equilibrium without the burden of considering *all* possible strategies, we restrict ourselves to two subspaces of possible strategy profiles, from which we will determine the alignment equilibria and Pareto optimal alignments:

1. *Random-action profiles:* Both α and β choose at each round the action to take randomly, according to independent and fixed probabilities of cooperation. These are analogous to mixed strategies in game theory, where actions are taken based on a fixed probability.
2. *Heterogeneous profiles:* β cooperates randomly following a fixed probability. α, in contrast, either cooperates or defects with probability 0.5 in the first round. In subsequent rounds, it follows one of these strategies:
   - *Tit-for-tat:* α's action in the current round is β's action in the previous round.
   - *Mostly cooperate:* α defects if in the previous round both agents defected. Otherwise, it cooperates.
   - *Mostly defect:* α cooperates if in the previous round both players cooperated. Otherwise, it defects.

   These are some of the most common strategies in non-cooperative game theory. We set that only one agent follows them in order not to condition the outcome of all transitions on the result of the first one.

Note that all of the strategies presented here are included in the set of reactive strategies [13], where behaviour is only dependent on the opponent's immediate past action.

4   Results

First, the results for the alignment under random-action profiles with respect to equality and personal gain are presented in Figs. 2 and 3 respectively. They are plotted as a function of the cooperation probabilities of both agents, which specify concrete instances of the individual random strategies e_α and e_β.

According to the definition of alignment equilibrium in Eq. (4), in Fig. 2 there is an infinite number of alignment equilibria corresponding to strategies satisfying $e_\alpha = e_\beta$ (here we only plot 10×10 strategy pairs). To see this, if we consider that the cooperation probability of agent β is e_β, then α's alignment is maximal when e_α is equal to e_β, and α has no incentive to deviate. Similarly if

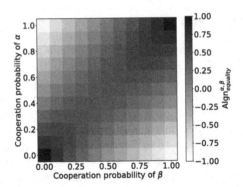

Fig. 2. Alignment of agents α and β with respect to value *equality*, Eq. (11), under random-action profiles.

we fix the cooperation probability of agent α, given the symmetry of Eq. (11). Therefore, an infinite number of alignment equilibria are found at $e_\alpha^* = e_\beta^*$.

It is unsurprising that the *status quo* with respect to equality corresponds to both agents having the same cooperation probability. It is worth noting that this result does not encourage any agent to increase its cooperation probability to enhance equality, but rather to act similarly to her peer.

The Pareto optimal alignment with respect to equality is found when either both agents always cooperate or always defect, since they always receive identical rewards and the Gini Index is kept to zero. So, actually, alignment equilibrium strategies with respect to equality do include Pareto optimal strategies.

As for alignment with respect to gain in Fig. 3, the maximum alignment for any agent is obtained when she defects and the other player follows a complete cooperation strategy. The alignment equilibrium, again considering only random-action profiles, is found at the position where both agents never cooperate. This is a consequence of the single Nash equilibrium of the stage game at the position (defect, defect), in combination with the definition of preference with respect to personal gain in Eq. (12) being directly related to the individual gains for a single round.

Differently from the results obtained for value *equality* where equilibrium positions were Pareto optimal, for value *personal gain* this is not the case. Starting from constant mutual defection, both agents could improve their alignment by turning to constant mutual cooperation instead, since they would attain larger gains at each round. This result is also due to the direct relationship between preferences with respect to personal gain and the actual rewards in each round, see Eq. (12).

This pair of strategies (both agents always defecting for all repetitions of the game) is the alignment equilibrium when both agents' alignments are computed with respect to value *personal gain*. An interesting observation is that this is also the alignment equilibrium when one player's alignment is computed with respect to equality, and the other with respect to gain. Let's consider the case where

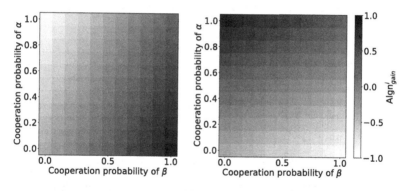

Fig. 3. Alignment of agent α (left) and β (right) with respect to value *personal gain*, Eq. (12), under random-action profiles. Note that $\text{Algn}^\alpha_{\text{gain}}$ and $\text{Algn}^\beta_{\text{gain}}$ are mutually transposed.

α's alignment is computed with respect to gain, Fig. 3 left, and β's alignment is computed with respect to equality, Fig. 2.

Regardless of β's actions, α's alignment is always maximised under null cooperation probability, so the preferred strategy to take is to defect in every round. Then, β maximises her alignment with respect to equality by imitating α, that is, always defecting as well. The result is that the only alignment equilibrium satisfying Eq. (4) for random-actions profiles is found at $e^*_\alpha = e^*_\beta = 0$. It is worth noting that the calculation for the alignment is specific to each agent in order to reflect their different priority values. Again, this alignment is not Pareto optimal. If both agents switched to $e_\alpha = e_\beta = 1$, α could enhance her alignment with respect to personal gain while maintaining β's alignment with respect to equality at 1.

A summary of the results presented so far for random-action profiles is displayed in Table 2.

Now, we look into the alignment with respect to a single value under heterogeneous profiles. The alignment for both players is plotted as a function of the cooperation probability of β, under the various possible strategies for α, for value *equality* in Fig. 4 and for value *personal gain* in Fig. 5.

Table 2. Summary of the results obtained for two randomly-behaving players, highlighting the position of alignment equilibrium strategies and their Pareto optimality.

Value for α	Value for β	Alignment equilibrium	Pareto optimal
Equality	Equality	$e^*_\alpha = e^*_\beta$	Included
Personal gain	Personal gain	$e^*_\alpha = e^*_\beta = 0$	No
Personal gain	Equality	$e^*_\alpha = e^*_\beta = 0$	No

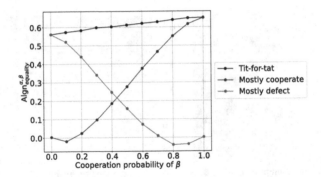

Fig. 4. Alignment of agents α and β with respect to value *equality*, Eq. (11), under heterogeneous profiles, depending on the strategy followed by player α.

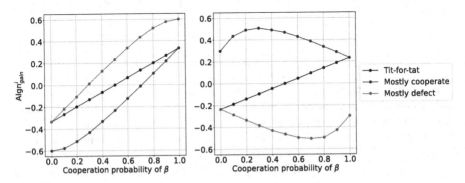

Fig. 5. Alignment of agent α (left) and β (right) with respect to value *personal gain*, Eq. (12), under heterogeneous profiles, according to the strategy followed by player α.

First, we focus our attention on the alignment with respect to equality in Fig. 4. In this case, the three strategies result in very distinct trends. *Tit-for-tat*, equivalent to imitating the opponent, leads to a very stable alignment with respect to equality, independently of the extend of collaboration of β. The other two strategies, *mostly cooperate* and *mostly defect*, result in alignments that are strongly dependent on β's cooperation probability. When β defects often (cooperation $\sim$0), *mostly defect* is the preferred individual strategy for α. In contrast, when β cooperates often (cooperation $\sim$1), *mostly cooperate* is the most suitable strategy for α. These results are in line with those obtained for random-action profiles with respect to equality (Fig. 2), where we observed that the alignment equilibrium was reached when both payers behaved similarly.

In order to find the alignment equilibrium from results presented as in Fig. 4, we must look for the position(s) such that: (a) For constant cooperation probability of β, *i.e.* by fixing the position along the x axis, changing α's strategy by switching line colour leads to a decrease in alignment; and (b) for fixed α's strategy, *i.e.* maintaining the line colour, the cooperation probability of β (the coordinate along the x axis) corresponds to a maximum along that line.

For heterogeneous profiles, the alignment equilibrium with respect to equality is found when β's strategy along the iterated game settles in cooperation (probability of cooperation equals 1) and α applies the *tit-for-tat* or *mostly cooperate* strategies, both of which result in α cooperating for all rounds of the game, except possibly in the first one. Neither β nor α would then have any incentive to unilaterally deviate.

Differently to the case of random strategies, where there was an infinite number of alignment equilibria (the positive diagonal), in this case there is a single alignment equilibrium that corresponds to the persistent collaboration of both agents along the iterated game, which is something clearly desirable from a social perspective. Then, the introduction of strategic directives for α has shifted the equilibrium with respect to equality towards cooperation. It is also worth noting that, in this case, the equilibrium strategy corresponds exactly with the only Pareto optimal position.

Second, we concentrate on alignment with respect to personal gain, Fig. 5. In this case, α's alignment is strongly dependent on the cooperation probability of β. The three strategies yield alignments for α that are monotonically increasing with β's collaboration. Also, the three strategies are always equally ranked. This means that, given a fixed cooperation ratio for β, the most aligned strategy is always *mostly defect*, followed by *tit-for-tat* and finally *mostly cooperate*. The strategies are ordered from least to most cooperative.

As for β's alignment, it increases linearly with its cooperation probability when α follows *tit-for-tat*. It displays a peak at low collaboration rates when α deploys *mostly cooperates*, and a valley at high cooperation probabilities when α follows *mostly defect*.

Again, considering only the heterogeneous profiles that have generated these results, there are two alignment equilibria with respect to personal gain corresponding to β not cooperating at all and α following either *mostly defect* or *tit-for-tat*. To achieve this conclusion, we first note that, for any cooperation probability of β, α always enhances her alignment by following *mostly defect*. Then, once α has settled for this strategy, the best choice for β is to always defect. These two observations lead to α following either *mostly defect* or *tit-for-tat* and β never cooperating. Given that β always defects, both these strategies converge to α always defecting as well, except maybe at the first round. It is worth noting that these equilibria are actually far from the maximum possible alignment for either agent. Nor do they result in a Pareto optimal alignment, since both agents could improve their alignment by having α follow *tit-for-tat* and β increase her probability of cooperation.

Finally, in an exercise similar to that performed for random-action profiles, we find the alignment equilibrium position when agents prioritise different values. Since players in this strategy profiles are not equivalent (α behaves in a conscious way while β behaves completely randomly), we must examine two possibilities: α prioritises *personal gain* while β prioritises *equality*, and vice-versa.

Table 3. Summary of the results obtained under heterogeneous profiles, highlighting the position of alignment equilibrium strategies and their Pareto optimality (Nomenclature for strategies: TfT: *tit-for-tat*; MC: *mostly cooperate*; MD: *mostly defect*).

Value for α	Value for β	Alignment equilibrium	Pareto optimal
Equality	Equality	$e_\alpha^* = $ TfT/MC; $e_\beta^* = 1$	Yes
Personal gain	Personal gain	$e_\alpha^* = $ TfT/MD; $e_\beta^* = 0$	No
Personal gain	Equality	$e_\alpha^* = $ TfT/MD; $e_\beta^* = 0$	No
Equality	Personal gain	$e_\alpha^* = $ TfT/MC; $e_\beta^* = 1$	Yes

For the first possibility, α will always need to follow *mostly defect* to ensure that her alignment with respect to personal gain is maximised, regardless of β's probability of cooperation. Then, in order to attain maximum alignment with respect to equality, β will settle on constant defection. Hence, the alignment equilibrium when α prioritises personal gain and β prioritises equality is the same as when both prioritised personal gain. Yet again, these strategies do not lead to a Pareto optimal alignment, since both agents could improve the alignment with respect to their prioritised values by having α follow *tit-for-tat* and β increase her probability of cooperation.

For the second possibility, α will follow *tit-for-tat*, since this strategy dominates the two others when it comes to equality, regardless of the cooperation probability of β. Given this observation, β will then enhance her alignment with respect to *personal gain* by always cooperating. At this position, α can resort to *tit-for-tat* or *mostly cooperate* indistinctly. This strategy profile is equal to the equilibrium found when both agents prioritised equality. In this case, it also corresponds to a Pareto optimal alignment, since α has achieved the maximum possible alignment with respect to equality.

It is worth pointing out that the alignment equilibrium positions under agents prioritising different values are driven by the player following the more conscious strategy, α in this case. That is to say that when α focuses on personal gain, the solution concepts are identical regardless of the value that β (the randomly behaving agent) holds in high regard. The same result is found when α focuses on equality instead.

A summary with the results analysed for the model under heterogeneous profiles is provided in Table 3.

5   Conclusions and Future Work

In this work, we have reviewed a formal framework that establishes preferences over the states in the world, and we have specified the computation of value alignment through the increase or decrease in preferences over states in a normative world. Some further study needs to be done in the theoretical front, but for the time being we have been able to implement this framework in the Iterated Prisoner's Dilemma model.

Inspired by the classical Nash equilibrium and Pareto optimality in game theory, we have introduced the novel notions of *alignment equilibrium* and *Pareto optimal alignment*. These solution concepts extend the existing definitions to account for different values beyond individual rewards and generalise to cases where agents may have different priorities. We have been able to identify both equilibria and Pareto optimal alignments in our Two-Agent Iterated Prisoner's Dilemma model, with respect to the values *equality* and *personal gain*. An interesting finding is that, under both strategy subsets under consideration, alignment equilibria positions with respect to equality include Pareto optimal outcomes, while equilibrium positions with respect to value gain do not.

This work intends to exemplify an application of the proposed model for the value alignment problem. Further work, built on it, remains to be done. First, on the analytical side, formal properties of the alignment equilibrium and its relationship with Pareto optimal alignments should be explored. Second, the model can be naturally extended to account for the introduction of norms, such as taxes, fines or the banning/enforcement of behaviour. An interesting outcome from such research should be the shift, if any, in the alignment equilibria positions. Finally, a third line of work should be focused on the development of methodologies to synthesise norms with optimal alignment with respect to values of choice.

Acknowledgments. This work has been supported by the AppPhil project (Recer-Caixa 2017), the CIMBVAL project (funded by the Spanish government, project # TIN2017-89758-R), the EU WeNet project (H2020 FET Proactive project # 823783) and the EU TAILOR project (H2020 # 952215).

References

1. Andrighetto, G., Governatori, G., Noriega, P.: Normative Multi-agent Systems, vol. 4. Schloss Dagstuhl-Leibniz-Zentrum fuer Informatik, April 2013. https://doi.org/10.4230/DFU.Vol4.12111.i
2. Atkinson, K., Bench-Capon, T.: States, goals and values: revisiting practical reasoning. Argument Comput. **7**(2–3), 135–154 (2016). https://doi.org/10.3233/AAC-160011
3. Axelrod, R.M.: The Evolution of Cooperation. Basic Books, New York (1984)
4. Bellù, L., Liberati, P.: Inequality Analysis: The Gini Index. Food and Agriculture Organization of the United Nations (2006). http://www.fao.org/policy-support/resources/resources-details/en/c/446282/
5. Chinchuluun, A., Pardalos, P., Migdalas, A., Pitsoulis, L.: Pareto Optimality Game Theory And Equilibria, vol. 17. Springer, New York (2008). https://doi.org/10.1007/978-0-387-77247-9
6. Cowell, F.A.: Measuring Inequality. LSE Perspectives in Economic Analysis. Oxford University Press, Oxford (2009)
7. Cranefield, S., Winikoff, M., Dignum, V., Dignum, F.: No pizza for you: value-based plan selection in BDI agents. In: Proceedings of the Twenty-Sixth International Joint Conference on Artificial Intelligence, pp. 178–184. International Joint Conferences on Artificial Intelligence Organization (2017). https://doi.org/10.24963/ijcai.2017/26

8. Gorrieri, R.: Labeled transition systems. Process Algebras for Petri Nets. MTC-SAES, pp. 15–34. Springer, Cham (2017). https://doi.org/10.1007/978-3-319-55559-1_2

9. Huang, L.: Nash theorem (in game theory). In: Encyclopedia of Mathematics. Springer (2002). http://www.encyclopediaofmath.org/index.php?title=Nash_theorem_(in_game_theory)&oldid=40004

10. Lu, Y.: Artificial intelligence: a survey on evolution, models, applications and future trends. J. Manage. Anal. **6**(1), 1–29 (2019). https://doi.org/10.1080/23270012.2019.1570365

11. Mahmoud, M.A., Ahmad, M.S., Mohd Yusoff, M.Z., Mustapha, A.: A review of norms and normative multiagent systems. Sci. World J. **2014**, 1–23 (2014). https://doi.org/10.1155/2014/684587

12. Miceli, M., Castelfranchi, C.: A cognitive approach to values. J. Theor. Soc. Behav. **19**(2), 169–193 (1989). https://doi.org/10.1111/j.1468-5914.1989.tb00143.x, https://onlinelibrary.wiley.com/doi/abs/10.1111/j.1468-5914.1989.tb00143.x

13. Nowak, M.A., Sigmund, K.: Tit for tat in heterogeneous populations. Nature **355**(6357), 250–253 (1992). https://doi.org/10.1038/355250a0

14. Osborne, M.J., Rubinstein, A.: A Course in Game Theory. MIT Press, Cambridge (2012)

15. Russell, S.: Provably beneficial artificial intelligence. In: The Next Step: Exponential Life. BBVA-Open Mind (2017)

16. Russell, S.: Human Compatible: Artificial Intelligence and the Problem of Control. Penguin LCC, New York (2019)

17. Schwartz, H.M.: Multi-Agent Machine Learning: A Reinforcement Approach. Wiley, New York (2014). https://doi.org/10.1002/9781118884614

18. Schwartz, S.H.: An overview of the Schwartz theory of basic values. Online Read. Psychol. Cult. **2**(1) (2012). https://doi.org/10.9707/2307-0919.1116

19. Sierra, C., Osman, N., Noriega, P., Sabater-Mir, J., Perello-Moragues, A.: Value alignment: a formal approach. In: Responsible Artificial Intelligence Agents Workshop (RAIA) in AAMAS 2019 (2019)

20. Sullivan, S., Philip, P.: Ethical theories (2002). https://www.qcc.cuny.edu/SocialSciences/ppecorino/ETHICS_TEXT/CONTENTS.htm

Election Manipulation on Social Networks with Messages on Multiple Candidates Extended Abstract

Matteo Castiglioni[1], Diodato Ferraioli[2(✉)], Nicola Gatti[1], and Giulia Landriani[1]

[1] Politecnico di Milano, Milano, Italy
{matteo.castiglioni,nicola.gatti}@polimi.it,
giulia.landriani@mail.polimi.it
[2] Università degli Studi di Salerno, Fisciano (SA), Italy
dferraioli@unisa.it

Abstract. We study the problem of election control through social influence when the manipulator is allowed to use the locations that she acquired on the network for sending *both* positive and negative messages on *multiple* candidates, widely extending the previous results available in the literature that study the influence of a single message on a single candidate. In particular, we provide a tight characterization of the settings in which the maximum increase in the margin of victory can be efficiently approximated and of those in which any approximation turns out to be impossible.

1 Introduction

Nowadays, there is increasing use of social networks to convey inaccurate and unverified information, e.g., hosting the diffusion of fake news, spread by malicious users for their illicit goals. This can lead to severe and undesired consequences, as widespread panic, libelous campaigns, and conspiracies. In the United States, for instance, there is an ongoing discussion on the power of manipulation of social media during the US elections in 2016 [14] and, more importantly, for future elections. Thus, understanding and limiting the adverse effects on the elections due to information diffusion in social networks is currently considered of paramount importance.

The problem of election control through social influence has been recently the object of interest of many works. E.g., Sina et al. [15], Auletta et al. [8], and Castigioni et al. [10] show how to modify the relationship among voters in order to make the desired candidate to win an election; Auletta et al. [2–4] show that, in case of two only candidates, a manipulator controlling the order in which information is disclosed to voters can lead the minority to become a

This work has been partially supported by the Italian MIUR PRIN 2017 Project ALGADIMAR "Algorithms, Games, and Digital Market".

F. Heintz et al. (Eds.): TAILOR 2020, LNAI 12641, pp. 205–211, 2021.
https://doi.org/10.1007/978-3-030-73959-1_18

majority; a similar adversary is studied by Auletta et al. [5–7], showing that such a manipulator can lead a bare majority to consensus with two candidates, but not with three or more; Bredereck and Elkind [9] study how selecting seeds from which to diffuse information to manipulate a two-candidate election.

In our paper, we focus on this last kind of manipulation, namely manipulation by seeding. More precisely, we assume that a manipulator can buy some locations on the network from which she kicks off a diffusion of (potentially fake) news aiming at altering the preference rankings of the voters receiving them to make the desired candidate to win the election. Wilder and Vorobeychik [16] have recently studied the case in which a manipulator spreads information on a single candidate to make her either to win the election or to lose the election. The authors also provided approximation algorithms to compute the optimal seeds for positive messages only or negative messages only. Similar results have been obtained also in [1,11,12].

However, in elections with more than two candidates, the assumption that the election control can be either constructive or destructive as well as on a single candidate only is too limiting. This is indeed exemplified by the setting in Fig. 1, characterized by five voters and five candidates, with c_0 denoting the manipulator's candidate and $c_1, \ldots, c_4$ denoting the remaining candidates. Note that each information is received with probability one regardless of the sender. Hence, we do not need to care about which nodes send positive or negative messages since all voters will always receive these messages. It can be easily observed that when a message (positive or negative) on a single candidate is sent (as considered by Wilder and Vorobeychik [16]), then the desired candidate c_0 cannot be made to win the election (at most, the election will end with a tie between c_0 and another candidate, both taking two votes). Instead, injecting the network with both a positive message toward c_0 and a negative message toward c_2 will result in c_0 being the only node with two votes, and thus the winner. Hence, differently from what happens in the setting of Wilder and Vorobeychik [16], the optimal solution can include positive/negative messages on candidates different from the desired one.

Our Contribution. We focus on the election control problem when the manipulator is allowed to use the locations that she acquired on the network for sending *both* positive and negative messages on *multiple* candidates. Our model essentially coincides with the one presented by Castiglioni et al. [10] and extends the one by Wilder and Vorobeychik [16]. It assumes that diffusion occurs according to a variation of the *independent cascade model* [13] able to capture the simultaneous spread of multiple messages. We also focus on the same objective studied by Wilder and Vorobeychik [16], that is to maximize the increase in the margin of victory of the manipulator's candidate c_0.

Under mild assumptions on how a voter revises her preference ranking given a set of messages, we provide a tight characterization of the settings in which the maximum increase in the margin of victory can be efficiently approximated and of those in which any approximation turns out to be impossible unless P = NP. Specifically, we prove that whenever there is a set of τ messages making the

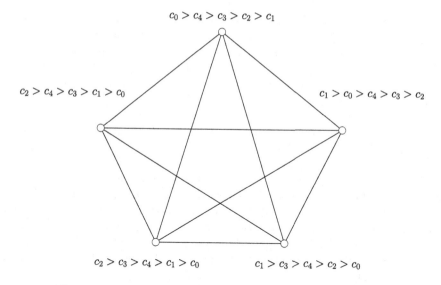

$$c_0 > c_4 > c_3 > c_2 > c_1$$

$c_2 > c_4 > c_3 > c_1 > c_0$

$c_1 > c_0 > c_4 > c_3 > c_2$

$c_2 > c_3 > c_4 > c_1 > c_0$ $c_1 > c_3 > c_4 > c_2 > c_0$

Fig. 1. Clique characterized by five voters and five candidates.

candidate initially ranked by a voter as the least-preferred one to the most-preferred candidate, then there is a greedy poly-time algorithm guaranteeing an approximation factor ρ depending on τ. A surprisingly sharp *transition phase* occurs, instead, when no such a set of messages exists. In this case, no poly-time approximation algorithm is possible, unless $\mathsf{P} = \mathsf{NP}$, even when the approximation factor is a function in the size of the problem.

2   The Model

We consider an *election control problem*, defined by a set of candidates $C = \{c_0, c_1, \ldots, c_\ell\}$, and a network of voters, modeled as a weighted directed graph $G = (V, E, p)$, where V is the set of voters, E is the set of edges, and $p \colon E \to (0, 1]$ denotes the strength of the influence among voters. In particular, with a slight abuse of notation, we denote as $p(u, v)$ the strength of influence of u on v. Each voter v has a preference ranking π_v over the candidates. We denote as $\pi_v(i)$ the i-th candidate in the rank π_v. At the election time, the voter is assumed to cast a vote for $\pi_v(1)$. For each candidate $c \in C$, we also denote as V_c the set of voters that rank c as first, i.e., $V_c = \{v \in V \mid \pi_v(1) = c\}$.

The election control problem involves a manipulator whose objective is to spend a *budget B* of messages to make c_0 win the election, by injecting in the network positive or negative information both about c_0 and about the other candidates. Namely, our goal is to find a set of *seeds* in V and a set of at most B messages sent by these seeds in order to maximize the increase in the margin of victory of c_0.

Specifically, let $S \subseteq V$ be a subset of voters and $I(s) = (q_0, ..., q_\ell)$ be a vector associated to each $s \in S$, where $q_i \in \{-, \cdot, +\}$, with $q_i = +$ ($q_i = -$, respectively) representing that s sends a positive (negative, respectively) message about candidate c_i, and $q_i = \cdot$ representing that no message is sent by s about c_i. For every $s \in S$, given a vector $I(s)$, we denote as $|I(s)|$ the number of messages $+$ or $-$ sent by seed s, i.e., $|I(s)| = |\{i : q_i \neq \cdot\}|$. We assume that $|I(s)| \geq 1$ for every $s \in S$. We also say that s sends *message* (c, q) for $c \in C$ and $q \in \{+, -\}$ if $I(s, c)$, i.e., the c-th entry of $I(s)$, is q. Given (S, I), its cost is defined as the cumulative number of messages sent by the seeds, i.e., $\sum_{s \in S} |I(s)|$. A solution (S, I) is *feasible* if its cost does not exceed B.

For each feasible solution (S, I), messages are supposed to spread over the network according to a *multi-issue independent cascade* (MI-IC) model. In this model, given the graph $G = (V, E, p)$, we define the *live-graph* $H = (V, E')$, where each edge $(u, v) \in E$ is included in H with probability $p(u, v)$. Moreover, for each candidate $c \in C$ and for each type $q \in \{-, +\}$, we keep a set $A_{c,q}^t$ of *active* voters at time t. These sets initially contain the seeds sending the corresponding messages, i.e. $A_{c,q}^0 = \{s \in S : I(s, c) = q\}$ for every c, q. Finally, at each time $t \geq 1$, we build $A_{c,q}^t$ as follows: for each edge $(s, v) \in E'$, we consider the set $M(s, v)$ of messages (c, q) such that $s \in A_{c,q}^{t-1}$ and $v \notin \bigcup_{i<t} A_{c,q}^i$; then for each (s, v) such that $M(s, v)$ is not empty, we add v to $A_{c,q}^t$ for every $(c, q) \in M(s, v)$. The diffusion process of the message (c, q) terminates at time $T_{c,q}$ such that $A_{c,q}^{T_{c,q}} = \emptyset$. Finally, the cascade terminates when the diffusion of each message (c, q) terminates.

The reception by voter v of messages do not only influence whether v will or not forward these messages through the network, but also affect her preference ranking. Denote with $R = \{(c, q)\}_{c \in C}$ a set of received messages. A *ranking revision function* ϕ associates each pair (π, R) to a new ranking π' obtained by revising ranking π with the set of received messages R. We study a general class of ranking revision functions that extends that one used by Wilder and Vorobeychik [16]. Specifically, when there is a single message on the network, the ranking revision is as the one prescribed by Wilder and Vorobeychik [16]. That is, a message $(c, +)$ causes that c switches her position with the candidate above, whereas each message $(c, -)$ causes that c switches her position with the candidate below. Instead, if v receives both $(c, +)$ and $(c, -)$, then, she discards them and behaves as if no message was received about c. When there are messages on multiple candidates, the ranking revision functions ϕ satisfy the following mild properties:

- if candidate c_j is the most preferred, then she keeps to be the most preferred when an additional negative message on an alternative candidate is received;
- if candidate c_i is the most preferred, then she keeps to be the most preferred when a positive message on her is received;
- given two possible rankings π, π' of a node v differing only for the position of candidate c_j, in π not being worse than in π', and given a message set R, if c_j is the most preferred in the ranking returned by $\phi(\pi', R)$, then c_j must be the most preferred also in the ranking returned by $\phi(\pi, R)$.

Given a feasible solution (S, I) and a live graph H, we let, for every $v \in V$, $\pi_v^*(S, I, H)$ be the ranking at the end of the MI-IC model. Moreover, for each $c \in C$, we also denote as V_c^* the set of voters that rank c as first at the end of the diffusion process, i.e., $V_c^*(S, I, H) = \{v \in V \mid \pi_v^*(1) = c\}$. Finally, the *margin of victory* of (S, I, H) is $\mathsf{MoV}(S, I, H) = |V_{c_0}^*(S, I, H)| - \max_{c \neq c_0} |V_c^*(S, I, H)|$, that denotes the number of votes that c_0 needs to win the election, if the first term is lower than the second, and the advantage of c_0 with respect to the second best ranked candidate, otherwise. Finally, the *effectiveness* of (S, I), denoted as $\Delta_{\mathsf{MoV}}(S, I, H)$ is the increase in the margin of victory for the choice of seeds and messages, i.e., $\Delta_{\mathsf{MoV}}(S, I, H) = \mathsf{MoV}(S, I, H) - \mathsf{MoV}(\emptyset, (), H)$. The election control problem consists in computing $(S^*, I^*) = \arg\max_{(S,I)} \mathbb{E}_H[\Delta_{\mathsf{MoV}}(S, I, H)]$, where expectation is taken on the probability of live graphs H.

An algorithm A is said to always return a ρ-approximation for the election control problem with $\rho \in [0, 1]$ potentially depending on the size of the problem, if, for each instance, it returns (S, I) such that $\mathbb{E}_H[\Delta_{\mathsf{MoV}}(S, I, H)] \geq \rho \mathbb{E}_H[\Delta_{\mathsf{MoV}}(S^*, I^*, H)]$.

3   Our Results

From our definition of ranking revision function, it is immediate to achieve the following monotonicity properties:

1. Given a node whose initial preferences are such that c_0 is ranked as the least-preferred candidate, either c_0 becomes the most-preferred candidate on receiving messages $\{(c_0, +), (c_i, -)$ for every $i > 0\ \}$ or there is no set R of messages such that c_0 can become the most-preferred candidate;
2. If the message set $\{(c_0, +), (c_i, -)$ for every $i > 0\}$ makes candidate c_0 the most-preferred one for a given ranking π when c_0 is the least-preferred candidate, then the same message makes c_0 the most-preferred candidate for any other ranking π'.

We then introduce the following definition that will characterize the approximability of the election control problem.

Definition 1. *The pair $(\phi, |C|)$ composed of a ranking revision function and a number of candidates is said* least-candidate manipulable *if, when c_0 is the least-preferred candidate for a node, message set $\{(c_0, +), (c_i, -)$ for every $i > 0\}$ does always make c_0 be the most preferred.*

Based on this definition, let us first state our inapproximability result.

Theorem 1. *For any $\rho > 0$ even depending on the size of the problem, there is no algorithm that on input instances of the problem that are not least-candidate manipulable, always returns a ρ-approximate, unless $\mathsf{P} = \mathsf{NP}$.*

Theorem 1 essentially states that whenever there is no way for making the least-preferred candidate for a node to become the most-preferred one of that node, then there is no chance that a manipulator designs an algorithm allowing her to maximize the increment in the margin of victory of the desired candidate regardless of the adopted ranking revision function.

We next show that the condition behind the inapproximability results is tight. Indeed, by dropping that condition, we can design poly-time constant approximation algorithms. Intuitively, the algorithm works by greedily selecting B/τ seeds and letting them to send the τ messages that make the least preferred candidate to be the most preferred.

Theorem 2. *Consider the set of instances in which $(\phi, |C|)$ is least-candidate manipulable. Call $\tau \leq \ell+1$ the cardinality of the smallest set of messages making c_0 be the most preferred for every initial preference ranking. There is a greedy poly-time algorithm returning a ρ-approximation to the election control problem, with $\rho = \frac{B-\tau+1}{2\tau B}\left(1 - \frac{1}{e}\right)$.*

References

1. Abouei Mehrizi, M., Corò, F., Cruciani, E., D'Angelo, G.: Election control through social influence with unknown preferences. In: Kim, D., Uma, R.N., Cai, Z., Lee, D.H. (eds.) COCOON 2020. LNCS, vol. 12273, pp. 397–410. Springer, Cham (2020). https://doi.org/10.1007/978-3-030-58150-3_32
2. Auletta, V., Caragiannis, I., Ferraioli, D., Galdi, C., Persiano, G.: Minority becomes majority in social networks. In: WINE, pp. 74–88 (2015)
3. Auletta, V., Caragiannis, I., Ferraioli, D., Galdi, C., Persiano, G.: Information retention in heterogeneous majority dynamics. In: WINE, pp. 30–43 (2017)
4. Auletta, V., Caragiannis, I., Ferraioli, D., Galdi, C., Persiano, G.: Robustness in discrete preference games. In: AAMAS, pp. 1314–1322 (2017)
5. Auletta, V., Ferraioli, D., Greco, G.: Reasoning about consensus when opinions diffuse through majority dynamics. In: IJCAI, pp. 49–55 (2018)
6. Auletta, V., Ferraioli, D., Fionda, V., Greco, G.: Maximizing the spread of an opinion when tertium datur EST. In: AAMAS, pp. 1207–1215 (2019)
7. Auletta, V., Ferraioli, D., Greco, G.: On the effectiveness of social proof recommendations in markets with multiple products. In: ECAI, pp. 19–26 (2020)
8. Auletta, V., Ferraioli, D., Savarese, V.: Manipulating an election in social networks through edge addition. In: AI*IA, pp. 495–510 (2019)
9. Bredereck, R., Elkind, E.: Manipulating opinion diffusion in social networks. In: IJCAI (2017)
10. Castiglioni, M., Ferraioli, D., Gatti, N.: Election control in social networks via edge addition or removal. In: AAAI, pp. 1878–1885 (2020)
11. Corò, F., Cruciani, E., D'Angelo, G., Ponziani, S.: Exploiting social influence to control elections based on scoring rules. In: IJCAI, pp. 201–207 (2019)
12. Corò, F., Cruciani, E., D'Angelo, G., Ponziani, S.: Vote for me!: Election control via social influence in arbitrary scoring rule voting systems. In: AAMAS, pp. 1895–1897 (2019)
13. Kempe, D., Kleinberg, J., Tardos, E.: Maximizing the spread of influence through a social network. In: ACM SIGKDD, pp. 137–146 (2003)

14. Office of The Director of National Intelligence: Background to 'Assessing Russian Activities and Intentions in Recent Elections': The Analytic Process and Cyber Incident Attribution (2017)
15. Sina, S., Hazon, N., Hassidim, A., Kraus, S.: Adapting the social network to affect elections. In: AAMAS, pp. 705–713 (2015)
16. Wilder, B., Vorobeychik, Y.: Controlling elections through social influence. In: AAMAS, pp. 265–273 (2018)

Process-To-Text: A Framework for the Quantitative Description of Processes in Natural Language

Yago Fontenla-Seco[✉][iD], Manuel Lama[iD], and Alberto Bugarín[iD]

Centro Singular de Investigación En Tecnoloxías Intelixentes (CiTIUS)
Universidade de Santiago de Compostela, Santiago de Compostela, Spain
{yago.fontenla.seco,manuel.lama,alberto.bugarin.diz}@usc.es

Abstract. In this paper we present the Process-To-Text (P2T) framework for the automatic generation of textual descriptive explanations of processes. P2T integrates three AI paradigms: process mining for extracting temporal and structural information from a process, fuzzy linguistic protoforms for modelling uncertain terms, and natural language generation for building the explanations. A real use-case in the cardiology domain is presented, showing the potential of P2T for providing natural language explanations addressed to specialists.

Keywords: Process mining · Natural language generation · Explainable AI

1 Introduction

Processes constitute a useful way of representing and structuring the activities in information systems. The Process Mining field offers techniques to discover, monitor and enhance real processes extracted from the event logs generated by processes execution, allowing to understand what is really happening in a process, which may be different from what designers thought [2]. Process models are usually represented with different notations that represent in a graphical manner the activities that take place in a process as well as the dependencies among them. Process models tend to be enhanced with properties such as temporal information, process execution-related statistics, trends of process key indicators, interactions between the resources involved in the process execution, etc. Information about these properties is shown to users through visual analytic techniques that help to understand what is happening in the process execution from different perspectives. However, in real scenarios process models are highly complex, with many relations between activities, which make them nearly impossible to be interpreted and understood by the users [2]. Furthermore, the amount of information that can be added to enhance the process description is also very high, and it is quite difficult for users to establish its relation with the process model. Additional analytics which summarize quantitative relevant

© Springer Nature Switzerland AG 2021
F. Heintz et al. (Eds.): TAILOR 2020, LNAI 12641, pp. 212–219, 2021.
https://doi.org/10.1007/978-3-030-73959-1_19

information about a process, such as frequent or infrequent patterns, that make it easier to focus on finding usual or unexpected behaviors, are also very useful [4]. Nevertheless, their correct interpretation is usually difficult for users, since they need to have a deep knowledge about process modelling and process related visual analytics. In this regard, some approaches have been described to automatically generate natural language descriptions of a process aiming to provide users with a better understanding of it [10]. These descriptions aim to explain in a comprehensible way, adapted to the user information needs, the most relevant information of the process. In general, textual information is complementary to process model visualization, which is the usual way of conveying information to users.

Natural Language Generation (NLG) [6,16] provides different methods for generating insights on data through natural language. Its aim is to provide users with textual descriptions that summarize the most relevant information of the data that is being described. Natural language is an effective way of conveying information to humans because i) it does not rely on human capability to identify or understand visual patterns or trends; and ii) it may include uncertain terms of expressions, which are very effective for communication [13]. Research suggests that in some specialized domains knowledge and expertise are required to understand graphical information [12] and proves that specialists can take better decisions based on textual summaries than on graphical displays [8]. With the integration of NLG and process model and analytics visualization, users with limited expertise on process modeling and analysis are provided with an AutoAI tool that allows them to understand the relevant information about what is really happening within a process.

In the state-of-the-art, techniques for process textual description focus on two perspectives. On the one hand, the Control-Flow perspective aims to align a Business Process Model Notation (BPMN) representation of a process model with its corresponding textual description [1,10,11,17]. The aim of this proposal is to, first, facilitate users to understand the process model structure and the dependencies between activities and how resources are used and second, detect inconsistencies in the process model such as missing activities, activities in different order, or misalignments in order to maintain a stable process model through the different stakeholders of an organization. The main drawback of these approaches is that they focus on hand-made processes (not discovered from real data) with a well-defined structure, and draw all their attention in the validation step of the process design phase. Preventing its application to process models extracted from real-life data, usually unstructured, with many relations between activities, including frequent loops, parallels and choices. On the other hand, Case Description techniques focus on generating textual descriptions about the execution of single activities or activity sequences that have been registered in an event log [5]. The underlying process model is not discovered from the event log, therefore neither the process structure is considered nor the relations between activities. So, these last techniques do not provide a faithful description of what has happened during the process execution.

In this paper, we present the Process-To-Text (P2T) framework, a process mining-based framework (the real process model is discovered from the event data) for the automatic generation of natural language descriptions of processes. Descriptions include information from both the control-flow, case and specially time perspectives, the later being usually neglected in the literature. P2T is based on a Data-to-Text (D2T) architecture [15] using linguistic protoforms (as a way to handle imprecision) that will be generated into natural language texts following a hybrid template-based realization approach.

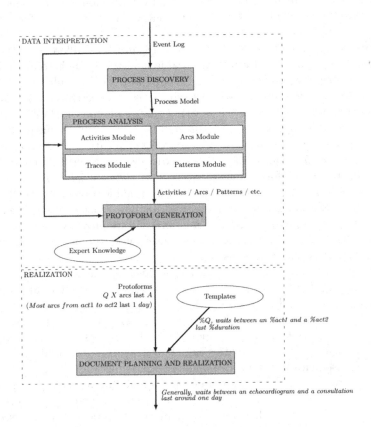

Fig. 1. Framework for the linguistic description of processes

2   P2T: A Framework for Textual Description of Processes

Figure 1 depicts the Process-To-Text (P2T) framework, for the automatic generation of textual descriptive explanations of processes. This framework is based on the most widely used architecture for D2T systems [15], which defines a pipeline composed of four stages: *signal analysis, data interpretation, document planning*, and *microplanning and realization*. P2T does not include the *signal analysis* stage since data input are not numerical, but event logs. Also, the *document planning* stage is subsumed in the *microplanning and realization* stage.

Process Discovery. The input of the data interpretation stage is an *event log*, defined as a multiset of traces. A trace is a particular execution of a process (i.e., a case), and it is represented as an ordered sequence of events, being an event the execution of an activity, which contains context information about the execution of said activity (e.g. timestamp, the case it belongs to, the resources involved in its execution, the process variables modified, etc.). However, the event log itself is not used as a direct input to generate the descriptions. Firstly, the process model has to be discovered from the event log by applying a process mining algorithm [2,3], which, traditionally have followed heuristic [19], inductive [9], or evolutionary computation [18] based approaches.

Process Analysis. Once the process model is discovered, the log is replayed (each trace is played over the discovered model) [2]. This gives us both temporal and frequency-based information about activities, arcs (relations between activities) and traces that can be as well used to extract frequent and infrequent behavioral patterns [4]. Then, this information is summarized into indicators (e.g. average duration and frequency of the relation between activities, average and mode duration of a path, changes of mean duration of an activity within a period, etc.) which are computed in the modules depicted in Fig. 1 in the process analysis phase. This phase is part of the framework and indicators are computed for any case or domain.

Protoform Generation. A protoform [20] is an abstracted summary which serves to identify the semantic structure of the object to which applies. In P2T, protoforms include fuzzy temporal references for providing information about the temporal dimension of activities, arcs, or traces. For example, the textual description *Most executions of activity α_1 last ten minutes in average more than those of activity α_2* is generated by the protoform Q B *activity lasts A*. This is an activity-related protoform where Q is the quantifier Most, B is a qualifier, in this case, activity α_1, and A is the summarizer used to describe activity α_1 *ten minutes in average more than those of activity α_2*. Note that behavioral patterns can be expressed through relations between activities, meaning that pattern-related protoforms are compositions of arcs-related protoforms. Protoforms have abstraction levels, as summarization does, this allows for a general abstracted summary to produce multiple different summaries depending on the knowledge used for its realization.

Document Planning and Realization. Its objective is to generate the natural language descriptions of the process, taking the protoforms, templates, and expert knowledge as inputs. In our model we follow a hybrid template-based realization, which uses some domain expert knowledge and is more rich and flexible than basic fill-in-the-gap approaches, but simpler and quicker than full fledged NLG system implementations. The SimpleNLG-ES [14] (Spanish version of the SimpleNLG realization engine) realization engine is used in this stage.

3   Case Study

We have applied our framework in a real case study in the health domain: the process related to the patients' management in the Valvulopathy Unit of the Cardiology Department of the University Hospital of Santiago de Compostela. In this Unit, consultations and medical examinations, such as radiographies, echocardiograms or Computed Tomography (CT) scans, are performed to patients with aortic stenosis in order to decide the treatment (including surgery) they will undergo. Other information like unexpected events (e.g. emergencies, non-programmed admissions) and patient management activities (inclusion in the process, revisions, etc.) are also recorded in the event log data.

Medical professionals have a real interest in applying process mining techniques to this process, since it allows them to extract valuable knowledge about the Unit like, relations between age, sex, admittance (emergency or normal admission) and the number of successful surgeries or delay between activities, the delays between crucial activities (such as the admission of a patient and its surgery) due to tests like CT scans or echocardiograms, the different paths of the process which patients with different attributes follow, etc. The main goal to reach with all this information is to reduce the delays between process activities, prevent the repetition of activities (loops in the process), minimize patient management time, optimize resources and most important, increase the number of successful treatments.

In Fig. 2 the model that describes this process is shown, it has been discovered from an event log with data on 639 patients.

Since medical, management activities and exceptions are recorded, and since patients' management depends on their pathological state, the frequency of each path (sequence of activities on a trace) in the process is very low (only the twenty most frequent paths from the 622 total are shown in the figure), giving place to a highly complex model. This makes it difficult for medical professionals to understand what happens within the process even when it is graphically represented. To solve this, linguistic descriptions of the main process analytics are generated, as shown in Table 1, facilitating the understanding of temporal relations and delays between activities and traces, which is the main concern of domain experts in this regard.

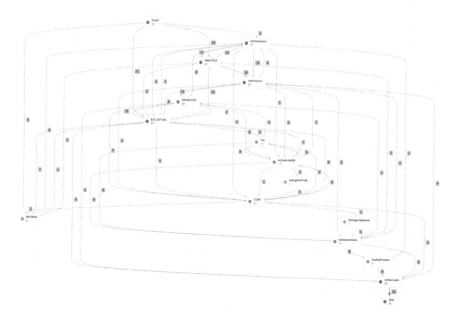

Fig. 2. Model of the Valvulopathy process represented with the InVerbis Analytics visualization tools [7].

Table 1. Textual descriptions generated for the valvulopathy process

- During the first half of year 2018, 52% less Surgical Interventions were registered compared to the second half of that same year.

- In the process, 78% less Surgical Interventions than Coronographies were registered

- Waiting time between Consultations is around 5 weeks and 6 days in average

- Waiting time between a Coronography and a CAT is around 6 weeks in average

- Around 7 weeks and 3 days after the Medical-Surgical Session a patient undergoes Surgical Intervention

- 6% of times, after the First Medical-Surgical Session, a Second Session is held around 5 weeks and 3 days later. On the contrary, 33% of times, patient undergoes Surgical Intervention around 7 weeks and 3 days later

- Patients who go through Assessment, Medical-Surgical Session and Surgical Intervention stay for 114 days in average at the cardiology service

4   Conclusions and Future Work

Our P2T framework integrates the process mining, natural language generation, and fuzzy linguistic protoforms paradigms for the automatic generation of textual descriptive explanations of processes, which include quantitative information (i.e., frequent and infrequent behavior, temporal distances between events and frequency of the relationships between events). A real use-case is presented, showing the potential of P2T for providing natural language explanations addressed to cardiology specialists about consultations and interventions of the patients of the valvulopathy unit. As future work, extensive human validation of the generated descriptions will be conducted with domain experts.

Acknowledgments. This research was funded by the Spanish Ministry for Science, Innovation and Universities, the Galician Ministry of Education, University and Professional Training and the ERDF/FEDER program (grants TIN2017-84796-C2-1-R, ED431C2018/29 and ED431G2019/04).

References

1. van der Aa, H., Leopold, H., Reijers, H.A.: Detecting inconsistencies between process models and textual descriptions. In: Motahari-Nezhad, H.R., Recker, J., Weidlich, M. (eds.) BPM 2015. LNCS, vol. 9253, pp. 90–105. Springer, Cham (2015). https://doi.org/10.1007/978-3-319-23063-4_6
2. van der Aalst, W.M.P.: Process Mining: Data Science in Action. Springer, Heidelberg (2016). https://doi.org/10.1007/978-3-662-49851-4_1
3. Augusto, A., et al.: Automated discovery of process models from event logs: review and benchmark. IEEE Trans. Knowl. Data Eng. **31**(4), 686–705 (2019)
4. Chapela-Campa, D., Mucientes, M., Lama, M.: Mining frequent patterns in process models. Inf. Sci. **472**, 235–257 (2019)
5. Dijkman, R.M., Wilbik, A.: Linguistic summarization of event logs: a practical approach. Inf. Syst. **67**, 114–125 (2017)
6. Gatt, A., Krahmer, E.: Survey of the state of the art in natural language generation: core tasks, applications and evaluation. J. Artif. Int. Res. **61**(1), 65–170 (2018)
7. InVerbis Analytics. https://processmining.inverbisanalytics.com/. Accessed 1 Feb 2021
8. Law, A.S., Freer, Y., Hunter, J., Logie, R.H., Mcintosh, N., Quinn, J.: A comparison of graphical and textual presentations of time series data to support medical decision making in the neonatal intensive care unit. J. Clin. Monitoring Comput. **19**(3), 183–194 (2005)
9. Leemans, S.J.J., Fahland, D., van der Aalst, W.M.P.: Discovering block-structured process models from event logs - a constructive approach. In: Colom, J.-M., Desel, J. (eds.) PETRI NETS 2013. LNCS, vol. 7927, pp. 311–329. Springer, Heidelberg (2013). https://doi.org/10.1007/978-3-642-38697-8_17
10. Leopold, H., Mendling, J., Polyvyanyy, A.: Generating natural language texts from business process models. In: Ralyté, J., Franch, X., Brinkkemper, S., Wrycza, S. (eds.) CAiSE 2012. LNCS, vol. 7328, pp. 64–79. Springer, Heidelberg (2012). https://doi.org/10.1007/978-3-642-31095-9_5
11. Leopold, H., Mendling, J., Polyvyanyy, A.: Supporting process model validation through natural language generation. IEEE Trans. Soft. Eng. **40**(8), 818–840 (2014)
12. Petre, M.: Why looking isn't always seeing: readership skills and graphical programming. Commun. ACM **38**, 33–44 (1995)
13. Ramos-Soto, A., Bugarín, A., Barro, S.: Fuzzy sets across the natural language generation pipeline. Progress Artif. Intell. **5**(4), 261–276 (2016). https://doi.org/10.1007/s13748-016-0097-x

14. Ramos-Soto, A., Janeiro-Gallardo, J., Bugarín, A.: Adapting SimpleNLG to Spanish. In: 10th International Conference on Natural Language Generation, pp. 142–146. Association for Computational Linguistics (2017)

15. Reiter, E.: An architecture for Data-to-Text systems. In: 9th European Workshop on NLG, pp. 97–104 (2007)

16. Reiter, E., Dale, R.: Building Natural Language Generation Systems. Cambridge University Press, Cambridge (2000)

17. Sànchez-Ferreres, J., Carmona, J., Padró, L.: Aligning textual and graphical descriptions of processes through ILP techniques. In: Dubois, E., Pohl, K. (eds.) CAiSE 2017. LNCS, vol. 10253, pp. 413–427. Springer, Cham (2017). https://doi.org/10.1007/978-3-319-59536-8_26

18. Vázquez-Barreiros, B., Mucientes, M., Lama, M.: Prodigen: mining complete, precise and minimal structure process models with a genetic algorithm. Inf. Sci. **294**, 315–333 (2015)

19. Weijters, A., Aalst, W.: Rediscovering workflow models from event-based data using little thumb. Integrated Comput. Aided Eng. **10**, 151–162 (2003)

20. Zadeh, L.A.: A prototype-centered approach to adding deduction capability to search engines-the concept of protoform. In: Proceedings Annual Meeting North American Fuzzy Information Processing Society (NAFIPS-FLINT 2002), pp. 523–525 (2002)

AI-Supported Innovation Monitoring

Barteld Braaksma[1(✉)], Piet Daas[1,3], Stephan Raaijmakers[2,4], Amber Geurts[2], and André Meyer-Vitali[2]

[1] CBS, Statistics Netherlands, The Hague/Heerlen, The Netherlands
b.braaksma@cbs.nl
[2] TNO, Netherlands Research Organization, The Hague, The Netherlands
[3] Department of Mathematics and Computer Science, Eindhoven University of Technology,
Eindhoven, The Netherlands
[4] Leiden University Centre for Linguistics (LUCL), Leiden University, Leiden, The Netherlands

Abstract. Small and medium enterprises (SMEs) are a driving force for innovation. Stimulation of innovation in these SMEs is often the target of policy interventions, both regionally and nationally. Which technical areas should be in the focus and how to identify and monitor them? In this position paper, we propose hybrid AI methods for innovation monitoring, using natural language processing (NLP) and a dynamic knowledge graph that combines learning, reasoning and knowledge sharing in collaboration with innovation experts.

Keywords: Natural Language Processing · Knowledge graph · Hybrid AI · Innovation · Policy-making · Human-machine interaction

1 Introduction

1.1 Innovation Scanning: Research Questions

Companies utilize innovation scanning services, such as Google Trends, TIM and Quid, to provide insights into innovation and technology trends. Such scans often use keywords, irrespective of human expert involvement, to measure real-time and emerging trends. However, such approaches are often inadequate when dealing with innovative novel phenomena such as emerging technologies or innovations as the terminology of some of the trends of interest does not yet exist or the meaning of existing terms in the area of interest changes over time [1]. Combined with the accelerating pace of technological innovation and social change [2], policy makers face the continuing challenge to navigate an increasingly complex space of strategic policy options [3].

In this position paper, we therefore explore ways to embed a hybrid AI-driven innovation monitor in the policy making process. To do so, we propose to detect trends in the innovation ecosystem using an innovation monitor in which there is close collaboration between an AI system and an expert that is able to explain its statistical findings, specifically in text. Using such an evidence-based, hybrid approach in the policy making process, it is essential for the AI system to be able to monitor the ecosystem, present innovations and to be embedded in the policy-making process. Therefore, the

© Springer Nature Switzerland AG 2021
F. Heintz et al. (Eds.): TAILOR 2020, LNAI 12641, pp. 220–226, 2021.
https://doi.org/10.1007/978-3-030-73959-1_20

first research question is of socioeconomic nature: *how to embed a hybrid AI-driven innovation monitor in the process of policy making?*

A complicating factor for such an innovation monitor is that the language used in innovative fields changes quite rapidly [1, 4]. The extraction of relevant terminology and definitions of emerging technologies in these fields is crucial, and – once linked to a semantic domain representation like a knowledge graph – can help to detect upcoming trends upon which policy makers can base their decisions. Therefore, the second research question is: *how to extract concepts from technical and socio-economic domains and associate them with a dynamic knowledge graph?*

We address our research questions in two pilots. The results and insights from these two pilot studies will be merged into a planned, principled approach for hybrid AI-driven innovation monitoring.

1.2 Pilot Study 1: Detecting Small Innovative Companies

In pilot 1, Statistics Netherlands (CBS) has developed a novel approach to detect innovative companies. The method detects them by studying the text on the main page of a company's website. Traditionally, innovation is determined at CBS by sending a questionnaire to a sample of companies. This approach, however, only focuses on a random sample of the large and medium-sized companies and completely misses the small enterprises, such as start-ups, that commonly develop and commercialize innovative technologies and products. Based on such evidence, innovation monitoring anticipates changes in the environment, interprets their consequences and develops future courses of action for responding the changes identified, but tends to miss the emergence of novel trends [5]. To better enable this, a logistic regression bag-of-words based model was developed by CBS based on the webpage texts of the companies included in the innovation survey.

The final model has an accuracy of 88% and contains around 600 stemmed words including word embeddings [10]. The approach taken to obtain the list of words was hybrid: it was generated automatically using AI, but required manual inspection for fine-tuning. The text-based method enables the detection of large, medium-sized and small innovative companies as long as they have a website. The latter was found to be the case for 99.9% of all innovative companies in the Netherlands. With the text-based approach the officially estimated number of large innovative companies by CBS, i.e. $19,916 \pm 680$, could be reproduced, i.e. $19,276 \pm 190$ [10]. This clearly demonstrated the high-quality results of the approach developed. For the small companies, a total of 33,599 innovative companies were detected in the Netherlands. Because location information is available, detailed maps of the Netherlands can be created displaying the distribution of innovative companies over the country (see Fig. 1) and within cities (not shown). In Fig. 1 the numbers of innovative companies are shown, at the municipality level, for the Netherlands. In a similar way, more specific models can be developed to detect innovative companies active in specific areas, such as 5G, hydrogen and mobility, for instance. This information can be embedded in the policy making process to enable policy makers to support decisions regarding how to spur and support early innovative trends in local or regional settings.

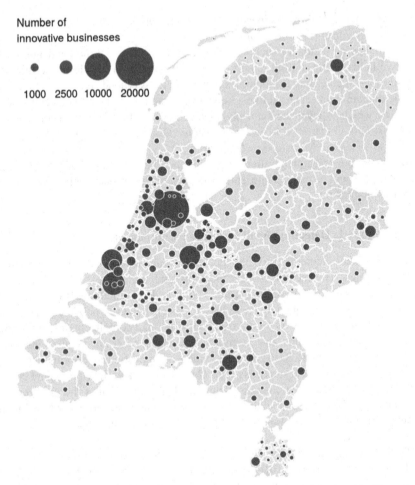

Number of
innovative businesses

1000   2500   10000   20000

Fig. 1. Estimated number of innovative companies, excluding those of the (semi-)self-employed, in the Netherlands at the municipality level. A total of 52,875 innovative companies are shown.

1.3   Pilot Study 2: A Hybrid Intelligence Approach

When trying to capture emerging trends in innovation and technologies for which the terminology of these trends of interest does not yet exist or the meaning of existing terms in the area of interest changes over time [1], ontologies play an important role. To capture both domain knowledge and the emergence of new trends, a hybrid AI method has been developed in which domain experts and machine-driven insights are reiterated to construct and refine an ontology and knowledge graph via a cyclic process [2, 7]. This hybrid AI method has been applied in a case study addressing Mobility-as-a-Service (MaaS). MaaS brings together the planning, booking and payment of all possible transportation options via apps. Such transportation options are not limited to trains, trams and taxis, but also includes shared bikes, cars and scooters. In our case study, we defined an ontology for MaaS, as follows.

First, domain experts created a 'seed' domain ontology through a structured knowledge elicitation process called MARVEL [8]. MARVEL, short for the Method to Analyse Relations between Variables using Enriched Loops, helped to structure and map relevant concepts and possible (inter-)relations between those concepts in a knowledge graph. This knowledge graph could then be transformed into web ontology language (OWL) for AI-supported foresight. Second, state-of-the-art AI has been used to gather data with so-called crawlers and scrapers: tools for obtaining data from websites and for cleaning up data. Data was gathered from a number of different sources, including ArXiv, Reuters, online journals and offline documents. The cleaned-up data was assigned to ontology nodes based on textual similarities with the data describing the ontology nodes, and stored in an index for retrieval purposes. The obtained insights are used to further refine the ontology. Based on human-machine interactions, missing knowledge is added or identified errors are removed from the ontology. This way, path dependencies, domain language or the over-reliance on past situations or experiences can be circumvented. Such an approach, whereby the expert knowledge base is combined with the machine's database (i.e. a hybrid approach between experts and machines) can significantly advance the quality of the outcomes [1]. Still, concept drift – or the degrading quality of ontologies over time – remains an issue. To address this issue, we propose the use of spatio-temporal entropy that takes into account both the spatial structure of an ontology and its evolution through time in terms of data coverage. The practical merits of this approach need to be assessed in an experimental, user-centric study we aim for as follow up of this work [9]. The outcomes can be used in the policy making process to enable policy makers to make decisions regarding early innovative trends.

2 Discussion of Results

When comparing the findings from the two pilot studies, we see opportunities to expand and combine both approaches.

First, it was observed in both pilot studies that the text-based model developed suffered from what is known as 'concept-drift'; that is, degrading quality of classification over time (see [11] for more on this). This is not an unexpected finding as one can expect that the words associated with innovation may change over time. However, this was solved in Pilot 1 by retraining the model on huge numbers of classified webpages, but still required regular checking of the model's findings [10]. In Pilot 2, a statistical, spatio-temporal approach for analysing probability distributions of external data (specifically, topics) over internal knowledge representations of domains has been produced. Topic drift, under such an approach, can be seen as a dynamic pattern within topics: the probabilities of words associated with a topic changes over time, and the difference between two word distributions at different time steps can be computed with measures like the Kullback-Leibler divergence [12], a method that underlies the spatio-temporal metrics developed in Pilot 1 [9].

Next, the results from both pilots indicate that more attention should be paid to international comparison. In Pilot 1, an international comparison revealed that a comparable web-based innovation detection approach also worked for companies in Germany [13]. A study performed in Sweden, based on the Pilot 1 approach developed for the Netherlands, incidentally revealed that this approach did not perform well in this country. The latter could be due to a behavioural difference of companies in this country or may be the result of the need for a more (language specific) advanced syntactical and NLP-based analysis. All in all, these findings indicate a need for a more dynamic approach which enables the inclusion of new topics in the original innovation detection model developed, a mechanism that can build upon our findings in Pilot 1, where low entropy scores of ontology topics covered with external data indicate necessary ontology repair, following Pilot 2.

Next, our findings also indicate the sensitivity of our model. That is, Pilot 1 excluded the findings for the (semi-)self-employed in the study [10]. This group of companies was found to be challenging to classify as it was observed that a very large percentage of them, compared to other small businesses, were classified as innovative. This suggested that self-employed people are more inclined to use words associated with innovation on their website and, hence, may be deliberately promoting themselves in a more innovative way.

Finally, our findings indicate the relevance of AI-supported innovation monitoring as an effective early warning system for policy makers. That is, an AI-supported innovation monitor helps to spot emerging topics and trends at a higher level of automation than before. Its hybrid and adaptive nature further allows the updating of information available to policy makers. This suggests promising avenues for the embeddedness of an AI-supported innovation monitor in the policy making process.

3 Conclusions and Outlook

In this position paper, we described two pilots addressing the analysis of innovation trends in society in order to address the overarching question how a hybrid AI innovation monitor could be embedded in the policy-making process while addressing the complicating factor that the language used in innovative fields changes quite rapidly. Our first pilot applies various NLP techniques to analysing company information to detect innovative ones, and identifies the need for addressing concept drift. Our second pilot develops a 'human-in-the-loop' approach to innovation mining, where human experts seed a domain ontology, which subsequently becomes enriched with externally harvested and automatically analysed data. The two pilots, although addressing different use cases and largely non-overlapping techniques, appear to pave the way for a combined set of techniques for future approaches to innovation analysis: advanced text mining (NLP) techniques combined with statistical methods for mapping out concept drift across the topics relevant to an innovation domain. As such, the results show the promise of an AI-supported, modular approach to innovation monitoring for policy makers. How to deal with the notion of 'concept drift' is an important issue when discussing innovation. We have observed that the indicator words we use to identify websites, belonging to innovative companies, change over time. This is a recurring issue with text-based methods. Policy makers are interested in following trends over time and they want to be sure that the quantitative evidence, used for proposing policy measures, is reliable and accurate. Our two pilots have produced metrics for analysing the coverage of the ontology and data, and we believe these methods can be used for addressing concept drift.

A question for future research is how to transfer methods developed in one language domain to another. This question is particularly relevant in the European multilingual context and a recurring theme for policy makers in the European Commission. How to deal with such linguistic issues, especially if we want to zoom in to specific topics like 5G-related innovations or the hydrogen-based economy in international, national and regional settings? Questions related to this are: What are internationally emerging trends? What are the primary topics in our region? Where are the geographic hotspots in our region?

A second question is if and how methods developed from an innovation monitoring perspective can be reused in other areas of interest or for other types of trends. For instance, is it possible to identify companies that try to move to a more sustainable (e.g. circular economy) based production method? Can we pinpoint the emergence of new types of business activities (e.g. servitisation) or production methods (e.g. AI-based)?

An important third question in this process is; what can be automated and what has to be left to human insight? And how can we make findings insightful for policy makers? Aiming for a hybrid AI approach – as illustrated in this study – sounds like a sensible way forward. By answering such questions, we will be able to create an AI-supported, evidence-based approach to help policymakers in their job to detect and stimulate innovative trends.

3.1 Outlook

In our future research endeavours, we aim to work with policy makers and other stakeholders from the users' side in order to better understand how to make the scientific results applicable and actionable in various settings. We have already engaged national, regional and local governments and other interested parties to find out what is the best way to present information. We listen to these stakeholders to understand their concrete questions, to get feedback on our results and to receive guidance on the way forward. We further aim to identify when and how policy makers wish to introduce AI-supported innovation monitoring into the policy making process, and how that introduction affects the policy making process in practice. We invite potential partners to collaborate to address such issues, e.g. in the context of the H2020 project TAILOR.

References

1. Geurts, A. et al.: Data Supported Foresight. Creating a new foundation for future anticipation by leveraging the power of AI and Big Data to go beyond current practice. TNO/Frauenhofer ISI whitepaper (2020)
2. Geurts, A.: A critical review of Alex Ross's the industries of the future. Technol. Forecast. Soc. Chang. **128**(1), 311–313 (2018)
3. Utterback, J.M.: Mastering the Dynamics of Innovation: How Companies Can Seize Opportunities in the Face of Technological Change. Harvard University Press, Cambridge (1994)
4. Cozzens, S., et al.: Emerging technologies: quantitative identification and measurement. Technol. Anal. Strateg. Manag. **22**, 361–376 (2010)
5. Mühlroth, C., Grottke, M.: Artificial intelligence in innovation: how to spot emerging trends and technologies. IEEE Trans. Eng. Manag. 1–18 (2020)
6. Himanen, L., Geurts, A., Foster, A., Rinke, P.: Data-driven materials science: status, challenges, perspectives. Adv. Sci. **6**(21), 1900808 (2019)

7. Smith, B.: Ontology. In: Floridi, L. (ed.) Blackwell Guide to the Philosophy of Computing and Information, pp. 155–166. Wiley, New York (2003)

8. Zijderveld, E.J.A.: MARVEL - principles of a method for semi-qualitative system behaviour and policy analysis. TNO paper (2007)

9. Raaijmakers et al.: AI-supported Foresight and bias: towards a hybrid approach. TNO working paper (2020)

10. Daas, P.J.H., van der Doef, S.: Detecting innovative companies via their website. Stat. J. IAOS **36**(4), 1239–1251 (2020)

11. Daas, P.J.H., Jansen, J.: Model degradation in web derived text-based models. In: International Conference on Advanced Research Methods and Analytics (CARMA), Valencia, Spain (2020). Accepted for publication

12. Kullback, S.: Letter to the editor: the Kullback-Leibler distance. Am. Stat. **41**(4), 340–341 (1987)

13. Kinne, J., Lenz, D.: Predicting innovative firms using web mining and deep learning. ZEW Discussion paper no 19-001, Mannheim, Germany (2019)

AutoAI

Semi-supervised Co-ensembling for AutoML

Jesper E. van Engelen$^{(\boxtimes)}$ and Holger H. Hoos

Leiden Institute of Advanced Computer Science, Leiden University,
Leiden, The Netherlands

Abstract. Automated machine learning (AutoML) is an increasingly popular approach for selecting learning algorithms and for configuring their hyperparameters in an effective, principled and fully automated way. So far, AutoML techniques have been focussed primarily on supervised learning scenarios. In this work, we extend AutoML to semi-supervised learning. Specifically, we propose *co-ensembling*, a generic procedure that uses unlabelled data to enhance the performance of high-quality ensembles of learners obtained from a state-of-the-art supervised AutoML system. Co-ensembling can be applied to any set of two or more base learners, and bypasses direct exploration of the large design space of semi-supervised learning algorithms. We demonstrate substantial performance improvements on multiclass classification problems by applying a single iteration of co-ensembling. On a large, diverse suite of multiclass data sets, single-step co-ensembling yields improved performance on 75% of the multiclass problems we considered, and achieves an average relative reduction in error rate of 7%.

1 Introduction

Traditionally, the application of machine learning techniques to real-world problems has required substantial human effort in finding and configuring suitable learning algorithms for the problem at hand. This approach is not scalable when considering the ever-growing range of machine learning applications, and the demand for machine learning systems that can be used with little or no human expertise has grown substantially. This has given rise to the field of *automated machine learning* (AutoML), which is concerned with automating the selection and configuration of machine learning algorithms for any given data set. AutoML is an important area within the broader field of automated AI (AutoAI), which aims to make AI methods easier to develop, deploy and maintain, with the goal of broadening access to high-performance, trustworthy AI systems. Recent advances in AutoML combine meta-learning, which reasons about the performance of algorithms based on observations from previous experiments, with Bayesian optimization methods [24] and ensemble learning [12].

Up to this point, research on AutoML has been primarily focussed on supervised machine learning problems, making use of only the labelled data to perform classification and regression tasks. In many real-world scenarios, however,

© Springer Nature Switzerland AG 2021
F. Heintz et al. (Eds.): TAILOR 2020, LNAI 12641, pp. 229–250, 2021.
https://doi.org/10.1007/978-3-030-73959-1_21

abundant unlabelled data is available in addition to the labelled data. By making certain assumptions about the structure of the input data, unlabelled data points can aid in the construction of better learners (see, e.g., [10,26,30]). This is the primary focus of the field of *semi-supervised learning*.

The dearth of research on automated semi-supervised learning can be partially attributed to the lack of standardized toolkits and environments; this stands in contrast to the situation for supervised learning, where broadly used toolkits exist (e.g., WEKA [14] and SCIKIT-LEARN [21]). Furthermore, semi-supervised learning is not applied as broadly as supervised learning, and no clearly defined set of methods is commonly applied in practice. Additionally, the design space of semi-supervised learning algorithms is potentially much larger than that of supervised learning methods. Although wrapper methods, which iteratively re-train supervised classifiers with unlabelled data augmented with label predictions, could potentially be incorporated into the algorithm and hyperparameter space relatively easily, their computational complexity—due to their iterative nature and the large number of unlabelled data points in typical real-world problems—presents a considerable challenge.

To overcome these obstacles, we propose to employ semi-supervised learning in a separate learning step, after constructing supervised classifiers using an existing AutoML system. We make use of the fact that the necessary conditions for ensembles of learners to be successful, namely *diversity* (i.e., learners do not make strongly correlated errors) and *accuracy* (i.e., learners perform well individually), match the necessary conditions for semi-supervised ensembling methods to succeed.

Our main contribution is a single-step co-training procedure that re-trains an ensemble of classifiers once, using labelled and pseudo-labelled data. The algorithm, which we call *single-step co-ensembling*, trains an ensemble of K classifiers on labelled data and uses each sub-ensemble of $K - 1$ classifiers to pseudo-label data for the remaining classifier. Each classifier is then re-trained on the labelled data and the pseudo-labelled data thus obtained. By applying only a single co-ensembling iteration on the entire set of unlabelled data points, we overcome a common problem with wrapper methods, where repeated pseudo-labelling iterations can introduce significant variance in performance and even degrade performance over the purely supervised ensemble [26].

We apply the co-ensembling algorithm to ensembles constructed by AUTO-SKLEARN [12], a prominent, state-of-the-art system for automated supervised learning. On a broad range of multiclass classification tasks, we demonstrate significantly improved predictive power of the ensemble with a single co-ensembling iteration. We also show that our approach outperforms multi-step co-ensembling: as the number of co-ensembling iterations grows, the performance improvements over the supervised ensemble diminish and variance grows. Using a single iteration of co-ensembling, we obtain a relative reduction in error rate of 7% on average. Crucially, our approach is robust: it improves performance on over 75% of the diverse set of widely studied multiclass data sets we used in our evaluation. On binary classification tasks, performance is not consistently improved.

The rest of this article is structured as follows. In Sect. 2, we provide background information on semi-supervised learning and AutoML, and give an overview of related work. We then introduce our single-step co-ensembling algorithm, along with a general framework for co-ensembling, in Sect. 3. Our experimental setup and results are presented in Sect. 4 and Sect. 5, respectively, followed by conclusions and discussion in Sect. 6.

2 Background and Related Work

In traditional, supervised learning problems, we are presented with a collection of l labelled data points $L = ((x_i, y_i))_{i=1}^{l}$, where x_i is the i-th data point and y_i is its label. Each data point is usually represented as a vector of real-valued features; the label is categorical in case of classification and real-valued in case of regression problems. Based on these data points, supervised learning methods attempt to infer a function that can successfully determine the label y^* of a previously unseen data point x^*. In semi-supervised learning, we also have access to a set of u unlabelled data points $U = (x_i)_{i=l+1}^{l+u}$. By taking advantage of some assumptions about the underlying data, these data points can be used to obtain improvements over purely supervised learners [30].

There are many semi-supervised extensions of traditional, supervised methods; for example, semi-supervised extensions exist of support vector machines [19], neural networks [20,22], and random forests [17]. Additionally, so-called *graph-based methods* [10] form an intuitive extension of nearest-neighbour methods to the semi-supervised setting: they propagate label information from labelled to unlabelled data points by constructing a graph over the data points. Lastly, there exists a class of semi-supervised learning algorithms called *wrapper methods* [26], which attempt to improve the performance of any supervised learning algorithm by iteratively re-training with artificially labelled unlabelled data (so-called *pseudo-labelled data*). Our work falls under this umbrella; in particular, it is closely related to the tri-training and co-forest methods, where multiple learners pseudo-label data using majority voting [17,28].

We apply our semi-supervised ensembling method to a strong ensemble of learners that is constructed automatically for any given learning problem using AutoML. In a nutshell, AutoML systems address the challenge of selecting learning algorithms and hyperparameter settings that work well for given learning problems. This challenge arises from the fact that no single learning algorithm is best-suited to tackle all learning problems; finding a suitable algorithm and hyperparameter settings for a given problem tends to be a difficult task, even for experts. Recent work in AutoML has shown that reliable, broadly applicable systems for automatic algorithm selection and hyperparameter optimization can be constructed that yield impressive performance across a broad range of supervised machine learning problems [12,16,25].

Technically, AutoML systems search over a large space of learning algorithms and hyperparameter settings in order to minimize an approximation of generalization error; this approximation is usually obtained via holdout or k-fold cross-validation. We denote the k training and validation sets used in this context as

$L_{\text{train}}^{(i)}$ and $L_{\text{val}}^{(i)}$, respectively. The loss of some learning algorithm A on the validation set, when trained on the training set, is then denoted as $\mathcal{L}(A, L_{\text{train}}^{(i)}, L_{\text{val}}^{(i)})$.

Let $\mathcal{A} = \{A^{(1)}, \ldots, A^{(R)}\}$ denote the space of available machine learning algorithms, and let $\Lambda^{(1)}, \ldots, \Lambda^{(R)}$ denote the space of their respective hyperparameter settings. Jointly, these give rise to a *configuration space*, whose elements are specific choices of a learning algorithm and settings for all its hyperparameters. The optimization problem tackled by AutoML systems can then be formulated as follows:

$$\underset{A^{(j)} \in \mathcal{A}, \Lambda \in \Lambda^{(j)}}{\text{minimize}} \quad \frac{1}{k} \cdot \sum_{i=1}^{k} \mathcal{L}\left(A_{\Lambda}^{(j)}, L_{\text{train}}^{(i)}, L_{\text{val}}^{(i)}\right), \tag{1}$$

where $A_{\Lambda}^{(j)}$ denotes learning algorithm $A^{(j)}$ with hyperparameter settings Λ. Traditional hyperparameter optimization approaches attempt to solve a restricted version of this problem for a fixed algorithm A_j. Examples of common hyperparameter optimization approaches include grid search, random search [1] and Bayesian optimization [24]. The more general task of combined algorithm selection and hyperparameter optimization is far more challenging, because of the size and structure of the configuration space to be searched, and is generally approached using Bayesian optimization methods. For neural architecture search, a subfield of AutoML concerned with finding a good neural network architecture for a problem at hand, other methods such as evolutionary algorithms and reinforcement learning are often used [9].

The first broad-spectrum AutoML system was AUTO-WEKA [16,25]; it is based on a configuration space that contains the machine learning algorithms and feature selection methods provided by the widely used WEKA platform [14]. The algorithm space underlying AUTO-WEKA contains several ensemble methods that can make use of arbitrary base classifiers.

A more recent, prominent AutoML system is AUTO-SKLEARN [12], which is based on the popular SCIKIT-LEARN toolkit [21]. AUTO-SKLEARN constructs ensembles of learners in two steps. First, it finds individual learners that perform well on the given supervised learning problem by searching a configuration space of preprocessors and learning algorithms. Then, a greedy ensemble selection procedure is employed, which iteratively adds the learner to the ensemble that minimizes the loss of the resulting ensemble [6]. Learners are in principle unweighted, but can be selected multiple times. At the end of the ensemble construction procedure, learners that occur multiple times are grouped, yielding a weighted ensemble. This approach to ensemble construction greatly reduces the size of the configuration space. Additionally, AUTO-SKLEARN employs meta-learning [4]: by running the optimization procedure for long stretches of time on a large, diverse set of data sets, a model is constructed for the posterior performance distribution conditioned on data set characteristics. This model is used for new problems, initialising the optimization procedure to promising configurations.

It has been shown that the performance of AUTO-SKLEARN compares favorably to AUTO-WEKA and HYPEROPT-SKLEARN [15] on a broad range of data sets [12]. Additionally, it won the 2015 AutoML challenge [13]. For this reason, we chose AUTO-SKLEARN as the basis for our work presented in this manuscript.

The intersection of AutoML and semi-supervised learning has received relatively little attention. To the best of our knowledge, the first work on this topic was published by Li et al. in 2019 [18]. They first use meta-learning to find promising configurations of semi-supervised learning algorithms, using data set characteristics based on the labelled as well as the unlabelled data. From these configurations, they select the configuration for which the algorithm produces the largest margin between its positive and negative predictions. To protect against performance loss relative to a specific baseline supervised learning algorithm, they compare the performance of this algorithm to the performance of the semi-supervised algorithm use cross-validation, and select the algorithm that performs best.

The approach we present here was developed independently of and in parallel to that of Li et al. [18]. There are substantial differences between both approaches. Most importantly, their optimization procedure operates directly on the semi-supervised learning algorithms, whereas our approach operates on the ensembles obtained using supervised AutoML. Unfortunately, at the time of the publication of the paper by Li et al., our experiments were already completed. However, we see a direct comparison between the two approaches as an interesting direction for future work.

3   Co-ensembling

The key idea underlying our approach is to enhance an ensemble generated by AUTO-SKLEARN using unlabelled data. Specifically, we employ a wrapper method that re-trains the classifiers in the ensemble using pseudo-labelled data from the other classifiers. Our approach falls into the group of wrapper methods, i.e., semi-supervised learning methods that use pseudo-labelling to re-train supervised classifiers. More specifically, it can be seen as a variant of co-training [3] with more than two classifiers.

3.1   Co-training Assumptions

All co-training methods rely on the *diversity* of the base classifiers, i.e., that classifiers do not make strongly correlated errors [29]. In multi-view learning, this requirement is satisfied by using uncorrelated or weakly correlated feature subsets. In single-view learning, diversity has to be enforced in the classifiers themselves. For instance, one can use base learners with different hyperparameters, or use different base learners altogether. In addition to the diversity requirement, co-training methods assume that the individual learners can, by themselves, yield accurate predictions. The former condition is commonly referred to as *independence*, and the latter as *redundancy* [29]. We note that these conditions coincide with the necessary conditions for supervised ensemble methods: the base learners need to be *diverse* and *accurate* [8].

Finding an ensemble of diverse, accurate classifiers for use in co-training is not a trivial task. We propose to mitigate this problem by applying the co-training paradigm to ensembles generated by AUTO-SKLEARN, making use of the observation that the necessary conditions for successful classifier ensembles are identical to the necessary conditions for co-training to succeed.

Algorithm 1. Co-ensembling

Input:
 Labelled data $L = ((\mathbf{x}_i, y_i))_{i=1}^{l}$ and unlabelled data $U = (\mathbf{x}_i)_{i=l+1}^{l+u}$
 Ensemble of classifiers $H = h_1, \ldots, h_K$
 Confidence threshold θ
 Maximum number of iterations num_iter
 Maximum number of pseudo-labelled samples per iteration max_pl
 Whether to retain pseudo-labelled samples in the next iteration $retain\_pl$
Output: Trained ensemble H'

 1: **procedure** CO-ENSEMBLING
 2: **for** $k = 1, \ldots, K$ **do**
 3:   $U_k \leftarrow U$
 4:   $h_k = \text{Train}_k(L)$
 5: **end for**
 6: **for** $t = 1, \ldots, num\_iter$ **do**
 7:   **for** $k = 1, \ldots, K$ **do**
 8:    $U'_k \leftarrow \{\mathbf{x}_i \in U_k : \text{Confidence}(H_k, \mathbf{x}_i) \geq \theta\}$
 9:    $U_k^* \leftarrow$ Select max_pl highest-confidence
      samples from U'_k
10:    $L'_k = \{(\mathbf{x}_i, H_k(\mathbf{x}_i)) : \mathbf{x}_i \in U_k^*\}$
11:    $h_k = \text{Train}_k(L \cup L'_k)$
12:    **if** $retain\_pl$ **then**
13:     $U_k \leftarrow U_k \setminus U_k^*$
14:    **end if**
15:   **end for**
16: **end for**
17: **return** $(h_1, \ldots, h_K)$
18: **end procedure**

3.2 General Co-ensembling Framework

We outline a simple framework for co-training using multiple classifiers. Our framework supports supervised base learners of any type, and does not use sample weighting, probabilistic predictions or bootstrapping. We dub this framework *co-ensembling*, referring to the application of co-training style optimization to any existing ensemble of classifiers. Furthermore, the framework we propose is generic and supports a wide variety of implementations.

 Pseudo-code for our co-ensembling procedure is provided in Algorithm 1. The general co-ensembling procedure for base classifiers $h_1, \ldots, h_K$ proceeds as follows. First, all classifiers are independently trained on the labelled data (lines 2 to 5). For each classifier h_k, we keep track of the unlabelled data points U_k that can still be pseudo-labelled (i.e., that were not pseudo-labelled in a previous iteration). This set of candidate samples is initialized to the set of all unlabelled data points. Then, in multiple co-ensembling iterations, we re-train each of the classifiers with the original data and pseudo-labeled data (lines 6 to 16); the hyperparameter num_iter controls the number of iterations.

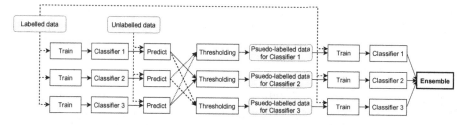

Fig. 1. Overview of co-ensembling algorithm with three classifiers and $max\_pl = \infty$. A single iteration is depicted. When more iterations are applied, the trained classifiers are provided with unlabelled data again, and generate new pseudo-labels.

In each co-ensembling iteration, all ensembles of $K-1$ classifiers pseudo-label samples for the remaining classifier. To select the samples to pseudo-label, the sub-ensemble $H_k = H \backslash h_k$, consisting of all classifiers in the ensemble except for h_k, is evaluated on all remaining unlabelled samples U_k for classifier k (line 8). From the samples on which the confidence of H_k (i.e., the fraction of the $K-1$ classifiers predicting the pseudo-label) exceeds a certain threshold θ, the most confident samples are selected up to a certain limit max_pl (line 9). Each classifier k is then re-trained on both the labelled samples and these selected unlabelled samples with their pseudo-labels from H_k (lines 10 and 11). If the Boolean flag *retain_pl* is set, the pseudo-labelled samples are removed from the set of remaining unlabelled data points U_k for classifier k (lines 12 to 14). An illustration of the algorithm is provided in Fig. 1. A PYTHON implementation of co-ensembling is available via https://github.com/engelen/co-ensembling.

The framework we have outlined is somewhat similar to *co-forest*, where an ensemble of K decision trees is trained by using sub-ensembles of $K-1$ classifiers to pseudo-label data for the remaining classifier. However, co-forest requires bootstrapping, to ensure diversity between the learners as well as to guide a heuristic stopping criterion based on the estimated generalization error. Our approach requires no bootstrapping, and ensures diversity via automated ensemble construction. Co-forest has been shown to be outperformed by supervised random forests as the number of base learners grows [11, Chapter 4].

3.3   Single-Step Co-ensembling

A substantial handicap of many semi-supervised learning methods is that they often only outperform their supervised counterparts or base learners in specific cases [19,23]. This is also the case for wrapper methods, such as co-training [17,26]. Moreover, the potential performance degradation is generally much larger than the potential improvement, especially if good performance is achieved with purely supervised learning.

The main cause of potential performance degradation in wrapper methods is their iterative nature: when the incorrect pseudo-labelling of a sample alters the decision boundary in an early iteration, this mistake can be amplified in subsequent iterations. Furthermore, the diversity of the set of classifiers, which is necessary for the ensemble to perform well, is explicitly weakened in each co-training iteration: when passing pseudo-labelled data between classifiers, the correlation in the errors they make will generally increase.

Our results (see Sect. 5) suggest a simple solution to this problem: we only apply a single co-training iteration, but use the entire set of unlabelled data (i.e., we do not explicitly limit the number of pseudo-labelled samples). The only constraint we impose is that the prediction confidence of the sub-ensemble is above some threshold θ, to ensure that only confidently predicted samples are pseudo-labelled.

4   Empirical Evaluation

We assess our co-ensembling approach by applying it to the ensemble generated by AUTO-SKLEARN; this allows us to directly compare its performance to the baseline provided by AUTO-SKLEARN. Our empirical evaluation is comprised of three stages. First, we investigate the performance of the ensembles produced by AUTO-SKLEARN, and show that using the ensembles in an unweighted majority voting scheme improves performance over the original, weighted ensemble. Next, we perform co-ensembling on this unweighted ensemble, and report considerable performance improvements on multiclass data sets. Finally, after we show that the performance improvements of co-ensembling diminish as the number of iterations is increased, we report the results from extensive experiments with single-step co-ensembling.

4.1   Experimental Setup

To be useful, AutoML systems as well as semi-supervised wrapper methods need to be applicable to a broad variety of data sets. We therefore evaluate the performance of our algorithms on a diverse suite of data sets with different characteristics, the *OpenML 100* [2]. This well-known benchmark collection consists of around 100 data sets, each containing between 100 and 100 000 samples. At the time of our experiments, it contained 52 binary and 45 multiclass data sets; further information on these sets is provided in Appendix A.

Our main experiments are conducted with 10% and 20% of the data being labelled; this constitutes the training set passed to AUTO-SKLEARN, while the rest of the data remains unlabelled and is used as testing data. Internally, AUTO-SKLEARN further subdivides the training set, using holdout validation to assess candidate classifiers. After AUTO-SKLEARN has constructed an ensemble of classifiers using each such training set, we evaluate the performance of this weighted ensemble as well as an unweighted version of the ensemble on the respective test set. Additionally, we compare the resulting performance to a popular baseline method, a random forest [5] with 100 trees.

We then apply co-ensembling to the unweighted ensemble, passing it the features of the available unlabelled data points (but, of course, not their labels).

In the semi-supervised learning literature, this is commonly know as the *trans-ductive setting*: the semi-supervised procedure has access to the features of the data points in the test set, but not to their labels. Our system produces a classifier defined over the entire input space, and is thus inductive, i.e., it can in principle be applied to new data points as well.

Since we need to split our data set into a small labelled data set and a large unlabelled data set to emulate common semi-supervised learning scenarios, the initial data set needs to contain sufficient samples per class. We therefore discard data sets with fewer than 10 samples per class on average when 20% of the data is labelled, leaving 91 data sets for our experiments. To obtain reasonably accurate performance estimates, we perform 10 independent runs of our pipeline for each data set and each configuration. In each run, the data is randomly partitioned into sets of labelled and unlabelled data points according to the specified proportions.

Our co-ensembling procedure is run with a varying number of iterations num_iter. In our final single-step co-ensembling experiments, the number of iterations is set to 1. No explicit limit is imposed on the number of data points to pseudo-label per iteration ($max\_pl = \infty$); in multi-step co-ensembling experiments, any pseudo-labels are retained ($retain\_pl = True$). We set the confidence threshold θ to 0.7 based on preliminary experiments; the setting of θ does not have a significant impact on the final co-ensembling performance (see Appendix C). We note that this fixed threshold can be considered to be more strict for data sets with more classes, where the labelling confidence can be expected to be lower.

Our experiments are conducted with AUTO-SKLEARN version 0.3.0. Each run of AUTO-SKLEARN is performed in a distributed manner on 8 computing nodes. Each node has exclusive access to one CPU core in a cluster of machines equipped with two 16-core, 2.1 GHz Intel Xeon processors (E5-2683 v4) and approximately 94 GB of RAM, running on the CentOS 7 operating system. One of these nodes is used exclusively as a controller, aggregating results from the other nodes and constructing the final ensemble. Each node receives a wall-clock time budget of 2 h (10% labelled data) or 4 h (20% labelled data); the time limit for each individual run (i.e., the construction of a single classifier) is limited to 10% of the total budget per node. RAM is limited to 2.5 GB per node.

4.2   Constructing the Final Set of Ensembles

Not all runs of our pipeline yield ensembles that are usable for our empirical evaluation. Of our 910 runs (10 runs for each of the 91 data sets) for each experiment, some had to be discarded. All selection steps are independent of the results of the co-ensembling procedure: we only omit infeasible and erroneous runs, which are identified as such before co-ensembling commences.

Firstly, the AutoML phase of the training process is susceptible to errors. In particular, AUTO-SKLEARN sometimes produces configurations that cause errors in SCIKIT-LEARN, and computing nodes may crash. After discarding crashed runs, we are left with 697 valid ensembles in the 10%-labelled setting and 710 valid ensembles in the 20%-labelled setting.

Table 1. Performance comparison of random forests, AUTO-SKLEARN (ASKL), and unweighted AUTO-SKLEARN on the OpenML 100 benchmarking suite. We report the absolute performance numbers as well as relative changes in error rate, averaged over all data sets; we also report win/tie/loss rates.

Method	Fraction labelled	
	10%	20%
Absolute error rates		
Random forest	0.196	0.173
ASKL	0.188	0.160
ASKL (unweighted)	0.182	0.154
ASKL vs random forest		
Mean rel. change	−6.4%	−14.0%
Win/tie/loss	42/0/32	51/0/23
ASKL (unweighted) vs ASKL		
Mean rel. change	−8.0%	−5.1%
Win/tie/loss	57/2/19	56/1/21
ASKL (unweighted) vs random forest		
Mean rel. change	−12.5%	−18.8%
Win/tie/loss	46/1/27	54/1/19

Secondly, co-ensembling requires two or more learners in each sub-ensemble to be able to estimate prediction confidence. Thus, three or more learners are required in total for co-ensembling to proceed. After discarding ensembles with fewer than 3 learners, we obtain our final set of 396 valid runs in the 10%-labelled setting and 496 valid runs in the 20%-labelled setting. We note that the number of valid runs reported above is based on the single-step co-ensembling experiments with a confidence threshold of 0.7. Due to the inherent stochasticity of the optimization procedure, the numbers can vary slightly for our other experiments.

5   Results

In the following, we present the results of the experiments outlined in the previous section. We first discuss the use of a weighted versus an unweighted ensemble of learners from AUTO-SKLEARN, before presenting our results on multi-step co-ensembling. Finally, we report the results from our extensive experiments with single-step co-ensembling.

5.1 Supervised Ensemble Weighting

In constructing the final classifier ensemble, AUTO-SKLEARN greedily selects classifiers that minimize the validation error of the entire ensemble until it can no longer be improved or a predefined ensemble size limit is reached [6,12]. Since classifiers can be selected multiple times, the resulting ensemble can be considered weighted. These weights are discarded in our co-ensembling experiments.

The results of the comparisons between the resulting unweighted ensemble, the weighted ensemble and random forests with 100 trees are shown in Table 1. Clearly, the AUTO-SKLEARN ensembles exhibit substantial performance improvements over random forests, and the unweighted ensemble consistently outperforms the weighted ensemble. On average, the error rates of the unweighted ensemble are 18.8% lower than those of random forests in the 20%-labeled setting. We note that in our comparisons with random forests, data sets with missing values are omitted, since random forests do not natively handle missing data.

We assess the statistical significance of our results by applying the Wilcoxon signed-rank test [27] with a significance level of 5% to the mean error rates observed on our data sets, as is common when comparing two classifiers on multi-data-set experiments [7]. We find that the performance difference between AUTO-SKLEARN and random forests is significant in the 20%-labelled setting, but not in the 10%-labelled setting. This could be explained by the lack of labelled data that AUTO-SKLEARN can use to evaluate configurations. The performance improvement of unweighted ensembles obtained from AUTO-SKLEARN over the regular, weighted ensembles and over random forests is significant for the 10% and 20%-labelled settings. Furthermore, the win/tie/loss rates clearly show that unweighted ensembles outperform both weighted ensembles and random forests in a large majority of cases. This shows that, even when using very few data points, AUTO-SKLEARN constructs high-quality ensembles.

5.2 Multi-step Co-ensembling

Before presenting our evaluation of single-step co-ensembling, which constitutes our most important result, we evaluate multi-step co-ensembling. Using the trained, unweighted ensembles obtained from AUTO-SKLEARN as a starting point, we run the co-ensembling procedure with $num\_iter = 20$ iterations. These experiments are conducted in the 20%-labelled setting. For each classifier in the ensemble, we initialize the set of candidate points to be pseudo-labelled to the set of available unlabelled data points. We emphasize that only the features of these data points are ever used during training—not their labels. We compare the performance of the resulting ensembles to the unweighted base ensembles after each iteration, assessing the mean relative change in error rate and its variance.

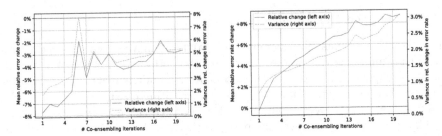

Fig. 2. Ensemble performance on OpenML 100 data sets, using multiple co-ensembling iterations, for multiclass data sets (left), and for binary data sets (right). We plot the mean and variance of the relative change in error rate between the unweighted AUTO-SKLEARN ensemble and the refined ensemble from co-ensembling.

The results are depicted in Fig. 2. Evidently, the performance improvement achieved by a single co-ensembling iteration is substantial for multiclass data sets: a mean performance improvement of over 7% is observed after the first co-ensembling iteration. However, as the number of iterations grows, this improvement decreases. Furthermore, the co-ensembling procedure is most robust in the first iteration, and variance in the relative change in error rate grows with the number of iterations. For binary data sets, performance is not noticeably improved; however, the procedure exhibits the same behaviour as for multiclass data sets when varying the number of co-ensembling iterations: performance worsens as the number of iterations is increased.

We identify two potential causes for this somewhat surprising difference in the performance of co-ensembling on binary and on multiclass data sets. Firstly, it is possible that an agreement of multiple base learners on a prediction is inherently more significant in the multiclass case: for binary data sets, it is more likely that a sub-ensemble of classifiers agrees on a prediction by chance, especially when the ensemble is relatively small. Secondly, it is possible that the ensemble diversity in binary classification problems is generally smaller than in multiclass classification problems. In that case, the base learners would often be unable to exchange useful information. Further investigation of these potential causes is beyond the scope of this work, but remains an interesting topic for future research.

Summarizing these results, the co-ensembling procedure achieves the highest performance when applied for a single iteration, as hypothesized in Sect. 3.3. This maximizes the mean improvement in error rate, and minimizes its variance.

5.3 Single-Step Co-ensembling

Having established the ability of co-ensembling to improve the performance of the ensemble constructed by AUTO-SKLEARN for multiclass data sets, we proceed to a more detailed evaluation of the performance of single-step co-ensembling.

Table 2. Performance comparison between unweighted AUTO-SKLEARN ensembles and ensembles obtained from single-step co-ensembling.

Method	Fraction labelled	
	10%	20%
Overall		
Baseline error (unw. ASKL)	0.177	0.151
Mean relative change	−2.2%	−3.5%
Win/tie/loss	45/2/31	42/2/34
Binary		
Baseline error (unw. ASKL)	0.158	0.144
Mean relative change	1.4%	−0.5%
Win/tie/loss	18/1/25	16/2/26
Multiclass		
Baseline error (unw. ASKL)	0.198	0.158
Mean relative change	−6.8%	−7.5%
Win/tie/loss	27/1/6	26/0/8

We conducted extensive experiments with single-step co-ensembling on the OpenML 100 benchmarking suite and summarize the results in Table 2. Consistent with our earlier findings for multiclass data sets, we observe an average reduction in error rate of 7.5% in the 20%-labelled setting and of 6.8% in the 10%-labelled setting. Especially compared to our earlier results on unweighted AUTO-SKLEARN ensembles *vs* random forests (Table 1), co-ensembling yields a substantial improvement in performance. Using a Wilcoxon signed-rank test with a significance level of 5%, we find that the performance improvements observed in the multiclass data sets are statistically significant, while the performance differences in binary data sets are not.

More importantly, single-step co-ensembling yields a substantial performance improvement for over 75% of our multiclass data sets, in both the 10%-labelled and 20%-labelled settings, indicating its robustness to the ratio of labelled to unlabelled data. Detailed evaluation of the performance improvements for individual data sets confirms this observation; the performance per data set is available in Appendix B. We note that, in our experiments, we imposed no explicit limit on the number of samples to pseudo-label ($max\_pl = \infty$). It is conceivable that this setting is ill-suited for scenarios where a much smaller fraction of the data is labelled. In that case, pseudo-labelled samples may dominate the training procedure, which may negatively impact performance.

We further analyse our results using a scatter plot (Fig. 3) of the performance differences between the unweighted ensembles produced by AUTO-SKLEARN and those obtained from co-ensembling. We consider runs with error rates between 0% and 10%, where most runs are concentrated. As the plot shows, co-ensembling is able to improve the unweighted ensemble from AUTO-SKLEARN in most cases.

Furthermore, it rarely produces ensembles with substantially reduced performance. The latter is an important feature of successful semi-supervised learning methods: users should be confident that the semi-supervised approach does not yield worse results than a supervised baseline.

The improvements obtained were not as pronounced in weaker ensembles as they were in well-performing ensembles, as is visible from the per-data set results in Appendix B. A possible explanation for this phenomenon is that the accuracy criterion (see Sect. 1) is not satisfied when the accuracy of the individual classifiers in the initial ensemble is low.

Overall, our results provide clear evidence that single-step co-ensembling is able to consistently improve the performance of strong ensembles of classifiers in multiclass data sets. Performance improvements are obtained for more than 75% of the multiclass classification problems we studied, and substantial performance degradation is rarely observed. Furthermore, since single-step co-ensembling retrains a given ensemble of classifiers, its time complexity is on the same order as that of the original ensemble: the original learning algorithms are always executed exactly one additional time (with additional data).

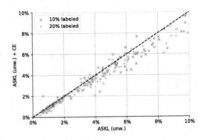

Fig. 3. Performance of unweighted AUTO-SKLEARN ensembles on multiclass data sets, and performance of these ensembles after running single-step co-ensembling, with error rates $\leq 10\%$.

6   Conclusions and Future Work

In this work, we have introduced a novel semi-supervised learning framework for training classifier ensembles. Our method, dubbed *co-ensembling*, iteratively introduces pseudo-labelled data to each classifier in the ensemble, by using the predictions of the sub-ensemble of all other classifiers. In an extensive empirical evaluation, we observed that this approach tends to show increased variability in performance as the number of iterations grows. Based on this finding, we focussed our attention on *single-step co-ensembling*, where the co-ensembling procedure is applied only once, considering all unlabelled data for pseudo-labelling.

Our experiments demonstrate clearly that single-step co-ensembling can consistently improve the performance of strong classifier ensembles on multiclass classification problems. Applying our co-ensembling method to ensembles constructed by AUTO-SKLEARN, a prominent automated machine learning system, we were able to consistently improve performance for a broad range of multiclass classification tasks. Firstly, we showed that using the ensemble constructed by AUTO-SKLEARN in an unweighted fashion improves performance over the standard, weighted ensemble. Secondly, we used single-step co-ensembling to reduce the error rate obtained by this unweighted ensemble by an average of about 7% in multiclass classification problems under different fractions of labelled data in the transductive setting. Our approach yielded performance improvements for 27 of the 34 multiclass classification tasks we considered when 10% of the data were labelled; for 20% labelled data, we achieved performance improvements for 26 of our 34 benchmark data sets. In binary classification, co-ensembling did not significantly improve performance. We identified two potential causes for this observation, namely lacking diversity in the ensembles for binary classification, and the fact that the probability of classifiers agreeing on a prediction by chance is higher in data sets with fewer classes. Overall, single-step co-ensembling achieves state-of-the-art performance across a broad range of multiclass semi-supervised classification tasks.

In future work, we intend to explore ways for improving the performance on binary data sets. One promising approach towards this end would be to incorporate the diversity of the ensemble explicitly in the AUTO-SKLEARN ensemble construction process, or even in the underlying Bayesian optimization procedure. Additionally, our findings provide strong motivation for additional investigations into ensemble diversity. With single-step co-ensembling, we have taken a first step towards automated semi-supervised learning. Our results and observations provide a good starting point and ample motivation for further exploration.

A   Data Sets

All methods we evaluate and propose are intended to be generic, robust machine learning methods, applicable to a broad variety of data sets. In that light, the algorithms should be evaluated on a large number of data sets with diverse characteristics. The OpenML 100, consisting of roughly 100 publicly available data sets, is a benchmarking suite that satisfies these requirements [2]. We note that this prominent benchmarking suite is subject to change; at the time of our experiments, three data sets had been removed from the benchmarking suite, presumably due to some inconsistencies in these data sets.

An overview of the data sets used in our experiments is provided in Table 3; it includes some data set properties, including the number of samples and the number of classes present in the data set.

Table 3. Data sets used in our experiments. The "ID" column contains the ID of the data set on the OpenML platform. The "Missing values" column indicates whether any feature values are missing in the data sets.

ID	Name	# Samples	# Classes	# Features	Missing values
1043	ada-agnostic	4562	2	48	
1590	adult	48842	2	14	Yes
458	anacat-authors	841	4	70	
469	anacat-dmft	797	6	4	
1459	artificial-characters	10218	10	7	
40981	australian	690	2	14	
11	balance-scale	625	3	4	
1461	bank-marketing	45211	2	16	
1462	banknotes	1372	2	4	
4134	bioresponse	3751	2	1776	
1464	blood-donors	748	2	4	
15	breast-w	699	2	9	Yes
21	car	1728	4	6	
1466	cardiotocography	2126	10	35	
23380	cjs	2796	6	33	Yes
1467	climate-model	540	2	20	
23	cmc	1473	3	9	
1468	cnae-9	1080	9	856	
478	collins	500	15	21	
29	credit-approval	690	2	15	Yes
31	credit-g	1000	2	20	
6332	cylinder-bands	540	2	37	Yes
37	diabetes	768	2	8	
23381	dresses-sales	500	2	12	Yes
1471	eeg-eye-state	14980	2	14	
151	electricity	45312	2	8	
188	eucalyptus	736	5	19	Yes
1476	gas-drift	13910	6	128	
4538	gesture-phase	9873	5	32	
1038	gina-agnostic	3468	2	970	
1478	har	10299	6	561	
23512	higgs	98050	2	28	Yes
1479	hill-valley	1212	2	100	
1480	ilpd	583	2	10	
1176	internet-ads	3279	2	1558	
451	irish	500	2	5	Yes
300	isolet	7797	26	617	
375	japanese-vowels	9961	9	14	
1053	jm1	10885	2	21	Yes
1067	kc1	2109	2	21	
1063	kc2	522	2	21	
1112	kddcup09-churn	50000	2	230	Yes
1114	kddcup09-upselling	50000	2	230	Yes
3	kr-vs-kp	3196	2	36	
40496	led-display-domain	500	10	7	
6	letter	20000	26	16	
1485	madelon	2600	2	500	
1120	magic-telescope	19020	2	10	

(*continued*)

Table 3. (*continued*)

ID	Name	# Samples	# Classes	# Features	Missing values
12	mfeat-factors	2000	10	216	
14	mfeat-fourier	2000	10	76	
16	mfeat-karhunen	2000	10	64	
18	mfeat-morph	2000	10	6	
20	mfeat-pixel	2000	10	240	
22	mfeat-zernike	2000	10	47	
4550	mice-protein	1080	8	81	Yes
1515	micro-mass	571	20	1300	
554	mnist-784	70000	10	784	
333	monks-1	556	2	6	
334	monks-2	601	2	6	
335	monks-3	554	2	6	
1046	mozilla4	15545	2	5	
24	mushroom	8124	2	22	Yes
1486	nomao	34465	2	118	
28	optdigits	5620	10	64	
1487	ozone-level-8hr	2534	2	72	
1068	pc1	1109	2	21	
1050	pc3	1563	2	37	
1049	pc4	1458	2	37	
32	pendigits	10992	10	16	
1489	phoneme	5404	2	5	
1491	plants-margin	1600	100	64	
1492	plants-shape	1600	100	64	
1493	plants-texture	1599	100	64	
470	profb	672	2	9	Yes
1494	qsar-biodeg	1055	2	41	
1497	robot-navigation	5456	4	24	
182	satimage	6430	6	36	
312	scene	2407	2	299	
36	segment	2310	7	19	
1501	semeion	1593	10	256	
38	sick	3772	2	29	Yes
42	soybean	683	19	35	Yes
44	spambase	4601	2	57	
40536	speed-dating	8378	2	120	Yes
46	splice	3190	3	60	
1504	steel-plates	1941	2	33	
1036	sylva-agnostic	14395	2	216	
377	synthetic-control	600	6	60	
1505	tamilnadu	45781	20	3	
40499	texture	5500	11	40	
1475	theorem-proving	6118	6	51	
50	tic-tac-toe	958	2	9	
54	vehicle	846	4	18	
307	vowel	990	11	12	
60	waveform-5000	5000	3	40	
1510	wdbc	569	2	30	
1570	wilt	4839	2	5	

B   Results Per Data Set

In Table 4, we report per-data-set results for our single-step co-ensembling experiments. The results in every table cell are aggregated over the individual runs for that data set and labelled data fraction.

Table 4. Co-ensembling results per data set. The column "ASKL (unw.)" contains the performance of the unweighted ensemble from AUTO-SKLEARN. The column "+CE" contains the performance of the ensemble obtained when applying single-step co-ensembling to the unweighted ensemble mentioned before.

Data set	10% labelled			20% labelled		
	ASKL (unw.)	+CE	Diff	ASKL (unw.)	+CE	Diff
Multiclass						
anacat-dmft	0.819	0.814	−0.6%	0.826	0.818	−1.0%
artificial-characters	0.378	0.380	0.6%	0.260	0.269	3.4%
balance-scale	0.155	0.124	−19.5%	0.110	0.108	−1.6%
car	0.092	0.086	−6.7%	0.062	0.056	−10.4%
cjs	0.023	0.025	51.9%	0.012	0.006	−51.9%
cmc	0.505	0.494	−2.1%	0.470	0.459	−2.3%
cnae-9	0.146	0.119	−18.0%	0.084	0.076	−9.5%
eucalyptus	0.475	0.464	−2.4%	0.401	0.394	−1.8%
gas-drift	0.012	0.011	−9.4%	0.007	0.007	−1.7%
gesture-phase	0.440	0.455	3.4%	0.411	0.431	4.7%
har	0.035	0.034	−4.7%	0.022	0.022	−4.0%
isolet	0.073	0.066	−10.0%	0.051	0.044	−12.0%
japanese-vowels	0.043	0.043	−0.7%	0.026	0.025	−6.0%
led-display-domain	0.352	0.343	−2.5%	0.300	0.285	−4.9%
letter	0.111	0.107	−5.1%	0.064	0.059	−7.5%
mfeat-factors	0.068	0.051	−25.9%	0.044	0.038	−12.7%
mfeat-fourier	0.199	0.193	−2.8%	0.168	0.162	−3.9%
mfeat-karhunen	0.064	0.050	−21.5%	0.038	0.033	−13.6%
mfeat-morph	0.307	0.306	−0.0%	0.281	0.281	0.1%
mfeat-pixel	0.091	0.064	−24.7%	0.038	0.032	−14.1%
mfeat-zernike	0.209	0.201	−3.5%	0.198	0.187	−5.5%
optdigits	0.028	0.024	−16.8%	0.018	0.015	−15.4%
pendigits	0.014	0.012	−13.0%	0.008	0.006	−15.3%
robot-navigation	0.019	0.019	−0.6%	0.011	0.010	−3.0%
satimage	0.124	0.125	1.2%	0.107	0.109	2.1%
segment	0.057	0.054	−4.8%	0.042	0.041	−1.4%
semeion	0.168	0.149	−12.2%	0.094	0.085	−9.1%
splice	0.063	0.063	−0.1%	0.051	0.052	2.2%
synthetic-control	0.043	0.024	−43.5%	0.028	0.023	−11.8%
texture	0.010	0.006	−34.9%	0.006	0.004	−30.5%
theorem-proving	0.493	0.502	1.8%	0.459	0.466	1.7%
vehicle	0.306	0.305	−0.3%	0.237	0.241	1.9%
vowel	0.473	0.418	−9.4%	0.228	0.221	−3.2%
waveform-5000	0.154	0.164	6.2%	0.139	0.142	1.6%

(continued)

Table 4. (*continued*)

Data set	10% labelled			20% labelled		
	ASKL (unw.)	+CE	Diff	ASKL (unw.)	+CE	Diff
Binary						
ada-agnostic	0.175	0.182	3.7%	0.161	0.159	−1.3%
adult	0.139	0.142	1.8%	0.137	0.142	3.5%
australian	0.180	0.207	13.3%	0.167	0.162	−1.8%
bank-marketing	0.102	0.103	1.7%	0.099	0.101	2.4%
blood-donors	0.280	0.281	0.1%	0.240	0.246	2.5%
climate-model	0.096	0.095	−1.5%	0.089	0.085	−4.2%
credit-approval	0.192	0.193	−1.8%	0.156	0.150	−3.6%
credit-g	0.289	0.284	−1.8%	0.272	0.269	−1.3%
cylinder-bands	0.402	0.435	8.5%	0.339	0.359	6.2%
diabetes	0.295	0.290	−1.3%	0.279	0.275	−1.2%
dresses-sales	0.459	0.443	−3.2%	0.462	0.465	0.7%
eeg-eye-state	0.071	0.065	−9.2%	0.057	0.057	0.3%
electricity	0.143	0.147	2.8%	0.111	0.117	5.3%
higgs	0.291	0.300	3.1%	0.288	0.301	4.5%
hill-valley	0.040	0.034	−47.9%	0.022	0.017	−46.7%
ilpd	0.328	0.333	1.8%	0.304	0.312	3.0%
jm1	0.192	0.193	0.3%	0.188	0.202	7.2%
kc1	0.162	0.162	−0.2%	0.156	0.152	−2.0%
kc2	0.145	0.166	14.7%	0.179	0.178	−0.1%
kddcup09-churn	0.075	0.075	0.0%	0.074	0.074	0.0%
kddcup09-upselling	0.050	0.054	7.6%	0.050	0.050	−0.2%
kr-vs-kp	0.036	0.037	2.4%	0.017	0.018	2.4%
madelon	0.292	0.290	−0.3%	0.213	0.221	3.5%
magic-telescope	0.136	0.137	1.1%	0.129	0.130	1.3%
monks-2	0.219	0.242	13.1%	0.072	0.076	20.4%
monks-3	0.092	0.086	−8.9%	0.042	0.039	2.9%
mozilla4	0.061	0.061	0.4%	0.054	0.054	0.9%
nomao	0.043	0.044	1.9%	0.038	0.041	5.8%
ozone-level-8hr	0.077	0.074	−4.5%	0.062	0.063	1.7%
pc1	0.074	0.072	−2.6%	0.078	0.077	−1.0%
pc3	0.167	0.150	−3.3%	0.122	0.119	−2.3%
pc4	0.118	0.117	−0.8%	0.102	0.102	−0.1%
phoneme	0.177	0.180	1.9%	0.135	0.140	3.4%
profb	0.376	0.361	−3.9%	0.360	0.357	−0.5%
qsar-biodeg	0.192	0.205	6.1%	0.164	0.167	1.5%
scene	0.021	0.015	−28.9%	0.015	0.012	−11.1%
sick	0.036	0.035	−2.3%	0.022	0.022	0.6%
spambase	0.069	0.069	1.1%	0.057	0.057	0.2%
speed-dating	0.150	0.154	2.4%	0.141	0.142	0.7%
sylva-agnostic	0.008	0.008	−6.1%	0.007	0.007	1.8%
tic-tac-toe	0.052	0.057	8.9%	0.052	0.029	−45.0%
wilt	0.016	0.017	6.3%	0.018	0.017	0.1%

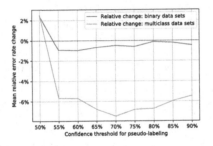

Fig. 4. Performance evaluation of single-step co-ensembling with different confidence thresholds in the 20%-labelled setting.

C   Confidence Thresholds

To investigate the influence of the confidence threshold θ, we conducted experiments with different thresholds in the 20%-labelled setting. The thresholds we evaluate range from 0.5, such that at least half of the classifiers in the sub-ensemble have to agree to suggest a data point for pseudo-labelling, to 0.9. The results of these experiments, shown in Fig. 4, indicate that no confidence setting threshold yields substantial performance improvements on binary data sets. The performance improvements are similar for all confidence thresholds. On multiclass data sets, the response curve for θ is unimodal, and the largest improvements are attained for $\theta = 0.7$.

References

1. Bergstra, J., Bengio, Y.: Random search for hyper-parameter optimization. J. Mach. Learn. Res. **13**, 281–305 (2012)
2. Bischl, B., et al.: OpenML benchmarking suites and the OpenML100. arXiv e-prints (2017)
3. Blum, A., Mitchell, T.: Combining labeled and unlabeled data with co-training. In: Proceedings of the 11th Annual Conference on Computational Learning Theory, pp. 92–100. ACM (1998)
4. Brazdil, P., Giraud-Carrier, C., Soares, C., Vilalta, R.: Metalearning: Applications to Data Mining. Springer, Heidelberg (2009). https://doi.org/10.1007/978-3-540-73263-1
5. Breiman, L.: Random forests. Mach. Learn. **45**(1), 5–32 (2001). https://doi.org/10.1023/A:1010933404324
6. Caruana, R., Niculescu-Mizil, A., Crew, G., Ksikes, A.: Ensemble selection from libraries of models. In: Proceedings of the 21st International Conference on Machine Learning, pp. 18–25. ACM (2004)
7. Demšar, J.: Statistical comparisons of classifiers over multiple data sets. J. Mach. Learn. Res. **7**, 1–30 (2006)
8. Dietterich, T.G.: Ensemble methods in machine learning. In: Kittler, J., Roli, F. (eds.) MCS 2000. LNCS, vol. 1857, pp. 1–15. Springer, Heidelberg (2000). https://doi.org/10.1007/3-540-45014-9_1

9. Elsken, T., Metzen, J.H., Hutter, F.: Neural architecture search: a survey. J. Mach. Learn. Res. **20**(55), 1–21 (2019)
10. van Engelen, J.E., Hoos, H.H.: A survey on semi-supervised learning. Mach. Learn. **109**(2), 373–440 (2019). https://doi.org/10.1007/s10994-019-05855-6
11. Van Engelen, J.E.: Semi-supervised ensemble learning. Master's thesis, Leiden University, July 2018
12. Feurer, M., Klein, A., Eggensperger, K., Springenberg, J., Blum, M., Hutter, F.: Efficient and robust automated machine learning. In: Advances in Neural Information Processing Systems, pp. 2962–2970 (2015)
13. Guyon, I., et al.: Design of the 2015 ChaLearn AutoML challenge. In: IEEE International Joint Conference on Neural Networks, pp. 1–8. IEEE (2015)
14. Hall, M., Frank, E., Holmes, G., Pfahringer, B., Reutemann, P., Witten, I.H.: The WEKA data mining software: an update. ACM SIGKDD Explor. Newsl. **11**(1), 10–18 (2009)
15. Komer, B., Bergstra, J., Eliasmith, C.: Hyperopt-Sklearn: automatic hyperparameter configuration for Scikit-learn. In: 31st ICML Workshop on AutoML (2014)
16. Kotthoff, L., Thornton, C., Hoos, H.H., Hutter, F., Leyton-Brown, K.: Auto-WEKA 2.0: automatic model selection and hyperparameter optimization in WEKA. J. Mach. Learn. Res. **18**(1), 826–830 (2017)
17. Li, M., Zhou, Z.H.: Improve computer-aided diagnosis with machine learning techniques using undiagnosed samples. IEEE Trans. Syst. Man Cybern. Part A Syst. Hum. **37**(6), 1088–1098 (2007)
18. Li, Y.F., Wang, H., Wei, T., Tu, W.W.: Towards automated semi-supervised learning. In: Proceedings of the AAAI Conference on Artificial Intelligence, vol. 33, pp. 4237–4244 (2019)
19. Li, Y.F., Zhou, Z.H.: Towards making unlabeled data never hurt. IEEE Trans. Pattern Anal. Mach. Intell. **37**(1), 175–188 (2015)
20. Miyato, T., Maeda, S.I., Koyama, M., Ishii, S.: Virtual adversarial training: a regularization method for supervised and semi-supervised learning. IEEE Trans. Pattern Anal. Mach. Intell. **41**, 1979–1993 (2019)
21. Pedregosa, F., et al.: Scikit-learn: machine learning in Python. J. Mach. Learn. Res. **12**, 2825–2830 (2011)
22. Rasmus, A., Berglund, M., Honkala, M., Valpola, H., Raiko, T.: Semi-supervised learning with ladder networks. In: Advances in Neural Information Processing Systems, pp. 3546–3554 (2015)
23. Singh, A., Nowak, R., Zhu, X.: Unlabeled data: now it helps, now it doesn't. In: Advances in Neural Information Processing Systems, pp. 1513–1520 (2009)
24. Snoek, J., Larochelle, H., Adams, R.P.: Practical Bayesian optimization of machine learning algorithms. In: Advances in Neural Information Processing Systems, pp. 2951–2959 (2012)
25. Thornton, C., Hutter, F., Hoos, H.H., Leyton-Brown, K.: Auto-WEKA: combined selection and hyperparameter optimization of classification algorithms. In: Proceedings of the 19th ACM SIGKDD International Conference on Knowledge Discovery and Data Mining, pp. 847–855. ACM (2013)
26. Triguero, I., García, S., Herrera, F.: Self-labeled techniques for semi-supervised learning: taxonomy, software and empirical study. Knowl. Inf. Syst. **42**(2), 245–284 (2013). https://doi.org/10.1007/s10115-013-0706-y
27. Wilcoxon, F.: Individual comparisons by ranking methods. Biom. Bull. **1**(6), 80–83 (1945)

28. Zhou, Z.H., Li, M.: Tri-training: exploiting unlabeled data using three classifiers. IEEE Trans. Knowl. Data Eng. **17**(11), 1529–1541 (2005)
29. Zhou, Z.H., Li, M.: Semi-supervised learning by disagreement. Knowl. Inf. Syst. **24**(3), 415–439 (2010). https://doi.org/10.1007/s10115-009-0209-z
30. Zhu, X.: Semi-supervised learning literature survey. Technical report 1530, University of Wisconsin-Madison (2008)

Transparent Adaptation in Deep Medical Image Diagnosis

D. Kollias[1,2(✉)], Y. Vlaxos[1], M. Seferis[1], I. Kollia[1], L. Sukissian[3], J. Wingate[4], and S. Kollias[1,3,4]

[1] School of Electrical and Computer Engineering,
National Technical University of Athens, Athens, Greece
[2] School of Computing and Mathematical Sciences,
University of Greenwich, London, UK
d.kollias@greenwich.ac.uk
[3] GRNET National Infrastructures for Research and Technology, Athens, Greece
[4] School of Computer Science, University of Lincoln, Lincoln, UK

Abstract. The paper presents a novel deep learning approach, which extracts latent information from trained Deep Neural Networks (Dnns) and derives concise representations that are analyzed in an effective, transparent way for prediction in medical imaging. A novel methodology is presented, in which deep neural architectures that have been trained to provide highly accurate predictions over existing datasets are adapted, in a consistent way, to make predictions over different contexts and datasets. Unified prediction is then achieved over the original and the new datasets. Successful application is illustrated through a large experimental study for prediction of Parkinson's disease from MRI and DaTScans, as well as for prediction of COVID-19 from CT scans and X-rays.

Keywords: Deep Neural Networks · Latent variable extraction · Transparency · Efficiency · Prediction · Adaptation · Medical imaging · Diagnosis

1 Introduction

Over the last few years, Deep Learning (DL) and Deep Neural Networks (Dnns) have been successfully applied to numerous applications and domains due to the availability of large amounts of labeled data, including healthcare prediction, visual analysis and recognition [7,9,18,19].

Transfer learning (TL) [32] has been the main approach to train Deep Neural Networks when only small amounts of annotated data are available. TL uses networks previously trained with large datasets (even of generic patterns) and fine-tunes the whole, or parts of them, using the small training datasets. A serious problem is related to TL: as the DNN learns to make predictions in the new dataset, it tends to forget the old data that are not used in the retraining procedure; this is known as 'catastrophic forgetting'. Moreover, when deploying

© Springer Nature Switzerland AG 2021
F. Heintz et al. (Eds.): TAILOR 2020, LNAI 12641, pp. 251–267, 2021.
https://doi.org/10.1007/978-3-030-73959-1_22

a pre-trained model to a real-life application, the assumption is that both the source (training set) and the target (application-specific) one are drawn from the same distribution. When this assumption is violated, the DL model trained on the source domain will not generalize well on the target domain due to the distribution differences between the two domains; this is known as domain shift. Learning a discriminative model in the presence of domain shift between target datasets is known as Domain Adaptation (DA) [24] and is targeted when dealing with non-annotated data.

In this paper we present a new methodology that alleviates the 'catastrophic forgetting' problem by generating a unified prediction model over different datasets, e.g., aggregated in different environments. At first, we extract appropriate internal features, say features **v**, from a DNN model trained with some dataset of interest. By introducing a clustering methodology, we generate concise representations, say **c**, of these features. Using these representations and the nearest neighbour criterion, we can then predict, in an efficient and transparent way, the class of new data.

According to this methodology, we apply the originally trained DNN to a new dataset, deriving a corresponding set of representations, through which we train a new DNN. From this new DNN, we extract a new set of features, say **v**′ and a concise representation **c**′. A unified prediction model is then produced by merging the **c** and **c**′ representation sets. Having achieved high precision and recall metrics in the derivation of each one of these representations ensures that the generated unified model provides high prediction accuracy in the derived representation space.

This modelling approach is of great significance when dealing with new non-annotated data, since it provides an alternative transparent way for prediction; it is shown that it can also create richer representations of the prediction problem. The approach can be thought of as a dynamic architecture, such as progressive networks, for domain adaptation and continual learning [26]; such methods do not provide transparency, which is achieved in our method via the clustering component.

The proposed methodology is applied for: a) prediction of Parkinson's, based on datasets of MRI and DaTScans, either created in collaboration with the Georgios Gennimatas Hospital (GGH) in Athens [31], or provided by the PPMI study sponsored by M. J. Fox for Parkinson's Research [23], b) prediction of COVID-19, based on CT chest scans, scan series, or x-rays, either collected from the public domain, or aggregated in collaboration with the Hellenic Ministry of Health.

The novel contributions of the paper are the following:

i) we develop an approach, extracting latent variables from trained DNNs, followed by appropriate clustering, which provides unified concise representations that can be analyzed in an efficient and transparent way for prediction,
ii) each concise representation set is linked to the respective input data (i.e., medical images, or scans, or other information), being, therefore, able to show - to the (medical) experts and users/patients - which were the main

(similar) cases on which the provided prediction/diagnosis was based; it is then up to the experts/users to decide whether they trust (this basis of) the diagnosis, or not,

iii) we successfully apply the proposed approach to different datasets in two healthcare problems: a) for unified prediction of Parkinson's based on MRI, or DaTscans, b) for unified prediction of COVID-19, based on chest CT scans, or x-rays.

2   Related Work

Recent research has focused on extracting trained DNN representations and using them for classification purposes [4], either by an auto-encoder methodology, or by monitoring neuron outputs in the convolutional or/and fully connected network layers [15, 34].

Such developments are exploited in this paper, combined with clustering, for diagnosis of diseases based on medical imaging.

Combining ANN, or DNN training with clustering has also been a topic of significant research. Surveys, focusing on different clustering methodologies and different combination ways can be found in [1, 25]; specific combinations can also be found in [12, 35, 36].

Here, our aim is to derive a unified latent representation and prediction framework, illustrating its successful use, especially in medical applications. The framework of interweaving ANNs or DNNs and clustering has also been examined in some former publications of ours [20, 33].

3   The Proposed Methodology

3.1   Extracting Features from Deep Neural Networks

Our approach starts by training a CNN or a CNN-RNN architecture to predict the status of data samples. Let us assume that we perform analysis of medical images, e.g., MRI and scans, collected in a specific medical centre, or hospital. As in [19] we consider a CNN part that has a well-known structure, such as ResNet-50, generally composed of convolutional and pooling layers, followed by one, or two fully-connected layers. ReLU neuron models are used in this part. In the case of convolutional and recurrent network, hidden layers with Long Short Term Memory (LSTM) neuron models, or Gated Recurrent Units (GRU) are used on top of the CNN part, providing the final classification, or prediction, outputs.

In our approach we select to extract and further analyse the, say M, outputs of the last fully connected layer, or last hidden layer of the trained CNN, or CNN-RNN respectively. This is due to the fact that these outputs constitute high level, semantic extracts, based on which the trained DNN provides its final predictions. Other choices involve features extracted, not only from high level, but also from mid and lower level layers [21]. In the following we present the extraction of concise semantic information from these representations, using unsupervised analysis.

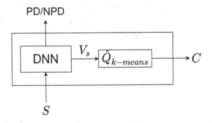

PD/NPD

Fig. 1. Dataset S is the DNN input; clustering of $\mathcal{V}_s$ produces representation C

Let us assume that a dataset S, including medical input images has been collected and used for training a DNN to predict the healthy, or not healthy, status of subjects. Let also T denote the respective test set used to evaluate the performance of the trained network. We train the DNN using the data in S, with cardinality N_s and, for each input k, we collect the M values of the outputs of neurons in the selected DNN fully connected or hidden layer, generating a vector $\mathbf{v}_s(k)$. A similar vector $\mathbf{v}_t(k)$ is generated when applying the trained DNN to each input k of the N_t test set:

$$\mathcal{V}_s = \big\{(\mathbf{v}_s(k), \; k = 1, \ldots, N_s\big\} \tag{1}$$

and

$$\mathcal{V}_t = \big\{(\mathbf{v}_t(k), \; k = 1, \ldots, N_t\big\} \tag{2}$$

In the following we derive a concise representation of these $\mathbf{v}$ vectors, by using a clustering procedure, such as the k-means++ algorithm [2] to generate, say, L clusters $Q = \{\mathbf{q}_1, \ldots, \mathbf{q}_L\}$ through minimization of the following function:

$$\widehat{Q}_{k\text{-means}} = \arg \min_{Q} \sum_{i=1}^{L} \sum_{\mathbf{v}_s \in V_s} \left|\left| \mathbf{v}_s - \mu_i \right|\right|^2 \tag{3}$$

in which μ_i denotes the mean of $\mathbf{v}$ values belonging to cluster i. For each cluster i, we then compute the corresponding cluster center $\mathbf{c}(i)$, thus defining the set of cluster centers C, which forms a concise representation and prediction model for medical diagnosis.

$$C = \big\{(\mathbf{c}(i), \; i = 1, \ldots, L\big\} \tag{4}$$

The procedure, of using dataset S to generate the set of cluster centers C is illustrated in Fig. 1. Since the derived representation consists of a small number of cluster centers, medical experts can examine and annotate the respective DaTscans and MRI images with relevant textual information. This information can include the subject's status, as well as other metrics. Let us now focus on using the set C for diagnosis in new subject cases, e.g., those included in the test dataset T. For each input in T, we compute the $\mathbf{v}_s$ value. We then calculate the euclidean distance of this value from each cluster center in C and classify it to the category of the closest cluster center. As a result, we classify each test input to a respective category, thus predicting the subject's status.

It should be mentioned that, using this approach, we can predict a new subject's status in a rather efficient and transparent way. At first, only L distances between M-dimensional vectors have to be computed and the minimum of them be selected. Then, the subject can be informed of why the specific diagnosis was made, through visualization of the medical images and presentation of the medical annotations corresponding to the selected cluster center.

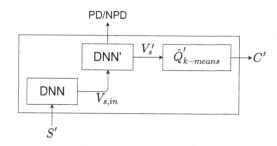

Fig. 2. S' is DNN input; V_s is DNN' input; clustering V'_s produces representation C'

3.2 Developing a Unified Prediction Model

Following the above described approach: a) we design a DNN (as shown in Fig. 1) and extensively train it for predicting a disease, based on image data provided by a specific hospital, or available database, b) we generate a concise representation (set C) composed of the derived cluster center representation that can be used to predict the disease in an efficient way. This information, i.e., the DNN weights and the set C, represent, in the proposed unified approach, the knowledge obtained through the analysis of the respective database S.

Let us now consider another medical environment, where another database related to the disease has been generated. Let us assume that it can be, similarly, described through the respective S and T sets. We will show how the proposed approach can alleviate the 'catastrophic forgetting' problem. Figure 2 shows the procedure we follow to achieve such a model. According to it, we present all inputs of the new training dataset S' to the available DNN that we have already trained with the original dataset S; we compute the V_s representations, similarly to (3), named as $V_{s,in}$ in Fig. 2. These representations, which were generated using the knowledge obtained from the original dataset, form the input to a new DNN, named DNN' in Fig. 2; this network is trained to use these inputs so as to predict the PD/NPD status of the subjects whose data are in set S'.

$$C' = \{(\mathbf{c}'(i), \; i = 1, \ldots, L'\} \tag{5}$$

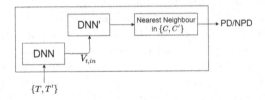

Fig. 3. Sets T, T' are DNN-DNN' inputs; $\mathcal{V}'_s$ classified through C and C'

In a similar way, as in Eqs. (3)–(5), we compute the new set of representations, named V'_s and through clustering the new set of cluster centers C': The next step is to merge the sets C and C', creating the unified prediction model. Using the two network structures (DNN and DNN' in Fig. 2), in a testing formulation, and the nearest neighbor criterion with respect to the union of C and C', we can predict the PD/NPD status of all subjects in both test sets T and T', as shown in Fig. 3. The resulting representation, consisting of the C and C' sets, can predict a new subject's status, using the knowledge acquired by DNN and DNN' networks trained on both datasets, in an efficient and transparent way.

In summary, we have trained the original DNN over a well defined input data space (i.e., large number of medical images, balanced data categories, etc.). Then we do not train the new DNN' with the respective (new) medical image data set, but with the concise representations - thus achieving lower dimensionality and lower risk of overfitting. Moreover, we take advantage of the knowledge of the originally trained DNN (which provides the input to DNN'). In this way, knowledge is scaled and interweaved between the two networks; it is not simply accumulated at their outputs.

4 Experimental Study

Our experimental study focuses on two different problems: i) prediction of Parkinson's over different datasets (one created in collaboration with the Georgios Gennimatas Hospital in Athens and another from the PPMI study sponsored by M. J. Fox for Parkinson's Research) based on MRI and DaTScans; ii) prediction of COVID-19 over different datasets (from the public domain and from the Greek healthcare system) based on chest CT scans, or chest x-rays.

4.1 Prediction of Parkinson's Based on MRI and DaTscans

In [19], DNNs were trained on a large Greek database to predict Parkinson's using DaTscans and MRIs, achieving a very good performance. The convolutional part of the network was applied to each image component, i.e., to an

RGB DaTscan image and to three (gray-scale) MRIs, using the same pretrained ResNet-50 structure. The outputs of these two ResNet structures were concatenated and fed to the Fully Connected (FC) layer of the CNN part of the network.

This structure has been able to analyse the spatial characteristics of the DaTscans and MRIs, achieving a high accuracy in the database test set, of 94%, as shown in Table 1. Then, a CNN-RNN architecture was trained on the database, including two hidden layers on top of the CNN part, each containing 128 GRU neurons, as shown in the Table. This has been able to analyse the temporal evolution of the MRI data as well, achieving an improved performance of 98% over the test data.

We started the experimental study of the current paper by training such a CNN-RNN network so as to classify the DaTscans and MRIs in this database to the correct PD/NPD category. We used a batch size of 10, a fixed learning rate of 0.001 and a dropout probability of 50%. We then applied the above-described clustering process, using k-means, to the V_s vectors extracted from the trained CNN-RNN architecture. Based on best precision/recall performance of the generated clusters, we selected to extract five clusters, two of which correspond to control subjects, i.e., NPD ones, with three clusters corresponding to patients. These constitute the extracted concise representation C set; consequently, C is composed of five 128-dimensional vectors.

Table 1. The accuracy obtained by CNN and CNN-RNN architectures

Structure	FC layers	Hidden layers	Units in FC layers	Units in hidden layers	Accuracy (%)
CNN	2	–	2622–1500	–	94
CNN-RNN	1	2	1500	128–128	98

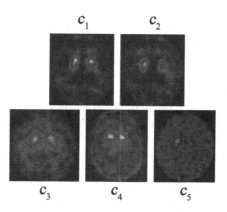

Fig. 4. The DaTscans of the 5 selected cluster centers: c_1 and c_2 correspond to NPD cases, whilst c_3–c_5 to progressing stages of Parkinson's

The DaTscans corresponding to the extracted cluster centers are shown in Fig. 4. Through the assistance of medical experts we were able to verify that the three DaTscans corresponding to patient cases represent three different stages of Parkinson's disease. In particular: the first of them (c_3) represents an early occurrence, between stage 1 and stage 2; the second (c_4) shows a pathological case, at stage 2; the third (c_5) represents a case that has reached stage 3 of Parkinson's. In the case of controls, there are differences between the first (c_1), which is a clear NPD case and the second (c_2), which is a more obscure case.

Following the above annotations, it can be said that the derived representations convey more information about the subjects' status than trained DNN outputs. This information can be used by medical experts to evaluate the predictions made by the original DNN when new subjects' data have to be analysed. The computed V_s representations in the new cases can be efficiently classified to the category of the nearest cluster center of C; the cluster center's Datscan, MRIs and annotations will then be used to justify, in a transparent way, the provided prediction. In case of new data, retraining of the deep neural network would be required, so as to retain the old knowledge and include the new one; this would be computationally intensive and possibly unfeasible. On the contrary, the proposed approach would only require extension of the C set with one, or more, cluster centers, corresponding to the new information; as a consequence, this would be done in a very efficient way.

Next, we examine the ability of the procedure shown in Fig. 2, using the trained DNN (CNN-RNN) architecture, to be successfully applied to the PPMI database [23], for PD/NPD prediction. Since the DaTscans were the basic source of the DNN's discriminating ability, we focus our new developments on the DaTscans included in the PPMI database. For this reason, we have retained 609 subjects from the PPMI database, excluding some patients for which we were not able to extract DaTscans of good quality. In total we selected 1481 DaTscans, which we combined with MRI triplets from the respective subjects, generating a dataset of 7700 inputs; each input was composed, of one (gray-scale) DaTscan and a triplet of MRI images.

At first, for comparison purposes, we trained CNN and CNN-RNN networks, similar to the ones presented in the previous subsection, from scratch, on the selected PPMI training set (6656 inputs). We used the validation set (1584 inputs) to test the obtained accuracy in the end of each training epoch. We then tested the performance of the networks on the test set (2028 inputs). The obtained accuracy was in the range of 96–97%, similar to the accuracy achieved by the state-of-the-art techniques on PPMI [34]. We also used Transfer Learning on networks generated in the first subsection of our experimental study, to initialise the re-training of the new networks. Similar results were obtained in this case as well.

We then applied the procedure shown in Fig. 2, to train DNN' with the V_s vectors extracted from the last hidden layer of the DNN that had been trained on [30,31]. The performance of the network was very high, classifying in the correct PD/NPD category 99.76% of the inputs. By then implementing the

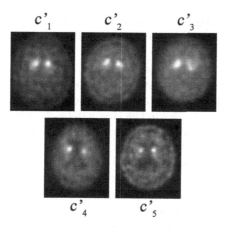

Fig. 5. DaTscans of the 5 cluster centers in C', with NPD at top and PD at bottom

clustering procedure shown in Fig. 2, we were able to extract five new clusters, three of which represent NPD subjects' cases and two of which represent PD cases. These cluster centers are 32-dimensional vectors. Figure 5 shows the DaTscans corresponding to the cluster centers c'_1–c'_5. Since the patients in the PPMI Database generally belong to early stages of Parkinson's (stage 1 to stage 2), it can be seen that two cluster centers, i.e., c'_4 and c'_5 were enough to represent these cases. Variations in the appearance of the non-Parkinson's cases can be seen in c'_1–c'_3 DaTscans.

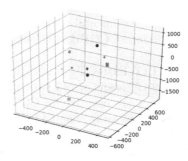

Fig. 6. The obtained ten cluster centers in 3-D: 5 of them (squares with red/rose color, & plus (+) symbols with green color) depict patients; 5 of them (stars with blue color & circles with black/grey color) depict non-patients (Color figure online)

We then applied the proposed merging of sets C and C'. It should be mentioned that the 5 centers in set C were 128-dimensional, whilst the 5 centers on set C' were 32-dimensional. To produce a unified representation, we made an ablation study, through PCA analysis, on the classification performance achieved in dataset [31], if we represented the five cluster centers in C through only 32 principal components. We were able to achieve a classification performance of 97.92%, which is very close to the 98% performance in Table 1. Consequently, we were able to generate a unified model consisting of 10 32-dimensional cluster centers. Figure 6 shows a 3-D projection of the ten cluster centers. The three (red/rose) squares denote the patient cases in the dataset [31] and the two (green) plus (+) symbols represent the patient cases in the PPMI dataset. The two (blue) stars represent the normal cases in the Greek dataset and the three (black/grey) circles represent the normal cases in the PPMI dataset. It can be seen that the PD centers are distinguishable from the NPD ones.

This has been verified by testing the ability of the unified prediction model to correctly classify all input data in test sets T and T', i.e., the data from both datasets. We found that there was no effect on the performance of the prediction achieved by each prediction model, i.e., C and C', when applied, separately, to their respective datasets. This shows that the unified representation set, composed of the union of C and C', has been able to provide exactly the same prediction results, as the original representation sets.

Let us further discuss the significance of the derivation of the unified cluster center set, for generating trustin our DNN-based diagnosis. Whenever a PD/NPD prediction is provided to a medical expert for a specific subject, it will also show the subject's DaTscan, together with the DaTscan of the center of the respective selected cluster. The latter will indicate what type of data were used by the system to generate its prediction. In this way, the medical expert, and the subject, could decide by themselves whether to trust, or not, the suggested decision.

4.2   Prediction of COVID-19 Based on Medical Imaging

In the following we present the experimental results obtained when applying the proposed procedure for prediction of COVID-19, based on, chest CT scans, or chest x-rays.

At first, we considered the COVID19-CT dataset [10], which is an open source public dataset, containing 349 CT scans of 143 patients positive for COVID-19 and 397 CT scans of people that are negative for COVID-19 (subjects that are normal, or have other types of diseases). The COVID19-CT dataset was split into training, validation and test sets, respectively containing 191, 60, 98 CT scans positive for COVID-19 and 234, 58, 105 CT scans negative for COVID-19.

In [10] the EfficientNet-b0, pretrained on Imagenet (including 5,288,548 parameters), was retrained and tested on this dataset, providing an F1 score of 0.78. Random cropping, horizontal flip, color jittering with random contrast and random brightness were used for data augmentation [17].

We applied the proposed procedure for latent variable extraction, using the same EfficientNet-b0 network, adding an extra hidden layer of 32 units. This size proved adequate in this case as well; consequently we extracted 32-dimensional representations. 5 clusters were generated, with their respective centroids shown in Fig. 7. The obtained F1 score in classification was much higher 0.842 (0.855 for the non-COVID case and 0.828 for the COVID one).

It should be mentioned that in [10] a much more complex network, DenseNet-169 (with 14,149,480 parameters), trained with additional images from the Lung Nodule Analysis dataset, was necessary for achieving a similar F1 score.

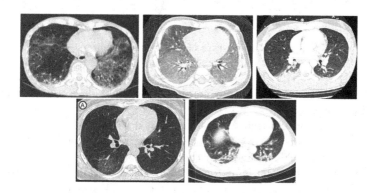

Fig. 7. CT Scans of the 5 cluster centers: non-COVID at top, COVID at bottom

Then we considered prediction of Covid-19 based on analysis of chest x-rays. We used two datasets, the COVID ChestXray dataset [5] and the Kaggle RSNA pneumonia dataset. The first dataset consists of data aggregated from websites such as Radiopaedia.org, the Italian Society of Medical and Interventional Radiology and Figure1.com. The second dataset is part of the RSNA Pneumonia Detection Challenge dataset. In total, the merged dataset consisted of images of subjects with pneumonia, subjects with COVID-19 and normal ones. The merged dataset was split into training and test parts, which contained 8629 and 955 pneumonia instances, 128 and 14 COVID-19 instances and 9766 and 885 normal instances, respectively.

We considered the COVID-Next network[1], which is a ResNeXt50-32x4d network, and trained it on this dataset, using data augmentation, based on vertical and horizontal flip, affine transformations (translation, scaling, shearing) and color jittering. COVID-Next achieved an F1 score of 0.93. We applied the proposed procedure, using the same network and transforms, adding an extra layer with 32 units. Five clusters of the derived representations were generated, with the respective centres being shown in Fig. 8. The achieved F1 score was 0.96, much higher than the state-of-the-art based on the same network.

The above verify that the proposed latent representation extraction and clustering procedure can further improve the current state-of-the-art.

In the following we investigated the problem of COVID-19 prediction based on series of chest CT scans; each series includes a pre-selected number of CT scans. We used two sets of CT scan series consisting of: a) 216 covid and 235 non-covid cases and b) 96 covid and 103 non-covid cases, including data augmentation. The mean number of scans per CT scan series was 45. The resulting

---

[1] https://github.com/velebit-ai/COVID-Next-Pytorch.

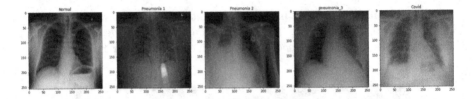

Fig. 8. Chest x-rays of the 5 cluster centers

size of the 3-D CT scan series that consisted the input data was 45 images of 512 × 512 pixels each.

The prediction system that we designed was a CNN-RNN architecture. The CNN part was the pre-trained EfficientNet-b0 network, as before; this sequentially received single CT scans from the 3-D input series. On top of that we added a layer with 128 GRU units for handling the evolution of CT scans within each input series. To deal with the input size of 45 CT scans, we added a fully connected layer of 32 ReLU units, with each unit receiving a concatenated input of 45 × 128 GRU unit outputs from the former layers, corresponding to the 45 consecutive CT scans of each series. This layer was followed by the output layer, providing the final prediction output corresponding to the respective CT scan series. Figure 9 shows the block diagram of the designed architecture.

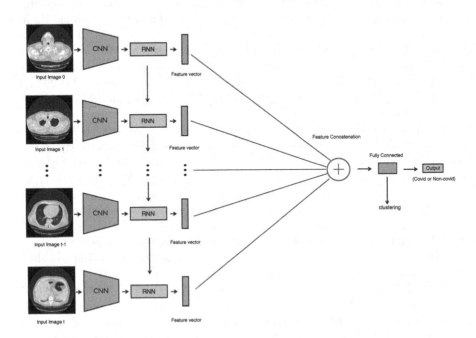

Fig. 9. The block diagram of the developed CNN-RNN prediction system

We trained this CNN-RNN network on the first GRNET dataset of scan series, splitting the dataset in training, validation and test subsets. Using 10-cross validation, the mean accuracy was 86,5%, with 85,7% for the Covid class and 87,2% for the non-Covid class. We then applied the proposed procedure of latent information extraction from the trained network and of clustering. We extracted three clusters, two for the covid-19 class and one for the non-covid class.

We then applied the proposed approach to train another CNN-RNN' network to classify the latent representations extracted when the CT scan series of the second dataset are passed through the former CNN-RNN, as shown in Fig. 2. We generated a new set of three clusters, two representing the covid and one representing the non-covid class, reaching an accuracy of 87% in predicting Covid-19 over this dataset.

As in the Parkinson's case, we merged the two sets of cluster centres, deriving a unified representation of six centres, as shown in Fig. 10 in 3-D plot. Here, the two crosses with blue color points represent the non-Covid centers, whilst the four circle with red ones represent the Covid centers. Through nearest neighbor classification, we showed that the unified representation set provided exactly the same prediction results, as the original representation sets. Figure 11 shows: (a) three images from the input CT scan series corresponding to a Covid-19 cluster center of the first dataset, (b) three images from the input CT scan series corresponding to a Covid-19 cluster center of the second dataset.

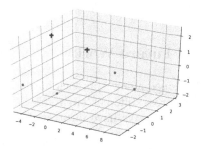

Fig. 10. The six extracted cluster centres: the two crosses with blue colour denote the non-Covid cases; the four circles with red colour denote the Covid cases (Color figure online)

The above-described experiments and the obtained results illustrate the ability of the proposed approach to provide very promising results over the examined datasets.

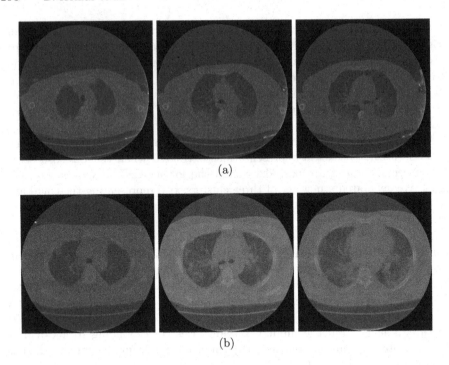

(a)

(b)

Fig. 11. (a) images from the CT scan series corresponding to a Covid cluster center of the first dataset, (b) images from the CT scan series corresponding to a Covid cluster center of the second dataset (Color figure online)

5   Conclusions and Future Work

In this paper we have developed a new approach for deriving efficient and transparent prediction models across different environments and contexts. It originated from our submission [16]. We have illustrated the successful application of this approach for medical image analysis and diagnosis of diseases, such as Parkinson's and COVID-19. Other applications are also possible, such as for predicting the outcome of ambulance calls [37].

We are currently extending the developed approach for unsupervised domain adaptation, using Bayesian formulations to provide the networks with self-training capabilities [28], while formulating it as a multi-objective optimization problem [11]. We are also investigating the use of capsules in the developed algorithms [6,29] so as to include feedback and model structuring in the generated models and representations.

Our future work will target to combine the data driven DNN representations with knowledge-based ontological representations [8,13,14,22], so as to generate formal explanations of the derived predictions, also including visual attention mechanisms [3,27].

Acknowledgment. We thank the Department of Neurology of the Georgios Gennimatas General Hospital, Athens, Greece, for providing the dataset with Parkinson's
data. The PPMI data used in the preparation of this article were obtained from
the Parkinson's Progression Markers Initiative (PPMI) database (www.ppmi-info.org/
data) and we thank them for this.

References

1. Aljalbout, E., Golkov, V., Siddiqui, Y., Strobel, M., Cremers, D.: Clustering with
   deep learning: taxonomy and new methods. arXiv preprint arXiv:1801.07648 (2018)
2. Arthur, D., Vassilvitskii, S.: k-means++: the advantages of careful seeding. Technical report, Stanford (2006)
3. Avrithis, Y., Tsapatsoulis, N., Kollias, S.: Broadcast news parsing using visual
   cues: a robust face detection approach. In: 2000 IEEE International Conference
   on Multimedia and Expo, ICME 2000, Proceedings of the Latest Advances in the
   Fast Changing World of Multimedia (Cat. No. 00TH8532), vol. 3, pp. 1469–1472.
   IEEE (2000)
4. Azizi, S., et al.: Detection and grading of prostate cancer using temporal enhanced
   ultrasound: combining deep neural networks and tissue mimicking simulations. Int.
   J. Comput. Assist. Radiol. Surg. **12**, 1293–1305 (2017). https://doi.org/10.1007/
   s11548-017-1627-0
5. Cohen, J.P., Morrison, P., Dao, L., Roth, K., Duong, T.Q., Ghassemi, M.: COVID-
   19 image data collection: prospective predictions are the future. arXiv preprint
   arXiv:2006.11988 (2020)
6. De Sousa Ribeiro, F., Leontidis, G., Kollias, S.: Introducing routing uncertainty in
   capsule networks. In: Advances in Neural Information Processing Systems, vol. 33
   (2020)
7. Esteva, A., Robicquet, A., et al.: A guide to deep learning in healthcare. Nat. Med.
   25, 24–29 (2019)
8. Glimm, B., Kazakov, Y., Kollia, I., Stamou, G.: Lower and upper bounds for
   SPARQL queries over OWL ontologies. In: Twenty-Ninth AAAI Conference on
   Artificial Intelligence (2015)
9. Goodfellow, I., Bengio, Y., Courville, A.: Deep Learning. MIT Press, Cambridge
   (2016)
10. He, X., et al.: Sample-efficient deep learning for COVID-19 diagnosis based on CT
    scans. medRxiv (2020)
11. Jiang, S., Kaiser, M., Yang, S., Kollias, S., Krasnogor, N.: A scalable test suite
    for continuous dynamic multiobjective optimization. IEEE Trans. Cybern. **50**(6),
    2814–2826 (2019)
12. Kappeler, A., et al.: Combining deep learning and unsupervised clustering to
    improve scene recognition performance. In: 2015 IEEE 17th International Work-
    shop on Multimedia Signal Processing (MMSP), pp. 1–6. IEEE (2015)
13. Kollia, I., Simou, N., Stafylopatis, A., Kollias, S.: Semantic image analysis using a
    symbolic neural architecture. Image Anal. Stereol. **29**(3), 159–172 (2010)
14. Kollia, I., Simou, N., Stamou, G., Stafylopatis, A.: Interweaving knowledge repre-
    sentation and adaptive neural networks (2009)
15. Kollia, I., Stafylopatis, A.G., Kollias, S.: Predicting Parkinson's disease using latent
    information extracted from deep neural networks. In: 2019 International Joint Con-
    ference on Neural Networks (IJCNN), pp. 1–8. IEEE (2019)

16. Kollias, D., et al.: Deep transparent prediction through latent representation analysis. arXiv preprint arXiv:2009.07044 (2020)

17. Kollias, D., Cheng, S., Pantic, M., Zafeiriou, S.: Photorealistic facial synthesis in the dimensional affect space. In: Leal-Taixé, L., Roth, S. (eds.) ECCV 2018. LNCS, vol. 11130, pp. 475–491. Springer, Cham (2019). https://doi.org/10.1007/978-3-030-11012-3_36

18. Kollias, D., Sharmanska, V., Zafeiriou, S.: Face behavior\a la carte: expressions, affect and action units in a single network. arXiv preprint arXiv:1910.11111 (2019)

19. Kollias, D., Tagaris, A., Stafylopatis, A., Kollias, S., Tagaris, G.: Deep neural architectures for prediction in healthcare. Complex Intell. Syst. 4(2), 119–131 (2017). https://doi.org/10.1007/s40747-017-0064-6

20. Kollias, D., Yu, M., Tagaris, A., Leontidis, G., Stafylopatis, A., Kollias, S.: Adaptation and contextualization of deep neural network models. In: 2017 IEEE Symposium Series on Computational Intelligence (SSCI), pp. 1–8. IEEE (2017)

21. Kollias, D., Zafeiriou, S.P.: Exploiting multi-CNN features in CNN-RNN based dimensional emotion recognition on the OMG in-the-wild dataset. IEEE Trans. Affect. Comput., 1 (2020). https://doi.org/10.1109/TAFFC.2020.3014171

22. Kollias, D., Marandianos, G., Raouzaiou, A., Stafylopatis, A.G.: Interweaving deep learning and semantic techniques for emotion analysis in human-machine interaction. In: 2015 10th International Workshop on Semantic and Social Media Adaptation and Personalization (SMAP), pp. 1–6. IEEE (2015)

23. Marek, K., et al.: The Parkinson progression marker initiative (PPMI). Prog. Neurobiol. 95, 629–635 (2011)

24. Mei, W., Deng, W.: Deep visual domain adaptation: a survey. Neurocomputing 312, 135–153 (2018)

25. Min, E., Guo, X., Liu, Q., Zhang, G., Cui, J., Long, J.: A survey of clustering with deep learning: from the perspective of network architecture. IEEE Access 6, 39501–39514 (2018)

26. Parisi, G.I., Kemker, R., Part, J.L., Kanan, C., Wermter, S.: Continual lifelong learning with neural networks: a review. Neural Netw. 113, 54–71 (2019)

27. Rapantzikos, K., Tsapatsoulis, N., Avrithis, Y., Kollias, S.: Bottom-up spatiotemporal visual attention model for video analysis. IET Image Process. 1(2), 237–248 (2007)

28. De Sousa Ribeiro, F., Calivá, F., Swainson, M., Gudmundsson, K., Leontidis, G., Kollias, S.: Deep Bayesian self-training. Neural Comput. Appl. 32(9), 4275–4291 (2019). https://doi.org/10.1007/s00521-019-04332-4

29. Ribeiro, F.D.S., Leontidis, G., Kollias, S.D.: Capsule routing via variational bayes. In: AAAI, pp. 3749–3756 (2020)

30. Tagaris, A., Kollias, D., Stafylopatis, A.: Assessment of Parkinson's disease based on deep neural networks. In: Boracchi, G., Iliadis, L., Jayne, C., Likas, A. (eds.) EANN 2017. CCIS, vol. 744, pp. 391–403. Springer, Cham (2017). https://doi.org/10.1007/978-3-319-65172-9_33

31. Tagaris, A., Kollias, D., Stafylopatis, A., Tagaris, G., Kollias, S.: Machine learning for neurodegenerative disorder diagnosis-survey of practices and launch of benchmark dataset. Int. J. Artif. Intell. Tools 27(03), 1850011 (2018)

32. Tan, C., Sun, F., Kong, T., Zhang, W., Yang, C., Liu, C.: A survey on deep transfer learning. In: Kůrková, V., Manolopoulos, Y., Hammer, B., Iliadis, L., Maglogiannis, I. (eds.) ICANN 2018. LNCS, vol. 11141, pp. 270–279. Springer, Cham (2018). https://doi.org/10.1007/978-3-030-01424-7_27

33. Wallace, M., Maglogiannis, I., Karpouzis, K., Kormentzas, G., Kollias, S.: Intelligent one-stop-shop travel recommendations using an adaptive neural network and clustering of history. Inf. Technol. Tour. **6**(3), 181–193 (2003)

34. Wingate, J., Kollia, I., Bidaut, L., Kollias, S.: A unified deep learning approach for prediction of Parkinson's disease. arXiv preprint arXiv:1911.10653 (2019)

35. Xie, J., Girshick, R., Farhadi, A.: Unsupervised deep embedding for clustering analysis. In: International Conference on Machine Learning, pp. 478–487 (2016)

36. Yang, B., Fu, X., Sidiropoulos, N.D., Hong, M.: Towards k-means-friendly spaces: simultaneous deep learning and clustering. In: International Conference on Machine Learning, pp. 3861–3870 (2017)

37. Yu, M., Kollias, D., Wingate, J., Siriwardena, N., Kollias, S.: Machine learning for predictive modelling of ambulance calls (2021)

Two to Trust: AutoML for Safe Modelling and Interpretable Deep Learning for Robustness

Mohammadreza Amirian[1,2], Lukas Tuggener[1,3], Ricardo Chavarriaga[1,4],
Yvan Putra Satyawan[1], Frank-Peter Schilling[1], Friedhelm Schwenker[2],
and Thilo Stadelmann[1(✉)]

[1] ZHAW Zurich University of Applied Sciences, Winterthur, Switzerland
{amir,tugg,chav,saty,scik,stdm}@zhaw.ch
[2] Ulm University, Ulm, Germany
friedhelm.schwenker@uni-ulm.de
[3] Università della Svizzera Italiana, Lugano, Switzerland
[4] Confederation of Laboratories for AI Research in Europe, Zurich, Switzerland

Abstract. *With great power comes great responsibility.* The success of machine learning, especially deep learning, in research and practice has attracted a great deal of interest, which in turn necessitates increased trust. Sources of mistrust include matters of model genesis ("Is this really the appropriate model?") and interpretability ("Why did the model come to this conclusion?", "Is the model safe from being easily fooled by adversaries?"). In this paper, two partners for the trustworthiness tango are presented: recent advances and ideas, as well as practical applications in industry in (a) Automated machine learning (AutoML), a powerful tool to optimize deep neural network architectures and fine-tune hyperparameters, which promises to build models in a safer and more comprehensive way; (b) Interpretability of neural network outputs, which addresses the vital question regarding the reasoning behind model predictions and provides insights to improve robustness against adversarial attacks.

Keywords: Automated Deep Learning (AutoDL) · Adversarial attacks

1 Introduction

The recent success of machine learning (ML) and deep learning (DL) has triggered enormous interest in practical applications of these algorithms in many organizations [23,24]. The emergence of automated ML (AutoML), which includes automated DL (AutoDL), further expands the horizons of such machine learning applications for non-experts and broadens the feasibility of exploring larger search spaces during development. Establishing trust in ML and DL models is thereby vital before they can be applied to real-world problems. Accordingly, trustworthiness has been recognized as the core concept for the applicability of

© Springer Nature Switzerland AG 2021
F. Heintz et al. (Eds.): TAILOR 2020, LNAI 12641, pp. 268–275, 2021.
https://doi.org/10.1007/978-3-030-73959-1_23

ML algorithms during the first TAILOR workshop at the European Conference on Machine Learning (ECML 2019[1]).

One approach in recent years has been focused on understanding the behavior of deep Convolutional Neural Networks (CNNs) by visualizing the network response in order to boost its trustworthiness [1]. However, there has always been a gap between state-of-the-art research in network architecture development and interpretability, with interpretability often lagging behind. Only more recent attempts incorporate interpretability into architecture design [20,21,30]. For example, architectures for image classification have been proposed which produce decisions in a more human-interpretable manner and hence shift the paradigm from maximizing performance to learning "the right for the right reasons" [20]. Consequently, incorporating interpretable model design into the growing domain of AutoML is likely to shorten its path towards practical applications.

In this paper, we present preliminary results that contribute to trustworthy neural network development and application in two respects: First, we report recent advances in AutoML and propose a unified architecture for multi-modal input data (audio and video) through an automated and thus repeatable development process, leading to safer architectures. Secondly, we introduce visualization techniques that improve the interpretability of a model's decision and show how they allow detection of adversarial attacks, improving the model's robustness and design. We argue that the feasibility and effectiveness of deploying AutoML methods contributes to improved trustworthiness. However, many challenges are still to be addressed in order to solve the tension between algorithmic automation and trustworthiness, especially in the case of algorithmic ensembles.

2 Automated Machine Learning

In this section, we present recent advances in automating the development and deployment of machine learning models, in particular CNNs, which have improved state-of-the-art performances by a significant margin in a wide range of applications such as audio processing [17], image processing [4] and natural language processing [8]. These successes come with the challenge of exploring a broad search space for hyperparameters and model designs. Therefore, an efficient search is not only a challenge in practical applications for non-experts, but also drives the need for automation in the research community. Under the umbrella term of AutoML, respective methods have already shown to be fruitful in hyperparameter optimization and model selection for traditional machine learning models [11], as well as in optimizing deep neural network architectures for computer vision [9].

Traditional AutoML aims at solving the Combined Algorithm Selection and Hyperparameter (CASH) optimization problem [11] and to build an ensemble of resulting models downstream to achieve the best possible performance with minimum computational and time resources. An intuitive and effective solution is random search. It reaches competitive results compared to more sophisticated

---

[1] https://ecmlpkdd2019.org.

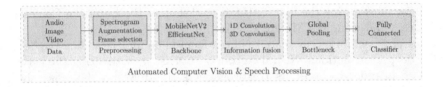

Automated Computer Vision & Speech Processing

Fig. 1. Block diagram of proposed automated audio-visual deep learning approach.

Table 1. Results for the automated computer vision challenge, comparing the proposed idea to other approaches based on the area under the learning curve metric.

Datasets	Automated computer vision 2 challenge					Final rank
	Dataset 1	Dataset 2	Dataset 3	Dataset 4	Dataset 5	
Winner (kakaobrain)	**0.6277 ± 0.0628**	**0.9048 ± 0.0517**	0.4076 ± 0.0139	**0.4640 ± 0.0443**	0.2091 ± 0.0122	1/20
Runner up (tanglang)	0.6231 ± 0.0449	0.8406 ± 0.0461	**0.4527 ± 0.0270**	0.3688 ± 0.0260	**0.2363 ± 0.0130**	2/20
Proposed (team_zhaw)	0.5418 ± 0.0340	0.8355 ± 0.0915	0.4110 ± 0.0072	0.3970 ± 0.0298	0.1677 ± 0.0052	8/20

algorithms when those are not pretrained [27]. Using the performance of previous runs on a given dataset to guide further model search motivates the idea of evolutionary optimization of the preprocessing and training pipeline [18]. Additionally, model selection and hyperparameter search can also benefit from the information of previous experiments on similar datasets through meta-learning [6].

With respect to automating deep learning, using a unified architecture for the automated design of CNNs in the context of computer vision for image and video data is proposed in [2] as an attempt to overcome the wasteful practice in ML to develop models independently for every new problem and data modality. However, meta-learning [28] and multi-task learning [5] demonstrate that the optimization process can profit even more from using many different tasks in similar modalities. We thus propose here an extension of the multi-modal architecture that encompasses audio data as spectrograms [17]. The resulting generic audio-visual architecture (Fig. 1) is appealing due to the following aspects: 1) it extends the state-of-the-art computer vision architectures to different modalities of data besides images; 2) the core information processing block (backbone) can profit from audio-visual information via multi-modal learning when the tasks are related; 3) the information fusion block can learn to combine multi-modal information using attention mechanisms.

The proposed approach aims at finding efficient models for a wide range of tasks on diverse datasets as fast as possible. Therefore, the generic architecture is accompanied with task-specific pre- and post-processing per modality to reduce architecture design burdens in practical applications. An earlier version of the approach competed promisingly in parts of the recent AutoDL 2019[2] challenge. This approach demonstrated a competitive performance compared

---

[2] https://autodl.chalearn.org/.

to state-of-the-art in terms of training speed and generalizing to unseen data. Table 1 presents the performance of the proposed method compared to the winning approaches on unseen datasets for automated computer vision where we achieved the 8th position out of final 20 entries. Similarly, the proposed architecture in Fig. 1 achieved the 4th rank amongst 9 entries in the AutoSpeech challenge for general automated audio processing. The proposed method is described in more detail and well investigate with extensive experimental results in [26].

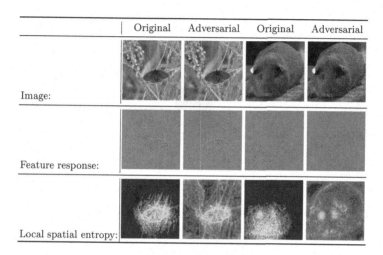

Fig. 2. Original and adversarially perturbed images from the ImageNet dataset [7], with attacks being clearly visible in entropy space but not yet in image space.

Table 2. Performance of similar adversarial attack detection methods. The Area Under Curve (AUC) is the average value of all attacks in the third and last row (this table is adopted from our previous research presented in [3]).

Method	Dataset	Network	Attack	Performance		
				Recall	Precision	AUC
Uncertainty density estimation [10]	SVHN [14]	LeNet [15]	FGSM	–	–	0.890
Adaptive noise reduction [16]	ImageNet (4 classes)	CaffeNet	DeepFool	0.956	0.911	–
Feature squeezing [29]	ImageNet-1000	VGG19	Several attacks	0.859	0.917	0.942
Statistical analysis [12]	MNIST	Self-designed	FGSM ($\epsilon = 0.3$)	0.999	0.940	–
Feature response (our approach)	ImageNet validation	VGG19	Several attacks	0.979	0.920	0.990

3 Interpretable and Robust Deep Learning

In this section, we present recent advances towards more interpretable deep neural networks, leading to increased robustness. One key in building trust in ML algorithms is to develop methods that explain the inner workings in a human-interpretable manner. Understanding the reasoning behind decisions of a trained model invariably improve the trust of domain experts. To achieve this for CNNs, several methods have been proposed [1] which can be used as guidelines to modify CNN architectures in order to obtain human interpretable decisions [30]. One of the best understood methods is the analysis of feature response maps computed using e.g. guided backpropagation [22]. Figure 2 illustrates how feature responses of CNNs, computed by guided backpropagation, can be used to visualize the regions where the network focuses at to take a decision.

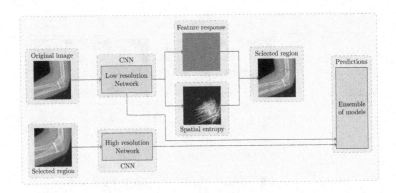

Fig. 3. Block diagram for a feature response-based adaptive zooming-in classifier.

Such methods to visualize the behavior of CNNs are mostly used to evaluate and compare the decision-making process of networks. Additionally, they also provide key insights to improve model design and robustness. For example, previous research demonstrate [3] that feature response maps are quite informative to detect adversarial attacks [25], which is an essential threat to the robustness and security of deep learning (Fig. 2). The feature maps depict the regions in the original image that contribute to the final decision of CNN, while the local spatial entropy images visualize the entropy of feature map activations in every 3×3 image patch. Simple thresholding of the latter yields a veritable detector for otherwise invisibly perturbed adversarial examples. The average local spatial entropy depicted in Fig. 2 provides a measure to detect adversarial attacks with competitive results compared to the state-of-the-art (compare Table 2).

Interpreting the decisions of CNNs can be applied beyond ensuring robustness and enabling trust to facilitate novel classifier architecture designs. As a demonstrator, we propose here the following multi-resolution classifier based on two CNN models (Fig. 3): Both models have the same input size but operate on the same image in different resolutions. The low-resolution model is trained first for an anomaly detection task based on the original full images. The high-resolution model then learns the finer details of detected anomalies based on a high-resolution crop of the region of interest around the first model's center of feature response. An ensemble of the two models can achieve promising performance in anomaly detection on the MURA dataset [19] of medical images.

Guan et al. present an alternative implementation of this idea, thereby improving the performance of thorax disease classification accuracy by using multi-scale information fusion [13].

4 Conclusion

When considering the future impact of deep learning in practical scenarios like medical image processing for diagnosis support, the issue of trust is paramount: Trust of the user/expert in the generated decision, and trust of the developer in the engineering process that currently is often unsystematic and difficult to repeat due to manual "grad student descent". We propose combining these two emerging ideas to address this trustworthiness tango, and present the following corresponding ideas: (a) AutoML to automate the model building process, thus making the vast design space searchable in a systematic manner. Our addition suggests a unified multi-modal architecture could be trusted for any audio/video/image classification task. (b) Visualizing feature responses of neural networks to give insight into the reasons behind classification results, thus helping concerned parties with the interpretation of a result in addition to providing robustness against adversarial attacks. Our addition shows that such interpretability measures can furthermore be beneficial to build novel classifier architectures by adaptively focusing attention on relevant portions of the input in a user-interpretable manner.

We see potential in further exploring this idea of combining the benefits of interpretability and automation in deep learning. Instead of building manually tweaked model architectures and attempting to interpret them afterward, let an AutoDL system optimize the hyperparameters of a more general architecture with built-in interpretability. This interpretability may also result from designing model-based methods that learn explainable representations [20,21,30].

Acknowledgements. We are grateful for support by Innosuisse grants 25948.1 PFES-ES "Ada" and 26025.1 PFES-ES "QualitAI".

References

1. Alber, M., et al.: iNNvestigate neural networks. JMLR **20**(93), 1–8 (2019)
2. Amirian, M., Rombach, K., Tuggener, L., Schilling, F.P., Stadelmann, T.: Efficient deep CNNs for cross-modal automated computer vision under time and space constraints. In: ECML-PKDD 2019, Würzburg, Germany, pp. 16–19 (2019)
3. Amirian, M., Schwenker, F., Stadelmann, T.: Trace and detect adversarial attacks on CNNs using feature response maps. In: Pancioni, L., Schwenker, F., Trentin, E. (eds.) ANNPR 2018. LNCS (LNAI), vol. 11081, pp. 346–358. Springer, Cham (2018). https://doi.org/10.1007/978-3-319-99978-4_27
4. Bianco, S., Cadene, R., Celona, L., Napoletano, P.: Benchmark analysis of representative deep neural network architectures. IEEE Access **6**, 64270–64277 (2018)
5. Caruana, R.: Multitask learning. Mach. Learn. **28**(1), 41–75 (1997). https://doi.org/10.1023/A:1007379606734

6. Chen, Y., et al.: Learning to learn without gradient descent by gradient descent. In: ICML, pp. 748–756 (2017)
7. Deng, J., Dong, W., Socher, R., Li, L.J., Li, K., Li, F.F.: ImageNet: a large-scale hierarchical image database. In: 2009 IEEE Conference on Computer Vision and Pattern Recognition, pp. 248–255 (2009)
8. Devlin, J., Chang, M.W., Lee, K., Toutanova, K.: BERT: pre-training of deep bidirectional transformers for language understanding. In: Proceedings of the 2019 Conference of the North American Chapter of the Association for Computational Linguistics: Human Language Technologies, vol. 1, pp. 4171–4186 (2019)
9. Elsken, T., Metzen, J.H., Hutter, F.: Neural architecture search: a survey. arXiv preprint arXiv:1808.05377 (2018)
10. Feinman, R., Curtin, R.R., Shintre, S., Gardner, A.B.: Detecting adversarial samples from artifacts. arXiv preprint arXiv:1703.00410 (2017)
11. Feurer, M., Klein, A., Eggensperger, K., Springenberg, J., Blum, M., Hutter, F.: Efficient and robust automated machine learning. In: NIPS (2015)
12. Grosse, K., Manoharan, P., Papernot, N., Backes, M., McDaniel, P.: On the (statistical) detection of adversarial examples. arXiv preprint arXiv:1702.06280 (2017)
13. Guan, Q., Huang, Y., Zhong, Z., Zheng, Z., Zheng, L., Yang, Y.: Diagnose like a radiologist: attention guided convolutional neural network for thorax disease classification. arXiv preprint arXiv:1801.09927 (2018)
14. Krizhevsky, A., Hinton, G.: Learning multiple layers of features from tiny images (2009)
15. LeCun, Y., et al.: Backpropagation applied to handwritten zip code recognition. Neural Comput. 1(4), 541–551 (1989)
16. Liang, B., Li, H., Su, M., Li, X., Shi, W., Wang, X.: Detecting adversarial examples in deep networks with adaptive noise reduction. arXiv preprint arXiv:1705.08378 (2017)
17. Lukic, Y., Vogt, C., Dürr, O., Stadelmann, T.: Speaker identification and clustering using convolutional neural networks. In: 2016 IEEE 26th International Workshop on Machine Learning for Signal Processing (MLSP), pp. 1–6. IEEE (2016)
18. Olson, R.S., Urbanowicz, R.J., Andrews, P.C., Lavender, N.A., Kidd, L.C., Moore, J.H.: Automating biomedical data science through tree-based pipeline optimization. In: Squillero, G., Burelli, P. (eds.) EvoApplications 2016. LNCS, vol. 9597, pp. 123–137. Springer, Cham (2016). https://doi.org/10.1007/978-3-319-31204-0_9
19. Rajpurkar, P., et al.: MURA: large dataset for abnormality detection in musculoskeletal radiographs. In: 1st Conference on Medical Imaging with Deep Learning (2018)
20. Ross, A.S., Hughes, M.C., Doshi-Velez, F.: Right for the right reasons: training differentiable models by constraining their explanations. In: IJCAI, pp. 2662–2670 (2017)
21. Sabour, S., Frosst, N., Hinton, G.E.: Dynamic routing between capsules. In: NIPS, pp. 3856–3866 (2017)
22. Springenberg, J., Dosovitskiy, A., Brox, T., Riedmiller, M.: Striving for simplicity: the all convolutional net. In: ICLR (Workshop Track) (2015)
23. Stadelmann, T., et al.: Deep learning in the wild. In: Pancioni, L., Schwenker, F., Trentin, E. (eds.) ANNPR 2018. LNCS (LNAI), vol. 11081, pp. 17–38. Springer, Cham (2018). https://doi.org/10.1007/978-3-319-99978-4_2
24. Stadelmann, T., Tolkachev, V., Sick, B., Stampfli, J., Dürr, O.: Beyond ImageNet: deep learning in industrial practice. Applied Data Science, pp. 205–232. Springer, Cham (2019). https://doi.org/10.1007/978-3-030-11821-1_12

25. Szegedy, C., et al.: Intriguing properties of neural networks. In: ICLR (2014)
26. Tuggener, L., et al.: Design patterns for resource-constrained automated deep-learning methods. AI **1**(4), 510–538 (2020)
27. Tuggener, L., et al.: Automated machine learning in practice: state of the art and recent results. In: 6th Swiss Conference on Data Science, pp. 31–36. IEEE (2019)
28. Vanschoren, J.: Meta-learning. In: Hutter, F., Kotthoff, L., Vanschoren, J. (eds.) Automated Machine Learning. TSSCML, pp. 35–61. Springer, Cham (2019). https://doi.org/10.1007/978-3-030-05318-5_2
29. Xu, W., Evans, D., Qi, Y.: Feature squeezing: detecting adversarial examples in deep neural networks (2018)
30. Zhang, Q., Wu, Y.N., Zhu, S.C.: Interpretable convolutional neural networks. In: CVPR, pp. 8827–8836 (2018)

Author Index

Printed in the United States
by Baker & Taylor Publisher Services